BEYOND THE FORESTLINE

THE LIFE AND LETTERS OF BENGT SUNDKLER

BEYOND THE FORESTLINE

THE LIFE AND LETTERS OF
BENGT SUNDKLER

Marja Liisa Swantz

GRACEWING
Studia Missionalia SVECANA LXXXIV

First published in 2002
by

Gracewing
2 Southern Avenue
Leominster
Herefordshire
HR6 0QF

ISBN 0 85244 560 1
ISSN 1404 9503

Typeset by Action Publishing Technology Ltd,
Gloucester, GL1 5SR

Printed in England by
Antony Rowe Ltd,
Eastbourne BN23 6QT

CONTENTS

ACKNOWLEDGEMENTS

Producing this book has been a long process. Living in Finland while much of the material was in Uppsala has necessitated the kind assistance of many friends of Bengt Sundkler's. I wish to thank especially the director of the University of Uppsala Archives, Viveca Halldin-Norberg, for the way she and her staff have made available the Bengt Sundkler collection for the writing of this work and I thank Åsa Henningsson for assisting with the pictures. Christopher Steed has provided steady support throughout the whole process, and I doubt whether this book would ever have appeared without his capacity to make things happen. I think warmly of Professor Carl-Fredrik Hallencreutz, who sadly is no longer here to see the publication of this volume. He, more than anyone else, responded to my requests for a Swedish, in particular, Uppsala, opinion on the writing of Bengt Sundkler's life story. He acknowledged and read each section promptly, making most helpful corrections and offering suggestions. I address my thanks to his wife, Katharina Hallencreutz, who also read the chapters I was constantly sending to their common e-mail address; I know that her opinion also influenced Carl-Fredrik's reactions.

I am grateful to Axel-Ivar and Kerstin Berglund for their hospitality during my frequent visits to Uppsala and for providing valuable background information as well as reading the manuscript and suggesting changes. I would also like to thank Sigbert Axelsson and Torle Furberg for meeting me several times, along with Carl-Fredrik and Christopher, to make comments and above all to advise me on how the book should be conceived. However, it is no fault of any of theirs if I have not followed their ideas at every stage. I am solely responsible for the result.

I owe special thanks to Tiina Ahonen who let me use her collection of articles and speeches of Bengt Sundkler. She also read the manuscript and made useful suggestions and corrections. I am also grateful to Gustaf Björck for his help in searching for information at the Swedish Institute of Mission. I would like to thank Jenny Oates for the laborious copy-editing of the book and for preparing the Indexes. I also owe thanks to the Church of Sweden Mission for providing a grant which facilitated the publication of the biography of Bishop and Professor Bengt Sundkler, who contributed so significantly to the work of the CSM.

Lastly, I thank profusely my long-suffering husband, Lloyd Swantz, for his patience in seeing this process through and my daughter, Eva Swantz-Rydberg, for the many ways in which she assisted me at different stages in the production of this book.

Marja Liisa Swantz

INTRODUCTION

Bengt Sundkler, a Swede, was a well-known missiologist and historian of non-European churches, specialising in African church history. He had served as a missionary in South Africa and Tanzania, and later the northwestern diocese of the Evangelical Lutheran Church of Tanzania called him to be their first bishop. Bengt Sundkler was a multifaceted person and a true international, long before the era of mass global-isation, which he saw coming in his later years.

Bengt Sundkler worked on his autobiography while he was writing his final major work on the history of the Church in Africa. He had various outlines, but reduced the text to an abbreviated version, leaving some chapter headings untouched or with only a few pages written. A brief autobiography forms the first part of this volume. In the second part I have made use of the earlier outlines which he sent to me in letters. The variety of other sources I explain below.

Any attempt to portray the lifetime's work of Bengt Sundkler and him as a person will inevitably be one-sided, narrowed down to aspects selected from a specific view of his personality and career. Firstly, the material and sources available shape the portrait, but the selection is also biased toward my own personal view of Bengt Sundkler, especially in his later years. As both editor and writer I further claim a certain commonality with his approach to scholarship and with his way of experiencing life in general, which I discovered first as a student and later as a colleague and friend. Here I attempt to describe my understanding of what that commonalty was. I direct the searchlight toward what I consider to be the keys to understanding Bengt Sundkler's life. This also influences the choice of quotations which form the core of the second part of the biography.

Four things oriented Bengt Sundkler in his life decisions:

Firstly, to the end of his life he remained a pastor, a shepherd of souls. He was ordained in the Church of Sweden in 1936, a church which he considered to be a bridge church within the Catholic, Universal Church: ecumenicity was the key to his being a pastor, priest and bishop. Christ was God's Mission into the world and for that reason, this Mission was the uniting factor for the Universal Church. This Mission entrusted to God's pilgrim people on earth was integral to the Church.

Secondly, Bengt Sundkler could not consider scholarship and history in isolation from people. In the final analysis, people were the actors in history. For him, people's ways of acting, living and thinking did not provide data with which he could verify his hypotheses, but rather formed the substance of his scholarship. He not only observed but also participated in the life of the people whose life and history he then wrote about. The leading concept was 'relatedness'. He called this an 'engaged approach'.[1] His methodology was grounded in a Participatory World View before anyone had theorised about participatory research as distinct from participatory observation.

Thirdly, Bengt Sundkler was an intense scholar for whom scholarship took precedence over most other concerns of life, but his scholarship was closely linked to practical life experience. Theory and practice were inseparably intertwined. In one of his interviews Bengt simply stated, 'In this miserable life of mine, theology has been worked out in the context of a living church.'[2] This close linking of theory and practice is, to my mind, the key to understanding Bengt Sundkler's theological and scholarly position in general, as a teacher of theology, and in his churchmanship. For this reason, his daily notes are significant for the story of Bengt Sundkler's life and work.

Finally, Bengt Sundkler was a creative writer who put into his writings his aesthetic experience of life. He found inspiration in liturgical services administered with reverence and devotion; in choral music; in Bach organ and piano recitals; in aesthetic, spiritual and intellectual enjoyment of listening to the radio or watching the television (often French television); in walks and bicycle rides; in the beauty of nature and freely shining sun while lying on his balcony, which he called his 'Tenerife'.[3] Above all, he found inspiration in the people who responded to him, who were alive and were open to the richness of life.

In all aspects of his life and work, communication, enthusiasm, encouragement, self-search, devotion and the wonder of life were some of the key concepts. To remain inwardly alive to his dying day was Bengt Sundkler's ambition. On 12 March 1967 he recorded in his diary a series of thoughts which startled him. It struck him to the core because it made him aware of a potential waning of inspiration.

Dr Fredrik Ysander insisted that I must take a month's holiday. He planned everything for us. He took us to his doctor's reception room (on a Sunday night) and we went through the whole [check up]. When we had gone through everything, he had something more to say. It was clear that what had transpired so far was only in preparation for this.

He had visited Africa on his way to India in the summer of 1939, stopping in Dundee, Natal, South Africa, where he had seen our work.

His outstanding memory of the whole trip was the morning he left Dundee. My wife Ingeborg and I were standing on the steps of our little house waving goodbye to him. He remembered this young missionary couple: their joy for work and their bright, friendly faces as they stood there seeing the guest off. 'Now I want you to travel far away and rest, so that I can see that joyful, happy look on your faces again.'

It was like a blessing of an old, charming man, a wise man, for us perhaps the last time we would see him. A moving moment. We flew to the Canary Islands for a three-week holiday.

Bengt said of himself in later years: 'I want people to think of me as a cheerful person.' When I meet people who have known Bengt Sundkler, more often than not their first remark is 'What a charming man he was!'

Bengt Sundkler wanted to write his autobiography as an accompanying volume to the monumental work of his last 20 years, the writing of the history of the Church in Africa. He started thinking about it at the same time as he began collecting material for his book on African Church History. From the outset he envisaged that the story of his life, written in a relaxed style, would be published at the same time as the massive history book. He returned to it time after time and enjoyed reminiscing on the many rich years he had experienced. He brought the great history to fruition, but sadly his own story was never completed.

In writing his autobiography Bengt Sundkler envisaged placing his life story into a larger perspective. The main theme is expressed in the title he chose for his autobiography, the concept of 'beyond', the ever-widening perspective from the Norrland forests and Vindeln village to the bigger town of Umeå, to Uppsala, the intellectual centre of Sweden, to England, to Africa, and eventually to the whole world; from the narrow bounds of northern pietism to broad ecumenical perspectives. On one occasion B Sr mused over the leading concept of his book, the 'BEYOND', in the following shorthand notes: 'Autobiography is called Beyond the Forestline: Beyond, because I was hedged and hampered by forest, by small-minded people, by Swedes, by narrow-minded missionaries, by church with walls and rigid doctrines.'[4]

'Beyond' meant for him embracing the world and its people. Beyond meant pioneering in an age and situations in which he was the first, or among the first, to challenge the customary and conventional. To begin with the 'beyond' was geographical, but it became also social, spiritual and ecclesiastical in the sense of ecumenical, international, global. Bengt Sundkler lived, made and wrote history. He worked crossing many borders, but at the same time, his 'going beyond' predicated not fully belonging anywhere: in Africa not being African, in Sweden feeling an outsider, in England not a native speaker, in Europe a northerner.

When considering his way of writing his autobiography, Bengt
Sundkler asked such questions as, 'What is the level on which to write
this story? What is the wider perspective it opens up to the reader in
which to look at someone's life?' One such perspective was what he
called 'discovery of Africa' or actually, 'rediscovery of Africa.' When
he started his work in Africa, the Nordic countries were yet by and
large to 'discover' Africa. For 50 years missionaries had been going
to South Africa, Namibia, Central Africa and Ethiopia, and stories
had been told of their work, but Africa had not emerged in people's
consciousness as part of the modern world. It belonged to those who
were sent as missionaries or 'knitted woollen socks', as the saying
goes, to support missionwork. Missions had to be brought into the
contemporary political scene and those with first hand experience of
Africa could assist in opening the way for the Nordic countries to see
their relatedness to and responsibility for Africa and the Third World.

Africa was not unknown in Sweden and certainly not among the
mission circles in the 1930s and 1940s. Even the university had recognised work done by Swedes in Africa by giving a pioneer missionary,
K. E. Laman, an honorary doctorate for his extensive anthropological
studies in the Congo as early as 1915. B Sr had also shared in the
wide protest of Swedes against Mussolini's takeover of Abyssinia in
1935–36. (Spiral notebook 1934–.) It shook concerned people in the
North, many of whom still remembered the impact of Haile Selassie's
visit to Sweden in 1924. But even so, the strong feeling of being out
of sight and out of mind, disappearing to an unknown future, was not
unreasonable for those who at that time, and even later, had chosen
as their career to work for long periods away from the familiar homeland. In this case the long eight years of isolation and separation
during the Second World War, which followed, added to the impact.

B Sr never for a moment regretted having left for Africa. Africa
became his destiny.[5] Yet he had definite grounds for thinking that
Africa did not at that time have the same prestige as the Orient in
academic circles. Oriental studies flourished in the universities of
Europe and preceded African studies by half a century or more. They
were worthy of learned scholarship and some of the most respected
members of the university staff were engaged in them. Western
history books often still presented Africa as a continent without
history in the 1950s.[6] Scholarship in Africa had hardly begun, it was
60–70 years behind. The tendency was to see that the gifted ones who
could discourse on the same level as the Eastern scholars and learn
difficult languages were oriental scholars or were sent as missionaries
to East Asia. (Interview 13 January 1978)

To these thoughts the interviewee could have added that the young
doctor in this specific case had raised many hopes and was expected
to continue toward professorship and excellent scholarship, since his
660-page dissertation had already been cited by the leading professor
of Church History, the critical Emanuel Linderholm, to be worthy of

a professorship. Africa had, however, already been imprinted in the mind of B Sr in his youth:

> I walked as if blindfolded, drawn by books I had read and following intuition. Decisive for me was E. W. Smith's book on Aggrey in the 1930s, Aggrey who challenged his countrymen in Ghana with high goals, 'You are eagles.' I had been tied to Africa step by step. (Earlier ms.)

On leaving for Africa, B Sr was already conscious of the wider task that the missions had. His frustrations during the first part of his career must be considered in this light. The mission environment to which he came was not yet ready to look at their task the way the fresh Doctor of Theology specialising in Mission History was beginning to see it. Such contradictions are apparent, not only in the story written with the benefit of 50 years' hindsight, to a certain extent they were already present in the field in the South Africa to which B Sr came with his wife. He saw them in a clearer light in hindsight, when interviewed at different times, thus perhaps expressing the situation in the South African Lutheran Mission more sharply than he would have done while working there.[7] He also regretted that he did not feel happy there: 'How sad that I did not feel happy in the South Africa years: for the Zulus were such wonderful people, the finest ever.' (Letter to MLS 25 January 1982)

Outline of the book

Bengt Sundkler was very particular about the outline of his books. He had a 'disposition joy', he took pleasure in working out outlines, in his own term 'dispositions', comparing himself to an architect. Disposition was to him like pillars in a cathedral, or structures in modern architecture. He admired the Finnish architects, Eliel and Eero Saarinen and Alvar Aalto, and had books on them in his library.

For his autobiography B Sr had the disposition worked out, but some of the chapters, to which the author had given titles, remained unwritten.

Bengt Sundkler's autobiography, in the form he left it, forms Part One of the book. He had written other more embellished versions, but toward the end of his life he wanted to write his life story in a flowing style and discipline his thought. He would only touch on events, thoughts and reflections without going into them in any great detail. He wanted his texts to be light and airy, a delight for the reader, and he lamented for ever that he did not come into this world with the English language as his birthright. To create beautiful form and flowing style were crucial to his literary mind. This sets demands which surpass my capacity as a writer who has had to struggle with both English and Swedish as foreign languages, yet I dare to attempt the task I have been trusted with. Having closely followed and encouraged B Sr in the writing of several of his books and having received numerous new versions for reading, I am certain the version we have to hand would not have been final. Some of the earlier parts would probably have gone back to the text.[8]

In Part Two, I comment on the chapters which B Sr himself had already written. I have made extensive additions and expanded many aspects which B Sr intentionally phrased in a concise style. I include some of the texts he himself had eliminated, because in my mind they broaden our understanding of the way he thought and felt in later life about the earlier phases of his life. I have included explanations of what B Sr writes in his account, based on his self-reflection and on my discussions with him. I have also added texts from his correspondence with significant people at the time thus giving a broader picture of their relationship. The chapter about his wife Ingeborg, which he wanted to write but never completed, I have placed where it belonged in Part Two. Particularly after reading Alan Paton's *Kontakion,* written in honour of his deceased wife, B Sr felt a great urge to write a chapter using a similar approach. He returned to the thought several times and consulted me on how to write the chapter, but we are left with shorter or longer sections and comments here and there.

When the second part of the book evolved I realised that I could not fit all the material into the outlined chapters. First I filled in the texts of chapters which were left with only headings in B Sr's own version, still using what were basically his own texts. I have changed several headings and out of one created several chapters and sub-sections. I have given sub-headings to sections in all the chapters to make the reading lighter, which was the writer's expressed goal. This is the case particularly with the chapter which B Sr had called 'Professor Among the Students'. His time as a professor in the university was long, but only part of it was 'among students'. He divided the time with many other activities and numerous travels. His time as a professor was periodically interrupted by his international duties and episcopal service in Tanzania.

In the additional chapters I portray Bengt Sundkler as the person I knew him, sketching his character as he sought to understand himself, what he yearned to be, his ambitions, his dreams and his relations with some of his friends and family. A sensitive addition is 'Travel into my inner self'. At the end I have added a chapter on Bengt Sundkler as a writer. In his later years he repeatedly said, 'I do not consider myself to be so much of a scholar as a writer.' He returned to the ambition of his early years when he had 'a passion for the history of literature' and literature itself. He also wrote poetry, although only few poems remain to tell us of this interest. I intend the last chapter to be a door to Bengt's personal 'workshop' as a writer. The quotes from letters and Free Associations offer an insight into his feelings, his emotional difficulties as well as his joys, and into his sensitivity for the beautiful things around him.

I make use of personal writings more extensively than Bengt Sundkler himself would ever have done, had he finished his own life story. He was sensitive about his public image as a person. However, from the time he took to write letters and to make at times surprisingly open statements, it was obvious that he knew these thoughts would become public. He was an internationale whose talking and writing was meant for a larger audience than his friends. He wrote his autobiography in English, even if he usually wrote his diaries in Swedish in order to be able 'to say things from my heart' (*att uttrycka mitt hjärta på svenska*). He gave this as a reason for reverting back to writing his diaries in Swedish after returning to Sweden from Bukoba in 1965. His diaries were written in English during his episcopal years in order to make them historical documents of the first years of the diocese, readily available to Tanzanian historians and writers. I hope the personal notes give further insight into Bengt Sundkler as the person he was, in his relationships to those near and dear to him, and in the life tasks for which he felt he had the calling.

To B Sr it was important to keep on 'crossing frontiers' and 'daring in order to know', two of his favourite thoughts captured in the names of two Festschrifts published in his honour by his friends, most of whom had been his doctoral students.

The birth of this book

In his will Bengt Sundkler suggested that I take over the 40 pages which he had finished and carry on writing to complete it. He did this knowing that I had access to several autobiographical sources which I itemise below. I describe here how I became involved with this task and how I have gone about it.

I met Ingeborg and Bengt Sundkler for the first time in 1951 in an Evangelical Student Conference in Uppsala to which I had come as secretary of the Student Christian Federation of Finland with a group of students from Finland. Professor Sundkler was the patron of the conference.[9] I gave there a little speech on my intention of going to Tanganyika as a missionary teacher, after which Ingeborg and Bengt Sundkler came and enthusiastically told me, 'We love all those who work in or for Tanganyika.' Later I received a letter from Ingeborg in which she gave me suggestions as to which books to read in preparation. I had already acquainted myself with 'the first modern book on missionwork in Africa' available in Scandinavia, Bengt Sundkler's *Ung Kyrka i Tanganjika* (Young Church in Tanganyika), the significance of which I only later came to realise. The next time I met Ingeborg and Bengt was two years later when they came on a visit to Ashira Girls' Teacher Training and Middle School on Kilimanjaro, where I by then had started teaching. The following year the first All Africa Lutheran Conference was held at the neighbouring Marangu Teacher Training College and as one of the hostesses I was there again to welcome B Sr as a speaker to the conference.

Eight years later, after I had married Lloyd Swantz, a Lutheran pastor from the USA, and started a family, we met Bengt Sundkler when we were working in Dar es Salaam. He had become the first Lutheran Bishop in Tanzania, Bishop of Bukoba. While attending the founding meeting of the Evangelical Lutheran Church of Tanzania and the opening of Luther House in Dar es Salaam in 1963 he stayed in our home in Luther House. Lloyd Swantz had been called to be a partner in planning the construction of the building and to start activities there. B Sr encouraged us to do research and work toward doctoral degrees. While my husband took his degrees in Syracuse University and the University of Dar es Salaam, I ended up doing my PhD degree under Bengt Sundkler at Uppsala University where I also became a docent. Bengt became a very close family friend. His wife Ingeborg died rather early, at the end of 1969, but a few months before her death she visited Tanzania and spent ten days with us on the beach of the Indian Ocean where we were then living.

Over many years I carried on a correspondence with Bengt Sundkler. I encouraged Bengt to write his autobiography and little by little he started working towards it. He made use of the opportunity to write parts of his life story in long autobiographical letters with the intention of including what he wrote in the autobiography. For 25 years he reported to me and my husband on his many travels and meetings with people. Correspondence became at times almost a daily exchange of ideas and experiences. Thus parts of the life story are taken from such letters. As the years rolled by and his major work on the African Church History demanded his time, interrupted by serious illnesses, B Sr acquainted me with the sources available for his biography, in the event that he would not be able to complete his story. I read parts of his and his wife's correspondence and he let me read his 'Free Associations' notes and parts of his diaries during my visits to Uppsala.[10]

After Bengt Sundkler's death I was hesitant to take on the writing of the biography by myself. I wrote to his friends and relatives asking them to advise me on how we should finalise the portrayal of the life of this great man, church historian, missionary, ecclesiastical leader bishop, teacher and communicative, warm personality. After a few discussions I decided to do the same as Bengt Sundkler himself did when he took over the writing of the history of the Christian Movement in Africa, as he first named his book on the African Church History. He was advised by two great historians of Africa, Roland Oliver and Terrence Ranger to go ahead alone, as he repeatedly told us. I made a similar decision and started the writing alone, aided by good advice from Bengt Sundkler's former doctoral students and close friends. I did this in the hope that later there will be others who will be inspired to take on the rewarding task and go into greater depth on the many aspects of this long, eventful and rich life.

I felt obliged to take on this work. I wanted to adhere closely to Bengt Sundkler's own words, narration and statements about his own life and thereby keep it in the form of an autobiography, using the first person where the texts were direct quotations from Bengt's own texts, indicating faithfully the sources, and indicating direct quotes with quotation marks. I was advised, however, by the ad hoc editorial committee, consisting of B Sr's close colleagues and friends, to separate clearly the parts which Bengt Sundkler himself had completed or partly written and to write the other parts clearly indicating that it was my portrayal of Bengt Sundkler.

In the last chapters in particular I have retained lengthy quotations from B Sr's own texts, but the choice of them must be read as the writer's view of the person, life and career of Bengt Sundkler. The reference group in Uppsala knew Bengt Sundkler as a different person from the man my selection of quotations presents him to be. We agreed that the book must be interpreted to reflect my personal view of the subject, bearing in mind that I am not a learned theologian nor do I know Sweden and Uppsala as they do as natives. I also want to make the reservation that the Bengt Sundkler I portray might not be what he himself would have agreed to.

My husband and I read several versions of the manuscripts in the process of writing *Bara Bukoba*, *Zulu Zion* and the last 20 years of the African Church History, and several lesser works in between. We shared with Bengt Sundkler the insight into, love for, and intimate contact with Africa. This is also the reason why I have called my part of the book 'Africa in His Heart'. B Sr used the expression 'Africa in Our Hearts' when he and Ingeborg were saying goodbye to the diocese in Bukoba and to Lake Victoria in the heart of Africa. It was also a theme which he frequently spoke on after he returned from his time as bishop of the northwestern diocese in Tanzania. No doubt he was thinking of his wife and himself but invited also the audience to share the sentiment. Together with him, I invite the readers of this volume to take Africa into their hearts and let the subject of this book, Bengt Sundkler, lead them to do so.

Sources for the biography

I have used mainly Bengt Sundkler's own texts for Part Two of this volume. For the most part they were taken from handwritten and typed sources and supplemented by interviews with his close colleagues and friends, Carl Fredrik Hallencreutz, Tore Furberg, Sigbert Axelson, Axel-Ivar Berglund, Christopher Steed, Kaarina Drynjeva and Erik and Birgitta Sharpe. B Sr's brother-in-law, Bishop

Stig Hellsten, had read the first draft of this part before his death and made valuable comments. He and his wife Ingegärd gave for my use the letters they had saved from Bengt and Ingeborg Sundkler. The diaries and many letters were written in Swedish often in somewhat unclear handwriting which at times made interpretation difficult, but after learning to recognise the standard abbreviations the translation became easier.

Interviews

Several people had interviewed Bengt Sundkler over the years, both publicly and in private, asking him to tell of his life, his theology, his vision of world mission and his relation to the Church in her ecum-enical, all-embracing dimension. I had interviewed him many times on different topics during his visits to our home. I posed very pointed questions and he was aware that this material was to be used for biographical purposes. I quote extensively from these interviews, especially in the last chapters. Almost all interviews are on tapes, to be kept safely in the Carolina Rediviva archives, the University Library of Uppsala.

Public speaking

As Bengt Sundkler celebrated his 70th, 75th, 80th and 85th birthdays and after his retirement at the age of 65, he was asked to leave his legacy to younger generations and to speak about the earlier years of his life and work. In his later years he repeatedly had the opportunity to relate how his last and the most monumental book on the Church in Africa came to pass. He did so eloquently and vividly, with slides, drawings on the blackboard, arms waving, at times labouring to get his point across, but mostly drawing the audience in with his own enthusiasm and warm relationship with the public. I remember him only once sitting down and more or less reading what he had written down. This was when he delivered his last public lecture a year before his death.

Diaries

Bengt Sundkler had kept a diary most of his working life. The decade of the1950s has only one or two diary books filled with short notes. The 1960s, 1970s and 1980s have one or two books for each year. The years in Bukoba are most extensively reported and written in English. The diary notes are often short, not many very personal. They were clearly written by a historian who knew that someone would study them and try to interpret them. The historians would put together B Sr's life from his own recording of the events and thoughts which he considered significant to preserve as a person who not only wrote but made history. He clearly checked the extent to which he would be personal in his writings.

Free Associations

B Sr had been advised by a psychologist friend to write freely more personal notes in free associations. The writing of them became less frequent when he confided in and through correspondence which increasingly replaced the need for the expression of personal concerns.

Letters

Another significant source is, of course, letters. The hope of having an autobiographical volume out in the near future does not permit perusal of the second largest collection of letters in the Carolina archives, categorised carefully by recipients and authors. The task would be too overwhelming at this point. I have consulted some correspondence, especially that between B Sr and influential personalities and family members of the early years. One can only hope that there will still be students even in this age of quick writing and fleeting scholarship who see the significance of history through the exchange of ideas between great personalities of the past.

There is also a rich source of letters addressed to me personally and to my husband. We continued intensive correspondence over the years starting from the end of the 1960s when I was finalising my thesis with B Sr as my advisor. In June 1982 Bengt wrote:

> I have been encouraged to attempt an autobiographical book. I would like to do it in the form of series of letters to you, and so I begin right in the middle...Well, I feel that I shall not be able to write the kind of conventional autobiography, decade by decade. I must try to see it in some other dimension. We shall see. (Letter to MLS 12 June 1982)

This expressed purpose of writing letters for the sake of recording one's life story already started in 1974. It has given me the freedom to quote from the writer's letters extensively, especially in the chapter 'Travel into my inner self'. This brings out the contrast and the inner change that B Sr went through when he became liberated by the African friends with whom he felt so at home, more so than in Sweden. Other notes which relate to B Sr as a person I have included in the last chapter where they illustrate the professional and inspirational processes of the writer and scholar.

Notebooks

Bengt Sundkler the scholar, for whom all situations in life were his field for research, always kept little blue or green, sometimes red notebooks in his pocket. In them he faithfully wrote down whatever anyone he talked with happened to say. With his associative mind he jumped at the ideas the discussant threw out that fitted in with whatever he was working on at the time. He referred to this capacity of his in one of his letters: 'I need to be reminded of the marvel that I can see, that these two eyes do computer-rapid combinations all the time and can help enjoy life so intensely.'[11] There were no wasted words to Bengt. He went through the notebooks from time to time, carefully underlining significant points and making use of them in his writing. The people he met in Africa got so used to the little notebook that when the subsequent missionaries did not jot down their sayings, they remarked that this foreigner lacked interest in their words.

Svensk Missionstidskrift (SMT)

Bengt Sundkler was the chief editor of the journal of the Swedish Institute for Mission Research for 20 years.[12] We can follow the development of his thinking and his current views in his lead articles and commentaries on the great events in church and mission.

Pastoral tasks

Bengt Sundkler was from his heart a shepherd and shepherd of shepherds, above all in Africa, but desirous to be so also in Sweden. As bishop and pastor he hardly ever refused to take on preaching assignments even in his later years. He preached regularly in St Per's church on the second Sunday in Advent, on the day he had assisted in the consecration of the church. He presided at the St Brigit jubilee mass and was the celebrant at the folk mass at the re-opening of Uppsala Cathedral after it had been renovated. He was always pleased when asked to preach in the cathedral. His sermon notes were seldom truly readable. His idea of the main thoughts crowded on paper the size of a thumb-nail or stamp is not far off the way his sermon notes appeared. They were outlined first in his notebooks and many sermon notes are available. He also often referred to his two episcopal letters written in 1962 and 1964 in Bukoba.

Dreams

Bengt was also a dreamer in a real sense. He was interested in the dreams of African pastors who in many cases had received their calling in their dreams. Bengt recorded faithfully his own dreams. Unfortunately I do not have Joseph's competence in interpreting dreams, but for someone else it is another potential avenue to look into the personality of the man whose profile we attempt to sketch through his own words on these pages, including a few dreams.

Personal communication

The rest of the material comes from our personal communication with an adopted member of the Swantz family and the discussion partner which Bengt Sundkler was as he laboured over and developed the thoughts for his books, starting with the Swedish version of *Bara Bukoba*. While he claimed to have been chained to his table for his last 20 years, he also needed desperately to communicate with partners to discuss the respective points he was working with. In his diaries and letters he refers to Carl Fredrik Hallencreutz more often than anyone else with deep gratitude and respect for having been such a partner. My husband and I served as a sounding board during his frequent visits to our homes in Africa and in Finland. He even kept up communication with our daughters and their families, and my nieces, through their visits to his home in Uppsala and his visits to them in the USA and Finland. On a personal note, I should also mention the magnificent dinner he organised in his home with his friend Kaarina Drynjeva, after I had defended my thesis, for nearly 30 people, including 13 relatives and friends from Finland, to whom he sent personal invitations.

In a letter of mine to B Sr in 1974 I find already an almost presaged thought in response to his expressed wish to write his autobiography:

> I shall put forth my inner wisdom and energy, whatever is there, to assist you in creating this book on your life. It has marvellous possibilities and I can hardly wait for you to start working on it. I wonder how much you dare to put into it and how personal you dare let it be. The art will be to find the right balance. (4 July 1974)

Handwriting

One difficulty has been in deciphering B Sr's handwriting. Many secretaries and archivists struggled with it during his life time, even he himself had problems with reading his earlier notes, as he remarks when preparing for another study tour in South Africa in June 1969. He states that the notes are enormously rich, but unfortunately they take time to decipher! But again, he did read what he noted down. (Diary 2 June 1969)

I end these introductory remarks with the words of a song, written originally in Luhaya language by pastor Sylvester Machumu from the Holy Ghost Church in Bukoba, B Sr's friend through 'ecumenics in banana groves'. They describe something of the spirit and experience which the two spiritual leaders shared:

> Vänner,
> vi går till stranden, och ser på havet,
> hur vågarna leker tillsammans ständigt var dag,
> det vägrar att vila.

Havet är mäktigt att verka och vill inte vila
eller, likt marken, att stelna.
Så ska vi kristna verka och vill inte vila
att Herren oss finner som vågen som lever och lyftes.

Friends,
we go to the shore and look at the waves,
how they ceaselessly play, day by day.
The powerful sea, it works and will not rest,
or like the earth, be still and stale.
So shall we Christians work unwilling to rest
that, the Lord will us find, like a wave,
living and lifted up.

Notes

1. A handwritten summary of what he had tried to accomplish in writing African Church History 1974–1990, given more fully in Chapter 11 of Part Two.
2. Interview by Tiina Ahonen 2 November 1990, for her Master of Theology degree. Unpublished thesis in Dogmatics *Bengt Sundklerin käsitys kirkon lähetyksestä* (B Sr's conception of the Mission of the Church) April 1992, University of Helsinki. I thank her for permitting the use of her taped interview. The tape is in the B Sr archives.
3. While others went to Tenerife in the Canary Islands he took his sun on his balcony, his Tenerife.
4. I use the abbreviation B Sr which Bengt Sundkler himself used of his own name and in abbreviating other names I follow the same rule. I abbreviate my own name Marja Liisa Swantz with MLS throughout the book.
5. 'I must take a stand on things African, because Africa has become my destiny.' This was written in a letter dated 29 August 1974 to MLS in reference to further work on Söderblom, which he felt he had to set aside and concentrate on Africa. This concentration perhaps kept him from taking a strong public stand on political matters not related to Africa.
6. Roy Preiswerk and Dominique Perrot 1978. *Ethnocentrism and History. Africa, Asia and Indian America in Western Textbooks*. (NOK Publishers: New York, London, Lagos) pp.105–19.
7. It is interesting though that Dr Danielson, who was there to meet the Sundklers in Dar es Salaam, still remembered in 1982 how glad B Sr was to get out of South Africa in 1942. (Discussion with Dr Danielson reported in MLS letter 25 July 1982 to B Sr.)
8. All the texts in the Part One are B Sr's own texts of his Autobiography which he completed, with no additions.
9. The conference was organised by *Sverige's Evangeliska Student- och Gymnasist Rörelse*, the patron of which B Sr had become.
10. I was for many years on the board of the Scandinavian Institute (now Nordic Institute) of African Studies which brought me to Uppsala in addition to the many conference and seminar trips, holidays and celebrations of various kinds. B Sr regularly spent holidays with our family and also made many official trips to Helsinki.
11. B Sr had been asked by Mrs Brillioth, a daughter of Nathan Söderblom and Archbishop Brillioth's wife, to read for a week to a General related to the Söderbloms, who was getting blind. When B Sr was doing it this wonder of seeing deepened his gratitude for being able to see. His remark about 'computer-rapid combinations' was not only in reference to physical seeing, it was the way

his associative mind worked. Furthermore, he became aware of how the blind in fact retain impressions and see things deeper in their way. (Letter 15 July 1974)

12. SMT now appears in English as Swedish Missiological Themes.

BRIEF BIOGRAPHY OF
BENGT SUNDKLER

Bengt Gustaf Malcolm Sundkler was born on 7 May 1909 into the
family of a retailer in Vindeln, along the rapids of Degerfors, in
northwestern Sweden. In 1928 he graduated from the Senior
Secondary School in Umeå, where the family had moved, and began
his studies in Uppsala University in 1929 where he graduated as a
Candidate of Theology in 1931. He studied for a year, 1931–32, in
Strasbourg and Paris. He was ordained as a pastor in the Church of
Sweden in 1936 and completed his doctorate in theology in 1937 with
a massive volume on Church History which contained detailed docu-
mentation and analysis of the three first decades of work for mission
support on the home front within the Church of Sweden. He also
studied several languages and attended anthropological seminars in
England and South Africa.

Bengt Sundkler undertook intensive archival work and fieldwork in
Africa, consulted missionary archives in Europe and USA, and
communicated extensively and intensively with well-known
Africanists throughout his research. In 1945 he became a docent in
Mission history and in 1949 was appointed Professor of Church
History with Missions. He headed the Swedish Institute of Mission
Research in Uppsala from 1951 until his retirement and was the chief
editor of the *Svenska Missionstidskrift* (*SMT*) for the same period. B
Sr combined scholarship with practical work and for him theory was
always closely linked with practice; he retired as professor in 1974.

In 1937, prior to their departure for Africa, Bengt Sundkler married
Ingeborg Morén, a teacher by profession and an accomplished pianist.
Bengt and Ingeborg Sundkler served as missionaries in South Africa,
Zululand, from 1937 to 1942 and in northwestern Tanganyika from
1942 to 1945. B Sr was research secretary for the International
Missionary Council (IMC) at its headquarters in London in 1948–49.
Between 1961 and 1965 he served as the first bishop of the
Evangelical Church in northwestern Tanganyika, later to become a
diocese in the Evangelical Lutheran Church of Tanganyika. B Sr was
a member of the Central Committee of the WCC between 1961 and

1965, a member and chairman of the Theological Education Fund from 1958 to 1963, and chaired the East African Church Union talks for several years while in Tanzania, as well as serving in the various committees prior to and following the unification of the Lutheran churches in Tanzania. Bengt Sundkler was presented with Honorary Doctorates from Aberdeen in 1967, Tübingen in 1968, Oslo in 1976 and Helsinki in 1990.

Sundkler published extensively. Internationally he is best-known for the ground-breaking book *Bantu Prophets* which sowed the seed for numerous subsequent studies on the independent churches in Southern Africa. B Sr himself wrote a revised second edition of *Bantu Prophets* and followed it up with another major book, *Zulu Zion and some Swazi Zionists*. On the African scene, he wrote *The Christian Ministry in Africa* and a study of his own diocese, *Bara Bukoba*, which epitomised the establishment of a church in Africa. His theological and historical treatise on the Church in South India was written to serve as a model for potential church unions in Africa, his own ecumenical passion and vision. *The World of Mission* with a revised second edition, originally written in Swedish and later translated into English, German and Finnish, was written as a text book for theological students, but is also of interest to other readers. He was frequently invited to speak at conferences, seminars and on courses, and contributed at a variety of gatherings. He became known as an inspiring speaker, and was favoured as a preacher and liturgist at church services.

Bengt Sundkler died in Uppsala on 5 April 1995, aged 86, after completing his major work, *The History of the Church in Africa*, which occupied the last 20 years of his life. The massive book, over 1,200 pages long, is a Cambridge University Press publication, co-authored by Christopher Steed as his assistant.

PART ONE

BEYOND THE FORESTLINE

Autobiographical Notes of a Northerner Turning South

Bengt Sundkler

1

IN THE FOREST

The Vindel River, rushing from the snow and ice of Swedish Lapland, burst its way through the immense forests of Norrland and formed at Vindeln a *degerfors*, an impressive cascade, a vast, glittering silver line through the endless dark green of the solemn vegetation. It was a memorable day when Mother allowed us, my younger brother and myself, to walk on our own to see the river and listen to the rumblings of the stream. I was about three at the time, in 1912, and my younger brother had just learnt to walk. The path down to the river was less than a mile through ferns and bracken. It seemed a long way until we arrived at the *nipa* (the steep sandy river-bank). We could see the river now, surrounded by forest which never seemed to come to an end. I looked and took it all in – 'What is there beyond the forest-line?' I wondered in awe. It was my first conscious question in life, a question which was to take me far, from northern Sweden to southern Africa and to South India.

A French literary critic, Roland Barthes, has suggested that every person has in fact only one question, varied and modified across the span of a lifetime, but remaining essentially the same enquiry. A paradoxical statement, to be sure, possibly mistaken, but I know one person of whom it could rightly be said. My fundamental question was formulated at this meeting with the river, 'What is there beyond the forestline?' This question has followed me throughout my life.

At the beginning of the century, we in Vindeln were surrounded by the forest, and embraced by it. Some people at Vindeln were known as *skogare* (foresters), from the highest official, the *jägmästare* (certified forester), to the lowliest forest worker. They all lived their life in and for the forest, and smoked the same little tobacco pipe, a cutty.

Together with others I discovered the forest in summer and in winter, always infinitely pleasing. In the winter one skied through the high white birch trees and the solemn fir trees, on soft snow or frozen crust. At times one could see a thin white pillar of smoke from some charcoal pile further north. You must not come too close to the burning pile, Mother warned, or you might fall into the fire. And then the spring, the early summer and the late summer: the delights of assorted berries: bilberry, cranberry, red whortleberry and the exquisite cloudberries in the swamps; and along the ditches arctic raspberries which I believe no longer grow, but which were a great delight then, long ago.

At this time – during the First World War – Vindeln was a stopping place for Same or Lapps, coming from the Swedish *fjields* with their herds of reindeer and staying for a few days. My first encounter with a non-Swedish language was listening to them when they came to my Father's shop to do their shopping. I also had the joy of going by *akja* or sledge, drawn by reindeer, an exciting meeting with a splendid people.

Vindeln society had its social differences: the rich forest owner, the prominent *jägmästare*, the doctor, the apothecary, the vicar. Then came the ordinary farmers who earned their living from forest-related jobs – charcoal and tar transport providing an additional source of income; and then the railway navvies who had been left behind in Vindeln as the building of the northern railway continued through the forests – and across the rivers and swamps – poverty-stricken families with large numbers of children whom one encountered at the elementary school. My Father's position as a shopkeeper fell in between these categories. In his shop, Father sold everything needed in the household at the time: salt and sugar loafs, American bacon, galoshes and clothes, along with a variety of other useful things.

Social differentiation was a fact of life in a small society such as that of Vindeln and was brought home to me quite unmistakeably in my first year at school. I was 6 at the time, and was walking home from school together with an older boy who told me that the following day he was to be 8 and he would like to see me with my younger brother at his birthday party. This was happy news to convey to our parents. It was an occasion for putting on our best attire, a navy blue sailor suit with a white striped collar. Father gave each of us a bag of sweets to present to the boy. Our maid took us by the hand, and off we went in great excitement. We arrived at the house and heard the happy throng of children rushing around. We asked to see Björn's mother. She came, looked at us and said: 'This must be a misunderstanding, there is no party here.' The door was shut, and there was nothing for us to do but to walk back home, rather dejectedly as I remember. We reported the outcome of our expedition to our parents and together with them tried to understand the situation. We formed a little family council together, and were thus given the chance to know our parents better.

It was on this occasion that Father explained his personal background. He was born out of wedlock, he told us. His father was a Swedish count, Captain Carl Gustaf Sinclair. 'We are different,' he mused, 'and,' turning to me, 'your third name, Malcolm, gives you away.' This was quite a discovery as far as I was concerned. I recalled the first day in school, when the children in the first class in primary school had to give their Christian names: Bengt Gustav Malcolm was, to that little audience a strange – and somewhat droll – combination, when the majority were named Kalle or Pelle or Ola.

Anyway, my Father continued, *his* father and mother had lived together with their son in the south of Sweden for a few years until my grandmother took her son away, moving first to Stockholm and later to Umeå in the north of the country. At the age of 13, Father begun to support his mother by working as an errand boy for a shop in Umeå. Later in Umeå we were to meet our paternal grandmother, a coughing, smoking old lady with a vast treasure-house of experiences and stories to tell. On two occasions, in 1913 and in 1919, my father visited his own father, meetings which meant much to him. In 1919 he cautiously changed his name to an approximation of *his* father's name, assuming the name of Sundkler. My Father was an interesting person with a remarkable memory, who would, on occasion, recite long nineteenth-century Swedish poetry by heart. He wrote poems himself, though not without a sentimental note, which made it difficult for us, his four children, to enjoy them. He was a staunch teetotaller and proud of the fact that he had never touched a drop of wine except for the occasional sip at Holy Communion.

While Father thus had 'a single parent', my Mother came from a large and lively family living near Sundsvall. We established the good tradition of making annual trips to visit our maternal grandparents, the whole family going by train, and later cycling the 230 kilometres to what seemed far south, near Sundsvall. Mother had 11 brothers and sisters. Ecclesiastically, my grandfather on Mother's side oscillated between the Church of Sweden and the Free Church, *Missionsförbundet*, a determining factor at each move being the attraction to or abstention from drink, from a permissive *folk* Church to the ascetic Free Church.

Grandmother on Mother's side was a charming old lady who arranged for one of her many daughters, my Mother, to go as a teenager to live with an aunt, a well-to-do, cultured lady who taught the sensitive young girl bourgeois values and manners. Through this Sundsvall family we were also exposed to emigration. My Uncle Frans moved to the United States, exchanging the lumber region of Sundsvall, Sweden, for the lumber region of Seattle, Washington State, USA. Mother was endowed with artistic skill, humour and optimism. She also retained a memory from her own confirmation: Bishop Johansson in Härnösand asked her for the meaning of the name Jesus, and she was able to render the formula in Luther's Larger Catechism: 'Saviour and Giver of Eternal Bliss'.

My experience of the social climate in Vindeln during the First World War should also be viewed in relation to the religious sphere. Vindeln was part of the Västerbotten 'revival' region, centred around Skellefteå and Piteå further north, but also further south. This was '*läsare*-land', the 'land of the Readers'. Strangely, I was to find that at precisely the same time – the end of the nineteenth century – as the Västerbotten Bible students were referred to as '*läsare*', the word was frequently used on the equator: *abashomi*, meaning Readers. There was a difference in meaning between the two. In Uganda the word for Readers referred to those who could read in a book; in Västerbotten – where the art of reading could be taken for granted – it denoted the Pietists, assembling in the villages in order to read the Bible and Dr Martin Luther.

In Västerbotten there was a distinction between 'old' readers – from the eighteenth century – and 'new' readers – from the beginning of the nineteenth century. Both were conservative and both sharply criticised the use of the 'new books', as 'new theology' or 'rationalisation', to be seen in the new translations and editions of Luther's catechism, and in the Swedish hymn book. The leading figure was Carl Olov Rosenius (1816–68), a renowned nineteenth-century preacher and editor of the monthly *Pietisten*. Characteristic of the religious activity in the region were the 'village prayers', *byaböner*; in the wide-spread local villages, often far from a central church, people assembled in the homes to read the Bible and Luther under the leadership of local 'readers'. Here whole generations of lay readers appeared, farmers also served as experienced preachers. They assembled in some big kitchen with its log fire and dim light while the lay leader explained the holy words. Some of these men developed a surprisingly astute grasp of the significance of central dogmatic terms, centred around the idea of being 'clothed with the righteousness of Christ'. These village prayer meetings eventually developed into local associations of the *Evangeliska Fosterlands-Stiftelsen* (*EFS*; the 'Swedish Evangelical Mission'), and the 'Bible True Friends', both influenced by Rosenius. The preachers were later ordained in the Church of Sweden and formed a highly salutary movement within the Church of Sweden, intellectually and culturally appearing as a 'reservoir of talent' in the population.

My parents were not part of this Pietistic movement, remaining rather distinctly churchy. In Vindeln-Degerfors the village prayer meetings also played a central role; my Father rented rooms for his shop and our family's flat from one Olof Hansson, '*Ol Hanscha*', who also served as a church warden. One day when I was about 8 years old, I paid a visit to the church warden's wife, '*Ol Hansch mora*'. Sitting with her in her big kitchen, she told me of the solemn verities of the faith, discussed in the village prayer meetings. She summed it all up, in her Degerfors dialect, in a happy declaration of the faith of the northern Swedish region: '*Ja Bengt, velken schoenen Gud ve hafva*' – 'what a great God we have', literally, 'what a beautiful God we have'. This was my first contact with the lay theology of the north.

SCHOOL YEARS

High school years in Umeå

In 1919 our family moved from Vindeln to the coastal town of Umeå, where my Father eventually established a grocery business. His main interest, however, was devoted to a club, Odd Fellows, where he was the 'chaplain', and where he recited by heart long passages of Swedish poetry. My first years in high school gave me a chance to practise the splendid sports of Norrland, skiing and skating, but in the main I attended to my school duties; I also picked up the good habit of collecting at the end of the school year such awards and scholarships as were available.

I soon discovered that there were effectively *two* high schools in Umeå, not just the ordinary one which led to the *studentexamen* (matriculation), but also another, unofficial, place of learning in the form of the town library, called the Minerva Library. The ordinary high school taught a number of languages, German, English, French, Latin and Greek, and of course Swedish along with Swedish and Nordic Literature. The town library was part of a very active adult education effort under the inspired leadership of one of the high school teachers, Dr Carl Cederblad. The Minerva Library had beautiful sets of reference books, especially in Swedish and Nordic Literature.

One day I saw in the bookshop window a new international atlas by Dierke, published in 1921 in Germany, and I was given it as a Christmas present. One continent seemed particularly interesting and alluring. This was Africa. I took a sheet of white paper and enlarged the map of Africa to double its size, with its lakes and rivers, its cities and countries, and fastened it up on my bedroom wall. Lake Victoria in the centre attracted my attention, particularly because of the *Caput Nili*, the head of the Nile, by way of a little river, Kagera, as the tributary. It seemed far away at the time. Later on it was to become my home for many happy years.

One Saturday afternoon I found myself in the school together with lector V. Hagström who, as a special privilege, took me to the teachers' own library. In a corner there was one lonely, uncut book, a doctoral thesis published in 1911 on radical Pietism in eighteenth-century Sweden. 'This is Church history,' he explained to me, 'you take it away for the weekend.' I cut it open, a large 500-page volume, and read it with fascination. One of the most interesting passages dealt with the so-called *Gråkoltarna* (the Grey Frocks) in Stockholm in the 1730s, impoverished, destitute Swedes of that period, appearing in grey coats. It seemed strange at that time. Was I ever to discover a parallel to this?

Very soon the history of literature became my passion, and much later when I approached the *studentexamen*, I took it for granted that I was to devote myself to the study of Nordic Literature. What could be more fascinating and exciting than Ibsen and Strindberg, and the Swedish-speaking Finns Runeberg and Topelius, writing in their mother tongue! It so happened however, that the headmaster of my secondary school – himself with a theological degree in addition to his doctorate – asked me about my plans after the *studentexamen*. Instead of waiting for an answer, he suggested that I study theology. I had shown a keen interest in the 'Student Christian Movement in Schools', its weekly meetings and its summer conferences and this seemed a relevant preparation for theology. My two younger brothers and sister all studied law – I was the only one in the family left with theology. Never for one moment have I regretted that choice.

A school's influence consists largely in its students and teaching staff. In the Umeå school I had two close friends who showed a particular interest in literature and writing. The first, Ingemar Wizelius, left Umeå after three or four years when his family moved to the south of Sweden. I felt his departure as a great loss. The other, Thorsten Jonsson, was the more original of the two. His father was the manager of an *EFS* bookshop in Umeå, a Pietist enterprise selling books to the public in the north. With this background Thorsten was insulated against Pietism. My own interest and passion was the history of Nordic literature – rather more so than the literature itself. Thorsten, on the other hand, lived close to modern literature, particularly that of the United States. Jonsson who died early, at the age of 50, has been the subject of a fascinating published doctoral thesis in Swedish by Per-Olof Erixon.[1] Both these friends of mine became well known internationally, as foreign correspondents for the leading Stockholm newspaper *Dagens Nyheter*, Thorsten Jonsson in the United States, Ingemar Wizelius in Central Europe. Wizelius is now well known as the editor of the annual yearbook of the Birger Sjöberg Society.

My high-school years held an additional interest because of the 'associations' which found a keen supporter in me: the literary group for which I acted as secretary, and the 'Student Christian Movement in Schools', of which I was chairman. The literary group collaborated over a modest journal and the secretary's weekly minutes were supposed to be entertaining. Fifty years later I have had an opportunity to re-read these literary efforts and was saddened by the immaturity of it all. The 'SCM in Schools' made me chairman of the group. This organisation was part of the Christian High School movement in Sweden, inspired by the so-called 'young church' movement (the *ungkyrklighet*). The local units were inspired by visits from highly competent travelling secretaries. In the summer there followed a week-long conference, with a splendid team of lecturers. I have never in my life been exposed to such gusts of rhetorical skill as during these summer conferences. This association proved to be fine preparation for the theological studies which I was to take up.

Notes

1. Per-Olof Erixon, *Ett spann över svarta ingentinget: linjer i Thorsten Jonssons författarskap* (Stockholm, 1994).

UNIVERSITY YEARS

Whatever values those high-school years may have provided, they could not match the opportunity of the university years. Uppsala, a university town north of Stockholm, in 1930 had some 30,000 inhabitants, 3,000 university students and a theological faculty of nearly 400. Theological studies at that time started with a preparatory exam in Greek, Hebrew and Philosophy, ordinarily taking between one-and-a-half and two years. I passed it in the spring term of 1929, and then spent the autumn term in the theological faculty devoted to Old Testament. This gave me the chance to read the most satisfying book provided by the whole Bachelor of Divinity course, Johannes Pedersen's *Israel*. This seemed a promising start to my studies and the examination results established my position at the university. I was in my parents' home in Umeå at Christmas 1929 when I received a letter from Professor Anton J. Fridrichsen in Uppsala. I had heard of him but never met him personally. The letter was an invitation to lodge with the professor in his home in Uppsala. I took my younger brother for a walk under the eternal stars of northern Sweden. I sensed the immense importance of the invitation, the potentialities of this unexpected letter, way 'Beyond' any expectations of mine.

In the attic of the professor's home there was a little room which became my home. Anton Fridrichsen was a Norwegian newcomer to Uppsala and Sweden who had chosen to leave the theological faculty in Oslo; he disliked its liberal theology at that time and was orientating himself to an emphasis on the Church in the New Testament. Professor Fridrichsen was a highly entertaining person, with a seemingly endless collection of stories. He received a constant stream of guests from all over Europe whom he had invited to lecture in Uppsala. The professor and his young amanuensis were obviously very different, but this did not seem to worry him. In February 1930 he summoned me for a planning session about my studies. He told me not to take my exams too seriously, suggesting that I should be finished with the Candidate exam in September 1931. He was pleased when I passed that exam in March 1931, with better results than he had anticipated. He planned a year in France for me – in Strasbourg and Paris – and followed my studies there with persistent interest.

It was Fridrichsen who first put me on the publishing track. In one of his seminars I discussed a few new books by German scholars on Infant Baptism and the New Testament. In the evening as we returned home he said, 'You showed a good understanding of those books. However, your own language is now Latin or German, rather than good Swedish. I shall show you.' So he took the phone to speak to the Uppsala publisher of religious books. 'Is that Thulin? Well, I have always felt that you need a good and fresh book on Infant Baptism in the New Testament. I have here a young scholar who is on the point of finishing a manuscript for just such a book. It is not ready yet – it will take another six weeks and then it will be ready for you.' The manuscript was ready in time, and the little book was, and remained, my only bestseller, possibly due more to its controversial subject matter than to any merit of mine. This set me on the path of constant writing and publishing. My next effort was in French, a highly original study of *Jésus et Les Païens* (Jesus and the Pagans), first published in the *Strasbourg Theological Review* and then, jointly with Fridrichsen, as a book, with Fridrichsen adding six pages on the problem in the Fourth Gospel. It was also Fridrichsen who suggested to me that I should do my doctoral work under Professor K. B. Westman, a learned historian of Christian missions. Fridrichsen understood the call of mission and of Africa. His own uncle on his mother's side was Johannes Johnson, one of the best-known Norwegian missionaries to Madagascar, and a noted hymn-writer.

All in all, the fellowship with Fridrichsen, brilliant professor and fascinating company, brightened my student years and made the 1930s a great time to be at the Faculty. Fridrichsen's influence on my university life was highly beneficial. It was an immense privilege to be guided by him, with his experience and wisdom, and to profit from his generous advice and encouragement. He lifted me out of my narrow little corner and showed me an international horizon. This emphasis on an international outlook was to be made through other situations later on, but it started with Fridrichsen. On reading again his countless letters to me in France and in Africa, I am amazed that he found time to keep in touch with me.

My university years formed me – and favoured me. It was good to come from the narrow world of the school and enter university life with its vast potential. I was to return later, in 1949, as a professor and was then able to enjoy an excellent time with the undergraduates and research students; and suffered rather a grim time, I must admit, with some of the academic staff of the faculty in the 1950s.

In 1931 I was received by Archbishop Nathan Söderblom. I had taken the Bachelor of Divinity exam at the end of March 1931. A Stockholm journalist picked up the story about my plans to study in France, and wrote about it in his newspaper *Dagens Nyheter*.

Somebody on the archbishop's staff read this and I was favoured with an invitation. It was an extraordinary privilege to meet him at the archbishop's palace, next to the cathedral. I had heard much about him, listened to him as an inspiring preacher and leader of worship and seen him in meetings and conferences; but all this was eclipsed by a personal encounter with the great man. He was indeed a great man, in Sweden and internationally, to be counted among such outstanding Swedes as St Bridget, Carl von Linné, Berzelius the chemist, Geijer the historian and Dag Hammarskjöld, secretary-general of the United Nations. Nathan Söderblom, scholar of the History of Religions and creative ecumenical leader – he called the first Ecumenical Conference to Stockholm in 1925 – was the ultimate international churchman.

He received me – I was 21 at the time – as if I were an old friend. 'Where were you born?' I mentioned Vindeln in the north. 'Vindeln,' he exclaimed, 'but my brother the agronomist is there.' A point of contact was established. He enquired about my studies and my idea of going for a year to France, to Strasbourg and Paris. He had special plans for me: the Church of Sweden had just decided to establish a chair of Ecclesiastical Law at the university and I should qualify for this post. He was to follow up this suggestion by writing letters of introduction for 'ce membre distingué de notre université' and personal encouraging letters to me at Strasbourg. I followed his wishes while I was in Strasbourg by attending, for a time, Professor Martin's lectures on Canon Law in the Catholic faculty, where I found myself surrounded by a hundred Catholic students, all in their long black cassocks. I soon found that while this Church Law was a splendid idea in itself, it was not for me and so I eventually withdrew, devoting myself instead to another life and another study – that of missions.

My meeting with Archbishop Söderblom took place at the end of March 1931. It was, I think, characteristic of his approach, to encourage young people in tasks at home and abroad. I was probably the last of them. Only a few weeks later, in July 1931, the great Archbishop passed away aged 65. I was eventually to write a biography of Söderblom, *Nathan Söderblom: his life and work*, published in 1968, and have also written other studies of him.

The Oxford Group

In the 1930s Uppsala was hit by the Spirit, in the form of the 'Oxford Group'. Associated with the name of an English university, this was a revival movement within the Churches, and had an Anglo-Saxon character. It spoke to the individual of sin and forgiveness and formed evangelistic teams and fellowships. The movement was brought from England to Uppsala by a young theological student, Hans Cnattingius.

Through his salutary personal influence it reached out to us with a refreshing spiritual power and conviction. I knew Hans Cnattingius well, and from the end of September 1933 became one of his closest associates. The Oxford Group gave me a solution to a personal problem of mine: 'The Holy Spirit must,' I thought, 'be something more than just the Third Person in the Trinity. What is this Holy Spirit? What does it mean to be influenced by the Spirit and filled by the Spirit?' I realised that I had a form of Pietism but not the spirit of piety. The personal message passed from person to person helped towards renewal and new birth. We were helped by English and Norwegian books on this subject: Geoffrey Allen's *He that Cometh: a sequel to 'Tell John', being further essays on the message of Jesus and present day religion* (1932) and [Kristofer] Sverre Norborg's *En märklig världsväckelse* (1933). Through the Oxford Group I discovered the value of team evangelism. Not the single performer, but the group, a team, could help to carry forward a convincing message of new life. I spent two intense years in this movement. On many occasions I had to rescue a meeting, a 'house party', by repeating my own miserable little conversion story. In the end it was too much; I withdrew, concentrating instead on my doctoral thesis, dealing with the interest in missions within the Church of Sweden from 1835–76, which was published in 1937. The finished thesis was some 600 pages long, and I found the work highly satisfying.

In the midst of this activity I was called for an interview by the acting Mission Director of Church of Sweden Mission (CSM). They were worried, he told me: no volunteers appeared any longer for work in South Africa, there were no missionary candidates. I had shown an interest in the CSM and participated in various student mission conferences in Sweden and abroad. There was now a job waiting for me as a theological teacher in Zululand. Could I help out? This was a decisive 'Beyond' in my life, 'Beyond' Sweden and Europe, and 'Beyond' the well-ordered academic life I had led hitherto. I felt also that the idea met me half-way, by a need for international involvement. I had read E. W. Smith's book on James Kwegyir Aggrey of West Africa, where Aggrey was telling his fellow Africans, 'You are eagles', and I felt greatly attracted by that message. What about 'a missionary calling'? Some, in fact most, of those whom I was to meet among missionaries in Africa held a Pietistic conviction of a special missionary calling, intimated by God in their heart. In my case the call was presented to me by a mission secretary, representing the Church, suggesting that I take on an international task where I was needed. Within less than a year the mission secretary approached me again. I should postpone working on my doctoral thesis; I was to complete this academic work later on, some eight years later. None of us realised then, in 1936, that in another eight years we would have to face a very different world, and a different Africa altogether. Just as important as all this was the change within myself. After changes and penetrating challenges to my life I was to become another kind of person. As it was I chose to complete the doctoral thesis within a year, by April 1937.

Then I met Ingeborg Morén. I first saw her and heard her speak at an Oxford Group weekend. Not that she was a 'Grouper' herself. She was fundamentally formed by a conversion at a Norwegian conference 'on biblical foundation', and anything else seemed to her inadequate, half-hearted, only second best compared with that experience. She was born in Johannesburg where her father was an architect–builder. When she was barely a year old, her parents moved back to Stockholm, where her father built prestigious buildings around the Oscar Church. She was a privileged young woman. Aged 16, she was sent by her parents for a year to Bournemouth, and she spoke English beautifully, I thought. She was devoted to England and English culture. In Sweden, before leaving with me for Africa, she taught English and Religious Knowledge.

Ingeborg was a rare beauty and 'had everything' – as the saying goes – except self-confidence, of which she had very little. I failed to dispel this. It was her African friends, Zulu Christians in Zululand, and Haya Christians in Bukoba, Tanzania, who took her by the hand and made her recognise her potential. In a crisis situation during the Second World War, in 1943, she was made headmistress of the teacher's training school at Kigarama. She managed this task very well, at the same time teaching English classes at this Swahili-speaking school during the most oppressive period of the equatorial day, between 2.00 and 4.00 p.m.

4

THE CHURCH AND SEGREGATION

In October 1937 Ingeborg and I spent four delightful weeks on a steamer from Scandinavia to Cape Town, and another two hot and dusty days and nights on a train from Cape Town to Dundee, a centre of Swedish mission in Natal province, South Africa. In the evening a group of friends welcomed us at an amiable dinner. We had at last reached our journey's end, and were ready to begin the task ahead. We heard singing outside: it was a Zulu school class with their leader, Mrs Mtimkhulu. She gave a little speech of welcome, and I tried to respond with a few words, as a matter of course shaking hands with her and some of her youngsters. Returning to the dinner table, one of the younger members of the group told me – rather pompously, I thought, 'It was a nice little speech you gave. Just one thing in confidence: here we do not shake hands with Natives.' As Ingeborg and I went to our room later in the evening, we walked rather wearily. Had we come to the wrong place? Had we arrived on the wrong planet, where social segregation seeped through even into the Church? Eleven years later that social system was intensified by apartheid, with its legal enactments and with complete differentiation.

The country was led at this time by Jan Smuts, prime minister, and by Jan Hofmeyr, minister of finance. The latter was of special interest to missions, dealing during the week with high finance and the international price of gold, and on Sundays devoting himself to his Sunday School class. In the mission it was taken for granted that Smuts and Hofmeyr were to direct the future of the populations in the country. In 1938–39, however, a new phenomenon appeared on the hills and in the valleys. Ox-waggons arrived – symbolic reminders of a tightening nationalistic programme, foreboding apartheid, although it was difficult to believe this in the 1930s. The relationship with the non-Europeans, so-called, was taken care of by a new organisation, the Native Representative Council, with Dr Edgar Brookes and Rheinallt Jones among the Senators. Was this Council anything but a 'toy telephone' appearing to be a piece of machinery for communication, but in fact mute and voiceless? In the same year, 1936, the

Christian Council of South Africa was founded with two Afrikaner pastors as president and secretary, to be replaced in 1939, as Hitler's war dramatically increased racial antagonisms.

The job intended for me at first was to substitute for a missionary who was going on a year's furlough to Europe. We had to learn to speak and write the Zulu language. The Lutheran missions had a good rule according to which their missionaries had to be able to speak the local language, rather than communicating through an interpreter. The old Swedish Dean (who had first arrived from Sweden in 1897) started us with two hours of Zulu grammar a day. He was well-acquainted with this subject, having actually published a book on it, a Zulu grammar in Zulu, an arcane thing to do at the time. As soon as possible we tried to apply this grammatical learning to practical speech. As a language student one was free to use any opportunity that came along. In 1938 we spent a couple of months living in a Zulu evangelist's home, at Makitika in Zululand. I wrote a little book in Swedish on this experience. Nothing could have been more helpful than this daily encounter with a local Zulu family, a congregation and a splendid Zulu leader, the evangelist Absalom Ndebele. He was a 'he-man', if ever there was one. When we climbed together the steep hills of Zululand, he would reach out his hand to pull me up, easily and surely, over a boulder. I liked him immensely. The Ndebele family had a house with three small rooms, of which we had use of one. In the evening, the family gathered round an open fire. This was our opportunity to learn Zulu proverbs and biblical phrases, all adding to our Zulu beginners' linguistic exercises.

We had other experiences of this kind in our first year of language study: I met with an Anglican priest in charge of St Augustine's Centre in Zululand. We were invited to spend a couple of weeks with him and his staff, learning Zulu in the process. It so happened that the lady president of the Anglican women's worldwide association, the 'Mother's Union', widow of Bishop Woods of Winchester, had come to visit the place. She was taken to 14 different outstations, and gave to each of them the same little speech, 'I have heard that you Zulu mothers have many children, ten or twelve children. But I have 600,000 children', etc. It was exceedingly fortunate for a student of the Zulu language that this little speech was interpreted by 14 different Zulu teachers at his or her outstation. Nothing could have been more instructive for the use of the forms of the Zulu language structure – the noun, the verb, the tenses, the constructions. It worked, and it was a pleasure to discover those Zulu connections and structures.

The stay at the Anglo-Catholic centre was helpful but not without problems. Dating from 1922 there was an agreement of 'intercommunion' between the Church of England and the Church of Sweden, but here at St Augustine's this agreement did not fully apply. In South Africa, they said, Swedes had fellowship with 'other Lutheran bodies' and therefore the Anglican priest-in-charge suggested that we had better abstain from partaking in the daily Holy Communion. This was a tough proposition, but we managed in our own way. We got up as early as any others, came to the beautiful cathedral and knelt with the others – but did not partake in communion. This problem, which was not of our making, made us eager to arrive at a worthy solution to something which should never really have been a problem in the first place.

This language-learning period soon came to an end – I realise of course that I could have used a much longer time for language study, but Ingeborg and I passed whatever there were in the way of tests, and I found myself occupying the position of Lutheran pastor in charge of the Dundee congregation. The job involved directing two Zulu pastors and some 20 catechists, and their local congregations, spread out among the African communities in the Natal coalfields. At the same place there was an Anglican priest, a Methodist pastor and a Dutch Reformed *predikant*, all European: they looked after white congregations while their Zulu counterparts served Zulu congregations. In the 1850s, Henry Venn of the CMS in London had suggested that missions should aim at church indigenisation – the 'three-selfs' criteria: self-governing, self-supporting and self-propagating churches – and these other churches acted in accordance with this fundamental idea. The Lutherans, however, moved cautiously, and in their case there was no parallel European congregation, as there was with the Anglicans, Wesleyan Methodists and so on. Here at Dundee the young Swedish Lutheran pastor, whatever his foibles, and no matter his inexperience in the language, was, as a white person, in charge. Nobody questioned this arrangement, and I too had to go through this experience.

I had two ordained Zulu colleagues, pastors Jonathan Sibiya and Michael Mzobe, the former hard as a rock, but most faithful once won over, the latter a brilliant preacher in the Zulu language, one of the four or five best preachers I have ever listened to in any language. Both men became my great friends. We planned the work together, formulating 'Preacher's helps' for the four quarters of the year, planning the work of catechists, youth groups, women and Sunday School leaders.

My time in South Africa between 1938 and 1942 introduced me to two very different Church situations, at Dundee in northern Natal and at Ceza in northern Zululand. Dundee was situated in a coal-mining area, and the 20 local mission outstations served African coal-miners, through the work of some 20 evangelists. Ceza in Zululand was part of what was then called a 'reserve', far away from the cities and mines. The population was largely traditional, a term indicating African traditional religion, but with hundreds of Christians attached to Roman Catholic, Anglican, Lutheran and Methodist centres (which were only accessible on horseback over the hills and through the valleys) and also to a rapidly increasing number of 'Independent' groups, mainly 'Zionists' as they called themselves.

The Swedish missionary exercised his influence through contacts with Zulu pastors and evangelists. Inevitably these men were far more knowledgeable about the local situation than any foreigner could hope to be, quite apart from the obvious fact that my Zulu co-workers were experts in the Zulu language, while the foreigner could at best achieve only an approximate linguistic grasp. For a religious group the language was, of course, decisive. I think it is fair to state that I had the best of relations with my Zulu co-workers. They honoured me by calling me by the name of a Zulu regiment, *uPhondolwendlovu* (the Elephant's tusk), and this is the name I still use in writing to my Zulu friends.

I learned as much as possible from these pastors, and I was amazed at the quality of the theological training they had received. The social and political situation of the African masses obviously provided an impetus for the Zulu pastor, an awareness of his role as inherited from Moses: 'Let my people go.' They were able to proclaim this revolutionary insight up to a certain point – and then leave it there, attempting to re-interpret the Moses-role. This brought them close both to the Old Testament and to the New Testament. I saw this especially in the person of the Reverend Michael Mzobe. I could never be sufficiently grateful for the chance to learn to understand and speak the Zulu language, a learning which enabled me to capture the thrust of his message. I was impressed when I heard Mzobe's sermons. Mzobe was able to turn an Old Testament text or a New Testament passage into a compelling message closely related to the life of his oppressed listeners. At our quarterly meetings with evangelists, women's groups, youth organisations, or Sunday School teachers we discussed matters of teaching, finance and discipline as well as filling the general role of pastor and missionary, visiting each outstation once a quarter. This was how the local church work was organised and looked after.

The Swedish Lutheran mission was related to the 'Co-operating Lutheran Missions' and it was interesting to know our partners from different Lutheran countries. Contact with the heavily tension-filled German home front of the 1930s was established by the visit in South Africa of the Berlin Mission director, Dr Siegfried Knak, well-known as the author of his invaluable book, *Zwischen Nil und Tafelbai* (Between the Nile and Table Bay), published in 1928, and as a leader of Lutheran German missionaries. A conference was announced to meet with Dr Knak, and as one would expect, the missionaries of the German and Hermannsburg societies attended. Among those present was one non-German, myself, keenly interested in understanding German attitudes at this particular point in history. The debate mainly concerned financial support through so-called *Devisen* (foreign exchange) and other practical matters; but specifically theological problems were not excluded. The leader of the Berlin Mission in South Africa was perturbed by the supposed differences in Lutheran orthodoxy between his own mission – also that of Dr Knak – and the Hermannsburg mission and said so openly, 'Why is it that we German Lutherans are divided among ourselves? Have we then two Luthers?' Dr Knak was not going to allow such liberties, '*Aber Herr P ... solche Sachen sagt mann nicht* (one does not say such things). *Setzen Sie sich* (sit down).'

The 'Co-operating Lutheran missions' – Norwegians, Americans, Swedes, Berlin and Hermannsburg Lutherans – had certain interests in common. One of these was a common Lutheran hymn-book. A committee with one representative for each mission was formed to look into the matter, with Dr Johannes Astrup, a Norwegian from the Evangelical Lutheran Church of America, as chairman. He had various interests to consider, but none so much as protecting the Schreuder memory: the extraordinary Norwegian bishop and missionary who had served in Zululand and Madagascar in the nineteenth century. There was also an African member of the committee, the Reverend M. J. Mphanza, representing the Norwegian Mission, an impressive Zulu pastor who played his particular role in this white group, that of agreeing with the chairman, saying respectfully '*Yebo, Baba* (Yes, Father).' For some unknown reason, I was the secretary.

The chairman led the proceedings by going through hymn after hymn, scrutinising it for proper Zulu and theological quality. Here was number so and so, Dr A. could not have been more critical: 'The Zulu language is poor, the theology atrocious.' As he uttered these caustic words he looked at the index at the end of the book and there to his consternation found that the writer was none other than the famous 'H. P. S.' himself, as indicated by the potent initials of Bishop Schreuder. It did not take him long to change tack, however. He now pleaded with the group, 'Well, gentlemen, I ask you to look more closely at this hymn. Can you possibly think of better Zulu than this one? And theologically? Could you find any other hymn expressing better the central idea of Christianity than this one?' Our Zulu colleague was persistently ready to agree, repeating his respectful '*Yebo Baba.*' So the matter was settled, and our committee could turn to the next hymn.

In 1939 Hitler's war broke out, involving everybody in southern Africa and northern Africa, in the desert. In Tanzania the German missionaries were interned, and the Lutheran World Convention invited neutral Swedish missionaries from various points in Africa to serve in Tanzania. Ingeborg and I volunteered, hoping to leave for Tanzania in 1941. I was about to quit Ceza and South Africa in 1941, but there was a sudden change of plan. At the Rorke's Drift Theological Seminary the Swedish theological teacher was bitten by a green mamba and, but for a combination of certain fortunate circumstances, would have died. His life was saved but it took him the best part of a year to recover from the effects of the poisoning.

I had to take over his job at the Theological Seminary, and thus spent what I was later to refer to as 'my ten happy weeks in South Africa'. This transfer was a gift to me. It meant doing what I had offered to do in South Africa, and Ingeborg and I found the time together with the 24 theological students – one or two from Zimbabwe – inspiring and refreshing. Here were young men who were ultimately to become leaders, bishops and rural deans in the African church. We were able to establish a constructive fellowship. This meant setting aside certain man-made restrictions which had been in vogue until then. The students were ex-teachers studying theology for a period of four years, this was their last year, leading to ordination. The teaching staff consisted of one American missionary, a Zulu pastor and myself.

It was a secluded little world, seemingly far away from South African society as such. Yet even at this church the facts of segregation – as practised by the Church – were evident. From the college we took over the missionary's house, a comparatively large building with two entrance doors, a main door and the kitchen door. We found that the students and their wives had never entered through the main door, and had had, in accordance with some unwritten law or rule, to use the kitchen door. The students were acutely aware of this inequality. Thus again the rule of segregation had invaded a central place in the Church, the theological faculty. Ingeborg and I immediately broke with this rule, if a rule it was, and every evening invited two couples for tea and sandwiches in the house, through the front door! We then had the chance to freely discuss problems related to the Church and to the faculty. I was simply too interested in these people to abide by any unwritten rules.

My special teaching at the College involved Old Testament, Church History and Practical Theology. I found this task interesting and received, I think, a good response. Teaching Old Testament in Africa is a great challenge. Many students recognise similarities between Hebrew thinking – the prophets Amos, Ezekiel, Isaiah and the others, not forgetting the Proverbs – and African patterns and traditions, and it is the theological teacher's task to discover these similarities and bring them to the fore. I found Church History to be at least as interesting to Zulu students as it was to Swedish students. I was impressed by the high standards shown in the written end-of-term tests.

In order to bring the subject of Church History closer to the reality of my students, I included in one test a question on Independent African churches to which we may have made some reference during that term. For my question I used the phrase 'The Sects in South Africa'. One of the students, the most original in the group, Titus Mthembu, gave a pithy answer: 'The one who calls others a sect, is a sect himself.' Needless to say, Mthembu and I became excellent friends, with his wide contacts in Zulu society, and he was eventually to help me considerably in my research on the 'Independents'.

Ceza, in Zululand, took us to a different world altogether, far from the towns and mines. Here the Swedish mission centre covered only ten

acres, its diminutiveness a forceful reminder of the Africans' hunger
for land. Within this space there was a church building, a hospital with
a couple of doctors, medical sisters and orderlies, and beds for patients,
a school soon to be raised to the level of a secondary school, staff
houses, and a stable for our two horses, an excellent means of transport
at any time but particularly in wartime. There was at Ceza an elderly
Zulu pastor, the Reverend Andreas Madide, and some 15 evangelists at
the district's outposts. Among them I found my friend and Zulu
language-teacher, Absalom Ndebele, and Absalom Buthelezi, father of
the present Lutheran bishop in Johannesburg. My work was basically
the same as in Dundee: leading a congregation; chairing quarterly
meetings for evangelists, youth leaders and women's groups; school
teachers' conferences; and the daily visiting rounds, on horseback, to
the outstations, all with their particular problems and worries, family
questions and financial concerns.

Ceza brought me closer to the people, so that I was able to formulate a fundamental question: How to adapt the Christian message to
these people, how to translate it into Zulu terms. Before I could even
formulate this question in my own mind, I was thrown into the midst
of it. It happened at an ordinary Lenten service in 1940. I gave a short
address, we sang a couple of hymns and prayed. After the service we
met under a tree outside the church. An elderly Zulu lady, Emelina
Simelane, came to me saying,

> Sorry, *Mfundisi* [Pastor], I left the church building in the middle of the
> service. You may have noticed that I left as we were about to sing. You
> announced hymn number 154. But that hymn is so strong that when I
> begin to sing it, I start to *qaqazela* [to shake] with my whole body. But
> here we are not allowed to shake.

This was a real challenge. I answered, '*Mame* [my Mother] this
church house is not my building. It belongs to God and to you. If you
must shake, do so here. You are free.' It was quite a decision on my
part. The meeting with that woman was an eye-opener to me. This
well-behaved Lutheran congregation was different from what it
seemed to be. It concealed deeper needs, about which I, the foreign
participant, knew next to nothing, and which I, as a priest, had to try
to understand.

If I needed a sociological laboratory to study Zulu Church life in
depth, I did not need to go far afield. I could just dig where I stood.
The laboratory extended everywhere in northern Zululand. In the
course of my ordinary Lutheran church work, I could combine interviews with charismatic individuals and groups, all in their white
uniforms. At High School in Umeå in 1927 I had come across a
doctoral thesis on the Radical Pietists in early Swedish society, called
'the Grey Frocks'. Here I was right among the Zionist 'White
Frocks'. I did not need to go far. I could go out on horseback at
dawn to find 100 or more Zionists doing their pious ablutions under

a waterfall. There I was able to establish contacts and get to know the local leaders of the charismatic movement. In most cases, these Zionists had previously belonged to an 'established' church. I had to try to understand the reasons for leaving an established church in order to form some charismatic group. As if this were not enough, I took the unorthodox step of inviting the Zionists to meet with the local Lutherans in the Ceza church. The church building was filled with white-clad Zionists, and we spent the whole time one day discussing the 'Holy Spirit', another day 'Baptism in Living Waters', and similar theological and personal questions.

For my ordinary church work we had a month's holiday and Ingeborg and I spent it with Audrey Richards, a sociologist at the University of Johannesburg. She was a brilliant student of the famous Bronislaw Malinowski and welcomed the idea of a study on the independent churches; her research seminars also provided a perspective on urban–rural relations in South African society as a whole. My own sociological training was sadly limited. To a certain extent I was able to overcome this handicap by relying on a recently published book dealing with related problems, Monica Hunter's (later, Wilson) *Reaction to conquest: effects of contact with Europeans on the Pondo of South Africa* (published in 1936), a study of the Pondo, whose situation was near enough to my Zulu reality. I could see how she approached the kindred Pondo local groups and this inspired my approach to problems in Zulu society, in the 'reserve', on the European farm and in the city. I extended the enquiry to include meetings with the Nazaretha, another sophisticated charismatic group. I needed to explore two main sources for this story, using local interviews to understand the present 'Zionist' situation, and studying the historical background to Ethiopian churches.

For the 'Ethiopian' sources, I had to wait some three years, after having returned to South Africa from Tanzania in 1945. This brought me back to the Rand and to Pretoria. I contacted Dr N. J. van Warmelo, government ethnologist. He gave me access to the thousands of enormous church files in the corridors of what was then the Department of Bantu Affairs. All church groups sent annual reports to Pretoria, in the hope of being accepted as 'recognised' churches, and I was able to benefit from this wealth of written material. This also provided me with factual information on the interrelations of these churches and the official reasons for their splits. It was Dr van Warmelo – a good Dutchman in South African employ – who suggested the name 'Bantu Prophets' for my study. I contributed a well-illustrated article to a magazine, *Libertas*, and called the article 'Black Man's Church', a title which at that time one avoided, preferring the phrase suggested by van Warmelo.

My ordinary church work at Ceza, and the interviews with the Zionists were, of course, carried out in Zulu. It became my most beloved Bantu language. I do not for a moment suggest that I was a good Bantu linguist but somehow my Zulu stuck and I enjoyed speaking the language. Later on I had an illustration of how deeply the Zulu language had lodged in my mind. In 1941 and 1942 I had initial contacts with Johannes Galilee Shembe and his Nazaretha church. In 1958, after 16 years spent in East Africa and Europe, I returned to the Nazaretha for a visit to their 'July Festival'. It was the most sacred occasion in their church year, the Sabbath. Some 10,000 faithful, all dressed in white, were assembled ready to listen to the great leader's annual message. I kept close to him and was seated at his table, keen to take down his message word for word. Hymns were sung and prayers said, and now I expected Shembe to rise in order to give his message, myself being prepared with a notebook and a pen. Then he turned to me and said, 'Now Dr Sundkler, we ask you to preach.' I took in the whole situation. These 10,000 men and women, what Bible word did they need? I thought of those hard-working people, despised and downtrodden in the world. Yes, I felt, I knew now what Bible verse to choose, the end of Matthew 11: '*Wozani kimi*', 'Come unto me all you that labour and are heavy-laden, and I will give you rest. Take my yoke upon you.' Those were meaningful words as a point of departure. I started out thus and continued speaking in Zulu for 12 loaded minutes, then sat down. Then Shembe rose and spoke on exactly that word, preaching for an hour and a half, an intense message on burdens that people carry: self-imposed or externally enforced. Then he sat down, saying to me, 'Thank you Dr Sundkler, your message inspired me.'

I close my 'Independent Church' section by suggesting that my chapters on the Charismatic Zionists were written with reference to interviews held between 1939 and 1942 in northern Zululand, while my acquaintance with the 'Ethiopian' groups relied on the masses of files in the 'Bantu Affairs' department in Pretoria, which I studied in 1945. In 1946, I took all this material with me to Britain and wrote 'Bantu Prophets' in the Africa Library of Selly Oak Colleges, Birmingham. I contacted Professor Raymond Firth at the London School of Economics and attended his seminars in 1946, which offered a wealth of ideas. I needed his help for I was haunted by doubts as to the value of my research. Dare I publish it? Once a week I travelled by train from Birmingham to London to take part in the inspiring Firth seminars. It was an exciting group to meet.

Bantu Prophets was published in 1948. I combined this with a new edition of *Bantu Prophets* in 1961 and a follow-up volume, entitled *Zulu Zion*, in 1976. There was a special concern of mine, the prosopographic approach, which makes this research important, namely the role of the personalities – not only of ideas and principles. In the twenty-first century, one is going to meet a new South Africa which will enquire into the role of African personalities of the past, and then it will be important, I hope, to study the role of distinguished African personalities in the 'Independent' churches.

Already in 1942, as we set out to move to Tanzania, along with my doubts I sensed the value of this research. I did something which stressed the importance I placed on these initial notes on 'Independent Churches', eventually to become *Bantu Prophets*. Just before leaving South Africa for new work on the equator, I wrote my will! On the whole it could be considered unusual for a 33-year-old to write a will, but this is what I did with reference to my 'Zionist' notes, and I include the will here. This was, after all, wartime; people died – that was common at the time. We were going to a place on the equator, and I had to assume that it was hazardous. So I felt that I should write my will, with regard to these 'Zion papers' of mine. Here it is, written at Ceza, Zululand, May 5, 1942:

> In case I should die in Tanganyika and will not be able to carry on the investigations re the Sects:
> 1. I would be glad if this material could be taken over by somebody chosen by Messrs Rollnick, Institute of Race Relations and J. F. Holleman, Stellenbosch.[1]
> 2. My successor for this very interesting and important project – I envy his being able to complete the work – will find a thorough plan of the whole work in two exercise books and then a lot of material on various aspects of this vast subject.
> I stress that I wanted to call the book *Black Church* with the important sub-title *an interpretation of the so-called independent churches in South Africa*. The historical viewpoint I have not dealt with – as it is not so important (respectful bow to Malinowski). I have tried to find relevant material for the life and faith of these Churches. They ought not to be understood in the dimensions of European dogmatics, but with the fourth dimension of Marcus Connelly's play about African-Americans, *The Green Pastures* (published in 1930).
> 3. I hope my successor will be a person with some influence who can get time for his work and study to do the work properly. Please do not spoil the work – it is so important – and could be a standard work for 50 years to come!
> Good luck, my dear successor – I would have loved to live and finish this and other pieces of work.
> So much to do – so little done.
> Your friend,
> Bengt Sundkler

Notes

1. Commentary, December 1994: Mr Rollnick, was a young secretary in the South African Race Relations Institute, Johannesburg, whom I met once, and then lost contact with. Hans [J. F.] Holleman, on the other hand, became my close friend. He spent some 4–6 weeks in his tent on our Ceza station and I learnt from him how a well-trained social anthropologist handled his study of northern Zululand material. Later on in life, Holleman returned to Holland and became professor at the University of Leiden and Director of the Netherlands Universities' Africa Studies Centre.

5

TO THE EQUATOR

Our 'Beyond' this time took us from South Africa to the equator. In June 1942 we flew by seaplane – the best kind of travel, I think – from Durban to Dar es Salaam, heading for Bukoba west of Lake Victoria. This 'Beyond' of ours – was it avoiding the unbearable segregation situation in the south? Above all it was an act of solidarity with an unknown, 'orphaned' church on the equator. Neutral Swedes on missionary service in Africa were invited to come to the rescue in a critical situation and I could not think of any other response than to accept the call.

The move from one African church in the south to another on the equator gave occasion to draw comparisons. Both were Bantu-speaking, yet there was already phonetically a great difference between the two languages. The Zulu language has vast vowels upon which the speaker loves to dwell, authoritatively and compellingly, a language for kings, judges and priests. The Luhaya language of Bukoba, on the other hand, has quick, rapid vowels tying its consonants to a glimmering weave of meaning, a language for brisk lawyers and counsellors.

Tanganyika was a mandated territory under the League of Nations, and the region west of Lake Victoria was officially ruled by eight local 'kings' or 'chiefs'. To this extent Bukoba was the 'show-window' of the political system of 'Indirect Rule'. To the occasional onlooker the system managed well; but there were sudden critical points when a 'king' was dethroned or dismissed by the British Governor for mismanagement.

The Haya Church became 'orphaned' during the Second World War. On seeing its missionaries removed from active missionary service, it insisted on its own African leadership. They elected pastor Jonathan Karoma as their leader, and he proved ideal for the purpose. In contrast I knew the capacity of the church in Zululand with people of good theological training and great ability. There was in South Africa, however, something untoward in the segregation policy of the country which did not allow African leaders to lead; something hampered them from doing so.

At this time, in the 1940s, the Zulu church was a women's concern. The men were away from home, working in the gold mines on the Rand or in the coal mines of northern Natal. The *Abasizikazi* movement, and the *manyano* movement as a whole in South Africa, brought out the very best in women's combined initiative. In South Africa, the Zulu church women had their own presidents and secretaries. In the weekly *manyano* day, Thursday, they encouraged one another with biblical addresses, joyful singing and urgent prayer. In 1942 there existed little in Bukoba to match the work done by the remarkable churchwomen in Zululand and in South Africa as a whole. In the Bukoba Church at that time a woman took the word only tentatively, seemingly embarrassed. This was to change radically through the East African Revival, which gave Haya women a new authority and a new freedom, and has helped to create a new atmosphere in the Bukoba church.

I came to a Hayaland ecclesiastically dominated by the Catholic Church: with surprising numbers of White Fathers whizzing around on their motorbikes and mopeds, and that was all I saw of them – 20 years prior to the good Pope Johannes XXIII – and the numerous White Sisters, serving as schoolteachers and medical sisters.

I also came to a Hayaland where German Protestant missionaries had been active. When the German missionaries were interned, only one old couple remained in Bukoba. The husband was 75 years of age and was allowed to stay on for health reasons. We got to know the old couple, Wilhelm and Martha Hosbach. Nobody could have represented the Protestants as well as they did. Mrs Hosbach had arrived in Tanganyika in 1890, and was called 'Mrs Europe' in Swahili as she was the first white woman to arrive, he came in 1893. In the 1940s and the 1950s he served the Bukoba mission as a treasurer, she established contacts with new German-speaking groups in Bukoba, Jewish refugees who had arrived via Germany, the Near East and Mombasa, to be placed for the time being in Bukoba. Mrs Hosbach was very musical, and invited these expatriates to musical soirées, playing Schubert and Schumann on her organ. We had breakfast with the old couple at 7.30 a.m. At the meal, Mrs Hosbach would suddenly ask: 'Have we prayed?' *Vater* Hosbach retorted tersely: 'At least I.' It took some time before I discovered that he held morning prayers at 6.00 a.m. every morning in the church, with a lively little address to the workers in town. He gave Swahili lessons to Ingeborg and myself. In December 1942, however, his health deteriorated abruptly, and finally Emil Kilimali, the driver, and I had to conclude that *Vater* Hosbach could not survive beyond the following day. We prepared accordingly. Expecting a crowd, I wrote addresses in English, German and Swahili about Wilhelm Hosbach, the blessed missionary. That day he pulled through. He lived for another 25 years, and died eventually at Oberkassel-bei-Bonn, a centenarian.

Bukoba, in the west of the country, was related to a wider federation of Lutheran churches. For one thing, we were close to the rapidly expanding Kilimanjaro Lutheran Church. This provided me with the opportunity to represent Bukoba in meeting with this remarkable Protestant Church on Mount Kilimanjaro, with its active communities on the green slopes of the mountain. The missionary in charge, Dr Richard Reusch, was a highly original personality. A Cossack from Kazakhstan and educated at Tartu University, Estonia, he was reputed to have climbed Mount Kilimanjaro 50 times. For somebody like Ingeborg and myself who tried just once, and then only managed to reach 15,000 feet, his was an impressive achievement. Among Chagga teachers I enjoyed meeting Stefano Moshi, who was later to become the first Lutheran bishop of the Kilimanjaro church. During the war he taught future school teachers. The Bukoba Evangelical Church, however, had its own history, which was also related to the Anglicans in Buganda. Kampala in Buganda was, in effect, our capital at the time, more so than Dar es Salaam which was situated on the coast and too far away for us in the west of the country. This was a creative period in the church in Buganda, and our visits to Kampala were inspiring.

The church consists of people. So it was in the Lutheran church in Bukoba, and it was my great privilege to co-operate with pastors, teachers and ordinary church people, men and women. From this period I recall particularly some of the preachers such as Jonathan Karoma, the chairman of the pastors and a charismatic personality. In his case, the traditional Bukoba religious heritage was determinative. As a preacher he used illustrations from the needs and conflicts of this traditional African religion which he knew so well. William Bwanuma was his young co-worker. He had started 'Buhaya's Hope', the name of the youth organisation in the church. They adopted an exceedingly practical approach, helping old and young alike, thus giving the youth leaders a privileged position. In the far south of the district I met with a young teacher, Sylvester Machumu, who impressed me greatly. He led his school class of 120 children with skill and enthusiasm. Twenty years later, when I returned to Bukoba as a bishop, I found that Sylvester Machumu had left the church fellowship and started his own 'Church of the Holy Spirit'. It then became my task to try to bring him back to the Church.

In 1941, the German Protestant missionaries were interned and removed from Bukoba. In the villages a rumour spread, claiming that Protestantism was forbidden by the colonial authorities. To dispel this rumour, my first task, together with Pastor Jonathan Karoma, was to make visitations to every Protestant village and community, in order to establish our presence and show our readiness to serve the Lutheran community. We were fortunate in having an excellent driver, Emil Kilimali, and a lorry. He took us to the main district centres from where we walked for daily encounters with the local churches. This was how I spent the best part of my first 18 months in the area. At the end of those visits to every district, having spent up to ten days in each central district, we gathered together the local leaders for a final conference which lasted two to three days.

This visitational approach provided us with a good chance to get to know the local congregations, and gave me daily the priceless opportunity to listen to Jonathan Karoma. I also gave a little biblical address in each place, in Swahili or Luhaya, but my homiletical effort was inevitably limited in comparison with Karoma's messages. It has been suggested that only the 'Independent' churches in Africa have had charismatic preachers, while the 'established' mission churches are represented by more wooden performers. Jonathan Karoma's unforgettable preaching refuted this observation. His personal background helped towards this: his elder brother was an *embandwa*, a priest-diviner in Haya traditional religion, and Jonathan started out in life as a 15-year-old messenger for his elder brother. Eventually a British District Officer came to hear of the boy, took care of him and placed him in a Protestant mission school.

As Karoma and I passed through Hayaland, reaching out to the local congregations, we found the little churches packed. Jonathan Karoma transformed the pious congregation into a crying, laughing group responding to his unforgettable message. In two books of mine, *Ung kyrka i Tanganyika* (1948) and *Bara Bukoba: Church and Community in Tanzania* (1980), I have given examples of Karoma's preaching, I shall not repeat this here. The sum total of it was that we were treated to unforgettable sermons by Karoma, with the Old Testament and the Synoptics of the New Testament being brought to life before our astonished eyes and ears.

To supplement the work in the districts, I announced a competition for pastors and teachers in writing an autobiography. I handed out exercise books and pens (these precious articles were rare in wartime) inviting each one to write on the theme 'Jesus Christ in my Life', in Swahili or Luhaya. To stimulate the writing I advertised that the three best in each district would receive a prize: first prize – three shillings, second – two shillings, and third – one shilling (as it was wartime there was not much money around). Nearly 100 of the autobiographies were thus collected, providing very valuable material for each writer and for my own knowledge of the spiritual situation in the Church. We also included autobiographies from the students at the teacher training school at Kigarama. These young men would claim for their future that, after taking their exam at the teacher training school, they would return to their home village to serve there as teachers. Very soon, however, the horizon of these young men was widened to cover the whole territory of Tanganyika.

Our activity was to some extent abated by a crisis at the Kigarama Teachers' Training School, some 30 miles north of Bukoba. The Second World War was raging, and this could not but affect the nerves of some. When the German missionaries were interned, a highly capable Swiss lady teacher was appointed headmistress of the teacher training school. She was herself psychologically affected by the war, and this took a dramatic turn. One evening, at school prayers, she announced, without consulting anybody else, that the following morning the school would close. All students and teachers were ordered to return to their home villages. Heavy consternation followed. Had her plan succeeded, it would have meant a major catastrophe for the school and the diocese as a whole.

One of the teachers, Onai Sengenge, took his bicycle and cycled through the night the 30 miles to Bukoba. Luckily it so happened that I was at Bukoba that night and was awakened at 1 a.m. by this news from Kigarama. I asked the driver, Emil Kilimali, to get ready and we drove through the night to Kigarama. At 5.30 a.m. we arrived, making as much noise as possible, ready to take over. Ultimately I was able to act on the orders of the Augustana Lutheran Mission, the body in charge of the 'orphaned' Lutheran churches in the country. I called the staff to an extraordinary meeting and asked for their help. Were they prepared to carry on with new management, in this case Ingeborg and myself? One of the teachers rose – he was later to become one of my best friends through the decades. Ernest Lutashobya, young as he was at that time, declared on behalf of his colleagues that they would gladly co-operate with me, convinced that together we were going to manage. The headmistress was moved to Bukoba and then to new friends in central Tanganyika.

Who was to take on the headmaster's job? This was decided by British officials in the colony's Education Department. Did I have the necessary pedagogical competence? I had a doctoral degree from Uppsala University but that had no pedagogic dimension to it. Very fortunately, Ingeborg had her Teacher's Diploma from Stockholm with her, and she was installed as the new headmistress, with responsibility also as a school nurse. She taught English, while I gave lessons in History and Geography, Current Affairs and Scripture. I gave three-and-a-half days per week to the teacher training school, and the rest to the Church through continued visitations to local congregations. Not surprisingly, it was a full-time job.

We were an isolated little teacher training school in the northwest corner of the country. Fortunately, the International Missionary Council had appointed an advisor for Protestant Schools, L. B. Greaves, ex-Methodist missionary in Ghana. In November 1943 he visited our Kigarama school, and nobody could have been more helpful and encouraging. He informed us that from the point of view of atmosphere and results, Kigarama was not managing too badly. It helped us to realise that Kigarama was a centre where the future leadership of the district, especially through a future staff of teachers, could emerge.

We had arrived in Bukoba in 1942 at a crucial point in the history of the Bukoba Lutheran Church. The very first signs of the

Evangelical Revival in East Africa – then often referred to as 'the Rwanda revival' – could be experienced in Bukoba. At Kigarama a local struggle was fought between the newly 'Saved Ones' and the stubborn conservative hard-liners. For New Year's Eve 1944–45 the two parties met for Holy Communion in the Kigarama Church. The atmosphere was charged, accusations were hurled across the floor in the church. I had been asked to lead the Communion service. I read the first part of the liturgy and then declared that, in the circumstances, I could not declare the General Absolution. They must carry on the struggle there and then, until they were reconciled. I left the building, telling them that I was prepared to return to them when they were able to forgive one another. After midnight I was called, and the Absolution was pronounced as a relevant and liberating declaration.

6

METROPOLIS AND AFRICA

In May 1946 I was on my way to Britain travelling by ship from Gothenburg. I sat on deck and looked at the sea. A few of my fellow passengers did the same. There was an English monk, in his black cassock. That must be Father Hebert, I thought, on his way home after discussions with Swedish churchmen whose books he was translating. Father Gabriel Hebert, SSM, was a leading member of the Society of the Sacred Mission, an Anglican religious order founded in 1893 by Father Herbert Kelly.[1] Father Hebert was something of a New Testament scholar, and had followed with keen interest Swedish New Testament research in the 1930s. 'Sundkler,' he mused, 'are you the son of Bengt Sundkler?' he asked. I explained my relation to that person, and we had a good talk together, about common interests in Sweden and Africa.

I was on my way to Selly Oak Colleges in Birmingham, where I worked on my 'Independent Churches' material. I had spent some months in Selly Oak before the war, picking up a little English before going to Africa in 1937. The Africa section of the Selly Oak Library was ideal for me, small and compact, with valuable studies on sociology and economics. The Africa collection was built up by the Missions professor at the Colleges, Charles Pelham Groves. I was allocated a room in the library next to his and we became good friends. Groves had served for some time as a Methodist missionary in Nigeria and then been invalided home after some illness.

This also gave me an opportunity to learn about the Selly Oak Colleges, founded by the Cadburys, one of the well-known Quaker chocolate families along with those of the Frys and Rowntrees. Soon I was to meet the head of the family, George Cadbury, son of George Cadbury senior and founder of the world-famous Bournville commercial and social enterprise. One day he made a tour of the Colleges, as his family helped finance the running of the place. As well as visiting the teaching staff he also came into my room. 'What are you doing?' I had heard of his ambition to see the Colleges used for Christian research, and I could honestly reply that I was doing research.

'Research,' he said, 'so you are doing research.' He pulled out his wallet and gave me two pounds. This was 1946, in the aftermath of war, and the money was worth three good meals.

My contacts with Dr Audrey Richards in Johannesburg during the war gave me the idea of paying weekly visits to the London School of Economics and Political Science (LSE) and Professor Raymond Firth's seminars. Firth had succeeded Bronislaw Malinowski and had an excellent group of young scholars who met under his leadership. Here were brilliant students who had returned to the metropolis from fieldwork in Asia, Indonesia and Africa, all ready to help me along. What some theological scholars could not see was obvious to Firth: the importance of a book on Independent Churches in South Africa. I was able to discuss my material with the professor and his research students and, above all, be encouraged by their faith in my task. This book on the Independent churches in South Africa was published in 1948, a second edition appeared in 1961, and a follow-up volume, *Zulu Zion and some Swazi Zionists*, in 1976.

I worked on my manuscript between May and December of 1946 and was then ready to take up another subject altogether. After the war there was intense interest in the theme of Church union in India. Why not write a book on the history of the Church of South India? In August 1947 I found myself again in Britain, ready to explore the debates on this Union between 1900 and 1947. I had a hunch that I should begin with the Methodists and their debates on the subject, so I went to see the general secretary of the Methodist Missionary Society and explained to him what I was trying to do, for which I would need access to records of the 50 years of debate in the archives. 'You don't need that, you know,' he suggested to me. 'It is all in our printed reports.' I thanked him for this valuable information, and left his room.

In the corridor I felt that it would be even wiser to see the person who really knew about the archives, the great man's secretary, so I went to her. She was more obliging: she took me to the window and explained that down there, I think eight storeys below, was the air raid shelter which housed the Methodist archives. It was an immense room which in 1939 had been filled, in each corner, with collections of letters from Africa and the West Indies – and South India. To combat the dust which had gathered in those war years, I went along to an outfitters and bought a pair of overalls. I then set to work; but this was only the beginning. I proceeded to the London Missionary Society, the Church Missionary Society, the Society for the Propagation of the Gospel, and to the Scottish Missionary Society in Edinburgh, collecting relevant, highly interesting material from all these sources, together with Dr Banninga's material from the United States.

I worked hard those days, from 2 August to the end of October and started writing on 1 November, continuing through Christmas. My manuscript on 'South India' was for various reasons left to 'mature' until the beginning of 1953. It became theologically my most ambitious work. Through Max Warren of the CMS, I was greatly helped by a young Anglican secretary, Douglas Webster, who spent seven weeks with us in Uppsala preparing my manuscript for publication. It was published in 1954 under the title *Church of South India: the movement towards union 1900–1947*. Douglas Webster became a very good friend, with an excellent taste for this kind of writing. My book was a learned thesis of some 450 pages. Douglas returned to London where he produced a series of 'What Is' books. *What is this Church of South India?* became a relatively good best-seller; *What is Evangelism?*, *What is a Missionary?* and *What is Spiritual Healing?* were also titles in that series.

My work on South Africa and South India opened the door for me to the International Missionary Council (IMC) in London, where I became research secretary from the beginning of 1948, succeeding Dr Charles W. Ranson. For decades the IMC was identified with the creative work of Dr J. H. Oldham, and the present incumbent was Norman Goodall, a British Congregationalist writing a doctoral thesis on the London Missionary Society 1895–1945, published in 1954. Oldham had given much time and infinite care to the interests of German missions, and his task was followed up in the Council by Miss Betty Gibson, a wonderful colleague and co-worker at the time. In connection with the IMC I met a missionary leader and statesman who was clearly a genius, Kenneth Grubb, later knighted, president of the Church Missionary Society. He had agreed to edit the first edition of a *World Christian Handbook*, 1949, and together with the Methodist historian E. J. Bingle and some others, I joined his team for that handbook. I have never watched the work, over the weeks, of a researcher as brilliant as Sir Kenneth Grubb. He had started his career as a young missionary in the Amazon basin and ranged all over Latin America. During the war he was made head of the Latin American section in the [British] Ministry of Information and later promoted to overseas controller of government publicity. When the Minister of Information, Brendan Bracken, told Winston Churchill that he 'had appointed an ex-missionary as Overseas Controller of my Ministry', Churchill replied, 'A very good thing, too; provided the man himself is up to it. If a missionary does not understand propaganda, what is he doing?'[2] Interestingly, there were similarities in the youthful experiences of Grubb and Bracken: both had absconded from school, Bracken from the Jesuit College at Mungret in Ireland, subsequently spending some years in Australia, and Grubb from Marlborough College, to join the Royal Navy before going to Latin America.

I had started at the International Missionary Council at the end of 1947 and Ingeborg and I moved to Britain, renting a house at Reigate in Surrey, south of London. We made many good friends there. My time at the IMC became short, less than two years. I suggested the Reverend Erik W. Nielsen, of Copenhagen, as my successor. From that central position he was then to stimulate missionary research for decades to come.

Notes

1. For information about Father Hebert's connections with the Church of Sweden, see Alistair Mason's *History of the Society of the Sacred Mission* (Norwich, 1993), pp. 162–88.
2. Kenneth Grubb, *Crypts of Power: An Autobiography* (London, 1971), p. 118.

7

AN INTERNATIONALE OF MISSIONS

Theological education – the training of pastors – was, and is, also a central concern for the churches in the Third World. In the first years of the 1950s the IMC sent four commissions to different parts of Africa to assess the needs in this field. Bishop Stephen Neill travelled on his own in English-speaking West and East Africa. One commission was sent to 'Latin' Africa: i.e., French- and Portuguese-speaking territories. The chairman of this group was Professor Searle Bates of New York, the other members were Professor Christian Baëta of Ghana, Frank Michaëli of Paris and myself from Uppsala. There were two other teams: Norman Goodall and Erik W. Nielsen to Southern Africa; and Frithjof Birkeli, then of Stavanger, and again Frank Michaëli to Madagascar. Each of the commissions published a report of its findings and, finally, I was asked to follow it all up with a comprehensive book, entitled *The Christian Ministry in Africa*, which was published in 1960.

Our Latin Africa commission started in May 1953 and spent some five months on our task. To see 'all of Africa' in this way was a great privilege. Africa is a beautiful continent. Sunrise and sunset, full moon and new moon over the vast areas of bush and savannah were a constant delight. It was wonderful to travel through the tropical forest in Zaire; or to see the thousand lights in the evening markets of West Africa – one example was Shagamu outside Ibadan – or the modern architecture of the Ivory Coast, or the ruins of San Salvador, or crossing the river Zaire, or again listening to hymns through an enthusiastically singing Africa; travelling in the footsteps of Prophet William Wade Harris on the border between Liberia and the Ivory Coast, and meeting with parts of Cameroon, its Protestant Douala and its Catholic Yaoundé. Through our visits we came close to the African churches. Very fortunately a prominent African, Reverend Dr Christian Baëta was part of our team. The rest of the team consisted of a white American, a Frenchman and a Swede. We all tried our best, but in 1953 nothing could beat the fact that the IMC had included this well-known African professor in our midst. I was moved when

hearing pastors and elders refer to him: *notre frère* – our brother.
They felt that they could understand him – not only because of the
happy fact that he spoke both European and African languages
remarkably well, but because they had much – namely indigenous
African experience – in common.

'You come too late – you should have come much earlier when
everybody was still asleep', was a reaction in Mozambique. 'Some
Europeans despise us. They know the alphabet from A to Z, but we
only know the first letter, A.' The tension with Roman Catholics was
strongly felt, not least in Mozambique. Protestants would refer to the
Catholics, using a pietistic formula, as 'the religion without law'.
Protestants had, of course, their 'law': against alcohol and tobacco.

Our 'Latin' commission started in May 1953. This was a unique
opportunity to see 'all of Africa', beginning in Belgium flying to
Zaire, then to Johannesburg and Mozambique, then on to the Belgian
Congo and Angola, and the French Congo, Cameroon, Dahomey
(with Ghana), the Ivory Coast and finally Liberia. The visit to Liberia
was extra. It was an English-speaking country. It also had the particular characteristic of surprisingly not being a colonial territory – a
distinction which was often made during our three weeks in the
country.

The trips were often exacting, but we were, after all, on a highly
important assignment. The commission came at the right moment,
1953; towards the end of the colonial period in Black Africa (exclud-
ing of course the countries in the south). Our visitations gave us the
chance to listen. We met with personalities and groups representing
the new, independent Africa, with all its expectations. In one country,
Ghana, the revolution was already in full swing: what happened there
could not but influence all the other countries and churches. African
villagers now had their radio sets which informed villages and cities
of developments in adjacent or distant territories involved in the most
important metamorphosis ever to hit the continent. We met the leaders
of Protestant churches, operating simultaneously in the *two* vast areas
of change: the political and the ecclesiastical.

8

PROFESSOR AMONG STUDENTS

9

BISHOP ON THE EQUATOR

These chapters were never completed.

A CONTINENT THROUGH
NINETEEN-HUNDRED YEARS

How long time would it take to write a Church History of Africa? A reasonable time was three or four years. In the way I first conceived the project it might have been achieved in such a 'reasonable time'. In 1974, I had just become a pensioner and felt that I should suggest to a few international friends the following idea. Some 20 Africa-oriented church historians, Africans and Westerners, should co-operate in writing a Church History of the continent: one continent, through 2,000 years or, as the case might be, 100 years. Somebody should serve as editor for the enterprise, but each writer had to take the responsibility of his or her own part of the work. The plan was simple and easily understood, and I had the satisfaction of receiving positive responses from the majority of my correspondents. One writer, however, voted against and this was the grand old man of African history, Professor Roland Oliver from the School of Oriental and African Studies, University of London. With all his experience of editing African history he warned, 'That kind of thing will not work. One person should write it. I suggest that you do it.' Eventually I accepted the task. It has taken me precisely 20 years, 1975–95.

A compromise between the two approaches was tried out in August 1977, when 25 historians, Africans and Westerners, met for three very productive days in Uppsala. We had the privilege of listening to unforgettable talks by Reverend Dr Ethelbert Mveng of Cameroon, Jacob Ajayi of Nigeria, Elizabeth Isichei, Richard Gray, Terrence Ranger, Marcia Wright, Richard Gray and Reverend Father Adrian Hastings – to mention but a few. Three years later I spent some weeks at Rhodes University, Grahamstown, South Africa. The discussions there opened my eyes more than ever to the interrelation of social history and Church history, more particularly with regard to Mfengu refugees and their reception of the new religion: drastic sociological change created in this group an openness towards new values. This should be compared with the Gqunukwebe Xhosa who, in the nineteenth century had their own ethnological reasons for accepting the new creed; they felt themselves apart from other Xhosa and took this

feeling with them into the church. The role of the Griqua is another
parallel showing a group reacting not as individuals but as a tight-knit
community in their approach to the new religion.

These cases were to form a key to the work throughout the continent, and the work on the nineteenth century enforced the idea of the
role of refugees in the acceptance of Christianity, already formulated
in the very first sentence of the book. In Uganda – Buganda and
Ankole – I met with 'refugees' supplemented to a corresponding role
of 'returnees'. When, after much consideration I decided to include
Madagascar, I could see the parallel between refugee–returnee
concepts in the southeastern islands of the Indian Ocean. The attitude
of the Malagasy queen, Ranavalona I, forced thousands to leave their
homes as refugees, moving by canoe or dhow from the central island
to the neighbouring smaller islands of Mauritius and Réunion, there
to remain for decades, only later finding their way back home as
returnees, in the 1860s.

Eventually a fundamental change in perspective was established: by
realising the role of the Catholic missions. I had the great privilege of
studying in the archives of the Holy Ghost Fathers, Paris, of the
White Fathers, Rome, and the Jesuits at Heverlee, Belgium, as well
as those of the Franciscans, the Capuchins and the Pallottines.
Showing great kindness the archivists of these missions spent long
hours during my ever-recurring visits in Rome, Paris and Heverlee.
These men helped me to see the role in the nineteenth century of
French Catholic missions, in the footsteps of Libermann and
Lavigerie, and others. The Catholic archives, and the persistent
advice given by their archivists, have provided vast amounts of new
material with which to characterise the growth of the Catholic
Church. My hope is, in this context, that this work of mine will
inspire any future African Church History to include *both* sides of the
picture.

There followed the history of the early development in North Africa
and in the 'Portuguese' period in equatorial Central Africa. The interpretation of the twentieth century was to a large extent dominated by
the new *Zeitgeist* of the latter part of the century, through Vatican II
leading up to the 'African Synod' in the spring of 1994.

For 13 of these 20 years of incessant work I was assisted and
greatly helped by Christopher Steed, a graduate in African history
from the School of Oriental and African Studies, University of
London. He has spent 13 years with me in Uppsala and wrote essential parts of chapters on West Africa, and on Islam. His bibliographic
expertise has been of tremendous help to the book.

This study was written by a Westerner and his young co-worker.
At the end of the work I realise that however much I hoped to underline the role of the African participant in the story, there are, in the
nature of things, important aspects of faith, worship and structure that
I may have missed. I hope that in the twenty-first century there will

appear a group of African church historians, who, through a corporate effort will be given the time and the means to produce a more fundamentally *African* church history. The great drama of the service of the Church in Africa deserves such an effort of interpretation. Some great foundation in the West might, hopefully, involve itself in this task.

PART TWO

AFRICA IN HIS HEART

The Life and Work of Bengt Sundkler

Marja Liisa Swantz

1

BEYOND THE ROOTS

The roots

In telling his life story, Bengt Sundkler finds a moment in his earliest childhood when a constant inner urge to reach 'beyond' became a conscious striving for clearer understanding of today's unknown. 'Beyond the forestline', the title he gave to his autobiography, expressed his urge to get beyond the binding influence his childhood and youth had on him, yet never rejecting his roots nor forgetting his family origins.

When beginning to write his life story, Bengt returned to Vindeln several times to try to recapture the sentiment and additional small incidents from his childhood. He found some who still remembered him, and as a son of the place he was also asked to preach in the local church. The experience of 'not belonging' had its first impact on him in an event which he recounted throughout his life, when a classmate from a wealthy family was celebrating his birthday, and he and his brother were turned away from the door. He came to realise he was different in a way which was concealed from others around him.

An echo of the past was reflected in his name – Bengt Gustav *Malcolm* Sundkler. He would have been an ordinary Johansson like thousands of others in Sweden and only common Bengt, the Swedish version of Benedictus, had his father not wanted to have his name in a form that revealed his forebears' British origins. His father changed the name Johansson, which he had inherited from his single-parent mother, to Sundkler, the closest Swedish variation of his father's, Count Sinclair's name. He also wanted to remind the son of the family's British origins by naming the son Malcolm, to be at least remembered on Malcolm's name day 28 March. (Letter to MLS 28 March 1974)[1] The son fell in love with British culture and felt at home in the Anglican Church, even if he scathingly criticised the inability of the British to apply their technical skills to the comforts of everyday life.[2]

When Bengt Sundkler wrote the biography of Archbishop Nathan Söderblom he paid attention to Söderblom's ideas of heredity. He

identified himself with Söderblom in many and varied ways which I
think is reflected also in the specific statements which he chose to take
up from Söderblom's relationship with his own father:

> Innumerable generations are behind the child in whose embryo the
> wonderful treasure lies dormant. Dangerous heritages, good heritages,
> weak heritages, subdivided in a thousand different ways, have produced
> diverse results in his forefathers. A combination and a mutual influence
> takes place from the natural gifts of his father and mother respectively,
> but also from earlier heritages ... The gift of genius bursts forth appar-
> ently as suddenly and unexpectedly as those phenomena which De Vries
> has called mutation ... We shall never be able to analyse perfectly the
> causes and elements of creative genius.

The quoted paragraph ends with a thought which returns the potential
for 'mutation' to Christian faith: 'Our Christian faith and our
constructive outlook on life and history know something more. They
know that God works in the complicated course of generations, and
that the right man is there to do his work, when he is wanted.'[3]

B Sr was careful not to compare himself with the genius of
Söderblom, yet interpreting Söderblom's career in the light of his
heritage gave him a direction from which to understand his own
person and personality. There is little doubt that his own heredity
touched some inner chord in him which could explain his interest in
people's background and roots in general, on the one hand, and his
interest in British scholarship and culture, on the other. In fact, after
writing this, I was surprised to find an explicit reference to this in his
1967 diary. After a disappointment in his relationship with his own
church, B Sr wrote in very plain terms about his close identity with
the British and his English heredity, although in the later years of his
life his intent even to move to Britain waned, perhaps together with
the weakening of the High-Church identity. (Diary 15 March 1967)

B Sr's own scholarship, as we shall see later, was based on personalities, people as actors in history. Knowing their roots and social
background was a natural departure point for understanding their
disposition and conduct in life, and not least, their influence in history
and society. He enlivened his writing with details fetched from anec-
dotal incidents which reflected the times and circumstances of his
subjects.

Intensive correspondence with the parents after the son left home
tells of their close relationship. This did not prevent the son from
remembering his relationship with the father at times in somewhat
darker shades, while he always described his relationship with his
mother more warmly. In a letter to his sister, Ingegärd, in 1982 he
expressed his thoughts in the following words:

> The older I become the better I understand that he [Father] did his best
> from his own starting point, but he was somehow locked, not free, was

not freed and happy and joyful. Life needs to be experienced as life in which one's spirit is constantly renewed. I would have wished him to have much more joy and inner freedom [sinne], be freed from all those ambitions and uniforms with which he surrounded himself. It was indeed a gift that Mother was so happy and even cheerful, not frozen in unnecessary ambitions . . . But we still can say that we had a good home which gave us all what we were due to have and even more. (Letter to Ingegärd 14 July 1982)

In another letter, B Sr reflected on his relationship with his father whom he found to be sentimental and full of self-pity. The father's reciting of Swedish poetry by heart at length irritated the son because of the tears that tended to accompany the recitals, 'He always broke down in tears when reciting Runeberg and Rydberg and over his own feelings. This was difficult to stand and stomach.' It created an atmosphere of thick sentimentality which the son came to detest throughout his life. There was often a tense atmosphere in the home from which his mother got relief in a sanatorium for some weeks, on at least two different occasions.

A small incident had a decisive impact on Bengt's relation to his father. 'I was 12 years of age when in my heart I said goodbye to him. I became grown up and old that day.' His mother was depressed and went to a rest home for six weeks. In a loving letter written while there, she generously praised her husband as being the better of the two of them. His father showed this letter to Bengt as a proof of his excellence. That incident marked the separation between father and son. 'I became old and alone in that moment.' Reflecting on this encounter later, Bengt felt that it turned him away from someone he officially loved and thus turned him into a hypocrite in the kingdom of love. Correspondence between the father and son continued, and remarkably, his negative reaction to his father did not lead to rejection of the calling to ministry in the church which his father also wanted him to take up. 'Father wished to see his son in the pulpit. In spite of this I did become a pastor and theologian. It just shows how strong the calling was.' (Letter to MLS 11 May 1971)

It is worth noting here that B Sr describes at length the father–son relationship of pastor Jonas Söderblom and his son Jonathan, who also took up priesthood out of a deep calling, tempted as he might have been to resist the wishes of his father. The latter had, like Bengt Sundkler's father, changed his name, in his case from common Olsson to Söderblom. Both fathers saw their hopes fulfilled in their sons. (Sundkler 1968:14–20)

Bengt's relationship with his mother was warm and his accounts of her were always very positive:

Mother came from a family of two brothers and ten sisters from a place so small that you would not call it even a farm. Her stay with an aunt in town gave her a taste of a life with a bit of refinement. While working in a store in Umeå she met her husband, when she was 25. She was born in 1883. They were married in 1908 and moved to live in Vindeln. She was full of life, full of joy, very temperamental, I thought. She could get very angry, particularly with my father. She was full of fun and regarded my father as strange. Father was serious, energetic, rather thin, and did not allow himself to be humorous ... Mother was very kind and encouraging. '*Om bara Bengt hade varit mera ordentligt, han skulle ha varit idealiskt,*' (If Bengt only would have been more orderly, he would have been ideal, she used to say). Very unfortunately I never managed that. After Father passed away Mother lived on for another five years.

When B Sr returned from South Africa in 1945 he found his mother in an asylum in southern Sweden. She had a kind of psycho-physio-logical disorder and stayed in care for two months:

I was very sorry to find my mother in that condition, even though the doctor said it would pass. She was in a state of apathy, her face and whole body had changed. She came out of it and lived until she was 80 years old. She had a gift of finding young friends. She was revived by her friendships with the young people. When she died in 1963 I happened to be in Uppsala from Bukoba and I took the funeral. When Father died I was in South Africa and could not return for his funeral. (Interview August 1988)[4]

When referring to himself, Bengt mentioned at times being neurotic. In analysing his home background and in interpreting his dreams he tried to come to terms with his own disposition and the potential causes of a certain over-sensitivity and even fears, which he also found hiding in himself. He brought out these aspects of family life in an effort to gain a greater understanding of his own reactions.

In talking about his family background, Bengt recounted many good moments they shared together which were reviewed in several family celebrations. The Nordic countries have invented a tradition of birth-day celebrations every tenth year after the person has reached his fiftieth anniversary. Three quarters of a century is also a cause for celebration, and in this age of honouring youth more than maturity, even the fortieth birthday has become an event of great attention by friends and relatives. On these occasions people can tell the celebrant what they have neglected to express in the course of everyday life. On such a day, in honour of his brother Folke, Bengt reflected on how Folke had been his first friend, and the playmate with whom he took his first steps into life in Vindeln and later on enjoyable walks through Hans-Göran valley down to Vindeln river and its roaring rapids. 'We lived together the intensive light and all too short summers of Norrland.' For his brother Lennart's 75th birthday Bengt wrote a poem describing the family in Vindeln and later in Umeå.

In writing about his brothers B Sr at times also recognised that his father's expectations toward his firstborn may have overshadowed the interest he showed to his other sons, Folke, and the youngest child, Lennart.

> I was the eldest of the three sons and a daughter. My father did to my increasing embarrassment and dismay adore me, not perhaps so much for what I was but for what I represented: fame for the name and the family, he thought. My father's admiration was always a problem, more particularly in relation to my brother, one-and-a-half years younger than I. He was, this brother of mine, always a good friend, and is so now. All praise bestowed upon me and my school and academic results therefore became a problem in my relationship with my brother. (Letters 11 and 23 May 1971)

His sister, Ingegärd, was born six years after Bengt, and he, as the older brother, always felt close to his only sister with whom he felt personal affinity and with whose family he maintained a close relationship. Bengt referred to his sister, the only daughter in the family, as being the most talented of them. His brothers made notable careers in the legal field, and his sister Ingegärd also studied law but majored in Political Science and took a special interest in social issues relating to children. After marrying she chose not to pursue a career of her own, preferring, as the musical and creative wife of Pastor, Dean and later Bishop Stig Hellsten, to devote her energies to the congregations in which her husband served and to her five children. From her youth she was acutely conscious of social injustices and found ways to work both on personal level and in public life for betterment of people's lives. As the brothers' and sister's children grew older, Bengt found much joy in communicating with them, meeting them in family gatherings and following their careers. (Interview August 1988; Hellsten, Ingegärd 1993)[5]

High school years in Umeå

From Vindeln on Degerfors – still today said to be the only *fors* (rapids) not harnessed to give power in Sweden – the family's move to Umeå meant a widening of their horizons. It was the first step 'beyond the forestline'. It awoke the intellectual interests of the young lad aspiring to learn more of the world; his high school not only began to equip him with language tools with which to communicate in the modernising world, it also looked back over history and Church history and taught the basics of Latin and Greek, soon to stand the young student in good stead when he took his next step on the road of learning.

During his high school years, the foundations were laid for the principal interests of Bengt Sundkler's life: his calling for scholarship within the realm of the Church and the discipline of history; and his interest in literature, the history of literature, and writing. It also introduced Africa into the realms of his imagination. The town library and the educational classes organised around it, which he called his second high school, served to broaden his literary horizons while his favourite teacher took special notice of the brilliant student's advanced interest in scholarship and took him many steps ahead in the history of the Church.

> But in the school literature course only Swedish literature was covered. I consider it a real loss that we never got into the works of Shakespeare or Goethe, nor learned the magic of their literary style, for which it was difficult later to compensate. Gustaf Theofil Engman was especially inspiring, a teacher in a class of his own, but remained distant as a person. [The main conservative daily newspaper] *Svenska Dagbladet*'s writer of feature articles Fredrik Böök – who later came to support the wrong politics – supplemented what one did not get at school. In 1925–28 I learned from Fredrik Böök brilliant style, elegance and how to grasp the subject. It dazzled me. I also remember a series of 'Journey around Swedish Parnassos, which came on a Sunday evening as Sven Lindman's part of a radio programme: It taught me how to summarise and close a presentation. (Letter to Ingegärd 14 July 1982)

In an earlier version of his autobiography B Sr enlarged on the occasion when his 'incomparable' teacher in Swedish language and literature history, Victor Hagström, took the eager student to the teachers' library,

> On that occasion he was to test my ability to grasp written sources. As a special privilege he took me to the teachers' own library, so far only admissible to the seemingly promising students. There were works I recognised, by Schück and Warburg, Blanck, Mortenson and others. In a corner there was a lonely book, a doctoral thesis of Emanuel Linderholm on Sven Rosén and his impact on pietism at the time of enlightenment, published in 1911 and still uncut. It was on radical Pietism in eighteenth-century Sweden. 'Linderholm's doctoral thesis gave me my first, and lasting, impression of a learned Church-historical work: its disposition, local Swedish perspective placed in an international setting.
>   One of the most interesting passages in this thesis dealt with an apocalyptic-kiliastic pietist movement, the so-called *Gråkoltarna* [Grey-Frocks] in Stockholm of the 1730s, these impoverished, destitute Swedes appearing in penitential grey coats. Rosén's dream of going to China and his work ending up in Pennsylvania were worked out into a book with carefully recorded references and sources. I said to myself: So this is the way to write Church history. Later in Africa I came face to face with 10,000 and later 100,000 blue and white 'kolts' in Zululand in the 1930s.

With hindsight it sometimes seemed to B Sr that too much time was spent on what could be gained from the high school years, compared to the haste with which he hurried through the basic theology degree.

In his letter (14 July 1982) to his sister he commented:

> Sometimes I have thought that I should have got one or two years of
> gymnasium (senior secondary) somewhere else, as a free student. The
> four years which I spent in gymnasium in Umeå were too much, espe-
> cially the last year which went back over material we already knew and
> consequently became extremely bothersome and unnecessary. But it is
> too late to complain about it now. Uppsala years lay ahead and they gave
> me freedom, new horizons and perspective.

Young Bengt's activity in student organisations presaged his future
tasks in life. The chairmanship of the Evangelical Student and High-
School Student Association in Umeå was the first step on the road to
Christian leadership, but it also prompted the Rector of the High
School to suggest to him that he study theology and become a pastor.
The student sssociation had also brought Bengt into contact with the
Luleå Diocese and its active mission centre in Skellefteå where the
students held summer conferences. The Diocesan youth were later to
adopt Ingeborg and Bengt Sundkler as their missionaries in South
Africa.

Bengt acted also as secretary to the literary group and – as he
reports – 'collaborated over a modest journal'. In his search for the
haunts of his youth he was disappointed with the standard of these
youthful efforts. Nevertheless, his companions in the group were
budding celebrities in the field. The literary group and the adult
education programme of the local library opened new channels of
knowledge, and above all, opened aspirants' eyes and ears to new
sources and new ways of acquiring knowledge.

A fundamentally significant stimulus for the 16-year-old was
reading the works of the philosopher Hans Larson, from Lund, whose
concept the 'essential detail' became a grounding principle in Bengt
Sundkler's approach to writing throughout his life.[6] Even when
sketching his autobiography toward the end of his life he uses this
kind of a key opener to his story: an essential detail serves as a chink
through which the larger scene can begin to open up.

Later, when B Sr read Chesterton with his student contemporaries,
he picked up another phrase, which became his motto, akin to 'essential detail': 'For anything to be real it must be local.' Thus Bengt
Sundkler's writing style began to develop in his early youth. This
style also worked its way into his research methods, and even into his
way of seeing the world. One early illustration of it was the atlas he
saw in the shop window and bought it. He was attracted to the map
of Africa. It inspired him to measure and draw the outline map of
Africa as a continent, in different sizes, a skill he still demonstrated
to his audiences in his old age when lecturing on African Church
History, Bengt Sundkler's last monumental work. However, the small
atlas in the shop window did more than provide a device for drawing
the map of Africa. It planted the continent firmly and permanently in

his imagination and his innermost self. First he lived in and worked for two corners of Africa, later through his scholarship and his travels he covered the continent from south to north and east to west. Finally, in his African Church history he completed the whole picture historically and geographically. The 'essential detail' through the 'real' and 'local' had done its creative work.

Notes

1. The father recognised the son born out of wedlock. The son met the father a couple of times. The half sister made contact with Bengt and Ingeborg Sundkler while they were in Tanzania and other contacts were kept up later in Sweden.
2. The history of the Sinclair family is written in a newspaper article, which was found in a large bound book of clippings entitled Professor Bengt G. M. Sundkler 1912–1950, located among Sundkler archived materials in Carolina manuscript collections.
3. Sundkler, 1968:20, quotation from Söderblom, *The Living God*, 1932:354–5.
4. I and my husband, also in the presence of Dr Festo Bahendwa, interviewed Bengt Sundkler when he fell ill while in Helsinki and was hospitalised for more than two weeks in Meilahti University Hospital.
5. Ingegärd Hellsten, *Erinringar från ett liv*, Umeå 1993. Her daughter, Cecilia Hellsten-Sandblad, has kindly let me read her mother's memoires.
6. Recorded interview by MLS 31 October 1985.

2

'GREAT TIMES IN UPPSALA'

Challenging encounter

Often when Bengt Sundkler was asked to recount his life experiences
on special occasions he referred to his student years as 'my great time
in Uppsala'. He offers us glimpses of this in the pages of his autobiography, to which I refer in my comments and add texts particularly
from correspondence with Professor Fridrichsen. B Sr worked hard
on his studies but he was also rewarded in ways which were not
enjoyed by every student, even if in a relatively small university, with
a teacher–student ratio of 1:8, teachers had more time for their
students, and the teacher's status could influence the careers of their
more talented protégés.

The Norwegian, Anton J. Fridrichsen, had been appointed professor in New Testament Exegesis at Uppsala just one year before B Sr
began his studies, thus the latter was one of the first students
Professor Fridrichsen housed. Others were to follow, among the most
noted of them were Fridrichsen's future successor Harald Riesenfeld
and the future professor and bishop, Krister Stendahl. Letters from
Professor Anton Fridrichsen, to which B Sr refers in his own story,
illustrate the close relationship between teacher and student. On the
one hand they indicate the independence with which the student
planned his life, in spite of the heavy influence of the elder man's
authority. On the other hand, the weight of this influence has to be
considered when Sundkler's own initial theological and ecclesiastic
orientation is analysed.

Earlier in this volume we compared certain similarities in the lives
of Bengt Sundkler and Archbishop Söderblom. Here it is worth noting
the differences, both in their respective study techniques and in the
environment in which they pursued these studies. While B Sr happily
depicts his time in Uppsala in glorious terms, he introduces
Söderblom's entry into the same university in a time of dryness.
According to Söderblom, Uppsala of the 1880s was experiencing its
driest period in history. While B Sr passed his exams and completed

his Candidate of Theology degree in two years, Söderblom took ten years to achieve the same, but his studies were thorough and widely read, and his time was filled with many other activities from which he emerged as a well-known leader (Sundkler, 1968:21–2).

The following Bengt Sundkler's sketches of his time in Uppsala and the personal connections he established supplement the picture he gives in his autobiographical chapters:

I came to Uppsala, a historical university town and ecclesiastical centre, in 1929. Apart from short absences, it was to remain my home until I finished my doctoral thesis in the spring of 1937 and left for Africa. I have repeatedly said that the 1930s were my great time in the Theological Faculty in Uppsala. The quarter of a century I later acted as a professor in the same faculty could not be compared with my years of youth in the university. It all depended on the chance opportunities that came my way.

The interest I had taken in Johannes Pedersen's fascinating book had given my Old Testament teacher cause to recommend me to Professor Anton J. Friedrichsen, who then sent me a letter of invitation to come and lodge with him. It was his custom to have some carefully selected students residing with him. He was professor of New Testament Exegetics and probably the most creative teacher at the time in the University.

Anton Fridrichsen was a round, jovial personality, who surrounded himself with a number of doctoral students and entertained foreign visiting lecturers. He was full of stories, one after the other, especially about German, French and at times also English professors.

I came to Uppsala as a pietist from Norrland and later, for a period, became a member of the Oxford movement, consequently I was very little of 'his type'. I still wonder how it was that in spite of the differences he always supported me in my work, giving his time and trust.[1] (Earlier versions of B Sr's autobiography)

On reading the numerous letters from Fridrichsen, some as long as eight typed pages, others written neatly by hand to B Sr in France and in Africa, the reader is amazed that he found that much time and interest to keep in touch with his student friend. Strangely for a reader today, the student's letters were addressed to *Farbror* (Uncle), and the teacher's letters sent to Strasbourg were addressed to 'Candidate Sundkler' and written in the third person, all in the style of the time: 'Sundkler already has a good understanding how to take the Archbishop's well-meant but inappropriate advice' (Söderblom had advised Sundkler to specialise in Church Law).[2] 'Look around the city and countryside of Strasbourg, read and speak French day and night, orient yourself to the circumstances in the Faculty, institutions, localities, etc.'

B Sr reflected later on the opportunities he had missed in concentrating too much on the studies to hand and not seeing what he was doing from a broader perspective. The following thoughts were enclosed as a hand-written appendix to B Sr's continuing narrative of his life story:

> In retrospect, perhaps I am hard on myself, but I do not like to recall
> ... that that very wonderful year, May 1931–June 1932, in Strasbourg
> and Paris did not influence me more than it did. I learned a lot of French
> and loved it, my first love to which I like to return. But I was not gifted
> enough and creative enough to make and retain important contacts with
> Alsatians and Frenchmen of my age, yet I was daily together with Theo
> Preiss, a very generous and I think creative theologian who died young.
> I did not keep up the contact later. Then the other half a year in Paris.
> I was hard-working, taking my diploma, enjoying it, and enjoying my
> little world in and around Boulevard St Michel that glorious spring. But
> so much happened in art and poetry and politics, and I suppose in
> Church life in France that year, and I was not really aware of it. I was
> too much keeping my nose to the paper, not looking enough around for
> perspective and discovery; too much interested in the immediate exam
> effect. Yet, I am perhaps too harsh on myself. It was a brief time, only
> slightly more than a year and I was just 22. (Letter to MLS 16 July
> 1982)

Fridrichsen came to see his student in Strasbourg. After his visit he encouraged Bengt again, now addressing him 'Käre Bengt' (Dear Bengt), who in turn continued to call him 'Uncle', in fact, even after his return from Africa. He kept on encouraging Bengt when he saw that the time abroad did not go without complications:

> I am very satisfied with the way you cope with difficulties and the list-
> lessness experienced by all who grapple with scientific work. I am
> convinced that you solve your task satisfactorily, both for yourself and
> for all who are interested in the difficult problem which you are tack-
> ling. As far as I can see, you have laid out your work quite correctly.
> Gradually the lines will become clearer and you will grasp your mater-
> ial. It is good that you approach the practical–theological problem from
> the religio-historical point of view, it makes your research meaningful
> and fresh. That you then study the rise and history of social thinking in
> Swedish proclamation is a good idea, don't let it slip away. (Letter from
> Fridrichsen 7 December 1931)

Fridrichsen stretched his flexible attitude even further when B Sr continued to write of his changing plans for the future. The reader is amused when reading his responses to the student's at times seemingly wild ideas:

> I will not in any way oppose it if you now wish to take the common road
> and become an ordinary 'bond licentiate' with a thesis about some

obscure preacher here at home. Just the opposite, I will encourage you to start working on your licentiate in the autumn: I think it will work well with your solid working temperament. You will see that the time in Strasbourg has not been completely wasted, after all. I give you full freedom and will give you all the support that is possible for me for your future career. (Fridrichsen's letter 15 January 1931)

In a letter six months later (1 July 1932) Fridrichsen had a reason to respond to B Sr's long letter and congratulate him in a card, this time for his intent to do (or possibly mainly write on) missionwork among the Lapps! 'Good luck for the mission among the Lapps ... a form of religion mixing Barth and Laestadius?' Clearly he was being sarcastic, but still encouraging.

B Sr added as a postscript to a part of his life story other reactions of his teacher's when he confided in him:

I should add to [my note about] A. Fridrichsen, my fatherly friend, when I 'witnessed' to him, that I had now been 'converted' and joined the Oxford group, he said: 'Well, Bengt, the leopard keeps its spots.' Later, as I told him, I was going out as a missionary, he was interested, his uncle John Johnson was one of Norway's great missionaries to Madagascar and a recognised hymn writer; but he did not like it. He wanted me to be a young professor of Practical Theology – but then, that was all fantasy – I was going to Africa. (Letter to MLS 16 July 1982)

After his time in France, B Sr acted more or less as Fridrichsen's amanuensis, *famulus*, in his doctoral seminars, administering some exams on his behalf and being very much trusted by him. He learned a great deal from it and above all, through Fridrichsen's seminars he discovered publishing, which subsequently became his overriding ambition. In reading his diaries one gets the impression that writing and publishing books drove him more than any other task throughout his life. He was always unhappy when time was spent without visible results in writing new volumes.

Of the birth of his second book, written in French, B Sr related in the hand-written account of his life quoted above (16 July 1982):

I wrote for Fridrichsen also the daring and a highly original study, *Jésus et les païens* (Jesus and the Pagans), first published in its entirety in the *Theological Review of Strasbourg* 1936, and then, together with Fridrichsen, as a book, with the latter adding six pages on the problem in the Fourth Gospel. I had read the great Norwegian Old Testament scholar S. Mowinckel (also an Oxford group member). He held a central view point of the Old Testament, on the New Year's Festival. I was fascinated by this, how one could organise that whole tome of the Old Testament around that Festival – and I suggested to myself, why not find in the New Testament a similar central seminal idea which ties the whole thing together. I tried with the *omphalos* idea: the temple, Zion, as the navel of the world. From there, remaining there, you can move the world. I could perhaps find a key, a solution to this central problem of Universalism vs. Particularism. Is Jesus universalist or is he particularist, is Mt. 28 or is Mt. 10 the answer? That had been the question. Well, the *omphalos* idea, I suggested, meant that staying in the centre Jesus changed the whole periphery. He is universalist precisely because he is a particularist. Then I had that written in French and it has played a certain role, perhaps.

In a long, beautifully hand-written letter sent to B Sr to Africa right after his arrival there, Fridrichsen tells the addressee that the study *Jésus et les païens* had raised a lot of interest and was in constant demand. He suggests that he sends to B Sr a list of professors on missions in different parts of the world so that B Sr can send the book to them. He also offers to send more books if needed.

I will break off for a moment here to refer to a later episode in this remarkable study. B Sr took exception to a view which his close friend, former student and successor to his chair, Carl Fredrik Hallencreutz expressed in his review of Bengt Sundkler's missiological scholarship in 1984: B Sr considered his idea of *omphalos*, the central concept which informs his interpretation of the ministry of Jesus, to be entirely his own. Hallencreutz rightly refers to David J. Bosch who shows an interesting parallelism and convergence of concerns between Sundkler's French exposée and the well-known German scholar Oscar Cullmann. Both published the same year (1936). It would appear that B Sr misread Hallencreutz's sentence: 'Bengt Sundkler applies what he has learned from Fridrichsen.' It seems to me that B Sr's account of what he learned from Fridrichsen concords with Hallencreutz's interpretation of Fridrichsen's antithetical teaching method, rather than suggesting that the concept of *omphalos* had come from Fridrichsen. (Festschrift 1984:11)

> I learned enormously from Fridrichsen. More particularly, I think, not to be afraid to think on my own, to dare to strike out with new things, new ideas. I always felt that in his seminar Fridrichsen, in discussing a New Testament problem, asked us to make a choice between two alternatives: A or B: which is the right one, which is the solution, and the answer was always – C. Now I am not at all sure that Fridrichsen would have recognised that phrase or that impression. That was, however, how I experienced him and his attitude to scholarly problems and it was this – the most important thing – which I learned from him, and for which I remain ever thankful. The idea of *omphalos* was of course an entirely original idea of mine. (Letter to MLS 20 July 1984)

To return to the Uppsala period, B Sr showed considerable independence in relation to his teacher, despite the fact that Fridrichsen had given his student the basic building blocks and courage to go forward on the road of scholarship. In his own story we learned how he came to choose mission over continued scholarship, but only after completing his great thesis on the history of the Swedish Mission Society in its 30 early years.

In a letter to Bengt in England, while B Sr was doing language study there, Fridrichsen showed that he had not given up hope that his student Benedictus would eventually continue his scholarly work. 'You have made a good choice and can now gain practical experience in mission service, before you again return to continue your scholarly work.'

Fridrichsen's letters to Africa were later sent to 'Dear friend Benedictus'. In them Fridrichsen kept B Sr informed about developments in the Theological Faculty. He followed the theological discussions in Lund and Uppsala and was unhappy about the secularisation of the Church which claimed the secularised nation as 'Christendom', but he also saw the same secular spirit creeping into the mission which made 'no distinction between the social welfare organisations and the mission organs'. He wrote detailed accounts of the progress of other theology students in writing their doctoral theses and their chances of being offered posts and being B Sr's competitors. He took it for granted that B Sr would follow Knut B. Westman as professor of History of Missions and he was unstinting in his praise of B Sr's competence. When the time came, however, the matter was not that simple.

During the war Fridrichsen told of his sorrow over his near and dear ones, particularly his brother whom he knew to be a Quisling.[3] He cared for individuals and saw to it that promising students did not fall by the wayside. In 1935 B Sr received a letter from Fridrichsen from Berlin (17 April 1935) asking him to visit a certain student who was trying to finish his candidate examination and give him a few hundred crowns so that he would not starve.

While working at Selly Oak on his book *The Church of South India*, and having been asked by the IMC to become their research secretary, B Sr wrote another letter to *Farbror* (25 August 1947) which shows the significance of the teacher's opinion to the younger scholar:

> Thank you very much for the letter of 21 August which I received this morning and hurry to answer right away. Above all I am glad that the thought about the IMC is agreeable to Uncle. I have waited to get that answer with great suspense before giving the final answer to IMC. I can now write to them a definitive letter, knowing that the plan is agreeable to the person whose judgement I value more than anyone else's ... I see this is a work with an unlimited horizon and great possibilities.

In his earlier manuscript B Sr describes the influence of another teacher who taught him to pay attention to the skills of presentation. Self-criticism of his own overly long, meandering and overly enthusiastic presentations fills the pages of the earlier as well as the later diaries. In 1977 he described his style of speaking as 'that strange and funny intensity of mine'. In the opinion of many this sense of being engaged in his subject made him a good speaker. B Sr indicated that Professor Tor Andrae's way of lecturing had served as a model for himself:

> Another teacher who left an impression on me was Tor Andrae. I tried to listen to lectures as often as I could fit them into my schedule, long after I already had taken the exams for Candidate of Theology in his subject. Andrae was an eloquent lecturer. He could take his starting point in some obscure example from a scholarly Hindu tradition, work it out carefully organising his material, and then lift out from it some fundamental, universal human conclusions. Good use of voice added to the fascination of his lectures, but above all it was the insight and overview of things that attracted listeners. For my doctoral work I, however, looked to another direction.

Caught by the Spirit

B Sr's memories of his relatively brief student-period affiliation with the Oxford group were highly ambivalent. He returned to the subject in different ways several times. While he recognised the spiritual blessing it had brought to him in personalising his faith, at the same time he also saw its limitations. He was later to encounter the same strength and limitations in his beloved diocese in Bukoba, Tanzania, in the East African Revival movement.

> For me, the budding theologian, my question had been all the time: This experience of a spiritual breakthrough, of conversion, about which the churchmen and the religious speak so much, what is it? This reference to a transforming power of the Holy Spirit, I realised I knew nothing about it. Then I was hit by it, through the most unlikely media, the Oxford Group, in the person of Hans Cnattingius, who became my greatest friend. From the end of September 1933 I became one of his closest associates. The personal message helped towards renewal and new birth. It provided me with a solution to my personal problem. Later in the struggle for academic preferment our friendship came to a lamented end. Another influential person in the Oxford group was Professor Arvid Runestam, a loveable prophet; some prophets are not loveable, they are too harsh and dictatorial for that. But A. R. was such a likeable and loveable and good man. I was absorbed into a happy and healthy friendship with these men.
>
> The Oxford group seemed to require that you retell your own spiritual experience over and over again, in order to move and win others. In the end it was too much. Without wishing to make a scene, I simply dropped out. Later, in about 1950, Professor Runestam told me that he had, after remaining faithful to the movement for a much longer time,

ultimately reacted in the same way. I withdrew, concentrating instead on my doctoral thesis. (Letter to MLS 12 July 1982)

The time in the Oxford group was also decisive from another point of view. In one such a meeting B Sr first met Ingeborg who later became his beloved wife, as recorded very briefly in his diary, 'He let me meet someone, and to meet her deep at heart.' The development of their story I leave for the chapter on Ingeborg. (Diary 3 August 1934)

Bengt had noted down a thought from Runestam in 1934 which had stayed with him throughout his life, 'It is easier to believe in God as the personal Saviour and Redeemer than to believe that God exists' but to that he added, 'To whom should we go, for Thou hast the words of life eternal.' I wonder if there was any word from the Bible that B Sr repeated throughout his life as often as the latter with which he commonly started his prayer in all the years I knew him. In this diary note he still strengthened the significance of the word by adding, 'Where else would we indeed go?' This was also the time when the students, Bengt among them, joined the opposition to Mussolini's Abyssinian war. (Diary note 6 August 1934)

In the long run, the repetitive concentration on personal experience in the Oxford group was too much for B Sr. His departure from the group was rather abrupt, but the influence of the movement spread wide and he was to encounter it later in different contexts. In fact, we shall see that his strong reaction to the Oxford group and group members found expression at times in dreams and coloured certain of his later relationships. As the years passed his attitude grew even stronger, especially toward the place where they later landed for language study in Walton-on-Thames which became to him a kind of epitome of the Oxford group. (Interview 31 October 1985)

Exciting doctoral work[4]

Bengt Sundkler was ready to continue his academic work toward a doctor's degree which had also been his teachers' wish since he started his studies.

I was drawn to write my thesis on Church history but it caused certain difficulties in Uppsala. The professor in the subject was Emanuel Linderholm. He had his good qualities, but as a graduate tutor he was known to be too temperamental and unpredictable. Other students wanting to do Church history had already gone to Lund. I wonder why they had not crossed the channel and gone all the way to Copenhagen which at the time had the excellent specialist in patristics, Jens Nörregaard.

While I was hedging about my future, Fridrichsen had other ideas for me. He suggested that I do my doctoral work for Professor K. B. Westman whose fine personality and great learning were highly respected in the university. Fridrichsen held the typically central-European view that the professor's standing in the university would influence the young student's position as a scholar.

Knut B. Westman was a learned Uppsala historian who had followed in Harald Hjärnes' footsteps, his subject being the History of Missions and East Asian Religions. He had been a rector in China in the 1920s and thus perhaps lost some of his spark and capacity to present his thoughts in a literary form in the field of his professorship; face-to-face he could present different issues brilliantly and with a fine perspective. As a learned and popular figure in the church and in society, coming close to being elected as the Archbishop of Sweden, he got appointed to many church committees and boards which perhaps took up too much of his time, leaving little time and energy for publishing. This also meant that I had to look for my actual training and inspiration for research and writing elsewhere, from other contemporary theses and studies, not least from the rich field of social studies of the Brusewitz school.

I turned to K. B. Westman and asked him to suggest a subject for my doctoral work. As it turned out, he had just received a letter from Stockholm from the secretary of the Swedish Mission Society. The Society was to celebrate its centennial festival in 1935 and needed someone to write its history. Westman thought that I could take up the task. It would not be a subject for a doctoral thesis, but a commemoration of the past.

I never produced a centenary festschrift. I found out soon that the first three or four decades of the society's history were full of dramatic central problems. As I worked with it I found that the interesting period was its first 40 years, and I wrote my thesis on *Svenska Missionssällskapet 1835-75*, (Swedish Mission Society 1835-75). It gave me an insight which helped me later with many other books I was to write: if one digs deep in one place and adds depth, one might strike gold. I found that an unlikely subject was a gold mine. I was fortunate in getting this task.

The University Library, Carolina, offered at that time a wonderful opportunity for interdisciplinary contacts. For me the contacts with the social sciences were the most important, particularly because their research often dealt with the mid-nineteenth century. I found a creative milieu in these circles. Another subject which became meaningful for me was statistics which was at that time located on the groundfloor of the Dekanhuset, where the Theological Faculty was also housed – so limited was space! This helped me with my statistical work which formed the base for my account of mission interest in Sweden through those 40 years in the nineteenth century.

The statistics covered every *öre* and *krona* [Swedish monetary units] in every diocese which had been given toward the mission work. I have now left all that material with the Carolina. Is it 'mission statistics?' No, because that would sound too boring. However, if you call it 'Earlier numerical indicators for the Swedish congregations' international awareness' it immediately becomes impressive and every figure significant. I dare to think that in years to come, perhaps in 2037 or 2057 some young scholar will make use of it and I think, this ancient work will cheer her or him up.

The statistics made the breadth of the church life understandable, and my thesis contains indications of that breadth. Let me take just one example: I worked out two different types of mission groups in the middle of the century, one the church-related type, often led by pastors, the other *ecclesiola* [church groups] type, led by laymen and based on mission societies, and I continue: 'The church-related type is the more common one, but does not because of it deserve less attention.' The pattern was different from the Norwegian scene where local mission circles supported a mission society. (Interview and information in Sundkler 1937:132)

Of the contacts with other sciences in the university the most significant was the advice which I received from a fellow researcher, Gunnar Heckscher, in social sciences, who told me how he managed his material. He had the whole thesis in a box on little cards. The cards followed the outline of his book and contained reference information as well as notes sufficiently extensively written out to enormously hasten the writing phase. I used to say that this fellow research scholar gave me half a day in explaining how he did it and it saved half a year of my work on the book and other books I wrote later. I followed his system right through the writing of all my books and taught all my research students to do the same – until I came to the last large one on ACH. The material for that was too extensive to be able to crowd it into one or two little boxes, but even then I had ultimately to resort to indexing the material.

The thesis on the *Swedish Mission Society 1835–75* [written in Swedish] provided an opportunity for me to learn many useful things for my future work. I was astonished by the rapid and penetrating changes that took place in such a relatively short time within the institution closely aligned with the church. Even the character of the society itself changed radically from 'inter-confessionalism' to 'confessionalism'. There was also a middle period, in which such a change took place, which I called 'new orientation'. These changes gave a clear structure to the 600-page thesis.

The book on the history of the Swedish Mission Society over its first 40 years was not only a study of how mission interest had grown in the Church of Sweden and in separate mission organisations related to the church, it was also a significant piece of history of the Church of Sweden and an analysis of a religious organisation using statistical and social science methodology:

The book was ready and published in spring 1937. I found the work greatly satisfying ... Two weeks after the defence I was on my way to England and then Africa, and another kind of existence opened up for me, taking me into another kind of a world.

B Sr had a very high opinion of his teacher and the supervisor of his thesis – K. B. Westman – as a person. He kept in contact with him throughout the years and, as we shall see, visited him up until the last weeks of his life, and was finally given the honour of performing the last rites at his death.

Thirty years on, B Sr recalls the day of his doctoral promotion as being one of the significant dates in his life (*ett högtidligt viktig datum i mitt liv*) in his diary notes of 10 April 1967:

> Thirty years ago on this day, I was 27 years old when I defended a huge tome entitled 'Swedish Mission Society 1835–75'. I remember the day very well as it gave me much satisfaction. The defence went well, if I dare say so. The first opponent was K. B. Westman. He had read my book thoroughly. The second opponent was O. B. Rundblom. He had such a hard time digesting my statements that 12 years later he collected his thoughts to respond in the form of an unfortunate thesis, to which he had devoted most of his time as a mission secretary in the CSM. I responded in turn seven years later in *SMT 1955* (in an article entitled 'When two became one'). The third opponent was Bengt Petri, now a (provincial) governor. An additional opponent was the statistician Docent P. Winsker.
>
> In the evening a dinner was served at the School of Home Economics. Emanuel Linderholm gave a speech as Faculty Dean. It was the last year of his life. He was very impressed by the thought that a person who could start teaching as a docent should go to Africa, 'Go then to Africa in the name of God,' he closed his speech in a somewhat tearful manner. [It was known by then that B Sr had committed himself to go to South Africa.] He also complimented Ingeborg on her fine Nordic name and on being so sweet and beautiful. Fridrichsen spoke as also our friends Hans Cnattingius and Öyvind Sjöholm. [Other guests are listed by name, among them family and relatives.]

Having several statisticians at the dinner broke with the usual custom. In B Sr's words: 'There was cross-disciplinarity already then, 1,000 years ago!' The new doctor got 2.5 out of 3, but Westman did not think there was any point in giving him the docentship yet, which commonly involved teaching duties, since B Sr was departing for Africa. B Sr was leaving for England in ten days time and could not do anything about it. Ingeborg, who had a better command of English and had not yet left for England brought the doctoral ring to Bengt when she arrived there later.

B Sr also reminisced on his financial situation at the time he was working for his doctorate. It appears that it was not uncommon for him to have to resort to personal sources in order to manage:

> As I passed quickly through the many tests and examinations I should have been eligible for some sizeable scholarships, but there was a kind of 'junta' in my student organisation, called Norrland nation, working against me. My father helped a bit and for the rest I took a loan. At the time of my doctoral defence I had a study loan of some 10,400 Swedish

krona from the CSM which I was to pay back with monthly cuts from my salary.

A decisive 'beyond'

The book on Aggrey had made a deep impression on the young school boy Bengt. It brought him into the fold of what he called the 'miserable little Student Missionary Association', the chairman of which he was for some years in Uppsala. That responsibility took B Sr to a Student Missionary Conference of the World Student Christian Federation in Germany in 1934 where one of the main speakers was Karl Hartenstein of the Basel Mission. This was one step along the way, even if it did not at that time lead to any comments on a personal interest in missions. In answering the question 'why' B Sr wanted to emphasise, at least in later years, that it was not a pietistic call but rather faithfulness to the Church of Sweden which led him to answer 'yes' to the challenge which came from the acting mission director Alm:

> The CSM had not been in a position to send out an ordained missionary with a proper, ordinary academic qualification for five years. That looked very bad – would I not come along. I responded, some kind of declaration of faithfulness to the Church of Sweden. Then of course, I was needed for I was to go to teach theology at Oscarsberg, Natal, and my theological degree seemed to make me the logical choice for that kind of a job. (Hand-written life story enclosed in a letter 16 July 1981)

B Sr responded to the question of how he got interested in Africa again in a taped interview in 1985 (31 October 1985 by MLS). He wanted to make it very clear that even if he had an initially pietistic approach to mission, he did not respond to the mission call because of the pietism which existed in northern Sweden and was strongly influenced by the Rosenian movement. B Sr had this to say:

> There was a wonderful link between pietism in north Sweden and Ethiopia, then called Abyssinia, where Swedish couples were sent out as missionaries. As I came from that place it could have explained my interest, but this would be completely wrong. I am glad that you ask about this so that I can make this quite clear. My parents and myself had nothing to do with that pietistic group. It was a self-contained group with its prayer house, even if part of the Church of Sweden. My father was a civil religion fellow, mother did not care about hymn singing and had nothing to do with pietistic warmth. Coming from Västerbotten does not explain it. My interest through secondary school was only the history of

Swedish literature. I loved it and lived in it and wanted to continue with it.

We have learned that it was his rector's advice which influenced him to go and study theology. This he went on to explain again in the interview.

After a period spent in England learning English there was a send-off on 18 September 1937. B Sr had earlier been ordained as a pastor in the Luleå diocese and so he and Ingeborg were sent out from there, having been adopted by the youth of the diocese as their missionaries. They went up to Umeå to take leave of the youth organisation and Bengt's home parish.

The local newspaper gave a lot of space to the reporting of the departure of a famous local son, in whose achievements it took great pride. The article helps us to understand the difference between the honour in gaining a doctorate in theology at that time and at that age and what it is today, and how strange it sounded to a commoner that the new doctor would, after all that, take off for Africa:

> Umeå resident has become a doctor of theology at the age of 27. Now he departs for Africa after a remarkable career with distinguished examination results and several valuable theological contributions in theological debates. His 614-page thesis is the first one on the subject of Mission history in Uppsala University. He is the youngest doctor to earn the doctor's hat in Uppsala University. The youth organisation will have its own missionary. (*Umeåbladet* 30 March 1937)

The Umeå newspaper also gave a penetrating report of the event at the Lutheran Missionhouse where B Sr gave a long speech on their future field and work. The reporting of the message is interesting to read for its conventional mission language on the one hand, and the forward-looking vision which was already developing on the other. The speech had many of the components which B Sr was to elaborate, deepen and evolve as his concept of mission developed.

It was reported that the missionary couple was going to undertake missionwork among the heathen, whose society had been static for centuries and who were now facing europeanisation through industry and, in the Swedish mission area, also through mining activities. In his 'touching and captivating lecture' B Sr showed the audience the breakthrough between the old and the new:

> Now the new time breaks through. Aeroplanes either drop bombs or come with medicine and mail to the tropical primeval forests ... To become like Europeans has become a new kind of religion there ...

Now Africa is a fermenting, dynamic society, in constant movement.

The lecturer gave an overview of the situation in Africa, where many
problems meet. He started with the land and labour problems as being
the most important departure points in learning to know Africa. He
emphasised the importance of land for the African economy. In West
Africa labour is not the same kind of problem that it is in East and South
Africa, where it is acute. There the race problem is a factor. One way
in which it is being solved is through communism. The only thing that
can bring the Black what he needs is the message which the mission can
mediate.

The political and economic troubles should not, however, hide the
most essential problem, it should rather serve to show that it is just
this situation which Africa now faces that demands the power of the
gospel. The special circumstances which prevail there must be taken
into consideration in the preaching of it. Missionwork must build on
firm ground. If the work leads only to the conversion of souls it
would not have been in vain; but the goal must be creation of a new
church, oneness [enhet], and there the tribe can offer a special opportunity for God's work.

After mentioning the importance of the medical mission and schools,
the speaker emphasised the necessity for co-operation. 'The work
requires good African leaders who, together with the missionaries, will
work for the christianisation of Africa.' The speaker warned against
romanticism and called for a sense of reality in mission vision.
Missionaries do not go out because they are adventurers, they go
because the love of Christ compels them to do so. (Umeåbladet 30
March 1937)

As we shall see, the couple was aware of the support they received
during their work, especially that of the youth in the Luleå diocese.
Eight years later the same paper would have occasion to report the
return of Dr Bengt Sundkler, not mentioning his wife, who had in fact
returned some months earlier.

Notes

1. In a later interview 31 October 1985 while discussing the issue of ambition
   B Sr refers to his pietism as follows: 'It was then a spiritual problem, in my
   pietistic time in the 1930s – because I was a pietist, but not in the Swedish sense
   perhaps.'
2. Cf. contact with Söderblom recorded in B Sr's own section. N Sm met B Sr after
   reading about his rapid completion of his Candidate of Theology degree in an
   issue of Dagens Nyheter in 1931 and adviced him to study Church Law. While
   B Sr was setting out to leave for Strasbourg Söderblom renewed his advice to
   study Church Law in a letter to B Sr (31 March 1931), but also asked him to
   take part in a course of five days for students in Geneva in September 1931 at
   the expense of the Ecumenical Council of Sweden and to visit on the way some
   of the big universities in Germany: Tübingen, Heidelberg, Bonn, Giessen,
   Marburg, etc.
3. During the German occupation Quisling was appointed by Hitler as leader of

Norway, and was consequently considered a traitor by patriotic Norwegians. Those who supported him were called Quislings.

4. This long excerpt is taken from the version of B Sr's life story I had in my possession. We do not know for sure which was the version he intended for publication. The final version was selected by his assistant Christop her Steed who knew best the location of his papers when he was admitted to hospital.

3

INGEBORG

Introducing Ingeborg Morén

Bengt had started to formulate this chapter on Ingeborg in his mind, but had not written it out. He had referred to writing such a chapter on several occasions. He had given me Ingeborg's personal writings to read so that, in his words, I could advise him on what to include in the chapter. I introduce Ingeborg where she comes into Bengt's life and tell of her role in work anticipating events which are later described more fully. We return to Ingeborg's life when her relatively early death approaches in 1969. Ingeborg's story is found in her numerous letters to Bengt, to her parents and brothers and to her friends. There are also pages of her diary which reveal her inner feelings. A good share of these are archived in Carolina Rediviva together with Bengt's papers, but at present access to them is restricted. Ingeborg was an excellent writer and her biography, based on her own writings from early childhood onwards deserves a special volume. In a later chapter I describe the intense presence of Ingeborg's death, quoting Bengt's diary notes, during the busiest university term and in the midst of moving house to their last home where Bengt continued to live alone until his own death 25 years later.

Privileged young woman

While still a member of the Oxford Group, Bengt and Ingeborg met and were attracted to one another. Bengt referred to Ingeborg as 'a privileged young woman' because of her family background and the chances she had had to prepare herself for adult life. Ingeborg was born on 27 June 1907 in South Africa, where her father, a construction engineer, had a business planning and building houses. Ingeborg, nicknamed Bojan by her parents, was brought to Sweden from South Africa as a baby when the family moved back to Stockholm. She described her father as being strict and somewhat scornful of his daughter's choices in life. Her father, Sture Morén (1878–1964) continued his work, constructing buildings around Oscar's church, as B Sr commented on his father-in-law's business. Bojan felt close to her mother, Anna Morén (born 1881), who to her sorrow died early, in 1940, while Ingeborg was in South Africa.

After completing high school, Ingeborg was given a chance to go to England to learn English in 1926–27. She went with a group of young women who stayed with families and took courses in language colleges at Bournemouth and later at Oxford. She spent also some time travelling in Europe. Her linguistic ability, which she later put to use in learning African languages, and learning French while staying in France, helped her to adjust to what life had in store for her.[1]

Ingeborg was educated as a teacher in Anna Sandström's Higher Teacher Training Seminar (*Högre lärarinneseminarium*), a very prestigeous higher education institution for the advancement of women at that time. She taught in Saltsjöbaden two years after finishing her training. Her fellow seminarian and close, lifelong friend Margit Persson, née Österberg, succeeded her in the same teaching-post and said in her funeral speech that Ingeborg's students had told of the deep impression she made on the students by her spiritual and dedicated personality. In Margit Persson's words:

> You can understand that if young people get that impression, then it must be something real, because they see through everything which is unreal and unauthentic. In her they had met someone who called forth and invited followers. Many other young people whom I have met who have known Ingeborg have said the same. (Funeral speech 25 November 1969)

After becoming engaged to Bengt, Ingeborg left her work and set herself wholeheartedly to assist him in gathering and organising the enormous mass of data that he had to deal with for his dissertation. In a letter to her in-laws she despaired at the growing disorder in her fiancé's cupboards, when he was trying to finish his thesis:

> You should understand that Bengt exists only for the child of his spirit and toil: the thesis. It is very understandable just now. It has been wonderful to see Bengt working at this time. When he is in action he develops extraordinary concentrated energy. Yes, you know. Nothing remains untouched and he draws everyone's attention in the library; no one can but notice him when he strides through the reading hall; around his table the air is loaded. It is a wonder that he is so well and in good temper.
> Yesterday we sent off a box of dirty clothes. His drawers and cupboard were so full of junk that we had to reduce it a bit. Just think. Bengt is a lucky owner of almost hundred pairs of socks! Just like the worst millionaire. Can you not be anything else but impressed by Bengt, in every respect?!! He is extremely nice toward me. (Ingeborg's letter to Bengt's parents 17 March 1937)

Ingeborg had a premonition of what it was to be married to a devoted scholar who time and again would excuse himself for throwing his whole being into periods of gathering inspiration while doing research and writing.

Mission rules for marriage

Ingeborg had no difficulty in making the decision to accept the mission call, but getting married was not a simple matter after they had agreed to go together to Africa. On the contrary, the mission board rules, formulated by the mission director and dated 28 January 1937, stated that a missionary must not, without special permission from the board, enter into matrimony before he (assumed to be the husband) had taken up his independent work in the missionfield. To quote the regulations:

> Extenuating circumstances which would allow an exception to this rule would have to be especially well-motivated; in general the rule has to be considered the normal practice from which exceptions could be made should especially strong factors so indicate. ... Such reasons would be that the missionary in question had already held an independent post at home and was over 30 years old.

Neither of these conditions pertained to B Sr. Exceptions had been made where the missionaries were sent to very specific tasks, such as a doctor to a definite place with known conditions where he would not be taking language studies. Another such case had also been a missionary going to teach theology in a specific place where the housing was organised and there was no question of changing the placement of the named person.

Indeed, the couple had quite a struggle with the mission board. On 12 January 1937 B Sr wrote a letter to them asking that the regulations be waived in their case and that they be permitted to get married before their departure. In sending the rules to them the mission secretary apologised, recognising that the rules were bound to sound too rigid, but he again emphasised that the rules would become meaningless if too many exceptions were made (mission director's letter 28 January 1937).[2] At the first meeting of the mission board in February their request to get married before their language-study period was put on the table. At the second meeting in April the board saw no reason why an exception should be made to the rules.

The head of the mission station in Dundee, Natal, Stig Falck, who was about to depart on a homeleave, wrote a letter explaining the mission board's position in greater detail, confirming that the paper the mission director had worked out gave the rules which were generally followed. Stig Falck wrote:

Concerning your marriage: The reasons I have so far heard against your getting married are the following: a) health; b) language; c) housing. Regarding the health there apparently can be some risk for the mother and child if the first delivery takes place before mother has acclimatised herself. M. A. (a Swedish midwife in Dundee) considers, however, this risk to be minimal. Regarding the language, it is said that the married do not learn the language as quickly as the unmarried, but this no doubt depends on the individuals. Have student marriages lengthened the study time in Sweden? Apparently so, and that is the reason why the married couple should not set up their own household. That difficulty can surely be helped by us inviting you two to eat in our household. As to the house, it might be a problem somewhere but not here. In conclusion: My view is that you should allow all engaged missionaries to get married before they go out. Their relatives and they themselves need to experience that joy. The young people themselves need to have the joy of facing the new experiences together. If the mission board decides that they should not set up a household before the language-study period is over, they would not mind at first living out of a suitcase, they would rather do that than live in different places. The latter seems to be unnatural, far-fetched and wholly unnecessary. Bring along a sewing machine and anything that will make your home look Swedish. (Stig Falck 30 July 1937 to B Sr in England)

The last point was followed when, before too long, Swedish furniture was ordered which later found its way to the Svenskbo in Durban, the Swedish resthouse for missionaries, and in the end was returned to Sweden!

The request was finally passed in a meeting in June, at the insistence of Bengt and Ingeborg, but it meant that they left for England for language study as an engaged couple and not married, and had consequently had some difficulty in finding a place where both could study. (Minutes of the Mission Board in April and letter received 27 July 1937)

Another issue was the loan B Sr had had to take out to finish his thesis. The mission board was not willing to shoulder it but agreed to deduct it gradually from his salary. The board reminded them that B Sr had already been granted the second highest salary rate among the missionaries. It could not be foreseen at the time that war would break out and isolate them from any possibility of getting regular salaries and paying debts. They had to resort to dependence on Ingeborg's father several times, and, as becomes evident from Ingeborg's letter, even asking for help from Bengt's father. When they later moved to Tanganyika (Tanzania), and the salary came from a different board, they had a reason to wonder how the debt at home was ever to be covered.

Ambitious language students

Ingeborg already felt at home with the English language because of
the time she had previously spent in England. For Bengt, who was
competent in French and German, getting acquainted with English and
England presented a new challenge which he took very seriously. The
time for learning the language became more complicated than they had
anticipated. Bengt left for England, travelling with the mission secretary, Bäfverfeldt, by boat to Harwich, arriving on 25 April. I quote
from a letter from Bengt to Ingeborg (27 April 1937), who stayed
behind in Sweden until Bengt could get things organised for them in
England:

> I find myself like a drop in the ocean here in London and can do
> nothing. The London School of Languages was a disappointment. I shall
> withdraw myself from there as quickly as possible. I have, however, to
> pay between four and ten pounds for some private lessons which I take
> instead of the class teaching which is worthless ... I have, in any case,
> to get organised, systematic training in English for myself.

Travelling by underground and on buses was at first stressful for
Bengt.[3] Living expenses and the cost of even poor lessons were high
in London. Bengt resorted to going to the language school run by Miss
Melin which was recommended by the mission. 'I threw myself into
the arms of Miss Melin in Walton-on-Thames', as Bengt expressed it
in a letter to Ingeborg. He felt caught between bad options. Ingeborg
came to Miss Melin, who offered cheaper boarding and free teaching,
but it turned out to be another mistake, 'another Oxford group
member', as we shall see later. Bengt escaped after two weeks, first
going to the Cochrane family, a private rural dean family of aristo-
cratic background at Yardley, near Birmingham, and subsequently
spent some pleasant weeks in Selly Oaks, Birmingham, leaving
Ingeborg to cope with Miss Melin in Walton-on-Thames, where
several Swedish missionaries were studying English.[4]

After two months in Walton-on-Thames, Ingeborg realised that she
knew enough English from her time as a young girl in England. By
that time Bengt had familiarised himself with British life sufficiently
to be able to establish his first contacts in the academic world. Bengt
wrote to Ingeborg to come to London, where he, as an ambitious
Doctor Upsaliensis had managed to arrange an audience with the
famous anthropologist, Malinowski, at the London School of
Economics. LSE later became familiar to him on many occasions,
first as a visiting student and later as a visiting professor. From there,
Ingeborg and Bengt would go to Oxford, familiar to Ingeborg from
her earlier years there. This would also be a way for Ingeborg and
Bengt to meet; they needed to meet, she should not think of saving
mission money! (Letter to Ingeborg 25 May 1937) Ingeborg went then

to stay with Bengt in Birmingham for several happy weeks, as she reports to Bengt's father of the time they had together, after returning home to Sweden (6 July 1937):

> But oh, oh! Where shall we get the money to buy all those books! In the meanwhile we imagine that we shall manage, if Bengt only will have his books and I my piano, what more will we need?!!!

In Kingsmead, at Selly Oaks, they had been exposed to the non-established free-church environment. In London, they had had contact with the High-Church Society for the Propagation of Christian Knowledge, SPCK. Bengt had then seen Ingeborg off to the boat on her return voyage to Sweden and to her family island of Manskär, where she was to spend the latter part of the summer with her parents. After seeing her off, in a letter to Ingeborg (5 July 1937) Bengt regretted that their plan to be on the island together in July had evaporated. The pattern for Bengt to sink in the world of books was beginning to form:

> There was clearly nothing that could be done about it. I have sunk in the world of books, I have read as much as possible in relation to Africa. Unfortunately it is only possible to browse through the books and get a rapid orientation, but I am convinced that even that is very useful. C. P. Groves himself has ordered books for us. I take part in Oxford Days 17–18 July.[5]

Bengt sent longing letters to Ingeborg every second day, yet he was convinced he simply could not leave England yet. He assures her that he misses her, even more so when he reads her descriptions of the peace and calm on the island, but sees no alternative to his continued stay in Birmingham. In a letter dated 20 July, he reports on the 'Oxford Days' where he had met many important Swedes, among them Yngve Brillioth and Manfred Björquist, and several others whom he lists by name. A week later he was to meet another famous anthropologist, Raymond Firth, later successor to Malinowski at LSE, and was hoping for a constructive meeting.

After receiving the letter from the Mission Office approving their marriage, Bengt rejoiced that they now could set the wedding date, call the banns immediately after his homecoming and make arrangements with the pastor. (Letter 27 July) 'I agree with you, it is wonderful to live. Because you exist.' (30 July)

Bengt returned to Sweden to join Ingeborg on her island. Their commissioning service for missionwork was held on 29 August. Ingeborg notes in her diary that at the commissioning of Bengt in Gammelstad in 1937 she gave a speech based on John 15:16, 'You did not choose me, but I chose you and appointed you that you should go and bear fruit.' She expressed her happiness about going to Africa, but felt that she was going as if in a dream.[6] Their wedding finally took place on 18 September, arranged by Ingeborg's parents and performed by Bengt's teacher and advisor, Professor Knut B. Westman, in Oscar's church.

On their thirtieth wedding anniversary, 18 September 1967, Bengt made the following endearing entry in his diary:

> This day 30 years ago Ingeborg and I were married in Oscar church, Stockholm (K. B. Westman). We celebrated the day with a dinner at home which I ordered from Martin Olsson, and added fine wine!
>
> I thank God for a good and noble wife, longsuffering and great in her gentleness (almost always!). Thirty years ago, on that beautiful Saturday in September 1937, with a fine and beautiful wedding feast which Ingeborg's father and mother arranged for us and their guests; 30 years in all lands of Africa, England and Sweden; 30 years of plans, work, and fellowship. How very rich and valuable. May God bless Ingeborg.

Less than a month after the wedding, on 15 October 1937, the couple was on a Swedish boat, M/S Tisnaren, sailing from Oslo to Cape Town.

Both Bengt and Ingeborg described the voyage in their letters. Ingeborg's attitude is that of a fresh missionary in a letter to her parents from the boat (11 November 1937). It deserves to be quoted here as it reflects the background from which Ingeborg started her work:

> Oh, how lovely and rich life is at times ... We have had worship services on all three Sundays. They are all heathen on board except one brother in the crew, who is a Pentecostal. Bengt took the liturgy and we sang hymns as best we could (without an organ). The interest has been quite considerable and I think Bengt preached very well all three times ... We are nearing Cape Town – the land of our longings [*våra längtans land*] ... all this you have seen.

At home in Africa

The mission board's fears that this linguistically talented couple would not study the language intensely were of course totally unnecessary. Aided by good tutoring from the long-time superintendent of the field and fine linguist, Dean A. R. Kempe, and given conversation lessons by a Zulu woman teacher, both quickly mastered the Zulu language which they soon learned to love.[7] Both took their exams in the time allotted for language study but had started their work even sooner. The husband described his young wife's success in learning the language in a letter to her father after nine months of language study (30 September 1938), 'I am very proud of her ... I can congratulate you on you daughter's very great and very well earned progress.' Ingeborg herself expressed equally her pride and joy about her success in the same letter, 'We both have passed our language exams with flying colours. I cleared my exam splendidly. I have broken the record and learned the language in nine months. For others the period has been at least one year.'

A year later Ingeborg wrote home expressing her excitement (30 May 1939).

> We have had a real Pentecost here. Bengt preached extremely well in the evening about the Holy Spirit, which we all need ... He will give the Holy Spirit into our hearts – so that we might live, really live – and shine as lights in the world and one day in Heaven.
>
> I have sewn Bengt and Pastor Sibiya each a Luther chasuble – so that they both could step before the altar dressed in their robes, really beautiful and both, of course, having also white stoles. We illustrated the text with a candleholder of seven candles for the altar and the candleholders for the congregation which were lit from the altar lights. The whole congregation were able to approach one by one to light their candle from the seven candles, a symbol of the Holy Spirit which like fire should so spread and burn in every person's heart – in the whole congregation.

Bengt praised Ingeborg's courage in getting around on horseback, as he was later to praise her driving fearlessly around in Bukoba and across the border into Uganda. He told how in Ceza, Zululand, Ingeborg was fully engaged in work. On horseback they visited the kraals, homesteads with cattle, talking with people. She visited the sick with the nurse and she taught English and gymnastics to the students in the school while Bengt taught them Bible knowledge. In a letter to the Hellstens he told of Ingeborg's participation in work in following terms (15 November 1940):

> Our church was in a terrible condition when we came here at the end of April. The building itself is hopeless and fortunately condemned to be rebuilt immediately after the war, in a wonderful Zulu style. We dream a lot about it and make sketches, but we had to do the best possible with what was there. We have renovated the church choir, got a larger altar, Ingeborg has created a wonderful small altar especially for children, with pictures and flowers which children themselves can put on it, and other such things. Ingeborg also sewed new vestments, and so the African pastors appear now always in white albs and stoles in tempera colours so much more fun to wear than the customary black colour, which is not meant for this climate and heat here. For the Advent Ingeborg will sew for me a purple chasuble which will also delight our congregation of nationals ... We do all such things very cheaply, my chasuble is going to cost 15–17 Swedish kronas, and it is going to be very beautiful. I know that beforehand, because Ingeborg has now much training. In recent times she has sewn 5–6 albs, most of them for the black pastors in our church.
>
> In Dundee, where life was very much more 'civilised' than in Ceza we did many interesting things together during the festival days, at

Easter and Pentecost. We started with processions, and worship services in the graveyard, with festive lighting which Ingeborg helped to develop in a modified African style. They were quickly adopted as part of the congregational practice in the whole synod which showed that something like that was very much needed.

At Ingeborg's funeral Bengt told in touching words of Ingeborg's warm fellowship with the people in Ceza with whom they had worked there:

> Ingeborg had for many reasons loved Ceza, which she had to leave behind, its wonderful Christian women among whom she found friends such as Andelina Nyandeni and others who came close to her. Daring rider that she was, she enjoyed tremendously riding swiftly over Zululand's rolling hills. But there was something in Ingeborg's inner history which bound her closely with the air and light and people in Ceza. In April 1940, the day before she and I were to leave the mission station in Natal and move to Ceza in Zululand, she received a telegram from Stockholm. It had taken three weeks to come and it informed her that her beloved mother had passed away. It was perhaps the heaviest sorrow in her life, but the sun above Ceza had 'healing under its wings', to speak in the language of the Old Testament Malachi. (B Sr funeral speech 25 November 1969)

The following years in Bukoba, Tanganyika, demanded rewarding professional service of Ingeborg. She was able to make use of her teaching qualifications, which were more acceptable to the colonial government's educational department than Bengt's theological doctorate. Ingeborg was appointed headmistress of the teacher training school at Kigarama and given teaching responsibility for the school in 1943. She thus became part of a rescue operation to secure the continuation of the school which B Sr considered to be the most important institution in the young church. She taught English classes (at this Swahili-speaking school) which meant that the teaching could be given by someone who had a working contact with the language, and not in a German accent as previously. Above all, however, she was a good mother to the family of 100 young African seminarians and ten teaching colleagues, most of whom later became leaders in government, church or schools. Ingeborg's motherly care was needed when the students occasionally had malaria attacks.

> In the congregation in Kigarama, and elsewhere, Ingeborg could become part of the first sprouting spring of revival in Bukoba, long before it blossomed fully. She understood what awakening was. Ingeborg's own fundamental experience in life was dated on the first page of her Swedish Bible: '8 July 1928'. Based on her own deep experience of conversion on that summer day she could recognise true spiritual life, in the East African Revival also. At the same time, this fundamental experience gave her certain critical principle which prevented her from

being carried away on all kinds of winds. (B Sr funeral speech 25 November 1969)

Wife of a scholar

'I was aware of Ingeborg's rare qualities and felt unworthy being married to her'; 'the world's most wonderful, sweet, beautiful, pure, best and most attractive wife', as Bengt expressed it in a birthday letter to her, adding that his innermost hope was to be able to be a good and helpful and supporting husband. (27 June 1938)

Bengt might not have been able to divide his time and attention as he would have wished to do as a devoted husband, but the correspondence between them was frequent when they were apart. The words and thoughts were warm, even when jotted down in a great hurry on small air letter forms in almost illegible handwriting. Bengt reported from his travels often and in great detail. Throughout his life Bengt recognised the spiritual strength he gained through his marriage to Ingeborg.

Time and again we find in his writings reflections of the great blessing that Ingeborg was for Bengt. The following was written after her death when Bengt was suddenly left alone:

> I think of our life together united in marriage. Ingeborg was a gift of God to me. She called forth new life in me. I was going my easy way in life, Ingeborg came into my life and challenged me to take life more seriously. For me it meant a breakthrough, God became alive again for me. I saw how He worked and that He was at work. Ingeborg, who had only one ambition, to live as she thought God wanted her to live, found it strange to walk side-by-side with a person so obviously driven by ambitions as me. Particularly in the many years in academic Uppsala: those books and articles and lectures so terribly important to me, were to her most often a waste of effort. What's the use? One could have spent the time instead in St David's chapel at Rättvik. In fact I did go there from time to time and found it immensely helpful to me personally to take retreats occasionally, and also to take part in the priests' retreats. But we had too little of that kind of a thing, she felt, without in any way nagging about it. It was just a void, I think she felt. I was deeply aware that I needed her to keep me on the way. Her image helped me to believe that there was purity, goodness, joy and also trust in this world.

The husband who was in the public eye for much of his life often felt that it was Ingeborg's lack of self-confidence which kept her out of the limelight and increased her loneliness. He wrote,'In Sweden she so often said that she was "tired". In Bukoba she received new strength every day and was glad and thankful. Her sensitive understanding of African life has been, throughout the years, a great challenge to me.'[8]

What in Ingeborg's letters to Bengt's parents before marriage was expressed in great humour turned to loneliness in later life. The loneliness would deepen as the time went on and was perhaps finally only fully reconciled at her death bed.

Inner longings

After returning to the academic atmosphere of Uppsala, and no longer intensely engaged in working with Bengt, childlessness probably became a greater burden for Ingeborg than for her husband. In his words:

> But that very fine woman, a saint on earth, had hidden resources. Ingeborg's reaction to not having children is possibly a variation of the attitude of many Western childless women of her generation who were groping for a place in life and not finding full satisfaction in married life, particularly as she found the husband absorbed and hard-working, and therefore not caring. She was a good pianist and she felt she had sacrificed her music, not finding a way of exercising her musical gift. She continued to take lessons while we were in Uppsala, living in a small flat on Luthagsesplanaden in the intermediate years 1946–47, and again after returning from Bukoba, but she could not satisfy her own ambition and in the end played only sporadically, to rid herself of her frustrations. (B Sr earlier manuscript)

Ingeborg wrote in her diary 23 January 1957:

> A child is not the deepest meaning of marriage. But why not be allowed to take part in creation. God who is so good, how can He allow a person to get married and not get a child? Think how much of an outsider a childless woman feels herself. Not any connection with Mary, Mother of God – how could we attain it – and yet ... It is beyond our understanding and yet I understand much ... One can lose oneself only in what one has been created for ... If I have been created a woman, why not to get the fulfillment of being a woman?

At the end of 1956 Ingeborg had occasion to express her loneliness in the diary which she kept. Bengt had not known that Ingeborg had kept a diary, as he recounted in a moving letter in which he informed their friend and Ingeborg's Anglican confessor, Father Hugh, about Ingeborg's death, inviting him to come to her funeral, an invitation he declined.

Ingeborg expressed her feelings of loneliness in her diary notes:

> Poor Bengt and poor me! I do not feel self pity, I only state a fact. There he sits in his Dekanhus, night after night, never at home – and here I am alone, day after day, year after year, longing for love and fellowship. What shall I do? I cannot solve this. I have to love in another way

... My longing for God becomes more total. I shall seek Him when
Bengt is not at home and be loving toward him when he comes home,
satisfied and glad in God's love. (Ingeborg's diary 11 December 1956)

Bengt and Ingeborg took retreats together, they went on holidays to
the Canary Islands, travelled and drove on long trips together, yet
Bengt became aware that they were gradually growing apart as he was
unable to reach Ingeborg's innermost self. In retrospect he said, 'I
could get irritated, we did not quarrel. I left her and went to do my
job. We did not talk through our deepest problems. We were so
different.' (Interview 1988 by MLS, n.d.)

Ingeborg did confide in some of her best friends with whom she
corresponded over the years. Of these friends, Margit Persson, née
Österberg, Margit Byegård, and Elizabeth Bernander visited her when
they were in Uppsala, and they also spoke at her funeral, expressing
how they had throughout been guided into deeper faith by Ingeborg.
(Funeral speeches and letter to MLS 16 March 1984)

Back to Africa

In 1958 Ingeborg returned happily with her husband to South Africa
when B Sr was asked to update *Bantu Prophets*. During that time
Ingeborg made a trip back to East Africa alone. This visit to the places
which had become dear to her prompted her to write, comparing
herself to a bird freed from its cage:[9]

> I am so happy. I am in good health and happy. I thank God the Heavenly
> Father, the little bird has flown out of her cage. She has flown up to the
> north, out of the cold South African winter [1 July] to the warmth and
> freedom of the north, from Johannesburg to Bukoba. I stayed overnight
> in Nairobi and Entebbe and am now in the bush in the Haya church
> field. We could only get here by a 4-wheel-drive jeep, to a Bible school
> recently started by a deaconess from Samariterhemmet [deaconess insti-
> tute] in Uppsala. We are the only two Europeans in this place. It is
> wonderful to be with her – and to hear everything that is happening here
> in the church which I know so well from working here.
>
> The most marvellous thing is that here this little person is creating a
> sanctuary of peace. What she could not do in Sweden is possible here.
> You know how hard the soil is in Sweden for the deeper religious life
> of the community type (if I may put it that way). And so God works in
> His many hidden and visible ways – and sends her out to bring about
> something which meets response. It is wonderful.

Bengt later became a bishop in Bukoba and he always considered
the time as the bishop's wife to have been the best for Ingeborg.
Together they were able to open the bishop's manse for people to
come on errands and visits, or for worship, Bible study and prayer.
The diaries of B Sr tell of an amazing number of local and overseas

overnight visitors to the manse and one can only imagine how much work it created for the hostess. Very fortunately, Ingeborg had prepared herself for this kind of service. In her papers we find a book of menus for dinners planned and served starting from 1929, long before she was married. Particularly after their return from Africa to Sweden in the 1960s, numbers of visitors and their names were recorded, and later we find also comments on whether the dinners were successful or whether they failed in some aspect. In one of these menu books there is a chapter written on 'English social life'. This indicates that she had learned this kind of formality, not only from her parental home, but also from her contacts with English society. It also gives background to her inclination toward the formality of High-Church spirituality. Bengt later recalled Ingeborg's role as the bishop's wife:

> Three years after this visit to Bukoba, Ingeborg came back as the wife of the bishop, now to a free Tanzania and an independent diocese. The four episcopal years in Bukoba (1961–65) were, I think, very satisfying to both of us, being similarly involved and engaged in a very great task, sharing the joys and sorrows, its seeming achievements and sad short-comings, to a very remarkable degree, day after day. I always felt that those years were, from the point of view of our marriage, the very best. (Letter to MLS 16 March 1984)

> During the years I had the privilege of being a bishop, Ingeborg was the ideal wife of an evangelical bishop: a great faithful believer, living in prayer and from Holy Communion, anxious to serve everybody in the diocese and doing so with joy and humour, enjoying it all. She trained people who were leaving to study abroad in England and America. (Recorded interview by MLS 1988 n.d.)

Ingeborg was visiting England when their great friend, one of the three candidates for episcopal election as the first African bishop in Bukoba, Ernest Lutashobya, came to England. She was able to greet him with *salaam sana* when he arrived in an unfamiliar world in order to start his studies in Canterbury, and she stayed there to get him well started.

As the bishop's wife, Ingeborg took charge of numerous practical arrangements, from building repairs to the planning and ordering of things not available locally. She would drive by herself to Kampala and get what was needed, while also visiting friends.

> Ingeborg enjoyed driving. She would take the car and drive to Kampala and back again. Once we were driving together and had a puncture at Kagera river. She said to me, 'Let me attend to this.' Suddenly 20 and then 200 people were looking on. Ingeborg went at it with speed and determination. A little boy standing there turned to a man and remarked, 'That is a man for you!' It was a poor attribute for me. There I let the woman do all the work. (Recorded interview by MLS 1988 n.d.)

Ingeborg also initiated a women's meeting for discussing the difficult problems faced by the Haya women. After one such conference she told her husband that she only then understood the subordinate situation of Haya women.

After returning home to Sweden Ingeborg was asked to speak to the Swedish Women's Mission Society (SKMF) about the women's situation in Bukoba. In referring to it Bengt did not recall her speech but in the diocese yearbook B Sr had described the conference and the women's situation in the following way (1965:70-1):

> Among ... all the courses conducted ... I mention here one in particualr, the diocese-wide women's course in November, full of promise for future. Our work in the women's world has not yet found its adequate form either on the level of the diocese or locally, apart from some good local initiatives. But this course showed that the situation is brighter than one is often led to believe. Quietly, but no less effectively for it, women have gained a new awareness which is fostered by the Church and Revival, and to a certain extent supported by the school and political organisations. Discussions and talks during the course showed also that in the equator diocese there is a richer stock of personal resources, especially among pastors' and teachers' wives, than was earlier known.

This led Ingeborg to remember the women of Bukoba in a special way in her will and to leave what remained of her inheritance to be used for their uplifting.

> Ingeborg felt she belonged to Bukoba. When I was at home, we used to take a walk along the shore of Lake Victoria, between 6 and 7 p.m., before darkness fell. Every time she said, in English (the language she loved): 'This climate suits me perfectly.' But she was also thinking then of the spiritual climate, the open, happy fellowship with African fellow-workers, both those she knew well and those she knew only through friendly greeting. She was a spiritually rich person with much to offer, who was able to flourish and grow within this good fellowship.
>   Africa takes and demands from a person everything that she or he has, an unreserved contribution of the whole personality. But far more than what Africa takes, Africa gives. Ingeborg was shy, and needed perhaps more than most an atmosphere of love, warmth and spontaneous response for herself to dare to give and grow and blossom. Bukoba diocese gave Ingeborg that milieu. This African group of Christian women and men were acutely aware of her spiritual qualities. They respected, honoured and loved her, their own 'Ma Ingeborg', more than was otherwise her lot in life. One can wonder endlessly how this happened. She did not give speeches or lecture to great audiences, and was not very special by people's usual standards. But she had an inner quality, a spiritual strength and honesty and an enduring faith. This did not escape those who daily worked with her and met her, Africans and missionaries of different nationalities. (B Sr at the funeral 25 November 1969)

In *Bara Bukoba* B Sr wrote:

> It was in the context of an Anglican tradition of spirituality and its Swedish variant that both Ingeborg and I had received our deepest spiritual experiences, and that tradition Ingeborg brought to the equator. It was largely thanks to her that we were able to hold on unfailingly to the regular early Eucharist in the bishop's chapel, and the tradition of prayer there. Wiser people advised against what initially looked like excess, but Ingeborg had a strong and dedicated will, an inner authority, and this, I believe, the people in Bukoba felt to be something valuable. She kept the weekly Holy Communion in the bishop's residence going with other pastors when I was not there. (Sundkler 1974:165–6)

> There were months during these Bukoba years when I lay ill in faraway Uppsala and was absent from the diocese. Then this brisk, calm Christian woman kept certain important work going, even just by being available and with a kind of indomitable determination to see to it that things got done. She saw to it that even then the customary Holy Communion on Wednesdays at 7.15 p.m. was celebrated in the chapel of the bishop's manse. As inevitable was the joyous *agape* meal in the form of common breakfast which followed the mass. It was enjoyed on the enclosed verandah which, on account of the ecclesiastic office of the occupant, was made more respectable by calling it the dining-hall and reception room. (Funeral speech of B Sr 25 November 1969)

Ingeborg continued her interest in teaching others how to keep the altarcloths clean and neat and how to sew new vestments, keeping their style in line with the simple beauty of African art. Even after they had left Africa, Bishop Bengt's successor Bishop Josiah Kibira, the first African bishop in the northwestern diocese, wrote to her asking for advice on the altarcloths and vestments in the new Bukoba cathedral, only a few months before Ingeborg died. We shall come to that time after many years of service in between, but I close this chapter on Ingeborg with words which Bengt spoke and wrote after her death because they so aptly describe the kind of woman she was:

> Ingeborg had two words of honour, both in her beloved English: care and concern. This to her was the function of the Church: to show care and concern in the name of Jesus. The more one learns of life the more one sees that this is not bad ecclesiology. How far such influence reaches, only God knows. There were at least some people to whom Ingeborg came close: some African pastors and teachers, pastors' and teachers' wives, some missionaries. At times fine students came from Kahororo school, with shining eyes and the problems of life, and Ingeborg rejoiced in their fellowship. Otherwise, she was there, available, for care and concern.
>
> In the international family in which Ingeborg worked there were some Danish co-workers. The prophet of Denmark, Sören Kierkegaard, once said, 'Heart's purity is to will one thing only.' '*Hjärtats renhet är att*

> *vilja ett.*' Ingeborg had a burning, intense will. It was sanctified to will one thing: the highest. (B Sr's funeral speech 25 November 1969)

Bengt could recall many memories of good moments they had shared together with Ingeborg. He realised that when Ingeborg died, not only had he lost his life's companion but that he would also miss the spiritual support which Ingeborg had given him:

> Bukoba was our common love. I often think of a morning in our Bishop's manse. Ingeborg sat embroidering one of her beautiful vestments. I came in and put on a record playing Handel's 'How beautiful are the feet of those who proclaim good tidings of peace.' Ingeborg looked up surprised saying that she had been humming the very same music. It was a precious moment in which we strongly experienced the commonness of our mission in the country we both loved.
>
> Ingeborg's death was a deep crisis. With all her beauty and joy and anxiety, Ingeborg had an inner authority which at once both compelled me and helped me (what I tried to do as a bishop in Bukoba is entirely due to her) and which sometimes was a little too much, too hard for me. (Letter 31 January 1972)

Five-and-half years after Ingeborg's death, on Ingeborg's birthday Bengt wrote:

> It is Ingeborg's birthday today. I look again at the very wonderful photo of her and think again of that very remarkable personality, so dedicated. I need her willpower and her immense dedication, and I thank God for what she meant to me and to so many. As you wrote about Bukoba and your visit there, I thought of Ingeborg's fine contribution to that diocese, very noble indeed. I am sure that she is thankfully remembered in many families and hearts. (Letter to MLS 27 June 1975)

Notes

1. Ingeborg's letter collection and her diaries, from which the information concerning the parents has been taken. (28 February 1957)
2. *PM utarbetad av t.f. missionsdirektorn, Sigfrid Alm daterad den 28 jan. 1937.* (Memorandum drawn up and signed by the deputy mission director Sigfrid Alm, dated 28 January 1937.) Later a footnote was added by hand by the mission secretary, A. Bäfverfeldt, about the board meeting decision on Dr Sundkler in June 1937.
3. B Sr had tendencies to claustrophobia which he reported from time to time. One experience was in a bus while on holiday in Bulgaria 1970, another in our small beach house in Dar es Salaam in 1973, another again in Bukoba in the dark, enclosed guest house during the Iddi Amin threat from Uganda, an occasion when the repeated Jesus prayer became important to him (Jesus Christ, the Son of God, have mercy upon me, now and for eternity).
4. Recorded interview by MLS 31 October 1985. Even in his dreams, B Sr returns to his experience with Märta Dahl as a representative of the Oxford groupers, as we shall see. It appears that coming to the Cochrane family happened by chance, after engaging in discussion with their son while travelling.

5. C. P. Groves had set up the Selly Oaks library, thus knew it thoroughly and was willing to order any books that B Sr wanted to read.
6. It appears that only the husband was commissioned and not the wife. This practice was later changed.
7. The setting for learning and the time with an evangelist at an outstation at Makitika while in Ceza were reported to the mission director by B Sr in a letter: 'Dean Kempe has been especially interested and stimulating teacher and Stig Falck has also set aside any free moment to teach us grammar.' (Letter 8 February 1938) 'We have had here at the station very good help from a woman teacher with whom we have had daily conversation.' (Letter 9 May 1939)
8. Quotations from an earlier manuscript in which the part of Ingeborg was more elaborated on.
9. B Sr's letter to the writer 16 March 1984: 'Thank you very much for reading these letters (Ingeborg's letters and diaries). I shall need your help in selecting passages for a chapter on Ingeborg in that autobiography of mine, if I ever get as far as that.' I have tried to be sensitive in selecting diary notes 23 January and 23 February 1957, 1 July 1958.

4

CHURCH AND MISSION IN THE SEGREGATED SOUTH

Initial shocks

Ingeborg and Bengt were sent off to South Africa from the central station in Stockholm, as was the custom, with a hymn singing by the friends who had come to see them off. To Bengt's dismay, because of what seemed to him unnecessary sentimentality, his father took the trouble to travel all the way to Oslo to see them off.

A letter written on board M/S Tisnaren (19 November 1937) on the way to Cape Town, sent home and copied to the home office, gives a glimpse of the impressions of travellers to Africa on their first long trip away from home. It also enables the reader to see the change that took place in the vision of Christian mission in Bengt Sundkler's own history. In his own story B Sr did not consider it necessary to highlight this, apart from referring to the fact that he started as a pietist from northern Sweden, but even then he emphasised that his own home background was not pietistic. I consider this point of departure significant for Bengt's later readiness to understand and feel with the revivalists in Bukoba and serve as their bishop. Both for Ingeborg and Bengt, their later High-Church piety and devotional life gained its spiritual strength from the personal spiritual experiences of their youth. From the boat Bengt wrote the following account:

> As the boat train was about to leave the central station the friends who had come to see us off sang 'Almighty fortress is our God.' – then as the group was singing *'Platt intet oss förfärar'* the train left the station and we were on our way out of Sweden. Not having made any such long voyages before it gave a special sensation to settle on the boat for almost a whole month's travel. We had exceptionally good luck with weather – in the Bay of Biscay it was a bit windy but it did not bother us, we have not been sick at all. We have had fine, sunny summer weather and since the coast of Spain we have been able daily to take a wonderful dip in a saltwater swimming pool. We have heard quite a few stories about the difficulties of missionary life and we have become convinced that a boat

trip can be a wonderful way of resting. Suntanned and rested we can step out of the boat on the shore of Africa.

We have also done something useful. I have been banging away on my typewriter for a couple of hours each day, glad of the chance to practice that skill further. On Sundays I have been able to organise services here onboard with quite a good attendance of both passengers and crew. I have met here men who had not been to church in over ten years. It has been wonderful to bring the gospel to them and to act as a seamen's pastor for a few days. There have been good opportunities to speak about God with people. On Sunday we plan to arrange a meeting with short witnesses by my wife, a nurse, a Pentecostal seaman and myself.

We look forward to our work with gratitude. We are prepared to meet difficulties, they must come, but we go with God and expect only to be used by Him. Judging from what I have heard and seen, it seems that the time for our missionwork in South Africa is critical. There is a turnover of staff, one epoch is ending, another is starting, something new is about to come. It can be quite wonderful to step into the work just at this time and pray only to God that the years down there can be used *ad majorem Dei gloriam*.

On 25 November 1937 they sent a cable informing the home board: 'Arrived Cape. Sundkler.'

In his own story B Sr tells of the first manifestation of apartheid which Ingeborg and he experienced directly after arriving at their first mission station in Dundee. This incident, so soon after their arrival, shook them thoroughly and affected B Sr irreversibly. He could not believe that a missionary, who five years earlier had left Sweden determined to change race relations in South Africa, could so soon have accommodated himself to seeping apartheid and say, 'We do not shake hands with the Natives.' The impression that he carried in his mind of the Swedish mission in Natal and Zululand, and perhaps of the Lutheran mission in general, was rooted in the initial shock he suffered.

In 1985 B Sr recalled a memory of this negative spirit in two Western missionaries in the theological seminary who 'had been overcome by the atmosphere and insisted on distance and certain segregation between white man and Africans who were learning white man's knowledge'. This was at the freer time when legislation was not yet as restrictive as in 1948–9. At that time it was self-imposed segregation. (Interview 30 November 1985)

I would venture to make the generalisation here that for someone with Sundkler's associative mind which worked through metaphors, icons and symbols, and if not emotions, at least intuitions, such impressions had a stronger effect on thinking than a discursive, Cartesian disposition would be prepared to suffer. On a prepared ground, inadvertently scattered seeds readily take root.

In 1938–39, soon after the Sundklers' settling in Zululand, they witnessed the kindling spirit of fear and hatred in the minds of many

Zulus. A new phenomenon, *Voortrekkerminnet,* was the cause. Large, heavy, Boer ox-waggons rolled slowly through the country toward the Blood River battlefield to reminisce about the past. Zulu parents on some outstations forbade their children from going to confirmation classes in Dundee in the end of the year for fear that something would happen to them on the road, teachers did not pick up their monthly salaries, being convinced that the Boers would drive over them on the way. The rumours were groundless but it was a foreboding of stricter apartheid (*Redogörelse för arbetet å Dundee* 1938).

These experiences soon after their arrival in the field prepared the newcomers' sensitive minds for their later awareness of the difficulties of being a White missionary in such a country. What took place in South Africa was intensified by developments in Europe where Hitler's war, as B Sr called it, dramatically increased racial antagonisms.

Learning the Zulu language and culture

Bengt's and Ingeborg's rapid progress in language study was made easier when they were able to follow their colleague in charge of the station on his trips to the outstations on Sundays. After two months they were able to report that, after a hard but satisfying effort to break into the new kind of language structure of Zulu, they were beginning to feel more and more at home in the new thought construction. A letter to the mission director, Gunnar Dahlquist, (9 May 1938) tells of the stay in Ceza:

> While living here in Ceza I have been able to assist with the liturgy in the Sunday services and have started taking some morning prayers in hospital. On Good Shepherd's Sunday I had to throw myself in the deep end. Josef [Sandström] was on a visit to an outstation on his way to a mission committee meeting in Dundee and left me with the whole lot, first taking people into the membership, then a baptism, liturgy and the sermon. I knew that our young supporters in the Luleå diocese were having a Sunday of prayer for the work in South Africa and I felt truly as if I were being carried by their prayers. It turned out to be a wonderfully rich day.
>
> Ingeborg has also struggled hard with the language and will tomorrow have her first morning prayer in the hospital. Before now she, like myself, has helped in youth meetings and in our stuttering Zulu tongue we have even tried to contribute something to them. We are particularly happy that we have been in good health all the time.
>
> We have also had a local teacher giving us training in everyday conversation in Zulu and we have made use of all the opportunities we have had here to talk with the natives. In general, it has been good to see real heathen villages [*hednabygd*] here. In Dundee you have to go a long way to meet a proper heathen [*hederlig hedning*]!

In learning the Zulu, Ingeborg and Bengt gained their first real introduction to African life while staying with the evangelist's family in Makitika. Of this Bengt wrote his first book on and in Africa, *En Ljüshard*,[1] *Makitika i Zululand*, printed in Uppsala in 1939:

> In the Makitika home, as the family gathered round the fire, each family member was expected to tell a story: *'Kwasukela . . .'*, it happened once upon a time, and so the evening went on. I was amazed at the smallest detail they could remember as they related their story, each story having a special message.

To move ahead in time, his success in learning the Zulu language helped to create the reputation B Sr had throughout his life of being a gifted linguist. When I first met him in 1951 he intentionally reinforced that impression by welcoming Nordic students to a conference in everyone's own language, including Finnish. B Sr's Latin was also very fluent and, on the occasions when he was the doctoral promoter on behalf of the theological faculty in the university of Uppsala in 1965 and in 1971, in the old tradition of the theological faculty he gave his promotional speech in Latin. Sundkler's considerable linguistic skills later enabled him to work in Bukoba in two quickly acquired languages, Luhaya and Kiswahili, and to move comfortably in the academies and archives of Europe utilising the major European languages.

With his ecumenical attitude toward work, B Sr was eager to see how other denominations worked and to get personally acquainted with their workers. As B Sr recounts in his own story, after some correspondence, Ingeborg and Bengt were able to visit St Augustine's Anglo-Catholic Theological Centre in Zululand on Whitsun, in June 1938,[2] after attending an evangelists' conference in Oscarsberg Lutheran Theological Seminary supported by the Church of Sweden Mission. B Sr tells in his own story about his second visit to the college, when he followed the world president of the Mothers' Union around and heard as many translations as she gave speeches. He recounts this in a letter to Ingeborg, at the same time inviting her to come there. He was prepared to come to fetch her, if no other way was found. He describes the impressive celebration of High Mass he attended but, as during the first visit, could not take part in the communion. (8 June 1938)[3] Even then, in his later life he refers to this occasion as the beginning of their appreciation of an aesthetically satisfying worship, celebrated with deep piety and devotion, and thus also their appreciation of the Anglican church.

B Sr corresponded with the mission director, Gunnar Dahlquist, for whom he had great respect. After two months in the field he wrote a letter in which he first thanked the director profusely and then expressed his ideas about the mission situation as he saw it to be. The letter gives an idea why some colleagues might have thought that this young doctor had to be put to his place. B Sr wrote as follows (8 February 1938):

[As to the mission situation] one does naturally reflect on it, and it seems to be quite serious. Some of the missionaries here question what the policy of the Mission Board in actual fact is in relation to South Africa. It would of course clarify the situation considerably if something of that nature were to be laid down, whether our mission has the intention of gradually withdrawing from here and putting the emphasis on some other field, or what its aim is. But while it is desirable for the Mission Board to have such a policy, also out here the mission and missionaries should organise their work and follow a definite plan for it. What is difficult here, when one learns to know the work, is the uncertainty about what the aims are. It is being said that we aim at an independent Lutheran Church, well and good, but when and how does one deem this to have been accomplished? The decentralised budgeting trials that Stig Falck has done here in Dundee, following the model made by Sundgren, have been particularly effective. From that point of view, in developing the congregation's capacity to support themselves, it has been quite instructive to study the bookkeeping in the Dundee parish. It has been great fun to follow how interested they have been at the outstations, when Falck has let the evangelists write on the blackboard the incomes and expenses for 1937. They could then see clearly where all the money goes, and they no longer need suspect that the money goes into the missionaries' pockets. These demonstrations are of course the cornerstone for the self-supporting church.

But when will this church be independent? I could not think of anything more inspiring than to line up a 10- or 15-year plan for our Zulu mission for the foreseeable future. I seem to remember having heard of some such plan within the Berlin mission ... Such a plan should be worked out in a few years and then we should settle down to carrying it out. Even if it were to turn out to be an unattainable dream it would in any case accomplish great things. Then we would at least have something to hold onto and to fight for. It would be accessible to both the Black and White missionworkers and it would do a lot to clear the air.

The letter moves to the question of Lutheran co-operation in South Africa. The writer is particularly annoyed by the fact that co-operation is thought to come about by what he terms 'generals' and is not the concern of the rank and file. Only the higher leadership had knowledge of other missions. B Sr commends the thought presented by his addressee that there should be a co-ordinating secretary, and common refresher courses should be organised for all Black workers in all the missions. He also welcomed the idea of carrying out a study of all the Lutheran missionwork and its needs, with the intent of sharing in the work. B Sr also hoped that he would be given time to visit the other Lutheran missions and learn of their work.

The letter prompted a long answer from Gunnar Dahlquist dated 12 March in which he expressed his surprise at the thought that the Mission Board would even contemplate leaving this area and moving somewhere else. As Swedish mission assistance still continues today, in 2001, in Zululand, perhaps it was a bit hasty to suggest moving out then, if that was what the writer meant. B Sr could also have hinted that the Board seemed to be more interested in the work in Rhodesia as another remark (see p. 90) on the Benjamin position of Rhodesia would indicate. The Board did not devote itself sufficiently to the basic problems in South Africa in its planning of the work. The main point in the director's answer was that according to the Board each field needed to have its own policy which evolved locally, since all the fields required different treatment. Dahlquist discussed the plans for the different sectors of work such as education, health and the personnel and their material   needs.   The planning B Sr proposed was different. It was on a level of general mission policy within the specific South African situation with its emerging race problems and well-educated African clergy. It is obvious that on arrival in South Africa, B Sr's insight into the situation there, and certainly two months after his arrival, was of a different nature from any situation that the mission was prepared to get involved in at that time. This evidently increased the differences between the newly arrived couple and the 'mission'; their respective interpretations of the word 'mission' seemed to differ.

However, in reply to the mission director's letter, a much humbler man writes back:

> I beg to thank you warmly for your very valuable and friendly letter of 9 May 1938. It was really imprudent and unnecessary on my part to express my views about the work of which I know nothing, so soon after arriving in the field. It was valuable to read your points about the youth work, self-reliant activities and co-operation. I have some questions about the education... (9 May 1938)

We must remember that the newcomer had behind him very extensive studies of the mission situation and consequently had a broad perspective. His reaction against the role of the mission and missionary in that situation still influenced him a decade later after he had returned to Sweden from Africa. It was the deciding factor when B Sr was asked to become the first bishop of the Lutheran Church in Zululand. He refused on the grounds that he would have to become the head, not only of the church but also of the mission, to which he often later referred to as the 'narrow, narrow Lutheran mission'.[4] As we shall see, B Sr aimed at a change in leadership giving full authority to the Zulu church.

On the other hand, from a letter sent home from Dundee we learn that the Sundklers initiated Saturday services in Swedish, first in Dundee and then in Ceza for the spiritual refreshment of the Swedish workers, followed by a gathering for afternoon tea in one of the homes. According to the annual report (*Redogörelse* ... 1938) B Sr had to write two months after taking over the mission in Dundee, there were 15 missionaries. A newcomer would probably feel sorry for their co-workers in such an enclosed situation. An old-timer might have been more reluctant to organise regular meetings based on a language which, at that time, only the Whites would have understood. After moving to Ceza B Sr wrote about their relation to the missionaries in a positive tone:

> We have a good time with our Swedish co-workers here in Ceza. The doctors, Dr Söderström and Märta Adolfsson are both as good and charming as one could wish. Then we have Dr Söderström's wife and two or, at times, three sisters. It is very helpful to have good relations in that respect. (Letter to the Hellstens 15 June 1940)

Much later, the question of services organised for Swedes in racial South Africa was brought up by the former missionary, Gunnar Helander who, in a period of harsh criticism of missionwork in 1960, attacked the Zulu missionaries in the Swedish Church paper (*Svensk Kyrkotidning*, nos 9, 10 and 12, 1960). B Sr reacted to the articles in what he later called a doctrinaire manner. Helander published a criticism of the Swedish missionaries in South Africa on the grounds of their racist attitudes in comparison with other denominations. Having himself taken a critical attitude toward some fellow missionaries' attitude toward apartheid and the Africans' place in the church, B Sr now defended the missionaries. Sundkler did not think that the Swedish public was sufficiently informed to understand the intricacies of the issue at hand. He also found that the polemics came from a man who himself had chosen to accept Bantu education in the mission schools and had served a Swedish-speaking congregation separate from the African congregation in Johannesburg.[5]

What is to me more interesting, however, is the down-to-earth approach that Bengt Sundkler adopted from the outset in his own work, despite his theoretical departure point. This approach, which in today's language could be described as grassroots or participatory, he was to deepen and develop further as mutual learning experiences when he studied the independent churches through participation in their services and inviting their leaders to his own parish church for common Bible studies. He combined his work with his study.

In accordance with this approach, B Sr rightly commended the financial planning by the elders and evangelists practised in small congregational outposts in Dundee. It is worth noting that this kind of approach is only now being introduced in development assistance work. It is being promoted as an experiment in village education planning by the World Bank, in district development programmes with the Local Government Reform Agency, and practised in specific cases, as in southeastern Tanzania, where villagers are given the opportunity to work out the budget for their educational needs and for village development in general. In this, as in the question of self-government of the churches, despite their shortcomings Protestant missions have been 30–50 years ahead of the international development organisations which still today have hard time relinquishing the leadership of their projects and programmes, and which call the concept of partnership a new one. ('Paths for Change', *RIPS*, Helsinki 1998: Swantz, 1998.)

When B Sr took over responsibility for the work after the language study period, he had already experienced situations in which he had been left to manage manifold congregational events. His placement was a great disappointment for him from the start. The young doctor of theology had come to teach theology. He was not entrusted with this task, for fear of his overly liberal theology, which he saw as the main reason. He came from Uppsala and had been a student of liberal Linderholm, and even Fridrichsen, who as a Norwegian was known to the Norwegian–American head of the theological seminary. This disappointment was even greater because B Sr had accepted the mission call specifically to teach theology. It is questionable whether he would have responded as positively had the offer been for general missionwork.

> In the narrow, narrow Lutheran world of the Zulu mission I was not given the job of theological training for which I was initially called. The great Lutheran leaders tried to avoid me – just because I came from Uppsala; it did not matter that I was strongly against Linderholm. This was the official reason. Another reason was that I was known to have close relations with the Africans and was best avoided. The thought that I was a doctor of theology was not popular. I was young and inexperienced and had to be cut down to size. One had to be put to one's place. South Africa was not a popular field, it was the oldest field and supporters were tired of hearing about it. Southern Rhodesia represented the future, the Benjamin of the missionfields, attractive. (Recorded interview by MLS 30 November 1985)

Later B Sr came to see that 'God works in mysterious ways'. He realised that he would perhaps not have come upon the beloved independent churches had he not met their adherents on the paths and hills and along the rivers of Zululand, nor would he and Ingeborg have learned to know the people personally the way they did when walking and riding around the countryside.[6]

In a letter to the mission office dated 29 January 1941, when he was expecting the Board's approval for their move to Tanganyika, Sundkler's attitude had mellowed:

> The congregational work is not always so encouraging, it seems at times like rowing in tar. But it is fun, especially here in Ceza with a good lot of evangelists with whom it is very good to work. And the home visits here, on which my respected predecessor laid so much emphasis, and which are indeed meaningful, provide an opportunity to ride around on horseback and sit down and be together with people and to try to understand their thought world. Should the Board set itself against my application, there is nothing more to be said. *Il faut cultiver notre jardin à Ceza*, There is the garden in Ceza to be cultivated, and it also truly needs it.

Back at home B Sr never would have been able to speak and write about Africa with the same devotion he did, had he not ridden among and walked with the Zulus and met them in their homes. In comparing the two tasks he made the remark that he would not even have had the wisdom and experience to deal with the church situation in Tanzania, had he not been able to make the comparison between the church he met in Bukoba and the older Zulu church in the environment of what he first had called sects. Even then, the ten weeks he finally taught theology were his happiest time in Zululand, as we shall see. The bishop who returned in the mid 1960s from Africa had developed close contacts with parishioners and 'zionists' since his stay in Zululand and could with inner confidence give one talk after another on 'Africa in our hearts'. (Diary 1965)

Dundee and Ceza - Local politics

In his own story B Sr tells of his time spent in two different places, in Dundee in the northern Natal coal-mining area, and in Ceza, in northern Zululand, in what was called a reserve. The different histories of the Zulu church and the Bukoba church, to which the Sundklers later moved, help us to understand the resistant attitude which B Sr developed toward the Swedish mission in South Africa, not toward the Zulu or the Zulu church. While he could appreciate his missionary co-workers and praise them highly for the work they did, he also recognised some basic weaknesses from the African standpoint. There were structural weaknesses which he did not consider to be the fault of his co-workers, rather of a system which needed changing. The system had produced a tradition which molded the attitudes of the missionaries. Sitting in the front row in services they somehow managed to control the behaviour of the congregation so that the members did not feel at home, they did not dare to 'shake' or feel free otherwise to express their emotions.

From the beginning, B Sr represented the view that the time of mission leadership was over in South Africa and its gradual elimination should have had a definite plan. The Christians must have felt more at home in what the established churches called 'sects' since they joined them. The fleeing of Christians to the 'sects' should have alerted the missionaries to the realisation that the church needed African leadership. Instead it made them afraid of what would happen to the 'pure Lutheran doctrine'should the Africans take over. With his ecumenical orientation, B Sr also criticised the 'narrow world' of the mission because of its weak contacts with other churches and even other Lutheran missions,'I modify my point. It was not more narrow than similar missionary situations elsewhere. The narrowness that struck me different was between a few young Swedes who were supposed to lead and control excellent African pastors.'

A few historical notes on the situation in Zululand from B Sr's own texts are in order here, especially because his approach to work and scholarship of the church had a strong sociological and historical bent:

> The political developments are not without importance for the attitude of the Zulu population to the missionary approach at Ceza in about 1905–10. Much of the subsequent history of Ceza can be understood in terms of Zulu opposition to white land-grabbing. The first Swedish missionary met with fierce resistance over the land question. Embittered men told the catechists in 1905 that the missionary had it in mind to 'steal their country'.[7] The mission station which was established in 1910 eventually extended over no more than ten acres (for church, hospital, school and manse).
>
> Both the Ceza central station and its nine outposts lie far from the beaten track. Roads into the district were built both by the mission and, in the interests of the gold mines near Johannesburg, by the Native Recruiting Corporation. A clinic had been opened by the mission in 1910. The first elementary school was opened at the central station the same year and such schools-cum-catechetical centres were established with varying degrees of success at the outposts. In 1915 the first ordained Zulu pastor had been posted to Ceza, as an assistant to the missionary. In 1938, the first medical doctor was placed at Ceza. (Toward the end of the 1950s the hospital had two or three doctors and a capacity of 135 beds, with an African nurses' school.)[8]

. . .

> The fate of Zulu kingdom and the drastic reduction of the Zulu country influenced, then and much later, the reaction of the Zulu population both to the religion of the Whites and to the presence of the missionary and his Zulu assistants. This could be gauged by the role played by the dethroned and deceased King Dinuzulu in the realm of ideas and dreams at Ceza. Eselina Zulu Simelane told me she was allowed by her father to visit the church only because it became known that the Christians in their holy house prayed for Dinuzulu and his return to Zululand. Andelina Ny, another leading woman, *umsizikazi,* at Ceza, had a dream of heaven in 1925, in which she was shown Dinuzulu, the beloved king.[9] During the Second World War it was still rumoured that Dinuzulu was alive and that he might one day return to power.
>
> At Ceza, the relationship to the white man's political power was possibly more complicated than in most other parts of Zululand at the time. In the 1890s the local chief of the ruling Zulu house was deposed, and the government appointed a hefty policeman at the magistrate's office in Nongoma as the new chief. This man, Shibelika Ndebele, knew only too well that he was not a chief of the blood but a government-appointed official (*induna yasebukwini,* literally, an official in the government book). He had to tread carefully in order to manage the situation. His political acumen was tested over the mission issue. What was to be his attitude to the missionaries and their new ideas?
>
> There were at least two levels of resistance against the influence of the Gospel at Ceza. The first pioneers, European and Zulu, had to fight

the sullen and determined aversion for the White man's religion and [resistance to] the White man's laws, that foreign and fearful power which seemed to undermine the whole fabric of Zulu society. This reaction was all the more acute because the first encounter coincided with the political development when the Whites removed Dinuzulu, the Zulu chief, from Zululand.

At first the women were even more determined in their resistance than the men. 'Our mothers', the combined woman-power in polygynous households, withstood the new religious ideas cherished by young men and girls, their pressure being directed particularly against the young girls joining the new community which emerged in their midst. The technical term for this transition to the dangerous foreign realm of the church was not very flattering: *ukundinda* was the Zulu word used by 'the mothers'. When it was discovered that a young girl had managed to break through the social control of the kraal in order to visit a church service, 'the mothers' had a phrase for it: 'The prostitute has gone for her lovers.' Sometimes the girls did not return; they found refuge at the mission station, having taken the definite step over to the new community. There was at Ceza, as in other parts of Zululand, a technical term for this flight of individuals from Zulu society over to the community around the mission station. It was called *ukweqa*, to jump. The mothers in the kraal were determined to see to it that there should not be too much *ukweqa*.

Over the years, B Sr had a habit of asking the same questions when he met people who had turned from their old beliefs to Christianity: What attracted them to Christianity? Repeatedly he got the answer that a factor of very considerable importance was the promptings of dream life. Asked again why he or she left the Lutherans or Anglicans for the new group, called Zionist, a person would often reply: 'I was shown this in a dream', and details of the dream would follow. In 1958 B Sr had a chance to return to his old friends in Ceza where the decisive influence of dreams was again confirmed. He asked the oldest members of the congregation what caused the first Christians to cross over from traditional religion to the Lutheran congregation. There were two things which stood out: healing and dreams:

The answer was often illness. The White Christ could heal through those He sent. That is why they joined the Christian group. But very often the crossing over also happened in response to a direct revelation of God in a dream. They saw a figure of shining light whom they recognised as White Christ, about whom missionaries preached. Or else they saw themselves dressed in a white baptismal dress, this because they had been told by God in a dream to dress thus. Then there was no discussion any longer, they had to stop all resistance and cross the border between the heathen society and the Christian Church and through baptism join the White Christ's new clan.

Interestingly enough, the colours in these call-dreams were always the same. As Eselina Zulu Simelane, now a Lutheran *umsizikazi*, had heard catechist Stefano Mavundla threaten his hearers: 'You are all going to burn in hell.' ... 'Then I dreamed about white clothes and asked to be received in the baptismal class.' Simon Xaba told me he had seen in his dream a sudden white light. It took form and was Jesus standing on short green grass, and exhorting him to be converted.[10] To the first generation there was one obvious interpretation of these symbols: 'green' stood for the green pastures of heaven, and 'white' for baptismal garments and a holy life (*ubumhlope*).

To B Sr it was evidence of the inability of the Lutheran missionaries to listen to the parishioners, or even to dare to ask them pertinent questions, that they put their men and women in black, the colour of the uniforms of pastor, catechist and prayer woman (*umsizikazi*). The cultural influence from the northern churches seeped through with consequences to which the missionaries were blind:

> The Zionists appropriated to themselves the white and green colours and put on white garments with green sashes and cords. The luminary visions in Zulu dream life – which seemed to resolve the hidden moral problems of the heart and soul – found a new, generally accepted point of reference: the Zionist prophet group attired in white. When the new generations in Ceza had their luminary dreams, it was for them a God-given revelation that they should join, no longer the Lutheran group dressed in black, but the Zionists in white uniforms.

Here the significance of Ingeborg's sewing of white albs and chasubles takes on a symbolic meaning. However important the leadership or other service given by the missionaries may have been for the situation at Ceza, B Sr recognised that the real clue was to be found in the position of the Zulu catechists and their impact upon the community. For the purpose of collecting more of the local oral traditions he returned to Zululand and Ceza in 1958 and again in the late 1960s, weighing and sifting the information he had gathered through time-consuming interviews and subsequent checking. He became convinced that Ceza was not an isolated case, it was typical of the whole younger church situation in Africa. The material available for the first two generations of the Church growth mainly reflected the contribution of the European missionaries in church, school and clinic; there was little reliable material in the way of biographies of African catechists, evangelists, pastors and leading lay people, and every passing day made it increasingly difficult to collect and collate this material.

The little study from which these quotes have been taken gives the kind of detailed information of individuals which the writer calls for. He also decided to include a chapter on Ceza in his *Zulu Zion* since the development of spirituality and forms of Christian expression are as important in the more established churches as they are in the independent churches, and the relationship between the two needs to be studied equally. In his enormous work, *A History of the Church in Africa*, B Sr then penetrated the history of the people who actually spread the gospel: the African catechists, evangelists, pastors and lay people, treating all the different types of churches on an equal footing. Against this background, the significance of the work of the African workers and the slowness of the mission to promote them becomes evident:

> When I made an attempt to gather information about the characters and personalities of the catechists at work in the Ceza area, I discovered that these seem to stand out best, in the memories of their parishioners, when seen in critical situations and in times of crisis.

Yet while being critical of the hemmed-in situation of the Lutheran mission-related churches, B Sr recognised their strengths:

> We must not forget the others, solid Zulu Lutherans, faithful and loyal, Zulu pastors, catechists, churchwardens and prayer women (*abasizikazi*) toiling tirelessly, building up their local congregations in the midst of both indifference and opposition from the surrounding community, and competition from other missions and separatist groups. Together they constituted a splendid group of Christian witness.

As a missionary in Natal and Zululand

B Sr's job in Dundee involved directing two Zulu pastors and 20 catechists and their local congregations. B Sr made the point that the Methodist and Anglican Zulu congregations were served by Zulu pastors and evangelists alone and did not have any missionary leadership. The situation of the Swedes was naturally different from that of the English-speaking missions, in which the missionaries were leaders of the English-speaking White and mixed population, many of whom did not know the local languages. In their case also separating the English worship services from the local language worship could have strengthened racial divisions.

When the Second World War broke out, it changed the relations of missionaries with their homes and the home office. Letters took a long time to reach their destinations and the sense of isolation was strong, with little knowledge whether the letters arrived or were lost en route. A letter which had been written in Ceza on 17 June came through to the mission office via Ingeborg's father on 27 November the same year. The message read:

> We are altogether fine and live in peace here in the countryside. Since we have no radio nor has anyone else here we seldom get any echoes from the outside world. We usually get newspapers and mail twice a week. For three days and nights we have had steady rain and wonder how long it will continue. It makes us even more isolated and the food situation becomes acute since the weekly bus did not go this week and

we failed to get supplies. It must be hard for you to imagine what it is like to be here down below divorced from everything, without radio and other such means.

Another letter reached home in mid November in answer to one written by Ingeborg's father on 6 October 1940, and a letter written 15 November 1940 was received 29 January 1941. I quote from Bengt's letter from Ceza written to his sister Ingegärd and Stig Hellsten on 15 November 1940:

By God's grace father's letter slipped through to us this week ... 15.09.–15.10. Ingeborg and I had a holiday in Pretoria and Johannesburg. It was a lovely time, we enjoyed the spring weather, all the flowers burst open and it was joy to live. But I mostly made use of the time for studies on the topic for which I have got Olaus Petri Foundation's research money of 2,000 Skr, a study of the more or less Christian native sects. There are 600 of them and what amounts to the spiritual situation in today's South Africa presents itself as a drastic caricature of Protestant denominationalism. My study of this topic is, I believe, a very important one and it touches a central mission problem.

B Sr had started to establish contacts with these groups which he initially called 'sects' but soon changed to calling 'independent churches'. The letter goes on to give a picture of the everyday life and work of a missionary, and also reveals a touch of sarcasm in his view of doing all this rather than teaching theology:

Today I have just finished the meeting with the evangelists which we hold every third week. This time we again had a church discipline problem around the sixth commandment; in questions of sex in Africa the church can perhaps expect the least results. We could translate your book on the subject, but it hardly would help. The problem is of another kind here ... It is difficult to write about it in letters and not be misinterpreted. The problem is the same as there, but seen in a different light, the same notes but different notation, and so also other melody. But when we move on to interpreting the Sunday texts, I love to listen to the evangelists' viewpoints on the texts and learn to think and speak in a Zulu way.
    There are thousands of other things to take care of: We have three buildings going up and one has to take care of the building materials and draw up building contracts, and elementary school teachers in the surrounding areas have to get their chalk and slates. Yesterday one of our cows died, we have to ascertain what killed it, and to dispose of it in the proper fashion. The store keeper threatens to stop taking care of the mail, we might have to start selling stamps for the district which means that I can make use of my theological studies by selling stamps. I hope it is going to be an easily learned skill!
    After a couple of days I drive to Ekutuleni to fetch Ingeborg who has been there for a rest, but it rains now and one has a hard time even with chains [on the wheels] on these non-existent roads. However, usually we

have the privilege of sitting on horseback and we gallop to the kraals, preach to the Christians and heathen alike, and return home sweaty, where the most wonderful thing is to open the tap and let the so-called cold water (which unfortunately never is cold since the pipes run on the ground and get hot under the sun) run into the bath tub. Only for four years have we had such comforts, what it was before them here, even I cannot fully picture. (Letter to Hellstens 15 June 1940)

The letters strongly reflect the lack of contact with what was happening in Europe. This was probably also related to the fact that Sweden was not engaged in the war nor was it being attacked nor occupied as the other Nordic or Central European countries whose missionaries would probably have felt a stronger concern for what was happening back home. Meeting with other Swedes was one way of fending off the sense of isolation.

B Sr recognised early the important role that women had played in the Swedish Zulu mission. This aspect deserves attention here.

The essential role of women missionaries

For the Swedish Church Mission Society's centenary publication (1974:71–118) Bengt Sundkler chose to write a chapter on the women's role in missions. In it the first women missionaries to Zululand played an important role. I select here a few quotes from the lives of certain women whose work seems to have attracted B Sr's attention specifically. As the relating African church workers' role in establishing the churches and spreading the gospel has been neglected, so have women's histories. Since B Sr was one of the first to heed this neglect, I believe it is in order to give him credit by including the following abridged quotes from his texts, with a few comments.

> The first Swedish missionary to South Africa, Otto Witt, was sent out in 1876. It was a time of crisis and war in Zululand. The first mission station, Oscarsberg, named after the king of Sweden, was right on the firing line for Zulu warriors, and Witt took his Mats out of school and returned home to the north for a time.
> At this time of retreating and frightened pastors, the one seeming to be more problematic than the other, a whole row of women came into the Zulu mission, striking figures, each in her own way, with personal style, stability and authority. Ida Jonatansson, Hedvig Posse, Beda Wennerquist (etc.) ... They came into the Zulu environment, where women did not seem to have much worth if her market value could not be counted in the number of cattle heads for bridewealth. They had to show what they were worth and what they could do.

B Sr chooses to write at length about Hedvig Posse. His reasons reflect the specific views he held and things he appreciated. In Hedvig Posse he saw a Swedish woman missionary of international stature.

B Sr had found that at that time there had been British – especially Anglo-Catholic – women missionaries, and some American congregational women missionaries from Boston who were daughters of highly educated and well-to-do families. Having family wealth, they were able to serve without a salary and contributed generously in the field of activity which they represented. Later they bequeathed their property to their mission. To be wealthy has been rare within the mission service, but what B Sr definitely valued in these wealthy women was the education and culture which they brought with them into missionwork.

Within the Swedish Church Mission, Hedvig Posse was the great Swedish corresponding figure to this kind of personalised missionwork. B Sr appreciated greatly the fact that this woman had the insight, after her arrival in Cape Town, to take a two-month study tour to the leading mission centres in Cape province and Natal. Thus she was able to establish more comprehensive contacts than any other Zulu missionary, male or female, before or after her, when starting her life's work. Personal relationships were important to her and she established permanent, caring friendships with male and female mission leaders in South Africa.

Hedvig Posse devoted her energy to Zulu girls. She had a particular ability to write Zulu hymns with and for the girls. In 1895 she published a song book for congregations and schools, printed in Stockholm, containing 100 hymns. The following year a music edition was published. Another skill which B Sr appreciated was Hedvig Posse's affinity with the Zulu language. She had a feeling for the accents in the language and resisted the temptation to try to rhyme the verses. Hedvig Posse was also aware of other needs. The Boer War on the one hand, and accidents occurring in the coal mines which had been opened at this time in Dundee district on the other, brought about in her the recognition of the need for a hospital for the Africans. With her resources she made available a house for the purpose and in 1899 created a hospital in Dundee which has served the growing African population, as well as Indians, coloured and many Whites ever since.

B Sr paid tribute also to the women missionaries serving in Ceza hospital, especially the 'Annas' – Anna Sandberg and Anna Skarin – who, as nurses, did the foundation work for 20 years and Dr Märta Adolfsson and sister Anna Berntsson, who followed with 30 years of service, between them creating a modern hospital with first-class training for African nurses. Again, what touched B Sr was the fact that Dr Adolfsson, who arrived in South Africa in 1936, already had nine years of medical training in Sweden behind her and one year in Edinburgh. In South Africa she was required to have three further years training to get certification. B Sr remarks on this:

One can imagine that some medical colleagues could have left her or his work in South Africa with such a prospect. Not so Märta Adolfsson. In the end she had thirteen years of doctoral training to start her work as a doctor in Ceza. This in a place of which most doctors in the world would have said that an education was wasted there.[11]

In his article B Sr describes how attendance at missionary conferences and mission boards was clearly the privilege of men and male pastors. While decisions were being made by men, women met in special women's meetings. Toward the end of 1920s the Mission Board had decided that women had a right to vote at conferences. Later, when more African men were participating in and manning the conferences, some of them remarked that they were not used to women's input in meetings.

> The new generation of women missionaries had, in the new epoch, to experience a new kind of patriarchal attitude, this time from African pastors and laymen.
> Some women missionaries eventually married missionary colleagues or pastors back home in Sweden. Ida Johansson, a primary school teacher from Sundals-Ryr in Dalsland, a deeply gifted personality, gave her first ten years to a school in Ekutuleni and then in 1923 became an exceptionally esteemed teacher in the teacher training seminar in Umpumulo. Three years later she married missionary Axel Berglund . . . Tora Smith . . . four years later married a Rhodesian agriculturalist, Johannes Bergman. Her support group at home had difficulties in accepting the change in her civil status . . . precisely because of this change, both Ida Berglund and Tora Bergman were able to give an essential mission contribution. As mothers they raised a new mission generation: Axel-Ivar Berglund and Tora and Sten Bergman.

B Sr notes that the school authorities were unhappy to lose such an excellent person as Ida Johansson in their teacher training system, but at that time it was unthinkable that a wife should retain an independent job. Even later in some missions it has caused difficulties.[12]

This diversion into the role of women in the Zulu mission and church is not, strictly speaking, part of B Sr's own life story in Zululand, but it is a small tribute to him for his part in bringing out the women workers' role in missions. I justify the inclusion of this as a female writer of his life story in appreciation of his foresight. B Sr held in particularly high regard the depth of Ida Berglund's relationship with the Zulu people. After her marriage her interest in the Zulu language and culture continued and she first introduced the young Sundkler couple to the secrets of the Zulu way of thinking. Her son, Axel-Ivar, later followed in her footsteps in disputing with the beautiful thesis on Zulu symbolism. (Berglund, 1976)

Home for the African soul

People in Ceza gave B Sr the far-reaching goal of 'knowing the African soul and making the church the home of the African soul', as he expressed it in an interview (MLS 13 January 1978):[13]

> New living forms had to be created to break with the African slavery to European forms. Easter services with joy and victory after the cross procession of Good Friday. Pentecost festivals where women were free to shake. Life of a community. Ingeborg had a good imagination and taste for African art forms and together we tried to adapt some liturgical forms which the congregation seemed to make their own. It was a hard struggle in an atmosphere narrowly focused on missionaries, mission without strategy and planning.

B Sr tells of his crucial encounter with Eselina Simelane, who did not dare to shake inside the church (see p. 21), the same Eselina who told the pastor how she first got permission to attend the Christian service. In the festschrift to honour B Sr on his sixtieth birthday, *Daring in Order to Know*, Axel-Ivar Berglund tells of another meeting between a woman from the parish and the young missionary, who now had become an authority in the parishioners' minds. It brings to life what happened in the meeting between human beings in their mutual search for truth. I quote:

> A woman of mature age, dressed in green and white, wearing fashionable headgear and equipped with two staffs of the kind required by ritual and tradition, stood upright and with authority ... The woman went on to say that she belonged to the local Ceza parish, but that she had been healed from barrenness by a prophet. Her healing had taken place at a pool immediately below a waterfall close to Ceza. Immersion in the waters of that pool, combined with physically exhausting exorcism with prayer and subsequent integration into the community of the officiating prophet had been her salvation.
>
> Besides the life-giving experience of healing, she recollected with equal enthusiasm that her baptism in the pool had been witnessed by no less a person than her Ceza parish priest, Phondolwendlovu himself. Fearing his wrath and expecting excommunication, she had avoided him. But one Sunday afternoon she ran into him, unexpectedly and unavoidably, along a path running between Ceza and Silanda. As custom demands, he had greeted her first. She had responded shyly and with some hesitation because she was afraid. But in a beautiful way he had neither hurt her feelings nor avoided the crucial issue when he introduced as a subject of conversation the question of baptism. 'He amazed me,' she said. 'Truly he amazed me! He did not scold nor excommunicate. He asked me questions pertaining to what had taken place there at the waterfall in the pool!', she said, pointing in the direction of the waterfall. 'I found myself answering clearly and calmly. Then he spoke of baptism in the parish church, explaining what happens. Then I spoke

again! Then he. It was not before the sun began casting long shadows that we parted, taking leave of one another, both as worthy human beings. I tell you, he amazed me very much! ... We shared as if we were of the same family, speaking nicely to one another without any bad words ... To this very day I remember him and his speaking. I listened frequently to him even in the church building after that meeting. He spoke clearly and with patience. He also listened. White people in general do not listen. But he listened. That is why I remember him very much.' (1984:25–7)

It was at such encounters that B Sr began to understand what treasures he had on his doorstep.[14] It was more than a scientific laboratory; it was human fellowship which became an unorthodox source of scholarship. In meeting these people, he recalled the 'Grey Frocks' of Sweden. Here they were, now 'White Frocks'. This was when he realised that 'God writes straight in crooked lines'. Of these meetings he recounted (Interview 31 October 1985):[15]

I got to know the Independent Churches instead of teaching theology in the college. From time to time I arranged meetings where Independent Church leaders met with pastors, evangelists and ordinary lay members of the Mission Churches. We had very stimulating talks, sometimes friendly, sometimes arguing rather heatedly, in the end agreeing to differ on fundamental theological and religious questions, such as the interpretation of the Bible, the role of baptism and purification rites, the Black Christ and scores of other problems. I attended preaching and purification services and other meetings of the Independent Churches, whenever my own regular mission work allowed me to do so.

There came a bad drought which threatened the planting. In the end the chiefs approached us: 'We must have a common prayer on the mountain,' was the request. My horse had disappeared, I went there walking up the mountain. Lutherans, Zionists and pagans were praying there. When we sang a hymn, rain started splashing on our hymnbooks. When I got back to the hospital, it was already raining hard. Mr Madide, the pastor's eldest son, made the remark, '*Ubu ye yooyo.*' (You returned with it.)

Adaptation to local custom was needed. Weddings were performed at the mission, we walked back with the party to the kraal in procession, round the cattle kraal and partook in celebrations. We were freer to do this in Ceza than in Dundee where there was more concentration of Swedish missionaries. Ingeborg felt she could not manage inviting them and feeding them. She could cry for half an hour after they had gone, because she felt she had not done it right.

The aim was to create the church as a home and place of fellowship. It was a search for human contact for both Ingeborg and myself. The African Christian Church provided this more than anything else. This is what the Church is for. We were two forlorn northerners, there especially for uprooted Africans, free to face contacts and found them important. Yes, Ceza was a happy experience.

Later experience taught B Sr that this concern for African liturgical forms and leadership, and these visions against Europeanised conventions for which the European missionary struggled, had eventually to be checked by true African initiative.

A new 'beyond'

Life held further experiences of 'beyond' in store, further challenges to respond to. In Tanganyika, which had been part of the former German East Africa, the German Lutheran missionaries were interned by the British colonial government after the outbreak of the Second World War. In December of 1940 the superintendent, A. R. Kempe, received the first communication from the Augustana mission director in Tanganyika,[16] George N. A. Anderson who, at the instigation of the colonial government, was inquiring whether it would be possible for any Swedish or Norwegian missionaries in South Africa to come and oversee some of the missions which had been left behind after the internment of the German Lutheran missionaries. B Sr recounts that he felt immediately that this was a call which he could not put aside without knowing more about it. He received the necessary information from Kempe and contacted Anderson directly, with the result that the Augustana mission's executive committee decided in its meeting on 27 December 1940 to extend the following call:

> That Reverend Bengt G. M. Sundkler ... be called on behalf of the Lutheran World Convention to supervise the Berlin Mission work in Tanganyika Territory for a period of two years at a salary of $1,400 a year, travelling expenses to and from the field to be paid.

B Sr wrote about his reasons for considering this call:

> The Lutheran World Convention (forerunner to the Lutheran World Federation) extended invitations to serve in Tanganyika to neutral Swedish missionaries at various points in Africa, and Ingeborg and I volunteered. I felt deeply and strongly the necessity in this difficult situation to be able to help so that the work of the Berlin mission would not go to pieces. I also felt that in that situation one's strength perhaps would be better used than in the place where no missionary would be needed of necessity – it turned out to be a great blessing to us. (Extract from an earlier version of B Sr's autobiography)

B Sr corresponded with Reverend Nordfelt from the *Evangeliska Fosterlandsstiftelsen* (*EFS*, Swedish Evangelical Mission Society), who was already in Tanganyika, in order to get more information. It seemed to him that Nordfelt should have taken over the Berlin missionfields in the southern part of the country and the personnel from South Africa would be needed for the Bethel missionfields in the

north. (Letter to Nordfeldt 29 January 1941) When they finally
arrived in Tanganyika, this was what actually happened.

In the earlier version of his life story, B Sr wrote the following on
the reaction of other missionaries to the Zulu:

> When I informed my fellow missionaries that I had been called to
> proceed to Tanganyika (Tanzania) to help out in a situation where all the
> German missionaries had been interned, I suggested that I knew of an
> ideal replacement for me, a pastor who had the advantage of speaking
> the language, Zulu, as his mother tongue, not laboriously memorised as
> was the case for the outgoing missionary. The man was Reverend
> Thomas Luthuli. The reaction of the missionary staff was at first
> discouraging: Was the African ready for such an appointment? Suffice
> it to say that the change at Ceza in 1942 proved at once to be highly
> invigorating and stimulating, both for the local Zulu congregation and
> for the Zulu church as a whole. Time was intertwined with expectations.
> The idea of 'not yet' implied lack of expectation. This lack of expecta-
> tion has been the most serious deficiency in the Western approach to
> Africa in this century, as well as in the White missions and their
> approach to the African church.

In his missiological writings, B Sr often returned to these two
thoughts: 'expectation' and 'not yet'. Lack of expectation had too
often led to the attitude of 'not yet' in the churches' process of taking
on their own leadership. B Sr mused also on an unexpected reaction
on the part of the new leader of the Ceza parish after he had handed
over the church books to Reverend Luthuli:

> I handed over the 'symbols of power', the church books with all the
> names of the Christians and statistics, in six columns, including the
> attendance at Holy Communion. I was found out. The book had space
> for six times, I had ticked out ten or even fourteen times. No, the book
> said six times and we had to do what the book says, were the instruc-
> tions. I had misunderstood the matter! (Interview 31 October 1985)

The time had not yet come for the Sundklers to leave South Africa.
While waiting for the final arrangements about going to Tanganyika,
the young doctor of theology was finally called to do what he originally had come for in Africa: to teach at the Rorkes Drift Theological
Seminary, 30 miles from Dundee. Its Swedish name was Oscarsberg,
after Oscar who was king of Sweden when the first mission station
was started in 1878 by Swedish Lutherans in South Africa.

Bengt spent ten weeks in the seminary from April until June 1941
(Interview 30 November 1985):

> I had my ten happy weeks in South Africa because of the very close
> contact that Ingeborg and I established with young couples. There were
> two Western teachers, Farup, the American head of the Seminary, the
> Swede, and a Zulu pastor in Homiletics (Practical Theology), to teach

25 students. They were there for four years for theological training, with a good library which represented a good collection of English Lutheran theological literature from the USA. Because I was a suspect person I was given subjects to teach which would not mislead the students, i.e. Old Testament, Church History and Practical Theology. It suited me well.

B Sr greatly enjoyed teaching his allocated subjects and saw in them a fine opportunity to learn more of the mind and life of his students and to enrich his already good knowledge of Zulu language. It became his most beloved Bantu language, even after learning Swahili and Luhaya in Tanzania:

New Testament and Dogmatics were taught by the American Lutheran, Farup, to ensure that the students got real Lutheran theology. In spite of the odds against me, we became good friends. We had tea and cookies at 11 a.m. Farup told the funniest stories and Ingeborg had a cause to remark that he had the biggest laugh in the southern hemisphere.

In my teaching and sermons in Oscarsberg I had this concern: 'How is the Church going to become a home?' In describing what the church is I used an illustration of the Zulu hut, which had three wooden pillars, all symbolic for the Zulu. I still have that sermon.[17]

The scholar Sundkler found his best assistants among these students for his further study when he returned to South Africa after his stay in Bukoba, and repeatedly thereafter, while he continued his scholarship on the Independent Churches.

Notes

1. 'A hearth of light' was the name given to the book by the publisher which B Sr was not happy with, *Makitika in Zululand* would have sufficed.
2. Invitation by Ms Hoddinot in a letter 28 April 1938.
3. Bengt urged Ingeborg to come by telling her that Ms Hoddinot had been impressed by her and wanted her to come. It is interesting to note that after the first visit there was no enthusiastic reaction to St Augustine. On his second visit B Sr was highly impressed by the High-Church mass and described it in glowing colours.
4. The Lutheran denominationalism and isolation from other churches were probably the main reasons why Sundkler used the term 'narrow' in relation to the Lutheran Mission. Another reason was the slowness to transfer the leadership to the Africans. There was still a parallel missionary conference with considerable influence not, as later in Bukoba, an African diocese with African leaders who insisted on calling the bishop of their own choice and missionaries who served under the church leadership.
5. B Sr brought up this issue in the context of being doctrinaire. Engaging in this debate had affected him in a way which later prevented him from engaging in polemic writings, even when he would feel inner urge to do so.
6. From a health point of view, travelling on horseback as much as eleven hours a day around the countryside was not good. B Sr contracted a bad case of amoebic dysentry which brought on kidney trouble. He was treated with injections once a day. The medication apparently affected him more than the illness and resulted

in kidney complications in later life.
7. Sandström, *Bland svarta kristna* 1935:24.
8. This and the following paragraphs are quotes from Sundkler, 'Response and Resistance to the Gospel in a Zulu Congregation', in *Basileia, Tribute to Walter Freytag*. eds. Jan Hermelink and Hans Jochen Margull. 1959, Evang. Missionverlag Gmb H. Stuttgart. See also for the same material in *Zulu Zion* 1976:244-74.
9. *Umsizikazi*. Lutheran prayerwoman, plur. *abasizikazi*. The name appears in the form Eselina in Zulu Zion.
10. J. Sandström, *Från den första kärlekens tid*. 1944:48.
11. The two women worked closely together and wrote a book about their work: Märta Adolfson and Anna Berntsson, *Ceza, a Roundabout Way to the Goal. Three Decades of Medical Missionary Work in South Africa*, Käppan 1984.
12. I personally found the policy in the American Lutheran mission very different from the Finnish one which in my time called both husband and wife as equal and individually paid missionaries.
13. By using what could be understood to be essentialised concepts, 'African soul' and 'African mind', B Sr wanted to emphasise the general differences in the style of music, art and thought between Africa and other continents. From all his writings it is clear that the local differences in culture and custom also formed one of his basic emphases within the church.
14. Axel-Ivar Berglund has also described these encounters beautifully in his article in the festschrift *The Church Crossing Borders*, 1969.
15. In recording, a part has been erased accidentally, of which I make a note in the transcription.
16. The Augustana Lutheran Church was a church established by Swedish immigrants in the USA.
17. It is likely that B Sr used the pillars to symbolise the three themes which he later was to use in his episcopal letters: 1. The Church as a home; 2. Inheritance of the church (continuity); 3. Renewal in the church (change).

5

TO ANOTHER AFRICA

'Beyond' – *to another world*

The next 'beyond' for Ingeborg and Bengt took them from South
Africa to the equator, where Bukoba lay 1° S, on the western shores
of Lake Victoria, the largest lake in Africa. They enjoyed the flight
as no other flight since. 'It was a wonderful way of travelling, every
minute of it unforgettably beautiful.' (Letter to SKM 6 September
1942). Bengt recalled this flight in his speech at Ingeborg's funeral in
1969 (with additions from a letter to MLS 16 July 1982):

> In June 1942 we left Durban by a wartime seaplane which flew low over
> the sea and the land strip of pure sand over the East African coast – the
> loveliest kind of air-borne communication ever invented, I think:
> Durban–Lorrenzo   Marques–Beira–Inhambane–Lindi–Dar es Salaam.
> We enjoyed the play of colours, I remember the string of pearls so very
> clearly. The Indian Ocean, brown nearest the coast, then emerald-green,
> and then deeper and deeper blue, under the eternal sun. The plane came
> down to refuel in the blue bay of Lindi, surrounded by green hills and
> the pure white sand beaches of southern Tanganyika. We flew over the
> innumerable rivulets which formed the vast delta of the Rufiji river
> before landing in the Harbour of Peace, emerging into the hot, bright
> sun. It was something the quick, high-flying jets can no longer offer
> passengers.

The couple was met by the superintendent of the Lutheran orphaned
missions, Elmer Danielsson who, in October 1941, had been elected
president of the Augustana Mission from the United States in
Tanganyika, and in that capacity had become the chairman of the
general committee on Former German Missions (FGM) (Smedjebacka,
1973:91). B Sr had already corresponded with him and his predecessor,
George Andersson, about the situation of the churches in Tanganyika in
order to acquaint himself with the work that faced them.

To receive the Sundklers there were also their fellow Swedish
missionaries Elizabeth and Gustav Bernander, who had responded to

a 'Macedonian call', as Gustav Bernander wrote about it. They had made a week's journey in a truck from Southern Rhodesia to arrive on the border of southwestern Tanganyika in July 1941. They then first toured the southern Berlin missionfield with Pastor Martin Nordfeldt from Swedish Evangelical mission (*EFS*), who had earlier experience in Ethiopia. He had been appointed by the caretaker Augustana mission to oversee the vast Berlin mission fields in the interior, work he shared with his energetic and capable wife. (Bernander, 1968) At that point the Bernanders were in Islamised Maneromango, 80 kilometres from Dar es Salaam, and Bengt and Ingeborg Sundkler were to spend their first intensive language study period with them.

For the first few nights the Sundklers stayed in the mission house next to the German-style Lutheran Church, a landmark of Dar es Salaam with its red roof clock tower, taken over temporarily by the Anglicans after the Germans were interned. They were then driven over the Pugu and Kisarawe hills to Maneromango, to begin their struggle with Swahili, which was later to become the official language of Tanzania.

Elizabeth Bernander was the best Swahili teacher the Sundklers could have wished for. B Sr always referred to Elizabeth Bernander in most complimentary terms, such a credit was she to the CSM. With her they got off to a good start in learning their second Bantu language. For work in Bukoba in the northwestern corner of the country there was still one new language to learn, Luhaya.[1] For Swahili they had six weeks in Maneromango. They found it a sleepy place where an African pastor named Josiah was holding the fort. A man-eating lion was roaming around, which prevented walks being taken for the purpose of making contact with people.[2] The work of the Berlin missionaries had already been interrupted for the second time, the first time during the First World War. The lack of continuity badly affected the Lutheran church work on the coast where Islam was making its way inland.

After five years the Finnish missionaries, Matti and Inkeri Peltola, were to come with their two children to continue the church work in Maneromango alongside the faithful Zaramo pastor Josiah. Inkeri Peltola wrote a Finnish book *Uzaramo*. B Sr used it later on one of the many times when he attempted to learn the language of the Finns whom he much admired.[3] Today the eastern and coastal diocese of the ELCT has a Bible School in Maneromango.

To get to Bukoba the Sundklers had to take a train to Mwanza and then catch a ship. On the way they visited the Singida area for a week, an area which was referred to as the Augustana missionfield in central Tanganyika. They descended from the train in Manyoni to be met by Dr Stanley Moris with a friendly, 'Isn't your name Bengt?' He took them to his and his wife Edith's home in Kiomboi. To the Sundkler couple a new experience was the big American double bed offered to them, a little detail Bengt has included in his narration of their new adventure into the interior. (Interview 26 December 1983)

They met several missionaries in their places of work (Eugene Johnsson in Ruruma, brothers Dean and Leslie Petersson, the latter working with agricultural projects) but the most significant contact was with Elmer Danielson who was doing pioneering work in Wembere. Of the experience in Singida, B Sr reported to his own mission office in the following manner (6 September 1942):

> I can never forget the strong impression which the missionwork of the Swedish daughter church Augustana [from the USA] made on me – even the buildings were the finest I have seen anywhere in Africa, but then they had also cost dollars. Above all it was wonderful to learn to know our relatives in person, especially the president, Reverend Danielson.

When they met Danielson he had just heard that his wife and six children – the youngest under two years – had been saved from the ocean after the Zamzam ship, on which they had been travelling to come to Tanganyika, had been torpedoed by a German warship.[4] For many weeks he had been made to understand that they had drowned with the ship when it sunk. (Interview 31 October 1985)

While waiting for the lakesteamer in Mwanza, the Sundklers paid a visit to an Africa Inland mission missionary, Mr Seawalker. This visit intensified B Sr's expectations toward the new phase in their life as he recalled this event and the sentiment with which they approached the shores of Bukoba (Interview 31 October 1985):

> We then went by slow train from Singida up to Mwanza and from Mwanza by ship taking us across Lake Victoria to Bukoba which we saw coming out of the water. As I approached that place I said to myself, 'I have had four years in South Africa. It has been an interesting time from many points of view. Not much has come out of it. We hope that here it will be much more fruitful and interesting. Above all, I shall regard every meeting with anybody here as of enormous importance for me and I shall regard everything that these people say as terribly interesting to me, to be written down in a larger volume in the evenings. I shall regard it as tremendously important to me to get to know them.'
>
> In fact, we were challenged on our way from Singida to Bukoba. We had stayed overnight at the African Inland mission with an old saint called Seawalker. He was an evangelical kind of a saint and a good, good man, but with a narrowness which was characteristic of that kind of conviction of Christianity. So he told me that he had two months earlier been through the so-called Bukoba field and seen what was left of Christian work which had been started by the Germans. He said there was nothing left. 'There is no life, they are all living in sin. It is a very sad place. I congratulate you, you will have a task ahead of you.' So I had that then in mind. I felt I was to know better than this man and that God had prepared for us something more joyful than this kind of a forecast that this old man gave of Bukoba.

We crossed the lake by a steamer on 14 July 1942.[5] The boat came in and waiting for us there was an African. He stood there and was looking for a young missionary couple. He identified these two people as the ones he was looking for. In fact, he was our very great future friend, Emil Kilimali from Usambaras, one of the three families that the Bethel mission had sent from the solid field of Usambara to the very dangerous field in Bukoba to keep them in good order up there. He was the driver of the mission. He had at his disposal a one-and-a-half ton lorry which could be used in spite of the fact that there was a war on. He was to take us all over Bukoba. I was going to regard what he and others said as enormously important, and I have been thinking of this ever since.

Mission politics

Bukoba, west of Lake Victoria, was to be Bengt and Ingeborg Sundkler's home for three years. B Sr wrote his letter home to the CSM from Ndolage, where they first settled to live, describing the new land and waters, but also of their hunger for news:

> We live now in Ndolage, 1,650 metres above sea level and 450 above Lake Victoria. In this hot land at the equator it is a wonderful gift to live quite close to the enormous inland sea, which Lake Victoria is. The whole Haya land is one gigantic banana grove ... We hunger for news from Sweden as an antelope thirsts for water, or a lion hungers for juicy prey.

At the outbreak of the Second World War in 1939 only the most suspect German Lutheran missionaries were interned, but in October 1940 they were all interned in camps; with only very few exceptions, most were held for the whole war in Oldeani, Tanganyika or in South Rhodesia, Zimbabwe.[6] Only one or two individual Germans returned in the 1950s to work together with Lutheran missionaries from other countries. When the other German missionaries working in Bukoba had been interned, Pastor Wilhelm Hosbach and his wife Martha Hosbach were left behind. Besides the Hosbachs only two German nurses were permitted to remain in Bukoba, one because of her poor health, the other to take care of the ailing widow of a German settler.[7]

Pastor Hosbach was not allowed to leave Bukoba town, but could visit the prison and take evening services in the Anglican church. Other contacts with the church had to take place in his own home, just outside town, to which the Christians had free access. (Bernander 1968:42)

In his own story B Sr gives great credit to the old German couple. B Sr held the German missionary much senior to him in high regard. In fact, in speaking about Pastor Hosbach B Sr referred to Nathan Söderblom's words when he spoke about evangelical saints: 'They are people whose life and work show that God lives. That definition came to one's mind when looking at Wilhelm Hosbach.'

Wilhelm Hosbach was referred to by people in Bukoba as Baba, by Germans Vater, father, and Martha Hosbach was Bibi Ulaya, Lady Europe. Bengt's interest in cultural activities drew his attention and admiration to Mrs Hosbach who, in the difficult, and in many ways deprived, situation in which she was living, established contacts with German Jewish refugee families from Hamburg and Vienna. They had made their way to Tanganyika via Cyprus and Persia (Iran) and Mombasa, and had been placed for the time being in Bukoba. B Sr was attracted to the idea that the difficult circumstances and potentially constraining relations were overcome with classical music which both groups appreciated. The musical Bibi Ulaya arranged musical soirées, playing Schubert, Schumann, Bach and Handel on her organ. In this act Bibi Ulaya demonstrated her total independence from the Nazi activities and attitudes in Germany at that time.

With the authority of superintendent in charge of 'enemy property' B Sr arranged it so that four or five refugee families occupied empty missionary houses in Bukoba town, others had houses in Ndolage and Kashasha. Those in Ndolage were given a field to cultivate, irrigated from a river. The refugees were later moved to Mwanza since the buildings were needed for school purposes and for African couples.

Potentially, there could have developed a real conflict between the young Swede and the old German pastor had the newcomer not had a genuine respect for people and been a skilled negotiator, and had the old man been more stubborn. I can appreciate the potential conflicts between the former 'owners' of the field and the newcomers since I also came to the former German fields while they were still being administered by the American Augustana mission, albeit ten years after the Sundklers' arrival. In his own account, B Sr was careful not go give any offence or demonstrate bias. He writes about his encounter with Dr Richard Reusch, who was at that time in charge of Lutheran missions in what was referred to as the northern area around Kilimanjaro and Pare. I also met him there, after my arrival in Tanganyika, at my first missionary conference which was held in his home in Nkoaranga, near Arusha, in 1952.

B Sr became the superintendent of the Bukoba church and in that capacity was *de facto* the leader of the church and school activities in the area, and was responsible for seeing that the property came to no harm. The superintendents reported to the Augustana Board of Foreign Missions which the Lutheran World Convention (later the Lutheran World Federation, LWF) via Lutheran World Action had appointed to be its agent for relief work in Tanganyika. While this was the case in principle, an agreement had been made between Pastor Hosbach and the representatives of the Former German Missions that the superintendent should do the work according to the principles and policies laid down by the German Bethel mission, and do it in accor-

dance with the wishes and advice of Pastor Hosbach, and not introduce anything new without his consent. This agreement had been
made with Pastor Hosbach by Dr Reusch and Reverend Danielson,
who had visited the field before B Sr arrived. Bernander, in his book
on the wartime assistance to the Lutheran churches, remarks that it
was to the credit of both Dr Bengt Sundkler and Pastor Hosbach that
this agreement document was never appealed to. (Bernander,
1968:47–8)

When B Sr arrived in Bukoba, he did not know that Reusch, 'a
great intriguer', had been to Bukoba before his arrival to prepare
Hosbach for his coming. Reusch had told Hosbach to report to him if
any problems arose with this Swede. In fact, Reusch was claiming
authority he did not *de facto* have. As a superintendent in Bukoba,
B Sr could make his own decisions and policy with the leading pastor,
Jonathan Karoma, and report the decisions directly to the Lutheran co-
ordinating organ. No reference was made to Dr Reusch in practice,
and the co-operation between the Swedish missionary and the veteran
representative of Bethel Mission caused no difficulties.

Dr Richard Reusch was a kind of legend, an ethnic German
Cossack from southern Russia, educated in Tarto, Estonia, and after
marriage to an American missionary nurse, a US citizen. He was a
small man who boasted an almost superhuman physical strength and
proved it through hard work and frequent climbs to the top of the
Mount Kilimanjaro. In the early 1950s he specialised in the Maasai
mission. He had recruited new young missionaries who had been
enthused by Reusch's eloquent challenges for the work among the
Maasai while he had been touring the Lutheran colleges in the USA.

German missionaries' belongings and books, which were considered enemy property, had been gathered into the attics of the mission
buildings. In Kigarama Teacher Training College, schoolboys had
taken the law into their own hands and made use of the property.
There was some tension between the British authorities and the
national pastors who had served under the Germans; they were
quickly accused by the British of having been Nazi supporters. Josiah
Kibira, the bishop of Bukoba *in spe*, who was a student in Kigarama
at the time, had told B Sr of a British teacher, who had thrown a
German flag against one of the Shambaa pastors, Pastor Hermas,
saying, '*Tazama kazi yako*' (See your work). The German flag in
itself did not indicate Nazism. Von Bodelschwing, the head of the
Bethel mission and the institutions for the mentally ill and handi-
capped, had endangered his life – 'over my dead body' – in resisting
Hitler's order to kill the mentally ill and disabled inmates in Bielefield
institutions.

In reading Bengt's letters to his wife at this time from his travels in
different parts of Tanganyika, often small hurriedly written airletters,
one is amazed how, even during the Second World War which forced
the colonial government to reduce its resources to a minimum, the

postal system still operated, bringing letters from one corner of the country to another, defying the poor roads and deficient means of transportation. B Sr sent his letters from his travels to other Lutheran areas where the meetings of the co-ordinating committees were held. Kilimanjaro and Meru mission stations looked to him like a paradise on the green mountain slopes. Bukoba retained, however, its special beauty and attraction for the Sundklers.

Mission of the African Church

In Bukoba B Sr began to think in terms of the mission of the African church. Here there was an African Church in the making. He took it upon himself to visit all the areas where the church had started work and to get acquainted with all the church workers. He also visited people's homes and began soon to feel that he was a co-worker with the African pastors, evangelists and lay people. It was important for the congregations to feel that they were not alone.

Not only in preaching but also in leadership, the charismatic Jonathan Karoma and his young 25-year-old assistant William Bwanuma, showed remarkable foresight. They had started a youth movement called Buhaya's Hope, in Luhaya *Omushubilo*, led by Bwanuma. Both male and female youth met together and took part in various Christian youth activities. B Sr gave the movement his full support. In *Ung Kyrka i Tanganjika* B Sr tells of the vision that these African male leaders had for the work among the youth, and the resistance which the movement met at a higher level. The church office received a letter from the local Sultan's court dated 12 September 1942. Excerpts from the letter give us the background to understand the significance of Karoma's letter to the Sultan.[8] Sections of both letters deserve to be quoted here. First the letter from the Sultan's office:

> On 31 August 1942 stories came to my notice [the secretary] concerning Buhaya's Hope which disturb both people and the Sultan. A Haya proverb states, 'Woman is a sheep.' She is kept in kitchen and eats there. Further, from the times past organisations have been only for men, there are no organisations both for men and women. The only right organisation for women is a school.
> But now we see that boys and girls meet together in Buhaya's Hope. This is a matter which gives many and also the Sultan fear. We hear that Omushubilo's aim is to help one another and others; this is not bad. But what is bad is to hear that boys and girls meet from 2 p.m. till 6 p.m. and if it is a festival day at the mission station or some festival of the organisation, girls come from their villages and play around until late at night in villages which are not theirs, since they cannot reach their villages before it gets dark. A proverb says: 'Evil has to be uprooted before it sets in. Truly, if boys and girls meet in this way nothing good

can come out of it.'

The Sultan has the power to prevent bad things that go on in the land. But since this organisation was started by the leaders of the mission, we beg you to ban this organisation or to change it to be for boys only.

Jonathan Karoma answered this letter, addressing it to the king and his secretary in Rwamishenye, Bukoba (abridged here):

Gentlemen, we thank you much for your letter – concerning stopping the Omushubilo work among the girls.

1. You quote our proverb: Woman is a sheep – True, earlier women were sheep. But now light has risen for them, so that they have also become same kind of people as we men. Look at their work:
   a. To give birth to children, and to assist at the birth. Sheepish?
   b. To bring up children. Sheepish?
   c. To look after the sick. Sheepish?
   d. To teach children. Sheepish?
   e. To hoe and to cook. Sheepish?

Gentlemen, if our women were to remain in a state of sheep who would do all this work then?

2. Buhaya's Hope was started by us Christians in the Kanyangereko congregation and no missionaries were there from the beginning. The organisation was started in 1937 in January and in these five years we have not found any foolish symptoms. If there are some individuals who have done something foolish they have done it on their own, not on account of this organisation. The organisations aims are:
   a. To teach God's word. b. Mutual help. c. Hoe and do handwork.
   d. Teaching of health and good kinds of plays, not bad. e. Good
   behaviour. f. Teaching the youth, boys and girls.

3. You Gentlemen ask us to put girls away from this organisation. But do the aims concern only men? I know that a builder in building a house of stones, puts up walls on two sides. If he builds only on one side the house would no doubt come crumbling down. We Christians think it is sad to be forced to teach only men and leave women to their fate as 'sheep'. . . .

6. Buhaya's Hope cannot be dissolved, and we cannot hinder girls and women from attending, as the Sultan wants. Even in schools boys and girls come together. In church men and women come together for teaching. We cannot hinder men and women from coming together.

7. In my view, 'Hope' cannot be dissolved, since it has got leaders who have witnessed that it is a good organisation. Our missionaries have told us that in their countries there are such organisations in order to help youth of both genders. . . .

Your true servant,
Reverend Jonathan Karoma

Mr Culwick, the district commissioner,[9] and Mr and Mrs Sundkler are mentioned as people who had witnessed that this organisation was a good thing and had become members of it. Their membership was used to support the legitimacy of the organisation. The main significance of it was, however, in the fact that it was not started at the instigation of the missionaries, but based on the concept of equality which was an integral part of Christianity.

B Sr had the highest praise for Jonathan Karoma's leadership and charisma of preaching to which he listened as they visited the congregations.

He was a charismatic personality as a preacher, a creative, homiletical preacher. In contacts with men and women intense, full of fun, laughter, humour, depth and understanding, centred on four gospels in which the fight against evil spirits was the same as in Bukoba. (Interview 8 August 1985)

In all his work, B Sr gave education very special attention. In his own story he tells of the struggle they had in order to retain the Kigarama Teacher Training College within the Bukoba Church. Since the mission schools were also under the authority of the colonial government, which defined the teaching programme and regulated the staff, ousting a headmistress who had been appointed by the government was no inconsequential matter. When the headmistress, Miss Boesch, used her powers to threaten to close the school, the government authorities did question the right of the mission to reassume leadership of the school, especially since the headmistress was a friend of the government school inspector. B Sr was later accused of interfering in school affairs without prior announcement of his intentions, but ultimately the matter was settled. Miss Boesch fled to Bukoba and eventually went to stay with her friend Miss Hancock in central Tanganyika. Miss Hancock, later to become a noted figure in Tanzanian politics, had visited the struggling school as a school inspector and sympathised with the work that the headmistress had done to keep the school going. The school had to produce its own food and was short of many necessities.[10]

B Sr announced a competition for pastors and teachers in writing an autobiography on the theme 'Jesus Christ in my Life'. The autobiographies provided very valuable material for B Sr's knowledge of the spiritual situation in the Church.

I quote what B Sr wrote on these autobiographies in *Bara Bukoba* (96-97):

When I study the brief autobiographical sketches written by young teachers in the early 1940s, I am struck by certain expressions of personal dissatisfaction with their spiritual condition. When these youngsters had first started school and had been baptised, they had mostly done so in order to achieve *maendeleo* [progress], to free themselves from the narrow confines of village society, to get ahead in life and share in the blessings of civilisation. But their studies of the Bible aroused new stirrings in them.

To be 'civilised' had ... been the dream of young Matia Lutosha – Lutosha's idea led him to baptism and elementary school and an early appointment [as a teacher] to a mission school. But the young man was distracted by many things, and his family's relative wealth offered spending possibilities which did not always tally with the rigorous words of the catechism. Soon he managed to acquire the art of skillfully balancing conformity to the Church and the material opportunities open to fortunate young men in Hayaland at this time. It was possible to hear the Word and yet to hear, not follow. For a time he gave up his job as a mission teacher. But the Word has a strange power, and suddenly it struck.

While listening to the preaching of missionary Hosbach something happened to Matia Lutosha. He wrote: 'Never in my life shall I forget what then happened. At that moment I made a resolution . . . I repented and vowed to leave my drinking companions. I destroyed my beer calabashes and began to feel hatred for drinking and the pleasures of the world, and I confessed my sins to the Lord God and asked Pastor Hosbach if I could be accepted as a mission teacher again, and this was agreed.'

For B Sr, individuals were significant in the development of the Church. He followed the lives of the students he met first while they were studying in Kigarama. One of them, Ernest Lutashobya, later became one of the episcopal candidates in Bukoba. B Sr talks of Ernest Lutashobya based on what the latter wrote on the theme 'Jesus Christ in my Life' and what he had experienced through dreams:

Similar, and yet different, was the conversion experience which Ernest Lutashobya had at about the same time. In 1938, while studying at the Kigarama Teacher Training College, he became seriously ill with some stomach complaint which the mission doctor could not diagnose. He had to leave the college and spend some time at his home in Kishasha, convinced that he was unlikely to recover.

That year he had two important dreams . . . The dream made him very much afraid and forced him to reconsider his spiritual situation. In the second dream he saw what seemed to be a full moon in broad daylight, '. . . and I stood there with other people, gazing up at it. Then I heard a voice from heaven saying: "Ernest Lutashobya must not be included amongst those who commit sins of fornication."'

During the time he was sick at home, Lutashobya wanted to help as much as possible and would take the sheep out for grazing. One day he took along a book in Kiswahili entitled *The Imitation of Christ*. 'Then I was given new strength and a new mind and new thoughts. I saw that I was not worthy to be called a child of God. I shed tears for my sin against God. I was almost beside myself that day. Then I began to hate the world and a new life began within me.' . . . Lutashobya's experience was not merely an early result of the East African revival which was just beginning at this time. But the combination of illness, solitude, dreams and a remarkable little book, the message of which was obviously written especially for one man in Kashasha, Tanzania, and only for him, led young Ernest Lutashobya to something which in retrospect can only be seen as a mighty spiritual breakthrough.

B Sr was sensitive to the dream life which we meet repeatedly in his writings on Africa and on the history of the churches in different parts of Africa. Dreams are individual experiences and focusing on them and their spiritual significance contrasts with the emphasis on the church as the ecumenical community which is the other side of B Sr's ecclesiology. He was building an African church but the concept of that church became a reality in the people with spiritual experiences.

Life was full of work for the lone missionary pastor among the African leadership. One of his sayings with which his friends were familiar was that he rested only in the Indian barber's chair in Bukoba town. It was a useful contact during the war, for from this barber Bengt could get any world news that was available in that distant corner of the world during the Second World War. The Sundklers did not have a radio and did not even dare to acquire one so as not to be accused, as non-British foreigners, of acting as informers for some foreign power.

While the missionaries were isolated and contacts with their homes did not work well, within the country they were able to communicate to some degree. As a member of the Lutheran Mission Council, B Sr visited the other budding Lutheran churches and missionfields, as they were still called at the time, where the Americans in the central and northern parts of Tanzania, and the Swedes from the *EFS*, in the southern highlands, were working. To and from Bukoba the missionaries and church representatives travelled by boat and train and by the few mission vehicles which took them to the local parishes and institutions. Chains on wheels were necessary even after a little rain and the journey could take extra days when stuck for hours on muddy roads.

B Sr's heart was in writing. He had thought of comparing the Zulu and Bukoba churches but decided to write a 'modern mission book' on the young church in the making. Right from the beginning it was clear to him:

> Not missionaries but the young church is interesting in what now happens in Africa. We need to have a radical change in our mission descriptions to what is essential. The young church to which the gospel has given birth, its faith and fellowship, interpreting the way in which the message has been adapted and received. (Sundkler 1948:6)

> After all the parishes and communities had been visited at least once I sat down in Ndolage to accomplish a plan which I had had since I left South Africa. Initially I wanted to write a comparative study of Zulu and Haya churches, but seeing how different the situations were I decided to write a modern mission book of a young church, the church in Bukoba. I had arrived in Bukoba in July 1942. In August 1943 I took a holiday and wrote the book in six weeks and sent the manuscript typed on thin copy paper to get it cheaply and quickly into the hands of the Church of Sweden Mission. After returning home in 1945 I found that nothing had

been done with the manuscript. I quickly reworked the book into a publication. That book, *Ung Kyrka i Tanganjika* [Young Church in Tanganyika], was never translated into English. *Bara Bukoba* (1980) was later translated to take its place but even today I feel that *Ung Kyrka i Tanganjika* was in its time, written in 1943, published in 1948, the first mission book with a vision of an African church in its relation to the colonial, national and local situation. In it I tried for the first time to show that Chesterton's words which I often have quoted were true, 'For anything to be real, it must be local.' (Interview 8 August 1985)

I quote from the *Ung Kyrka i Tanganjika* (1948:5–7):

> Nowhere does [Chesterton's] word fit better than in describing the work of mission and life in young churches.
>
> My interest has been to describe the young Haya church itself. Mission has been there and has done its groundwork. But I have been in a position to learn to know the church in a time when almost no missionaries have been working there. What thus matters is naturally the church itself and everything is viewed from the standpoint of the church. In interpreting the life of this church I have tried to catch the fourth dimension of reality, the church situated in its everyday and Sunday life, with thousands of connections with the whole reality of the Haya society. I have striven to give the Haya church its characteristic tone through personal quotes and local descriptions. If we could hear the young church express itself through sermons, its own songs, dreams, autobiographies, minutes from meetings, the interpretation would come alive and colourful, and above all, bring us close to real life.

Mission accomplished

B Sr's mission vision had been transformed from emphasising the pietist conversion of individual heathens in the heart land of South Africa, of which he wrote in his letters to his young supporters in Luleå, to a vision of the Church in Africa finding her way of being African, not simply a copy of a White church. In his practical ministry he tried to live out the reconciliation between the piety of an individual and the church as the mission.[11]

Eventually the war was over in Europe. The Church of Sweden Mission had taken steps to send new missionaries to Bukoba. Ingeborg and Bengt Sundkler were permitted to leave for a vacation which they had planned to spend in South Africa, initially with the idea that they would still return to finish their term in Bukoba. They travelled through Rwanda, Katanga in Belgian Congo, North and South Rhodesia (Zambia and Zimbabwe) to Johannesburg by buses and trains. It took more than a week to travel from Bukoba to Elizabethville in Katanga (Lubumbashi in the present Republic of Kongo) and from there by train to Johannesburg via Lusaka and Salisbury, now Harare. It must have been quite a tiring journey, but

B Sr had his reasons for making that trip. He was eager to continue his research on the independent churches in Pretoria. While there they received a letter from the mission director in response to their request to return home, informing them that Ingeborg could return to Sweden for health reasons. She managed to get a place on a poor ship from Beira and was on her homeward voyage after a strenuous time of work and travel.

B Sr also received a letter from the home office permitting him, if he so wished or if a doctor so advised, to make the same voyage, but he felt that he still had work to do before leaving, and there was space only for one on board the ship.[12] His ambition was to finish gathering material for his book which he initially called *Black Man's Church*, a book on the 800 independent churches. This was his last opportunity to find the material in a manageable form. On a later visit he found that the new computerised system would not have permitted the kind of study he was then able to make. He was anxious to get back to writing and scholarly work, with his eye on the professor's chair from which Professor Knut B. Westman was due to retire before long. He returned after intense work in the archives in Pretoria, three months after Ingeborg. (In another interview 8 August 1985 the period mentioned was half a year.)

The newspaper in Umeå, Sweden (n.d.) under the heading: 'Dr Bengt Sundkler in Sweden again after 8 years' stay in Africa' gave the following interesting account of a ship arriving with a load of exotic food items which had been missing during the war and now gave significance to this postwar event:

> The long-awaited, transatlantic ship, Gullmaren, arrived on Monday morning in Gothenburg with a valuable load which consisted of, among other things, 500 tons of oranges, 2,000 tons of ore, 600 tons of cocoa, 100 tons of mahogany, 1,100 tons of copra, and 300 tons of wine. There were 13 passengers on board and seven of them were missionaries returning from different mission societies who came back after many years of work in Tanganyika and the Belgian Congo.

In the meantime Ingeborg had spent a well-earned summer holiday on her family island in Manskär and then prepared a mission flat for them in Uppsala on Luthagsesplanaden.

Soon after his return Bengt Sundkler became a docent of Uppsala University. He was called to speak in Oslo, at the opening of the Egede Institute, on the task of mission research. The institute had been launched by Olav Guttorm Mycklebust who had become a professor in the Menighetsfakulteten in Oslo. The Sundklers had come to know him when he was principal of the Umpumulo Teacher Training College in South Africa while they were there. A Norwegian newspaper recorded B Sr's message which stressed the necessity for co-operation between the Nordic libraries, institutes and journals. He also spoke of the need to start a similar Institute for Mission Research in Sweden; indeed, it later became his task to establish and to lead such an institute. On this occasion Bengt Sundkler's message emphasised a theme which was to be central to all his scholarship and active work in building the Universal Church in Africa: research was to be practice-oriented and should, whenever possible, be done by those who had experience of practical missionwork. To quote: 'Docent dr. theol. B. G. M. Sundkler expresses *inter alia* the importance of missionwork as a personal prerequisite for mission science and the actual problems which the Swedish mission research faces.' The article continues to quote Sundkler's lecture directly:

> Much can be learned from books and journals, and I have the deepest admiration for those mission experts who often devote their knowledge to these. But in the context of missionwork there is the fourth dimension of reality which only those who have done missionwork can understand ... Similarly I see the task of mission research essentially to be practice-oriented research, which means that it deals with problems of what significance missionwork actually has. It is also tied to the question of presentation and the thought values of the people among whom the mission works ... Mission research should also interest itself in sociological viewpoints of problems in the field – to study the structures of African society and find potential for grounding the Christian Church as a part of that society. (Newspaper report in Oslo paper 1945, n.d.)[13]

Notes

1. In the Haya language the *lu*-prefix indicates language while *mu*- and *ba*-, singular and plural, signify people. In Swahili the corresponding prefixes are *ki*- for language and *m*- and *wa*- for people.
2. Recorded interview by MLS 31 October 1985.
3. B Sr often regretted that he had not in his youth crossed the narrow straights between Umeå and Wasa and attempted to learn the Finnish language. He had many Finnish friends and gave them praise words such as, 'These remarkable Finnish people, strong enough to resist Stalin, humble, open, living,' and then referring to the famous architects and Sibelius, and several Swedish-speaking Finns.
4. The story of six children being saved after swimming in the ocean for an hour – the mother with the baby – is one of the miracle stories of missionwork, recorded in a book called *Zamzam*. The family was taken to Lisbon and then sailed back to the USA. The youngest, Lois Carlson, née Danielson, later returned to Tanzania as a missionary social worker in Dar es Salaam.
5. In another account 29 July is given as the date. 14 July is in the letter to SKM/CSM 6 September 1942.
6. The number quoted varies between 132 and 172, apparently depending on whether the wives were counted. Those who remained had to sign a 'Parole' document to declare the trustworthiness and their movements were restricted to their area of residence. (Bernander 1968:19)
   It should perhaps be remarked here that the Roman Catholic Church did not

need to intern their German or Italian missionaries because within the system of convents of priests and nuns the bishops were accepted as guarantors of their fellow workers. One cannot avoid thinking of the political power that the RC Church wielded. This gave the Catholic work a great advantage. Another example of the superior authority of the RC Church over the British colonial government authorities was the immediate take-over of the Kidugala Church and mission in the southern highlands by the government for the Polish Catholic refugees. The African Lutheran congregation not only lost their church administration headquarters but also the caretaker missionary director Nordfelt's home and office with immediate effect. With no prior notice they had to vacate their church and quarters to the Poles and had to worship from there on in a mud and wattle building which they hurriedly constructed with the help of a meagre compensation. Bernander rightly comments that the spiritual care of the Polish refugees could have been arranged in a less disturbing manner. Considering the size of the RC mission stations throughout the country and the land acquisitions which they did not give up even later after the Land Commission's recommendation in the 1950s, one can question why such distress was caused to the already troubled Lutherans. This is one example of the quarrels in certain locations and disagreements that occurred between the Catholics and Protestants, not to say that the issues were purely one-sided. I have no evidence that the Catholic Church was involved in the above measure, but this is what it seemed to people. In fact, there was a rumour in Bukoba, before B Sr came, that the government had forbidden the Lutheran church to operate, and the place was overrun by Catholic priests. I stress here that B Sr himself was very careful not to mention anything which could have in any way discredited another denomination. Having witnessed the rebuilding of the Lutheran church in Kisarawe near Dar es Salaam, amidst Muslims, I could feel for the people in Kidugala. Also the Lutheran Christians in Kisarawe had suffered from the take-over by the district commissioner of the two-storey missionary house and the pulling down of their particularly sturdy church building. The congregation of 150 Christians had to worship in a mud hut which was all they could afford to build with the compensation they got. (Bernander, 1968:51–4) The large mission headquarters and residences of the Berlin Lutheran Mission in Dar es Salaam were also torn down near the Magogoni ferry on the excuse that it was a place for a hotel. The hotel has never materialised and at the time of writing this the place is still vacant.

7. I have added this detail from John Moris' unpublished account of his mission service in China and Tanzania where he served as a doctor in Singida, Bukoba and Usambara missionfields. He came to Ndolage six months after the Sundklers and was living with his family in Ndolage at the same time as the Sundklers.

8. Calling the king 'Sultan' indicates Islamic influence. Both Muslim and Haya traditions forbid the meeting of young men and women together which was the main reason why the Sultan interfered with the youth movement.

9. Culwick and his wife wrote later an anthropological work *Ubena of the Rivers*, while he was district commissioner in that part of the country.

10. B Sr was to meet Ms Boesch again when he returned to Bukoba as bishop of the northwestern diocese. She had settled in Bukoba for her retirement and sent for a Swiss woman, Elsy Dietiker, to be her personal helper. Elsy Dietiker followed the missionaries from Bukoba to the Swahili language course in Dar es Salaam and ended up as a promoter of Christian literature affiliated to the Anglican church in Morogoro, herself working under a Swiss Bible mission society.

11. B Sr was aware of the role of the church also when leaving for Africa but he wants his readers to understand clearly the new emphasis he had gained.

12. In another later interview B Sr remarks that he could not get place in the ship which Ingeborg took and thus had the chance to remain. (31 October 1985)

13. The undated newspaper article is quoted from a book of clippings prepared

possibly by B Sr's father and presented to Bengt in 1950. The book is in the Sundkler archives in Carolina under the cover title *Professor Bengt Sundkler 1912–1950*. It includes photographs of B Sr as a child and of his parents as well as scenes from Vindeln and Umeå.

6

'DIFFICULT TIMES IN UPPSALA' – THE 1950S[1]

A programme for mission research

After returning from Africa Bengt Sundkler became a docent and a senior lecturer at the University of Uppsala in 1945. He started giving lectures on mission history, but his heart was aching to get at the material on independent churches in South Africa and to write of his new vision about the Church and mission. He soon got that chance and in his own story he tells of his voyage to England in May 1946 and his experiences at Selly Oak Colleges in Birmingham. After finishing the manuscript of *Bantu Prophets* (published in London in 1948) he was ready for another sojourn to Britain in August 1947, in order to start working on another book altogether, this time on the Church of South India. Both books were of intense personal interest to him, but they were also aimed at gaining expertise for the professorship in Church history, especially missions. The broad international scope of his work led him into the International Missionary Council (IMC) as a research secretary and to moving to England with Ingeborg for two years, 1948–49.

In August 1949 Bengt Sundkler returned to Uppsala from England, to be ready to take up the job as a university professor on 1 September. He gave his inaugural lecture as the Professor of Church History with Mission History on 5 November 1949. In it, he outlined the tasks facing mission research (*Missionsforskningens arbets-uppgifter*). The lecture was published as the first volume in the Swedish Institute for Mission Research (SIM) series (*Skrifter utgivna av Svenska Institutet för Missionsforskning 1, 1952. 1*) which was established by him. In it he presented his leading themes as a teacher and researcher quoted below:

> History only comes to life – when presented as an interaction and interplay of living people. History is not made only of ideas floating in mid-air, but people with their prejudices and fears, their ambitions and ideals.

History, and here that part which is church or mission history, does not exist just to divide the past into periods.

History teaches us above all to understand and to judge, with sympathy and insightful co-living [*inlevelse*] to lay a bridge of understanding across to another human being, to another time, another people and another race.

Our own time is one in which the views and meanings coagulate and get stale soon after they have been expressed. They become hard, without the finer nuances, intolerant . . . Therefore we need today more history, not less history, history about the living past which gives us a perspective on our own situation and becomes a roadsign to the future.

My own subject 'Church History with Mission History' is an indication that research and teaching are to be directed both to the old tradition of the Church and to continuity when the new structures of the Church of Christ are being erected in new lands. In the name of the professorship for this special field of theological research, I would like to see tension and interaction between tradition and new creation, the tension and interaction which characterises university studies as a whole and through which culture is both preserved and renewed . . .

The world political situation . . . has had a radical change of accent in mission development in Africa and Asia . . . from missionfield to missionchurches, from European-led missionwork . . . to the young church with its own history and specific problems of African or Indian Christians. So far, missionary scholars have been assumed to be only linguistic or ethnological scholars. There, one could guarantee that their contribution would be counted as science. But in fact, the whole mission reality in its total dynamic tension is what concerns Christian mission. So far, it has had space and justification only when presented in bright colours and sentimental mission stories . . . The richest task now is the mission situation itself, the contact itself between traditional religion and the Christian message, contact and conflict areas between traditional society, its customs and faith and the young congregations and church, as well as what the life of faith in the young congregations and church is like. These are no less legitimate or scientifically significant than other scientific interests . . .

So far attention has been directed to missionaries – much more relevant in history of the Zulu church are South African land legislation, urbanisation and clan struggles. Arnold Toynbee has, in his *Study of History* wanted to show that the growth of cultures is furthered between what he calls challenge and response . . . cultures moving to new ground is a brilliant example of this . . . When the church moves out overseas and is transplanted onto foreign soil, so-called mission churches will change . . . Before too long we will face the demand for something that we will call universal Church history. We cannot be satisfied with national or provincial Church history.

The whole of Church history from the oldest time goes forth as a stream of life and is bound to what is happening today within the young churches. At the same time, the whole history of the Church is often as if gathered together in a young church. Denominational characteristics which were developed in northern Europe, Great Britain or the USA become, in new tropical forms of growth, adjusted, and develop further . . . As an example one could cite the Church in South India.

The programme which B Sr outlined for mission history in Uppsala he had also worked into the programme for IMC. He was succeeded in his post in IMC by a Dane, E. W. Nielsen, who took up the programme and developed it skilfully. B Sr commended the excellent research work initiated and carried out by J. Merle Davis in a special department of the IMC founded in 1930, the Department of Social and Industrial Research and Counsel, in his article 'Fact-Finder for the Kingdom' in *World Dominion*, in which his own emphasis was also well-stated (Sundkler, 1948:203-6):

> The research programme of the International Missionary Council must never allow itself to be academic and remote from life, but should be closely related to actual practical problems of the younger Churches. This approach also serves to strengthen the National Christian Councils and to give them a vivid demonstration of the need for research in the field of the Church's life.

Professor's chair 'with' or 'without' missions[2]

The process of becoming a professor had not been easy. There had been considerable opposition to having Mission History included in Church History in the Theological Faculty. Extending Church History to include the history of the younger churches did not sit well in the conventional concept of the discipline. Learning history through field-work and relating research to the practical needs of the churches did not fit the scientific scheme of the faculty. I highlight some of the events because of the difficulties B Sr faced in the process, and its effects they later had on him.

At the instigation of Archbishop Söderblom, a collection had been taken in the Church of Sweden in 1919 and 1920, including a fund from the Church of Sweden Mission, to create a private chair for History of Missions and East Asian Religions in the University of Uppsala. Knut B. Westman, who had been in China for seven years and had the necessary academic qualifications, filled the post. In 1945 the chair was no longer private, it was changed to 'Church history, especially missions' and as such it was to be declared open. The argument was put forth at the very last moment that the chair should be called 'Church history with mission history'. 'With' was in the course of the debates weakened to mean 'without'. (The opponent even used a phrase 'minus Mission history'.) Within the Swedish Missionary Council there was an interest to safeguard donations which would guarantee the continuation of teaching of Mission History at the university. Gunnar Westin, Emanuel Linderholm's successor as Professor of Church History, being a Baptist, was very supportive of a government-supported chair in 'Church History, especially with missions'. Three other professors, Widengren, Engnell and Lindroth, were not so keen on combining Church History with Mission History and found it convenient to argue that if a full chair for Mission History were later to be established, the person now appointed should be one more fully competent in Church History rather than placing the emphasis on missions. Tore Furberg has shown in his article, 'Bengt Sundkler, pioneering Uppsala mission scholar', (*Kyrkohistorisk årskrift*, 1997) how the opposing professors demonstrated a lack of knowledge of field methodology in social analysis, which had been used by B Sr, and because of this they called the scientific quality of his work into question.

B Sr applied for the post together with Hans Cnattingius, who had introduced his good friend Bengt to the Oxford movement. B Sr did not deny his competence as a church historian on Swedish Church History, but he had no competence in Mission History. As we have learned, B Sr had written on Swedish Church History, on the Church of South India and on the independent churches in South Africa.

At the time B Sr was in London and from there wrote a 30-page statement in his own defence, while the struggle went on in Uppsala. In the customary academic mode, both applicants tried to convince the decision-makers of their superior qualifications over the other candidate. Both had supporting statements from British scholars. It amazes an anthropologist to read that Professor Widengren and others who opposed B Sr's appointment questioned the competence of the well-known British specialists in the field of African studies (Raymond Firth, Audrey Richards, Max Gluckman, Daryll Forde) all of whom had highly praised B Sr's *Bantu Prophets*, the first version of which had appeared in 1948. The argument, based on the claim for objective science and formulated as a critique of fieldwork methods, is familiar to field researchers committed to human or social causes who take as their departure point practical needs in social studies.

The process lasted nearly a year. Of the three experts the faculty had selected, two were church historians and one had expertise in mission history. They declared Bengt Sundkler very competent and Cnattingius incompetent as he lacked competence in mission history. In the faculty meeting the votes divided equally (3 for Bengt Sundkler and 3 for Hans Cnattingius), one declared both competent but declined to state a preference, (in the university council he voted for B Sr).

The resistance was largely against Mission History. Several newspapers took sides, either for putting the emphasis on Mission History (in south Sweden) or against it (in Uppsala and in some Stockholm papers).[3] The argument was put forth that the experts had given missions too large a share in their assessment. This influenced the decision of the university council, in which the majority turned against B Sr (13 against, 9 for) on the basis of that argument.[4] The final word lay with the chancellor of the university, Professor Engström, professor of law, who placed Bengt Sundkler first. In his judgement the referees chosen by the university could not be ignored. The king's appointment came in May 1949.

Sadly, B Sr had to face another encounter with Cnattingius when the latter, together with Sven Göransson, applied for the main professorship in Church History, the chair left open after the retirement of Gunnar Westin. B Sr was called upon by the faculty to act as one of the three experts who would assess the scholarly merits of the candidates. He spent weeks in 1955–56 studying the works of both and came independently to the same conclusion as the two others in the committee that Sven Göranson should be recommended to the post. Personally B Sr found this very trying. Cnattingius thought that for moral reasons his former friend now should have supported him. It was very hurtful when Cnattingius' wife phoned Sundkler following the decision and congratulated him on having crushed Hans. In B Sr's words, 'this decision was one of those harsh facts of academic life where one's judgments on academic competence are frequently queried'.[5]

This process was one of the factors which made the 1950s difficult for B Sr. In his diary notes, letters, and in private discussions the effect of this came up occasionally even if he never had any doubts as to his competence for the work he had been appointed to do.

A professor with international commitments

As we see from the agenda below, which B Sr has included in his diary of the 1950s, B Sr's teaching was frequently interrupted by his international duties and the necessity to travel to get his research material in the countries on which he wrote:

1950/51	India 15.11.50–05.03.51;
1951	Breklum, Germany 07.–10.06.
1952	Willingen and Hannover
1953	London, Paris, Brussels; whole of Africa 30.05.–22.12.
1955	November–December East Africa, Marangu LWF conference
1956	January–February Bossey Switzerland, lecturing
1956	May 5–6 weeks Oxford, Professor Evans Pritchard
1957	December–August 1958 Ghana, South Africa, Kenya, Tanganyika, Uganda
1959	January Helsinki, 100-year jubilee of FMS
1959	Roskilde student conference
1960 25.01.	Scotland: Edinburgh, St. Andrews
1960 20.08.	Bukoba 50-year jubilee, Kenya, Uganda.
1960 08.12.	Dar es Salaam, Salisbury University, IAI.
1961 22.12.–26.12.	Johannesburg
1961 26.12.–1.1.	Nairobi, Makumira, Bukoba, Uganda

This travel schedule is ample illustration of the difficulty B Sr must have faced at a time when international travel was not nearly as easy nor as common as it is today.

In his second year of teaching B Sr made a long trip for field studies in India, and soon after that he had a leave of absence to serve on an international commission on ministry in Africa. When he returned home, he taught on a part-time basis, in order to have the time to write up and publish the commission's various reports. He lectured and attended conferences and meetings in a number of places in the 1950s. Towards the end of the decade he took further leave in order to update *Bantu Prophets* which took him and Ingeborg to Africa for a period of eight months. When the new decade of the 1960s started with three-and-a-half years of absence as bishop in Bukoba, one year granted at a time, it is not surprising that his colleagues were somewhat upset by, and perhaps even envious of, all these privileges bestowed on him. The time of large-scale internationalism had not yet arrived and Uppsala was a parochial place into which an internationale of missions did not fit well.

In addition to B Sr's full schedule of travels and teaching, his diaries include plans from time to time for his literary work for the coming months and years. Several of these never materialised when plans were changed because of external assignments. Quite commonly, festive days gave B Sr some quiet time for outlining his plans for writing, while others were celebrating. For instance, on St John the Baptist's Day (the Nordic Midsummer Day) 1952 the list consisted of the following:

> To finalise the Missionforsknings arbetsuppgifter (Tasks for mission research)
> Book on IMC Conference in 1952
> Mission and Church (outline given)
> Baptism
> Church Union in India
> Swedish book on India
> England's Colonial Politics
> Lines of Development in Swedish Missionwork 1940–52
> Nordic Mission

Professor among the students in the 1950s[6]

Bengt Sundkler was known as an inspiring lecturer who brought a fresh crop of ideas with him from Africa and from the world centres of learning. He enjoyed communicating with students and found his best friends among them. He felt he had something important to share with them. He and Ingeborg frequently invited students to their home, and in general, they gave the impression that they were interested in them as individuals and in their future work and careers. B Sr encouraged the students to continue higher studies and ended up having the largest number of doctoral dissertations within the faculty as the years went by. Listening to sermons, he detected weaknesses in the theological training of the faculty which led him to include in his informal and formal teaching aspects which were not strictly speaking in the Church or mission history programme. He remarked that interpreting the Old and New Testaments and knowing the place of mission in the teaching of Systematic Theology was also fundamental for understanding the meaning of the Church as mission. His concern was for a living Church in the world, not just for scientific discipline. Later in his career he was glad when he was able support his own views on the research perspective from which he viewed history by referring to Gunnar Myrdal's line on objectivity in the social sciences: Everyone has some bias, a view of life and the world, which leaves its impression on the scientific work. It is important to make that bias explicit and deal with it objectively (Myrdal 1970:55).[7]

The following texts are from B Sr's fragmentary diary written in 1956 (pp. 32–41), when he was reviewing activities related to his work in the theological faculty as a teacher and professor during the early 1950s:

I tried to make my teaching interesting and compelling and to expand it through the Swedish Institute of Missionary Research (SIM) which I started. I published books, as professors were expected to do, and edited a scientific journal *Svensk Missionstidskrift*.

Åke Holmberg was the secretary of the institute for two years which was a great help. In 1954 Holmberg went to teach in Tanganyika for two years, which left me alone to manage the institute and the journal.

From September 1954 till May 1955 I was the dean of the Theological Faculty. It started poorly, I was not accustomed to faculty affairs. But starting from November the whole mood changed, even Widengren and Engnell had been increasingly generous and kind and we have co-operated well. On 31 May was the promotion of honorary doctors. Professors Dumezil and L. Andberg were promoted and I came to know both very well which was a rich experience.

Of great value for me has been to work together with Sven Göransson, a noble man and very knowledgeable. I have good co-operation also with Riesenfeld, Åke Andren and Herb Olsson. As a person, Engnell has also been exceptionally pleasant.

Geo Widengren, professor of the History of Religions, and Ivan Engnell, professor of Old Testament Studies, had earlier numbered among B Sr's critics. Harald Riesenfeld was Fridrichsen's successor, Åke Andrén was the young professor of Practical Theology and Herbert Olsson was professor in Ethics.

As teaching was only one of B Sr's interests and duties the reader begins to sense a conflict when his own research, writing and international engagements began to pull him in different directions. One gets the impression that he felt closest to those students who responded to his own line of thinking and could in turn help him to think through what he himself was writing at the time. His teaching, preaching and speaking grew out of his writing. 'For me writing is creating and I am unhappy because I am not literary, actively creating.' This thought we find expressed for the first time in his diary for 1950 and later repeated in various ways. In order to write, however, he had to have the material. He refers on several occassions to the fact that in Uppsala great emphasis was laid on material and its correct usage. He had living material, not only material in archives, as was usually the case among historians.

Completing the book on the Church of South India

One urgent task for B Sr was to revise the manuscript and publish his book on the Church of South India, a serious theological work about realising ecumenics in practice. He had barely started work as a professor when, after just one year of teaching, he squeezed in four winter months' of fieldwork in India and adjusted his teaching schedule accordingly. He needed the time in order to work the initial South India manuscript into a solid book. He travelled by ship, stopping in Tel Aviv, via the Suez Canal to Bombay. In Delhi he stayed in an Anglo-Catholic centre of the Cambridge brotherhood.

Coming from the background of Africa, India seemed to him a strangely exotic country. Comparisons with Sweden and Africa seem exaggerated in retrospect, but B Sr was not the only one who has had that impression, as strange as it might seem to the great number of highly educated Indians. Of this experience he reported to his father:[8]

> The days here in the tropical heat of Calcutta have been extremely varied and have broadened my horizons. India is a fantastic land. Africa seems quite Western and civilized in comparison with this totally strange world which one meets here. Above all, it is the influence of the Hindu religion which gives it this exotic character. In Benares I saw thousands bathing in the holy Ganges river, in dirty and muddy water, but these people seemed to have felt good in that holy water. I took a boat on the river and saw the burning of the bodies and circled to see the numerous temples along the river.
>
> Politically India is of course very interesting now. Hunger and a shortage of housing make easy room for communism. Masses of people sleep on sidewalks and sleep well. Hundreds of thousands of refugees is a big problem. Nehru does what he can, but India is in need.
>
> On Wednesday I shall go to visit the Norwegian Santal mission in Santalistan, on Friday to Tagore's Santiniketan and on Monday night to Nagpur. It is good that I can fly to most of the places here for the trains are dirty. Even First Class is like a cattle car in old, clean Sweden. But I am getting a lot of material for articles and books and I am grateful to

be able to see India because a mission professor must have seen India in order to know something about it. There might come a time when it is not so easy to come to this land. (Letter to his father from Calcutta 27 November 1950)

When proceeding to the south B Sr had the opportunity to meet Indian and missionary leaders and to learn something of the life and social and economic background of the Church. He interviewed a number of the most important persons in the Faith and Order movement, people whom he knew quite well beforehand through their correspondence. He had read about them and their writings in the various archives of mission societies, while he was writing the first edition of the book.

In place of mere plans, proposals, schemes of reunion and shelved declarations the fact of the realised union in the Church of South India became a challenge for the whole ecumenical movement. Christians longing for greater unity in the universal church had been asking whether all this talk about ecumenicity was perhaps a smoke-screen behind which the old trenches were being dug still deeper. In this setting the mere fact of such an accomplished union of different denominations (Anglican, Congregationalist, Methodist and Presbyterian) in the Church of South India was meaningful. The meaning of that fact had to be read in the life of the Church itself. It could also be grasped through a study of some of the criticism launched against the Church of South India on which Sundkler's book elaborates, such as the Derby Report of 1946. (Sundkler, 1956:345–7)[9]

To B Sr's great disappointment the Lutheran churches stayed outside the South Indian Church Union. He gave credit to the Lutheran missionaries in South India who tried to persuade their home churches to understand that the Lutheran influence on the Church of South India would be greater if it came from within rather than from outside. The fullness of Christian tradition could better be experienced if it could be viewed from within the church, after the separate churches had come together.

B Sr considered the book on the Church of South India to be theologically his most ambitious work, a learned thesis of some 450 pages. It was published in 1954 under the title *The Church of South India: the movement towards union 1900–1947*. Another revised edition came out in 1956. The earliest version of 1947 was not published as such: '*The Church of South India* was an ideal task for me. It concerned the total Faith and Order problematic from the view point of ecumenical relations and the accomplished Church Union in South India, the most important church union project in the Third World in the twentieth century.'

B Sr often made a special effort to find alliterating concepts to fix an idea in the minds of the readers or listeners. In analysing the achievement of the Church Union he focused on three central concepts, Expectation, Experience and Exception. These concepts he briefly elaborated on in the following few statements:

> The time factor plays a central role in the forming of expectation concept. The range of expectation measured in units of time ... is decisive. Expectation of imminent union; Experiencing the spiritual gifts in Holy Communion; and Exception proving the Rule – these were the three keys that opened the locked door ... Anticipation and expectation became operative words – intercommunion as an anticipation of real unity – this was their solution ...
>
> This expectation was a religious experience. Bishop E. J. Palmer's attitude to the problem of intercommunion was expressed in many letters of advice to Anglican leaders in South India. In Palmer's words: 'I cannot help thinking that one cause of the distress about the statements (on intercommunication) is the opinion of some that an ecclesiastical rule admits no exception. But that opinion has been refuted once and for all by our Lord's teaching on the divine law of the Sabbath. (*SMT* 1987, Vol.57:3,73–81)

Union was possible before full agreement was found on doctrinal ground in expectation of fuller understanding of each other's stand when experiencing communion together. Christ had approved an exception to what was considered ecclesiastical hard rule, similarly it was possible to make an exception and accept the Christian brothers and sisters from another denomination and find togetherness in practice.

On returning from India the lectures had to be crammed into the rest of the term. In spite of the interest that a professor fresh from the outer world could raise, time had to be stolen for writing, as a letter to his father indicates:

> My lectures are well attended and I enjoy working on lectures. The difficulty only is getting sufficiently concentrated time for writing books and articles. This matter must not become stressing, but it does happen at times ... I have to work with my notes from India. It is a huge but interesting task. Part of it will be worked into an English book, but partly I want also to produce a smaller book in Swedish. If only God gives me strength and health, I will do it. (Letter to his father 22 March 1951)

In the first years of his professorship B Sr did not produce new books, but was very active in writing in *Svenska Missionstidskrift* (*SMT*), the Swedish mission research journal and other journals, basing his scholarship on his experiences in practical missionwork, on lectures in conferences and universities, and revising the manuscripts and books written earlier.

In July 1952 the LWF organised its World Assembly in Hannover which B Sr attended. He reported to Ingeborg who herself had just returned from a visit to Holland:

It is very interesting here, much better than I could have expected. We have an interesting Section II here about world missions where I am in the chair. In my sessions we have a very good time on mission. I have much to do with the drafting committee. Berggrav [Bishop from Norway] preached on Sunday in German, a very fine sermon ... A new acquaintance is Arne Bendz, we have become real good friends. I showed him your picture with which he fell in love of course. He recognised you from Oscarsberg. He is going to Sumatra Batakland as a theology teacher, has a theological doctorate from Yale, a brilliant young man. We get much joy from being with one another.

I changed my hotel a couple of days ago, it became too expensive. I left the hotel to Birkelis, etc. They can stay in their fine hotels as far as I am concerned. I went outside Hannover and now stay with a Mrs Reich, a pastor's widow, I think, in Dürren. It is a thousand times better than in the hotel.

No time to see Hannover but the conference is fruitful. Today Berggrav will speak about the State and the Church. Wingren spoke yesterday about mission, brilliant, dangerously erroneous, excellent English. Nygren funny, speaks Bohusian [dialect of Bohus in Sweden] when he stammers his German. Now a new chairman is going to be elected, probably Hans Lilje who is an excellent leader and speaks fine English. Hungarian communist priests will speak now at least for an hour. It is going to be exciting. (Letter to Ingeborg July 1952)

The letter continues with loving words on how wonderful it is going to be at Manskär Island after Bengt comes home. Greetings to Ingeborg were sent from Swedish and Bukoba friends.

Before the term begins we find B Sr again in England, getting some more information about the Church of South India. If India had its faults, so did Britain, compared with the progressive homeland of Sweden. He writes to Ingeborg:

12 September 1952 Westminster Hotel, Chester. I have now made my way to Chester in order to interview Bishop N. H. Tubbs in the morning. He was in Tinnevalla in the 1920s and has taken part in the Church Union negotiations in South India. Wednesday evening and Thursday I was in Birmingham. I stayed with Colonel D. and had my meals with the Ws. The room and food were quite miserable. They had unpleasant iron locks on the doors, and I was wakened up 12 at night with a noise which could have shaken an elephant. And food, I ate guest house food, which you know, but have then taken my own food, a bit better, with butter and cheese: now I am beginning to be obviously old! On the whole I think they have incredibly hard life here in England, Birmingham and the Black Country. What can we say: everything is covered with wet soot, grey rain overall, absolute hell. But also here in Chester, there is green around although the city itself is so unnecessarily industrialised and ugly, except for the cathedral which I have gone to see. People are the type of proletarians which I thought can be found only in Russia, but they are found here in masses.[10]

I stay in a hotel near the station, and have had good meals and coffee in the lounge, where I have found the first warm spot for a long time. I go to London tomorrow and hope to be with the Bingles for the weekend. I met C. P. Groves, very touching. They greeted you warmly. She is absolutely wonderful, affectionate and good. Write to her, if you have time.

A letter dated 15 September reports the visit to the Bingles where they, together with the sons, had attended two services. The food had been good, and while the wives of men B Sr met earned often the remark that they were sweet, Margaret Bingles was 'unusually enjoyable and charming'. Next he moved to 112, Lexham Gardens near Lambeth Palace, a move he was not looking forward to but which was necessary.

On a commission to Latin Africa

Soon after B Sr returned from India and completed writing the book on South India in 1953, he was called to take part in a Theological Commission on the Ministry in Latin Africa. He was able to take one university term's leave, making a total of seven months absence from Sweden. This was a rewarding task, allotted to him because of his earlier services in the IMC. It took him back to Africa and gave him a new perspective on parts of Africa he had not visited before, still less studied.

While Bengt Sundkler had been research secretary for the IMC he attended and played an important role in their conference in Whitby in 1947 and later in Ghana in 1958. I shall return to them in a later chapter. From Whitby he was given the task of preparing three research programmes. The first one concerned the African family and marriage, a research task which the IMC undertook together with a group of anthropologists and other researchers. The second was to look at pastoral training in the younger churches and create an overview of the situation in Africa where this question was really pressing. The third concerned the churches in the West in relation to the younger churches. It dealt with the question of how the churches were enabled to see their mission task and take it up seriously. All these questions were of practical importance to the churches and the organisations which sent out missionaries. A leading principle of the IMC was that research should have a practical orientation and contribute to actual and central mission problems. The research staff was in close contact with the National Christian Councils all over the world and worked together with the World Council of Churches. Many of the tasks outlined were carried out after B Sr had left IMC. (*Vår kyrka*, 22 April 1948)

In his autobiography Bengt Sundkler has described his travels for the commission on pastoral training and ministry in the churches of 'Latin' Africa, i.e. the French- and Portuguese-speaking countries and

Liberia. Again, characteristically, he emphasises the importance of having had Professor Christian Baëta from Ghana with them, if only for six weeks, while the other three were from Europe. Other members were Professor Searle Bates from New York and Frank Michaëli from Paris. B Sr, who liked to learn the maximum from any travel he made and to use any opportunity he had for communication, made the point that Father Michaëli was an exceptionally valuable company. He writes:

> It gave me a chance to learn again French properly and I got a better grip on how to give a lecture. He as a Frenchman was an ideal speaker – himself originally a mathematician; very clear, crystal clear in his presentation; for my chaos it was wholesome and challenging.
> The travelling was highly demanding, physically and mentally. Sleeping in the same room with loud snoring Bates was often almost unbearable. Furthermore, he never responded to what one said, and I belong to those who need to hear some echo to what I utter. But I tried my best to be loyal, after all, we were on a highly important assignment. Our 'Latin' commission started on 1 June 1953 and lasted six months. I was back for Christmas. (Review of the first part of the decade in diary 23 December 1956)

His concluding thoughts from his report on ministry in Africa reflect the revolutionary period in the history of Africa in which the commission visited the churches.

B Sr wrote first a report of the commission's observations and was later asked to collect the information from all the missions together in the volume *The Christian Ministry in Africa*, which finally appeared in 1960.

B Sr felt that the writing took too much of his time, amidst his many other duties, but he appreciated the experience of getting to know such a variety of churches. It helped him tremendously when he later became bishop of an independent church in Bukoba. He was also able to verify his earlier observations about the significance that dreams held in Africa, of which more in chapter 7.

While Bengt was touring in Latin Africa, Ingeborg visited the missionfields of the Mission Covenant Church of Sweden in the French Congo. (Interview 8 August 1985) After that Ingeborg and Bengt visited Tanzania (then still Tanganyika) together and they reported to Bengt's parents from Kilimanjaro (9 December 1953):[11]

> Warm greetings from Tanganyika. We have a wonderful time here. I have now travelled through the whole of Africa, South, Central, West and East Africa. We might make an effort to climb Kilimanjaro. I have learned more than I can say during this trip and will be writing one book in English and another in Swedish on Africa. I am now reading the proofs for the book on South India. I will be returning on 12 December, Ingeborg will stay on for 5–6 weeks more to enjoy the warmth. Just now we are staying with good friends whom we know from our earlier stay

in Tanganyika, Dr and Mrs Danielson from the Augustana Mission. He
is the leader of the large Chagga church on the wonderful slopes of
Kilimanjaro.

Now I begin to feel that it will be wonderful to come home again.
When I return from here I will have lived out of a suitcase for seven
months! Often quite irksome, but on the whole quite pleasant.

Back to teaching

Ingeborg stayed in Tanzania and Kenya to weather the winter. We can
follow B Sr's activities in Uppsala from Bengt's correspondence with
her, urging her to collect materials as he would have done had he been
there:

> 2 January 1954. I went for a few meals to the Hellstens, to the Falks at
> New Year's and visited the Brillioths, Anna Söderblom and Siri
> Dahlquist, Birgitta and Henry (Weman) one night. They spoke of
> Helander like all people here. They have not talked about anything else
> for the entire autumn and now they can get new speed and do nothing else
> . . . I hope that you contact the UMCA people and their nunnery. Cut out
> carefully from papers everything important that happens, be so good.

Several letters refer to the issue of Dick Helander, a former
colleague in the faculty who had become bishop in Strängnäs. Court
proceedings were carried out against him which shook the Church and
society. He was found guilty of having by the means of anonymous
letters made false accusations against other candidates, including his
professional colleague Professor E. Lindroth. This was one of the
issues which made the decade difficult for B Sr, but also other things
came up which touched him even more closely. He was rumoured to
be a candidate for three different dioceses in Sweden and two in
Africa. Only for two of them did he allow his name to be put forward
as we shall see further on.

> 23 January 1954. Tingsten spoke about South Africa here yesterday, and
> was clever. It was the same old thing but was energetically presented.[12]
> Gunnar Pleijel came home with me and we talked about his licentiate
> study. I think I have found a fine topic for him and we can work well
> together. Furberg will come here today and we shall talk about his licen-
> tiate work. Arne Forsberg who has been in Paris and now is a curate in
> Sofia will also do his licenciate for me. It is fine.
>
> Yesterday the Aftonbladets correspondent in Eskilstuna phoned me
> about the episcopal election, which you remember, and asked if I
> 'become a candidate as a bishop for Stockholm'. I was very surprised
> and let him know that the question had no connection with me or with
> reality at all. He knew, however, that there was some interest for it in
> the diocese. I answered that I shall, to the extent of my ability, devote
> myself to my professorship and not have other aspirations. So you see

things are moving in the country. In today's paper we read that Giertz and Cullberg do not contemplate coming to Stockholm. Herrlin will probably get the post.

30 January 1954. You have it very hot there in Tanga. It is good to know that you are not here. It is very cold, and the weather is going to get colder, it comes from Russia of course! I have been down with a cold for three days. It has been a problem, I should say, to get food. A town messenger has brought dinner from the Homeassistant school, but lunches I have had to get for myself. It has been quite tricky, but I have managed. Today I have been up and taken part in the faculty meeting. I have talked with Bennetsson and Brundin and talked about their studies. A while ago Kihlström was here. He was so happy about your presence in Vadstena and sends his greetings to you.[13] Bennetson thinks he should stay home and study before going to Bukoba because of a problem with housing there but I tried to reason with him that he should leave on 1 May. Holmberg leaves on 1 July for two years.[14]

1 February 1954. Yesterday we had the committee meeting for the Jerusalem society. Then I had dinner at the Brundins and we talked about mission strategy. If one only gets the chance to shout 'dynamic mission strategy' one has done very well. Further, one has to mention at least that such and such a person does not have a sufficiently strategic view etc., so one makes an immense impression.

5 February 1954. We have had demonstration lectures for the post in Practical Theology. Kjöllerström, Rosenquist and Maliniemi as experts, the latter two from Finland ... Generally rather dull lectures but I stayed to listen to all of them. [Comments on each candidate given, Hans Cnattingius being one of them.]

I have worked well this week. I have had four seminars and one lecture. One lecture I had to cancel because of a dinner with the experts in Gillet. I have further written some reviews and articles. Today I shall devote the whole day to the Executive Committee of the Mission Board. I have a seminar also in Swahili, four fine students: Åke Holmberg, Else Orstadius, Tegneus and Lic. Simonsson, the latter a linguist specialising in the Tibetan language. I am going to have seven or eight sessions with them. It is great fun, as you well understand.

As we have seen, friends and neighbours occassionally invited the lone professor for dinners and lunches in the absence of Ingeborg, but he also made an effort to entertain in spite of the inconvenience:

7 February 1954. Hedquist from Lövanger has been here for a week. Yesterday I invited him for breakfast in our flat. It was an enormous effort. There are endless things to think about, even if it means only remembering cornflakes, eggs, salt and coffee, the table cloth and serviettes and all such things, which one does not need when one manages by oneself. I was secretly very proud of my effort, but he seemed to have taken the whole thing as totally self-evident!!!

I am going to have an evening broadcast on 'Meeting New Africa' at the beginning of March. I am working hard on it. I have also a lecture about 'Young churches in Africa' at the annual parish festival. Lindeskog will talk about Jerusalem where he spent seven weeks in autumn.

15 February 1954. On Saturday I was in Göteborg for a lecture for the Society of Christian Education at Margareta School, and it was a very delightful contact.

I hope to be free from most of the things from 1 April on to write a book then.

I hurry to be back from Lund and Aarhus to meet you at Bromma [aiport]. It is wonderful that you go to Nairobi and stay at the CSM guesthouse. You asked what you could do there to help me. Above all clippings from newspapers. Try to get hold of numbers of the *East Africa Standard* for a couple of months back and cut out articles and news about race questions and Maumau, church and politics, and whatever you think would be of interest. You will probably be able to get some help from someone in collecting old papers and devote a couple of hours to this with someone's help.

The All-Africa Conference in Marangu

Between 12 and 22 November 1955 the Lutheran World Federation (LWF), under the leadership of Fridtjov Birkeli organised its first All-Africa Lutheran Conference. This brought 150 delegates, speakers, visitors and guests to Marangu in northern Tanzania (then Tanganyika) from different Lutheran churches in Africa, which at that time numbered some 1 million members. B Sr was one of the speakers, giving lectures on 'Strengthening the Ministry' and 'The Church and its Environment'. Marangu was the first common effort of the Lutheran churches to come to grips with the issue of the translation of the gospel into African mode and thought. B Sr refers to this in a significant article (*Svensk Kyrkotidning* 29 January 1959) in which he challenges the Church of Sweden to get hold of the new mission vision in the new world situation and to forget the old ball game of concepts of 'our mission field', 'our natives' and let them rattle and tumble down, *ramla och skramla*. The world situation had totally changed, in India, in China, in the new nationalist emerging states of Africa. How was the Church to meet the situation?

B Sr had attended the International Missionary Conference in Ghana 1958 and he quoted its chief message: 'The Christian world mission is Christ's, not ours. Before all our efforts and our activities, before all our gifts of service and devotion, God sent his Son to the world.' B Sr comes back to this thought time and again. The article is written for the Sunday of Candlemass. Mission is the 'candlemass' for the world: Christ is the Light of the world, He is there before, *ante*. This is not a statement in a conference. It is the reality which the mission translates in local situations. The baptised individuals and a group of outcasts in an Indian village are the body of Christ in that village, they are the mission of Christ. It is not a mission of some white foreigners. He kept this message when the general tone turned to what was termed 'social gospel', although right from the outset he had also responded to the social challenge.

Mission is not only a translation from a European language and culture to another language for Africans to learn another culture. As part of mission we first learn their language and their values, their longings and their need. Translation is not meant to stop at the external signs, at changing liturgical forms or confession, or even at certain Christian life forms. It is worked out in the *ashrams* searching for Indian forms of communion, or the struggle of the Batak church in Sumatra where God the Father is set in relation to the Muslim religious milieu in which the church lives. The Second Article's teaching of Christ is confronted by Indonesian messianism, and the Third Article faith is placed with certain forms of Indonesian spirit beliefs. In Marangu then an attempt was made to begin to formulate *Confessio Africana*. B Sr makes a reference to Bishop Heinrich Meyer's book on the subject, *Bekenntnisbindung und Bekenntnisbildung in jungen Kirchen* (Bertelsmann, Gütesloh, 1953).

In an article in honour of B Sr, Birkeli referred to Sundkler's second lecture in Marangu as having been, in the opinion of the African delegates, the most 'African' presentation in the conference (Birkeli, *Aftenpost*, 12 August 1975).[15] In his lecture on 'The Church and Environment' B Sr started in true African fashion from the beginning, the first covenant in Genesis 1:26, the fall and the corruption on the earth:

> At that lowest point of history of mankind, God called one man out of darkness, Abram. (Under the new and lasting covenant) Abram struck his tent and journeyed until he came to foreign country of Canaan, and east of Betel he pitched his tent. And the Lord said: 'Look now toward heaven and tell the stars.' Gen. 15:5–6. (The Hellenised Judaism also claimed first that it was universal, missionary-minded, but) they forgot the tent under the stars of the night and retreated into an Ark anchored in their own people alone. (It was the Christian church as the Ark of the new promise that was left with the universal task.) ... it carries with it in the Ark a responsibility for the whole of the environment, for the whole of God's world ... Abraham's role is carrying the tent, through the desert, toward the Land of Promise ... In the New Testament, the term 'tent' is used for the abode of Jesus Christ, as He identifies Himself with mankind. 'The Word became flesh and dwelt (or, rather, pitched his tent) among us.'[16]

Faithful to his approach, B Sr then moved to speak about the Church in the village and in the new Africa, making reference to the great Afro–Asian Conference in Bandung, Indonesia in 1955, where the visions of the independent Asia and Africa were drawn. Sundkler continued his message emphasising points familiar to the reader from his other texts:

[The] task of the church is twofold: prophetic warning and apostolic identification. (We) The church is called to pitch the tent of identification in the soil of the people ... At this Lutheran conference of African churches we must remind ourselves of the task of interpreting in the terms and expressions and thought forms of the particular tribal, village, or urban community. ... to translate the given Gospel into generous and rich African terms of expression relevant to the whole life in Africa.

B Sr promoted the 'strategy of the dedicated group of sufficiently high spiritual quality,' (do we hear an echo of the 'Oxford Group' of his youth here?) 'Healthy tension between the altar and the pulpit'; 'this church with its altar and the pulpit should always be on the move'. The new territory is not only geographical, there is the new Africa to move into, 'as an ark of worship with its altar, as a tent, our outgoing witness'. (Marangu 1956:113–19)

Organising a large conference was no easy task with the resources available in Marangu at that time. When we, as residents in Marangu and neighbouring Ashira, first heard about the plan to run such an All-Africa Conference in Marangu we had grave doubts about it all, but ultimately everything went without serious mishap – apart from the bedbugs which had come with the mattresses borrowed from Moshi! The speakers were accommodated in the two small hotels Marangu and Kibo. Bengt wrote about his stay to his wife on 14 November:

I sit here and listen to Reverend Mathibela from Rhodesia reading a paper on the African heritage. It is rather dull and uninteresting, so I take time to turn to you instead. We have it good here. We live in Kibo hotel together with distinguished Americans and beloved Zulus, such as Simon Mbatha and others. He is a wonderful man and he remembers you very well and greets you warmly. I have had a long discussion with him and took copious notes. You will be amazed by his attitude. Political oppression is not our worst enemy, rather our own weaknesses (sex, prostitution) etc. Tomorrow I shall have my lecture on the strengthening of the ministry. It is not easy, as you can understand, to be bound to the manuscript which one has written months ago! Viking serves as an interpreter into Swahili; he is very fast and skilful.

Through the open window birds sing, responding to one another and their song is much more beautiful than people's theology! You would enormously enjoy being here and wandering idly in nature. You do remember exactly what it was like here in Marangu.

As one of the hostesses to the Marangu conference, with no relation to Sundkler's role in the conference, I cannot resist the temptation to remark here that this was an entirely male conference. Among the participants there was only one woman. In the *Marangu* report (the writer of the report is not indicated) in Section Seven, 'Interlude', Mrs E. Marealle's speech on 'The Women in Tanganyika', was reported on one page. Mrs Marealle was the wife of the Chagga Paramount Chief Thomas Marealle and a former student of our Ashira Girls School. Her topic was the only one relating to women, and it was included in the discussion section. Mrs Marealle's name is not given in the list of speakers nor is she in the list of participants or visitors.

In the report there is no mention of the practical arrangements, nor of the army of women teachers, missionary wives and students of the girls' and boys' schools who made the whole effort possible in conditions not suited to such conferences. There is no mention of the male or female heads of either of the teacher training colleges, who carried the main responsibility for the arrangements. It was a time when men still thought that food came to the table because it was women's work to make and serve it.[17] It was a miracle that in those conditions all the arrangements could be made, and simultaneous translation could be even provided in four languages: Swahili, English, French and German.

Before his excursion to Marangu, B Sr also visited Uganda and Bukoba. After the conference he met the UMCA staff in Korogwe and then writes from the Anglican centre in Magila a letter to Ingeborg (26 November 1955):

> It is absolutely wonderful here. I stay with the bishop and had a very rewarding afternoon and evening with him and a good little man Eliot who is a treasurer. The stay here is a great relief after two days in Korogwe UMCA – uha! Bishop Baker has just now gone on a safari. We had a mass in his private chapel at 6.30 this morning. Very fine. The mass was in Kiswahili, even when we were only three Europeans there. Eliot will take me to the sisters' convent this morning. Last night the bishop took me sightseeing. The ringing of Angelus 6 o'clock was immensely peaceful, as if the clock would have echoed peace over the whole neighbourhood. I have read much here.

B Sr ended up in Kenya, spending six weeks on the trip, which he described as being significant for his work.

Before getting fully started with his work in Uppsala, B Sr had six weeks of lectures on Africa to 36 pastors from different parts of the world in the Ecumenical Centre in Bossey, Geneva. He mentions particularly three people whose presence brightened his stay. He became especially friendly with Reverend Gabriel Setsiloane, BA Math, Virginia OFS, South Africa, the new principal H. H. Wolf, whom he learned to appreciate, and Ilse Friedenburg, a High-Church German lady, a phenomenal linguist and a specialist on the Russian Orthodox Church. He also visited WCC headquarters and *Mission Swisse pour l'Afrique du Sud*. Ingeborg joined him for two weeks and had a wonderful time, after first receiving seven letters from Bengt urging her to come. They both returned to Uppsala on 10 February 1956. On his return Bengt wrote the diary review of the first years of the decade and turned his attention to his first post-graduate doctoral students. In Bossey B Sr had met Peter Beyerhaus who had a Swedish wife and thus connections with Sweden. He was impressed by Beyerhaus's ongoing dissertation work and encouraged him to terminate his studies in Uppsala. In 1956 Beyerhaus became B Sr's first doctoral student to defend his thesis in missiology, Bengt Sundkler was his examiner. B Sr looked with concern on the later missiological development of Beyerhaus, with which he did not agree.

Students again

As Peter Beyerhaus was the first student to defend his thesis under him, B Sr worked hard to see to it that the thesis truly passed the standards. Other doctorands preparing their theses were Tore Furberg and Rolph Sjölinder.

> In February 1956 I had come back to Uppsala after my travels to East Africa. I read Peter Beyerhaus's licentiate thesis and discovered he could present it as a doctoral thesis if he added to it Nigeria. He started working on this extremely demanding job for him and for me.
> In July 1956 I spent ten days with Peter Beyerhaus in Norrköping struggling with his doctoral thesis. We managed it somehow.
> After that I spent two weeks with Ingeborg on her Manskär island.
> Beyerhaus' defence was set for 1 December and Bishop Heinrich Meyer was asked by the faculty to be the opponent. He fell ill ten days before and I had suddenly to fill his place. He got 2 out of 3. Sven Göransson had serious questions but out of loyalty toward me let it pass. It made me in turn support his judgment of his own students, although there were cases in which I had serious criticism.
> Tore Furberg and Rolph Sjölinder work well with their doctoral theses. For me personally it is especially satisfying that Furberg has taken on the history of the Church of Sweden Mission in 1874–1901 as he thus continues from where I left off in my own doctoral thesis. It is also good because I had already given the topic to two others (Samolin and Pleijel) from University of Göteborg, both of whom have given up the work. Furberg is a fine person and will do well. Sjölinder should also go far. He is younger than Furberg and as a curator of the Norrland student nation (with 1,500 students) has become aware of his ability. Per Janzon is especially talented but unfortunately I cannot now give him much help on the topic in patristics [early church fathers]: I wish I could take on the theme about Baptism and Mission in the first 300 years, but it must be left until after my fiftieth birthday, if I ever live that long. (Diary to close the year 1956)

A Kenyan student, John Williams, turned up having been brought into the country by the Moral Rearmament group (MRA), descendant from the former Oxford Group. B Sr took endless trouble in trying to help him, but the story ended badly. B Sr called it a serious warning for himself. The student ended up starting a John Williams company with the money he received. Later he became the Ambassador for Kenya in the Nordic countries, turned up as a candidate for a doctorate in another subject and was promoted.

Another notable doctoral candidate was Johannes Aagard from Aarhus, Denmark, whom B Sr regarded highly:

> Johannes Aagard has been here since September 1957 and will stay till July 1958. He is a grand fellow, young, 29 years old, mature, sharp, quick and very kind and considerate to me. I have been warned against him by Torben Christiansen [Church historian in Copenhagen] and Erik W. Nielsen, [Bengt's successor in IMC in London] but I could not wish for better. I like this sure touch of his and he is a good theologian. Will turn into an excellent missiologist. He has helped me a lot with my own book, and he seems to think I have helped him a little. He is very appreciative of my efforts to try to help him. As we go to Africa he will live in our flat for six months.
>
> Tore Furberg is now my assistant in SIM, excellent and considerate. He works on CSM 1874–1901, just the subject which I have hoped for a long time to have well treated by somebody. I have been working on *Svensk Missions Atlas* [Atlas of Swedish Missions] together with Gudmar Sommarström and managed to get that out with fine graphic work. I am making preparations for Ghana, but I do not have as much time as I have to attend to SIM, etc. (Diary December 1957)

In a letter to his brother-in-law, at that time Dean in Luleå, B Sr expressed disappointment at not having been invited to a pastors' meeting in Luleå at which two of his students, Hedquist and Tore Furberg were presenting their pastoral theses, based on work for which he had been the adviser. He had been asked by one of the examiners for material, but he had not received an invitation to the meeting, although he was listed as a pastor of that diocese since he was ordained there. I mention this to show B Sr's continued interest to be counted as a serving pastor in the Church of Sweden. The letter continues to tell of another pastors' meeting to which he had been invited where Nils Karlström, Archbishop Söderblom's last personal secretary, was to present his thesis:

> I beg to mention these things to show my personal interest for this particular pastors' meeting and I rejoice that such clever men lead the discussion on mission in the meeting in question.
>
> There were supposed to be two pastoral meetings oriented towards mission this year, but the Skara meeting has been postponed. I have had much to do with Nils Karlström's thesis for the Skara meeting and have had a very friendly invitation for that reason to the meeting, long before the postponing of it now. In general, I am in contact with Rolph Sjölinder who will soon go back to Scotland again to continue with his

thesis, with Stiv Jakobsson who is for the same reason in London, and with missionary Carl Johan Hellberg, who has now finished his licentiate and will defend during his next home leave, and I hope that Furberg will also be finished soon. At present I have two Zulu pastors here, Mhlungu and Mbatha. They help me with the Zulu texts. (Letter to Stig Hellsten 9 August 1959)

The Sundklers were preparing to go to South Africa, but before that they attended the IMC conference in Ghana. This I will elaborate on in the chapter on the Internationale of Missions.

Revisiting Bantu Prophets

Bengt Sundkler's first edition of *Bantu Prophets in South Africa* had been published in London in 1948. He had been in personal contact with the independent church leaders and members and spent time in the South African archives before returning to Sweden in 1945, but he knew he had only begun to tap the rich sources and had much more to learn. Ten years later, in 1958, another opportunity to return to South Africa opened up when the International Africa Institute, London, gave B Sr £1,000 for six months in Africa to prepare the second edition of *Bantu Prophets*. For the faculty another leave of absence seemed somewhat excessive.

Most of this time was used for field and archival work in South Africa. This also gave Ingeborg a chance to return to South Africa and to make a prolonged visit to Tanzania and Bukoba. We can read about this second period of field research in the introduction of the reworked edition of *Bantu Prophets in South Africa* (1961), reprinted in 1964:

> On the invitation of the International Africa Institute and its director Professor Daryll Forde, I had the opportunity to revisit South Africa for eight months in 1958, with a view to preparing a second edition of this book. My research was once again concentrated on the Separatist Church conditions among the Zulus: on the Rand, in Natal, and in Zululand proper. But there was some widening of the scope of our research. Through the help of Dr J. F. Holleman, Director of the Institute for Social Research of the University of Natal, I was given the chance to visit Swaziland. I paid attention to Swazi Zionist and Ethiopian Churches in Swaziland and on the Rand. Here was a cultural and religious situation very similar to that of the Zulus – as Northern Nguni they are closely related. Yet there are significant differences in the fundamental factors: land, kingship, political situation. (1964:5)

In the earlier version of the book, B Sr had written that forms of worship in these independent churches were like bridges to tradition. When he returned to South Africa to study the same groups 13 years later he no longer saw it that way. He understood that from their point of view they were moving forward, away from their tradition. 'Anyone who listens to them in their decisive moments can hear what they have to say.' (Letter to MLS 12 April 1975)

The Sundklers arrived in Durban on 11 April and departed for Zululand on 1 May. On 19 June B Sr wrote from Durban that in the cold South-African winter he had suffered from a bad cold and stayed in bed for a week with high fever. Ingeborg was to fly to East Africa at the beginning of July and Bengt mid-August and they intended to be back in Sweden for 1 September. Their return was postponed until 1 October because B Sr wanted to update his knowledge of the Christian Council of Kenya. (The second reason for postponement was that he wanted to avoid attending the Church Assembly in Sweden and so 'avoid extra trouble', even if it cost him an extra month's salary.) He liked his stay in South Africa (Letters to Stig Hellsten 19 June and 7 August 1958):

> I am having an enormously good time out here with my studies among the churches and sects. The whole night between Easter Saturday and Easter Day I spent in Orlando 'native' town, going to bed only at 8.30 a.m. after having taken part in everything from sect dances to Anglo-Catholic early vigil and mass. Ingeborg and I stay now in an Anglo-Catholic retreat house (St Benedict, Rosettenville). Ingeborg has also had a wonderful time in the Irene Retreat house near Pretoria.

In early April 1960 B Sr wrote again to his brother-in-law Stig Hellsten explaining why it was possible to shorten his terms and stay away for such long periods:

> I have as little lecturing as possible and have primarily a research professorship, which suits me well. At the same time, I am very much engaged on two African fronts: South Africa and East Africa. I have proposed to [Archbishop] Hultgren that the Church of Sweden would designate the sixth Sunday after Easter this year, 28 May, a Sunday of Prayer for South Africa; the Church of England has her day of prayer the 31 May, which is actually a weekday, Wednesday. (7 April 1960)

It appears that B Sr continued to absorb many ideas from the Anglican church.

A favoured speaker in the 1950s

The diaries tell of frequent requests for speaking engagements which B Sr accepted with a sense of a mission, as he had something to say to the Swedish audiences. For his whole life he aspired to excel as a speaker, to walk in the footsteps of Söderblom and Tor Andrae, the teacher he went to listen to in his student days for that very purpose. He constantly commented on and criticised his own performance, but he also commented on the audience as well as other preachers, lecturers and speakers. He was not tied to a written script, although he usually prepared quite carefully, especially for public performances. This freedom of delivery led to lengthier and more enthused and inspired rhetorics which he subsequently regretted, preaching to himself on how he should have behaved. I limit the quotations here to the 1950s and return to the topic later:

7 January 1950. I spoke at the Swedish Women's Mission Society meeting about 'Black Messiah and White Christ'. The hall was packed. I think it went quite well, although I kept on for an hour. I could have managed in 50 minutes but was given an hour to speak.

10 January 1950. In the evening I spoke at the Free Christian Student Movement at their annual meeting in Lidingö about 'The State and the Church'. Unfortunately I went on too long, over an hour. Worry about it unleashes my desire to write again in the diary in order to clarify this matter for myself.

LESS IS MORE! P. von Rohe has thereby given a modern functionalist life ideal. I am too heavy. I have to throw out a lot of dead weight. I am not daring enough just to give indications, hint at things. I must learn now to speak briefly and to the point. I think of course that the Swedish public is ignorant about the missions; one cannot assume that they know anything. They have no associations with which one can connect, at least I think so, but I may misjudge them. In any case, I hardly underestimate the audience. I have to throw overboard all long introductions which steal half of my time. I have to learn to be brief and snappy.

On 13 January I shall speak at the Rotary Club in Stockholm for 20 minutes. It is a useful exercise, something I should have learned 20 years ago. I will become unknown – and I do not want to become unknown – if I am known to speak for too long. I often make small excursions, deviations left and right, they take too much time. Then there are no proper conclusions, I offer no solution.

God protect me from this danger. Less is More – it must also be my ideal in my manuscript for the Christian Ministry in Africa. It should apply to every lecture. I have vowed to learn this. It is about time, high time too. It implies aiming at the core problem and then, with two or three main points, promptly working straight through first one point, and then the others directly thereafter. I have a tendency to throw in illustrative asides that pop into my mind. I want to be specific since I detest generalising speeches about Asia and Africa which leave the audience wondering whether the speaker has ever been there. But there can be too many specifics and it takes too much of my time. The clock must totally dominate my presentation.

Bishop Ward should be my ideal. He can stand up and talk about any topic in the exact time allotted and produce a really well-worked-out conclusion. With me, I rattle off instead a few scattered end points.

The desire to create good form grows ever stronger in me. I am sad when it does not show, does not take shape, the spoken word with me.

I think I somehow succeeded on 7 January when I spoke about Black Messiah and White Christ. But it is not enough. I must make it a rule without exception to look at the clock and its five minutes periods, as something decisive. I must have time to prepare all my presentations so that I have time to discard all unprepared associations which crowd my thoughts.

Nine years later B Sr was again invited to speak at the Rotary Club, a meeting which the king also attended. After the occasion he reports briefly with no regrets:

13 January 1959. I was invited to the Stockholm's finest Rotary in Grand Hotel. The king was present and was a very interested listener. I spoke about Africa in 1959, about mission and church against the background which nationalism etc. implies. The President was A. Dalen, a very interesting personality.[18]

The brevity of these comments is astonishing after such a performance for celebrities, and after having such worries beforehand about the presentation. We can study the speech given in the presence of the king, and several other longer speeches during those final years of the decade, in an article (*SMT* 47, 1959:23–34) entitled 'Christian Church in New Africa'. Skilfully chosen metaphors, observations B Sr made on his travels and collected in hundreds of small notebooks, which he then perused and underlined for easy access, formed the core of his presentations. They were more than illustrations. The associations which they brought to the fore contained the essence of the message.

The article – as most likely the speech – began with a play on words: 'Now' and 'new' (in Swedish: 'Nu' and 'ny') as the magic words in Africa at the end of the 1950s, starting with the case of Ghana:

[A well-known scholar] Dr J. B. Danquah had every chance for victory to hand ... He had created a well-organised political party, the United Gold Coast Convention, with a well-thought-out programme, all embracing seven postulates, aimed at 'self-government as soon as possible'. He had influence, connections with power-yielding Black and White, and he had formulated 'seven postulates'. In short, he had everything – except one thing.

Kwame Nkrumah, an upstart, stranger in his own land – after ten years of absence from the Gold Coast in 1937–47, active in the United States and England – pressed the hidden, forgotten [in Swedish 'gömda, glömda'] NOW-button, which turned out to be the 'open sesame', which opened the door to the new kingdom of freedom. 'Self-government NOW', – with three capital letters – became the readily understood programme. One practical password in place of seven learned postulates – and Ghana was born, the first independent African state in the latter half of the twentieth century.

'We find ourselves at the start of an adventure', said Nkrumah to the All-Africa Political Conference which he, using the visitor's right, assembled in his capital Accra in the year 1958. One meets the same attitude wherever one goes in Africa today.[19]

The speaker, Bengt Sundkler, played further with the words Now and New. The new Africa was on its way to the villages in Africa, new things were happening for the first time. The first pastor lifted the village to a different status. 'I remember when Pastor X. came to our village. It was for the first time in history', as told by one of the hundreds of school pupils writing essays on 'The pastor in my home parish'.

And naturally he was right. For the first time in the history of a village the first school, the first pastor, the first nurse, the first agriculturist, the first railway stop, or perhaps rather, the first airfield, the first democratic elections, the first study group. 'For the first time in history', 'in the beginning of the adventure' – NOW is the acceptable time – this is the notation for the NEW time melody in today's Africa.

B Sr went on to talk about another important FIRST, another great event with metaphoric significance: Bandung 1955, which collected the people of Asia and Africa onto a common front against the white world's colonialism. 'Here the coloured people's world, folkworld, joined in an emotionally loaded united movement.' The host leader, Sukarno of Indonesia, formulated the new unity into a key statement, 'We unite here race and religion.' This slogan, so hard for nations to demonstrate in practice, Bengt Sundkler as the speaker then used from a mission viewpoint.

The speaker referred back to that powerful personality, Cecil Rhodes, as the symbol for the power of colonialism in Africa. The speaker also loved maps and used them skilfully in his speeches. Here Cecil Rhodes, in his residence 'Groote Schuur' in Cape Town, stood in front of the map of Africa, marked in large sections with red, signifying the British Empire. He exclaimed, 'All that red. It is my dream!' And the map was drawn in straight lines, so that Ewe peoples were divided between the Gold Coast, French and English Togo and a bit of Dahomey. The Fang tribe found itself divided between the Cameroon, Gabon and the Congo. B Sr continued, 'Now the Bandung-clock has rung quarter past twelve and the map in Africa is drawn anew in different colours, no longer in straight European lines.'

This was said in 1959 when even the northerner turned south had his dreams. The straight lines have not disappeared, if anything they have dominated more than any Black or White would have wished, but the differences from the past remain crystal clear.

The speaker went on to bring out the impending tensions between the old tribalism, and the new Africanism, how the old culture comes to town, described in lively details from newspaper clippings, whether a big evil fish buried by an army of traditional practitioners, led by a woman, (*SMT* 46) or demonstrations of the vitality of African dance performed before dignitaries. This is where the Church played its important role, as the new home, the new tribe in urbanised and changed conditions where the old home was lost. This is also where the church came with its healing and education.

There were moments of success, but there were also moments of regret:

At the Swedish Women's Mission Society [SKMF] conference in Uppsala. I gave a talk on 'World Mission in 1945–69'. It seemed awfully dissatisfying afterwards. Why must I present myself as a good-for-nothing professor who cannot finish, who goes on and on. God have mercy. I had spent a ridiculous amount of time preparing. I should not allow myself to waste time in preparation, and even then it was not satisfactory, I think. It was a simple, elderly public, very respectable and touching people, but not exactly my public. Some nice people thought it was a splendid lecture, but I myself was terribly dissatisfied. I got a headache from loss of self-esteem.

[Diary] 22 March 1969. The headache is gone but self-accusations because of the lecture yesterday do not leave me! I have devoted endless time to this: Why? Why? I should be skiing instead or do something else more reasonable. Of course: try to speak peacefully, wisely, convincingly, not the exaggerated way I clearly do, an expression of my sorry temperament or queer personality. I heard Dr Kerstin Dahlin speak about Ndolage hospital: clear, clear, quiet, collected; extremely well. One was glad that we have such fine doctors in Bukoba as the Dahlins are. She did not say everything she knew, or had information about, but what she said, she said well.

Tonight there was a Laurentius Petri Mass in the cathedral, a wonderful choir, Ragnar Holte [a fellow member of the faculty] was the celebrant, together with Öyvind Sjöholm [a good long-time friend of B Sr] and Bryn Widmark. Sjöholm mentioned that my talk had been good and his wife had been fascinated with it. So it gave a little comfort that at least some few drew some benefit from my efforts. I took part in the closing dinner. Afterwards Barbro Johansson [missionary friend from Bukoba] came home and we talked mostly about Africa.

In other chapters the themes which B Sr developed when giving speeches continued to be developed into written articles and chapters. Here my intention has been to demonstrate B Sr's way of formulating his speech and finding his illustrations, but also to show his ambition to speak well.

Difficult times in Uppsala

The return to his home country and finding his place in the Church of Sweden and in the academic environment were difficult for someone like Bengt Sundkler who had been personally fully involved, both theoretically and practically, in the central and real issues of Church and life on both a global and a local scale.

Personal notes in diaries, letters and Free Associations express some of the anxieties B Sr experienced after he had chosen to become a professor rather than continue missionwork in Africa. During his 'difficult time' in Uppsala B Sr felt that he was 'being pushed and buffeted about in this faculty, or so I thought, and felt generally dissatisfied'. (Letter to MLS 14 July 1982) In a diary note B Sr questioned whether his anxiety was caused by having made the wrong decision (29 June 1950):

> Deep down I believe that there is the conflict about whether I did right in taking up the professorship. I should be in Tanganyika, not here. I have not got a grip on this professor's work, I have not worked with my whole personality on it, only superficially.

After getting aquainted with all the activities which were crammed into the 1950s it is difficult to understand why B Sr in his later years always spoke about this decade in such negative terms. The fact that he had spent more time away from Uppsala than there might in itself be one reason why he never really felt 'at home with himself', as he once expressed it. The following two sections are based on his reflections in diaries and letters:

> Despite the numerous rich experiences I try to understand why the 1950s have taken on that dark and dismal colour in my memory. It is indeed strange that I should have such a recollection of sadness and heaviness from the first time as a professor here. I am sure there are also other dimensions to remember. I suppose it is in contrast to the decades which followed: the creative and happy years in the 1960s, being a bishop for a few great years and then walking for another three years or so with Nathan Söderblom, preparing a book about him.
>
> In comparing that kind of life with the tough times in Uppsala in the Theological Faculty of the 1950s, such years must appear only second- or third-best. And in my memory I have allowed the impressions in the faculty sessions together with those seven or eight professors to crowd everything else out ...
>
> Strange: I have written out in my diary in lead pencil a draft about this struggle in the university and in the faculty, but I cannot afford the strength and time now even to type it. I cannot be bothered by that which once was such an important and very heavy burden on me. Now all that seems to have lost its interest to me.
>
> I had a session with Hallencreutz yesterday over this, and he told me of lectures I had given at that time that meant something to him and I suppose to others. (Letter to MLS 12 June 1982)

Finding reasons why the 1950s were such a difficult time was no longer an acute concern for B Sr, yet he kept on returning to that era and comforted himself with the thought that the students also then had received something from their teacher.

The thought of losing time is repeated perhaps more often than any other thought in B Sr's diaries:

> '*Tidens räkenskap* 1950-1961'. Rendering account of time.
> '*Ack med tiden, tiden,*
> *när den är förliden,*
> *kommer ej igen.*'
> (Oh, but the time, time, when it is gone it never returns.)
> 'This minute that comes to me over the past decillions. There is no better than it and now.'
> 'Time is irreplaceable. Waste it not!'

These quotes open the diary book of 1950-60. The last quote is repeated in the diaries over and over again. B Sr had the urge to accomplish, having been called to write and to produce, and for that no time should be wasted. He did not lament his failures as a teacher, but rather as a scholarly writer, as a member of the academic community and a public figure.

B Sr found, as so many other returnees, that having been absent from the home country for a considerable time it was not easy to find his proper place in society and Church. In many and varied ways he continued to feel an outsider. On his return he had agreed to become president of two organisations, the Evangelical Student- and High-School Student Movement (*Sveriges Evangeliska Student- och Gymnasist Rörelse*), and the Christian Education Organisation (*Kristen Fostran*), 'both of them conservative'. It was as president of the evangelical students that he led the Nordic student conference in Uppsala in 1951 where I met Ingeborg and Bengt for the first time. He wrote afterwards about his involvement in these movements in a somewhat disparaging tone:

> I went along without much enthusiasm for this kind of attitude but trying to be helpful all around: That was the only way of finding a home for one's search for priesthood. The other alternatives seemed too superficial at the time, at least to me ... But as I went along I never identified myself with these organisations wholeheartedly, and therefore never gave the kind of leadership for which these people were looking. (Letter to MLS 14 July 1982)

At the beginning of the last year of the decade B Sr's plans had changed from what they were at the start, in 1952, but in part they contained the same unrealised works, with some title changes:

> [I must] Take time for a long-term planning of work, and work the details into a frame which I believe I can manage - aware at the same time that conditions change quite a bit, but that God speaks also in them

and through them. I have to squeeze much into this year:
  Missio – a handbook for students and study circles
  Christian Ministry in Africa
  Bantu Prophets
  Why not a book on India: Voices from the East (*Röster från Öster*)
  And necessarily a book on Africa: Now it is Africa's turn.
  In order to clear all this, health and balance are needed.

From B Sr's letter to his parents at the end of the last school year of the 1950s we can see how full the planned programme for the rest of the year was:

We have had an interesting and enjoyable term which has just closed with [doctors'] promotion in Aula [University Main Hall], and we are now planning our summer programme. On Whitsun we go to Manskär for a short while. June 14–16 we both will go for a pastors' meeting in Skara. Bishop Sven Danell invited me to come there a couple of months ago. I am to comment on a thesis on a mission theme presented there. 28 June–2 July we shall be in Ransäter where I lecture at a Geijer Society course. Then Ingeborg goes to Manskär and I to Storlien, July 4–7, to lecture for a course on Christian Education, but hope to return soon to Manskär and Uppsala. July 25–August 15 I shall be in Edinburgh and St Andrews for conferences. Ingeborg should also be in England during that time. I shall most likely fly to Tanganyika at the end of August for a couple of weeks. After the autumn term, on 9 December, I shall travel to Rhodesia for a two-week conference at Salisbury University. From there I continue to South Africa where I shall spend Christmas and New Year. Other than this, we are going to be in Uppsala.

The plans changed. A completely new chapter opened up with a call to Bukoba which was to transform B Sr's personality and life.

'Travel into my inner self'

Questions of motivation, ambition and failure on a personal level, lay hidden somewhere in the depths of B Sr's personality, and they were not easy to tackle. He was going through periods of anxiety and inner struggle, the cause and depth of which he could not fully clarify for himself. The efforts he made to get to the root of his inner turmoil he called '*travel into my inner self*'. One of the psychologists whose help he sought had advised him to write Free Associations whenever he felt particular need to release these inner pressures. I feel justified in recording some of the inner searching in retrospect because B Sr explicitly stated that he wrote letters for autobiographical purposes.

  An outside observer would have suggested that the pace of his life, the numerous outside engagements involving frequent and extensive travels, would have been enough to exhaust anyone. In trying to interpret this phase in B Sr's life, I consider his statement 'I belonged to a different category all together from the other members of the faculty' to be one of the keys to it. The reasons he gave as being 'an internationale of missions', a scholar belonging to a different category from others, having left Africa behind and finding the domestic academic scene relatively unresponsive to international concerns. This can perhaps be best understood by others who have gone through the same kind of a change of 'life world'. For Bengt Sundkler it was particularly hard because of his intense need to communicate and the sense he had of lacking a response in Sweden. In one way, this could be seen as an expression of a general human experience of alienation, which some individuals in changing situations find more trying than others. B Sr made this explicit:

My struggle about the professorship did not end with the appointment. As an internationale of missions, even as a scholar, I belonged to a different category all together from the other members of the faculty. Leaving the international work, and above all, leaving Africa was not an easy adjustment for me, not even for Ingeborg. In my diary I find notes about a continuing inner struggle, trying to get to the roots of it. I was glad I could write my struggle down in diaries. Writing in itself was then, as it still is now, a healing process for me. Yet there were deep crevices in my innermost soul I failed to reach. (Letter to MLS 12 June 1982)

Both Bengt and Ingeborg found the retreats to be the right places for them to meditate and to seek inner peace. Hjälmseryd and Rättvik were two places where they found solace, but also St Julian's in southern England and also in Limuru, Kenya, while in East Africa. I quote from Bengt's letters to Ingeborg from the Hjälmseryd retreat in May 1952.

These weeks are a wonderful gift for me which I use in prayer and self-examination to seek to start a new life. I believe that it is succeeding. Pray for me ... There is a wonderful small twelfth-century church here which has been totally forgotten but was restored in 1933. Very beautiful. Hector is a wonderful priest and soulcarer. Very refreshing and pious and fine. Can you not stop here on your way home? Take a car in Sälvsjö and stay here for a few days, it would be a very good idea. You should see Hjälmseryd, which is a very special church centre.

I hope, in all simplicity, to be able to go into the High Church [*det högkyrkliga*] seriously, without return. I believe it is as if it were created for me, it would mean doing it from the depth of my innermost intention and aim in life [*syftning*], to be Lord's priest and nothing more. I read English and Swedish soulcare literature for self-examination, and stay long periods in the church. I also go for walks. On Wednesday I walked for two-and-a-half hours. Tomorrow is Sunday. One has no idea about the calendar, only the church calendar here! Actually quite a wonderful rhythm of life.

Bengt was again in Hjälmseryd in January 1954 'It is an unbeliev-
able weakness in our church that a person like Hector cannot be given
better conditions to devote himself fully to his important task. [He had
to teach outside the centre to make a living.] Ours is an ailing church
in my opinion.'[20]

In 1956 B Sr finds that he has made a leap away from his state in
1950. He thinks he has found a form suitable to him to express his
spiritual yearnings and life:

> When I read now what I wrote during the first part of the 1950s I think
> of the months May and June 1952 with enormous gratitude for what they
> meant for me, a travel into my inner self. Totally decisive for my spir-
> itual life, three weeks on my knees in church. General confession, new
> start. The repeated contacts with Ingvar Hector, the best pastor in
> Sweden, as I deservedly call him. I became conscious of the catholicity
> of the Church, confession, communion, objectivity, that is my line.
> (Review of the early 1950s in B Sr diary 1956)

B Sr had experienced the universality and catholicity of the Church
in the mission of the Church. The Church incarnated Christ who
was God's mission into the world, to be the light of and in the
world.

> Mission is important for me because it incarnates the catholicity of the
> Church. I am sorry to say that some of my restlessness is left from 1950.
> Not so much restlessness as an inability to concentrate, in spite of the
> fact that I know this is life and happiness for me. But I have grown much
> since 1950, I see that I now have more peace, deeper inwardly, quieter
> and more carefree joy. (Diary 23 December 1956)

Writing was of central significance to B Sr in all phases of his life.
Not to be able to concentrate and see results was a cause of constant
anxiety for him, as we shall see later; it was also a worry in the
1950s. He had befriended some doctors whose reception rooms he
frequented, not always waiting for consultation hours but making use
of the friendship at other times of the day. In this, as in several other
major and minor incidents, he acted on strong and fleeting impulses
which he at times later regretted.

> I visited Dr John Björkhem, Saltsjö, Duvnäs. I had to talk with a good
> and wise person about my lack of concentration and my inhibitions in
> work. It was a good and pacifying situation, a good moment. Now I am
> thinking of getting *Bantu Prophets II* started at full speed. In the evening
> I listened to Lacretelle commenting on becoming a novel writer.
> Sincerity, devoting oneself entirely, totally, that is the recipe, it applies
> also to research work and studies, it seems to me. (Diary 1 December
> 1957)

In a letter February 1954 to Ingeborg who was in Tanganyika:

> I have been reading Bernanos' *Les Carmelites*, a very moving drama.
> He is a fascinating author. You remember his *Country Priest's Diary*. It
> would be very worthwhile if one could take more time to read more
> literature and follow questions relating to art and art history. I must start
> civilising myself more, you know!

B Sr felt increasingly that writing a diary was helpful to him and
from the year 1959 we can follow his day-to-day activities and
thoughts through his diaries:

> There were long periods in the 1950s when I could not keep diary. In
> 1959 I began in earnest. I need a diary for the sake of my soul, to clarify
> what is happening with me when the years fly past, so unbelievably fast.
> (Diary 11 January 1959)

Bengt Sundkler returned repeatedly to his 'difficult years' in the
1950s in later life, in letters, in diary notes and when being interviewed. He tried to penetrate his own personality and to understand
better the reasons for his actions and the sources from which he had
sought refuge. He became more critical toward the High-Church tradition, finding it too rigid, too uniform; he sought to become spiritually
free and liberated and appreciated openness in communication. After
his years as a bishop he also took a different stand from that of his
High-Church colleagues on the question of the ministry of the Church,
particularly on the question of women as priests. His constant remarks
on how each service he attended had been conducted reveal the need
to experience spirituality in every act of devotion and piety. He paid
similar attention to the content of sermons and freely expressed his
appreciation, or lack thereof. Here I quote some of the reflections
about the 1950s expressed in hindsight in the 1970s and 1980s.

B Sr wrote in retrospect about the 1950s in letters in 1973:

> I went to an ordinary check-up with a doctor some two weeks ago, and
> he found everything absolutely perfect, heart, lungs, everything. I just
> mentioned to him that I used to have this kind of anxiety which now is
> over and gone with. This also led me to High-Church lines and gave me
> that kind of a 'uniform' into which I somehow fitted, at least for some
> time. In fact until the time of my episcopal Bukoba years.
> The 1950s were unhappy for many reasons. I spent, for instance,
> untold years and energy on writing that book the *Christian Ministry in
> Africa*. It was a difficult book to write, but I wonder now why I should
> have at all bothered. My forte is straight history, such as the book on
> *Church Union in South India*, and perhaps biography, for I felt
> completely at home when writing on Nathan Söderblom. (Letter to MLS
> 2 March 1973)

My extensive travels, first to India, later on behalf of the Commission on Theological Education to Latin Africa took me out of the narrow parochial sphere. With my international experience and connections I had many other duties outside the faculty and university. I was involved in the resurgent Swedish influence in African affairs, in conferences and discussions. The travels in Africa, longer periods teaching at the Ecumenical Centre at Bossey as well as giving lectures and doing research in Britain were challenging experiences for me, but they took their toll.

Well, this time I take up a fundamental theme in my life, accommodation or doctrinaire insistence on a principle. Theologically the 1950s here were a very doctrinaire period. There was a doctrinaire streak in my make-up, having been influenced by the High-Church movement, and by my contacts also with the Anglicans in England, although they of course must not be held responsible for whatever aberrations I may have shown: they were always so very kind and helpful. (Letter to MLS 14 July 1982)

We have already referred to the public debate which B Sr got into with Gunnar Helander, former missionary in South Africa (p. 89). Sundkler implied that he was not psychologically strong enough to endure difficult public debates and that he would rather accommodate people. From time to time he referred to issues which he would have liked to comment on but refrained for fear of losing his mental stability. B Sr indicated that in later years he mellowed and saw life in a spectrum of many colours. He referred to Paul Tillich's influence on his thinking in the same letter but was going to elaborate that aspect later:

The accommodating tendency has become increasingly strong in me. It has perhaps something to do with my early life, measuring myself against the impression I had of my father. He was most often very rigid, could burst out into immature statements and then of course would fall prey to sentimental tendencies, all of it abhorrent to a young person. Eventually, I think, I tried to overcome any tendency towards rigidity, and trying to see that one has to try to understand all kinds of conditions of men, and that is perhaps what I call accommodating. (Letter to MLS 14 July 1982)

Nothing is easier than to let time fly past. I have a task to perform. No one else sees it. I am spoiled enough to think that people should give me encouragement for good deeds. What a bad joke, what a shameful attitude. No, I must in God and with God have my own inner strength, the wisdom to know that whatever the world does or does not think, I have my own line, and I have to a considerable degree the chance to follow it. I have so few ties, no responsibilities, no official obligations, totally forgotten by the church which I had wanted to serve – that much freer, also in my conscience, to carry through my literary ambitions.

I have my tasks, I have to grasp them anew, insist on them in my mind, face them. [Lists them again.] They seem to be a lot, but with discipline, order and secret joy in working I can do it. (Diary 19 October 1969)

In interviews on 7 August and 31 October 1985 B Sr discussed changes that had taken place in his person:

> There is this weakness in my character. I have gathered that in this intel-
> lectually difficult milieu you express yourself in a somewhat ironic way
> about other people. That goes to explain why some people have seen me
> as an ironic person. This is sad, particularly if I think of myself as a
> confessing Christian. I hope that in more recent years this has changed
> altogether. I think of myself as a happy person, and I hope to give the
> impression of being a happy person, an encouraging person all around.
>
> I have been told after the event of things that cannot be rectified. I
> had this little institute of mine where we had some good typists, some
> came for a few weeks. They saw me only as a professor who rushed by
> and never gave them a thought. Doris Falk, my long-time secretary at
> the institute, initially had great difficulties with me as an inconsiderate
> professor. I have been told this by Doris Falk with whom we later
> became good friends. In one or two cases I later tried to rectify things
> but did not succeed. Sad and bad, one can only pray that it will be taken
> care of by God himself.
>
> Of course, Ingeborg felt this nervousness and these problems I had
> more than anyone. To carry that burden, that is the only thing. But it
> was something about Africa and the African way of meeting others that
> disarmed me and made me enormously happy and thankful to be staying
> with these people, a privilege for me. I must say in my defence that the
> milieu of the 1950s in which I was living in Uppsala was very harsh,
> very difficult, two or three people sitting there doing everything they
> could to make things difficult for me. I suffered from the dead weight
> of sullen criticism and lack of encouragement in that early period. It
> hindered me so much. I should have overcome this, I did not.
>
> The background to this? I was 36 years old when we came home. This
> problem of not having children, Ingeborg felt this as an enormous
> problem. We were trying to help it, but it did not work out as we had
> hoped. That became a burden to us both and to our relationship. We
> then went to England in 1947–48, and found yet another life, an inter-
> esting stage of life. Ingeborg and I had close contact and work together,
> not altogether satisfying because of the conditions in which we lived. We
> were living far from London, one-and-a-half hours in a packed train in
> the morning. A miserable, cold house. IMC did not look after the people
> from outside. Other secretaries had been pastors in Anglican or other
> parishes and had places to go.
>
> I am now aware that writing a diary would have been of great help
> for me in getting some clarity into my life, it was unfortunately not easy
> for me.

B Sr had a deep sense of having a call to be a pastor or priest; he loved to preach, as we see from notes in his diary during the Epiphany season in 1959.

> I preached the Epiphany sermon for myself since no one asked me to
> come and preach. God, I must preach. *Kann auch ein Pastor selig*

werden? Ja, aber nur als Pastor! [Can also a pastor be saved? Yes, but only as a pastor.] (Diary 6 January 1959)

Reflecting back B Sr referred to the self-criticism which was recorded after every presentation as a kind of 'inverted competition'. A quote from Charles Pegny in the diary for 1950–60 expresses something of B Sr's feelings: 'Quarante ans est un age terrible! Forty is a terrible age.'

Looking toward a brighter 1960s

After closing the spring term of 1960, the difficult years seem to be over:

> I am much aware that I have dwelt only on the difficult sides in my past life, while there is much to say for the bright side, particularly after 1960–61.
> I have spent too much time in self-critique, to no effect. I am dissatisfied with everything I say or write. It is miserable. I overrate my own importance and significance. What I do does not measure up to the image which I paint of myself. That is why I torture myself for nothing, which gives no joy to anyone, least to myself. (Diary 22 March 1969)

> But what was wrong? I was generally dissatisfied with my achievements at the time. I did not aim at big enough things. I tended to think that if only I had had some encouragement, I could have done better. This is another way of admitting that I was not strong enough then. I compare this with later periods when all my writing has been radiated by the immense support and insight and help which you and Carl Fredrik Hallencreutz have given me. (Letter to MLS 29 February 1982)

The reader cannot fail to note the frequency with which B Sr refers to his good and intelligent friend, former student, later colleague and then successor as the professor of missions, Carl Fredrik Hallencreutz. He played a very important role, starting from the latter part of the 1960s, in providing the support and response which B Sr obviously depended on for his scholarly and literary work. It would appear that B Sr had lacked that kind of constant communicative and intellectual support in the difficult decade of the 1950s.

I end this section on the journey into Bengt Sundkler's inner self with a quote from an interview and a letter to the writer with a glance toward the better years which lay ahead:

> At last the 1950s came to an end through the call to Bukoba, and this proved to be a salvation to me: a new and happy solution for me as a person. Through the contact with the generous people in Bukoba it became a personality transforming experience for me. 1960s brought two liberating and joy giving experiences into my life: Meeting with the

African Church in Bukoba and getting to know the personality of Nathan
Söderblom. (2 March 1973)

Notes

1. Information not otherwise indicated is based on interviews by MLS 13 January
   1978 and 7 August 1985 and autobiographical notes attached to a letter dated 16
   July 1982.
2. The account is put together from several interviews and earlier written accounts
   by B Sr. I follow the interview recorded on 31 October 1985 and Tore Furberg's
   article of 1998, where other sources are not mentioned.
3. Letter to B Sr's father, Gustaf Sundkler 15 August 1949.
4. The university council consisted of the heads of all the faculties who were not
   knowledgeable about the substance and quality of the applicants' work. They
   could thus be convinced by external arguments.
5. Review in the early 1950s in diary 1956:31–41. I record this since it affected
   B Sr's psychological well-being afterwards.
6. From the beginning of the 1950s B Sr began intermittently to keep a diary. Many
   notes do not have a date, at times even the year is not obvious. The quotes in
   this chapter are from the diary for 1950–60, unless otherwise indicated.
7. Myrdal, Gunnar, 1970. *Objectivity in Social Research*. Duckworth & Co. Ltd,
   London. 'Disinterested social science has never existed and, for logical reasons,
   can never exist.' p.55.
8. The whole trip is well recorded in letters to Ingeborg and in a diary, not quoted
   here.
9. The 'Derby' report (of the Bishop of Derby), The South India Church Scheme,
   1946.
10. B Sr himself was at the time a Social Democrat in Sweden.
11. Ingeborg had flown to the Cameroon where they had agreed to meet. From there
    she flew to the French Congo and the Belgian Congo where she had Swedish
    missionary friends from the Mission Covenant Church *Missionsförbundet* (SMF).
    They met in Usumbura (Bujumbura) Burundi whence they drove to Bukoba and
    then on to Machame, Kilimanjaro. They also visited the Ashira Teacher Training
    College where I was teaching at that time.
12. Herbert Tingsten of *Dagens Nyheter* had written a strong critique of South Africa
    after the 1948 elections and several articles in his paper. He had been surpris-
    ingly positive about the CSM.
13. Vadstena was the seat of St Brigit nunnery where services were held in commem-
    oration of her on certain festive days.
14. Åke Holmberg later became Professor of History at Gothenburg.
15. 'Bengt Sundkler – *Hans liv och hans diktning*' (His Life and Writings).
16. Parts in parentheses contain the meaning, rather than word for word quotes from
    the lecture.
17. I quote from the history of the Ashira Girls School: 'The First All-Africa
    Lutheran Conference . . . came as a crowning glory to our year's work. The girls
    contributed by offering hands and feet in preparations and felt greatly honoured
    to be able to sing at the first Sunday's service. The entire Ashira staff played a
    part in the preparations as well as the daily work connected with the conference.
    The greater load was carried by the Marangu Teacher Training Centre . . . Ashira
    housed about 50 delegates. We prepared our dormitories by whitewashing walls,
    making new mattresses, and borrowing steel beds. The girls sewed 260 new
    sheets and 139 pillow cases. Ashira staff members were assigned the information
    and registration responsibilities. In addition to receiving and registering delegates
    we set up a checking service for valuables and larger amounts of money, a lost

and found department. At the desk we offered information about travel, exchanging money, laundry service and also managed incoming and outgoing mail and sold stamps! We prepared the packets of pertinent programme materials, meal tickets and room assignments. We also provided a canteen through which we sold tea, coffee, breads, cookies and candies. Missionary wives ... provided and served all the meals ... Most of the daily requirements came (i.e. had to be brought) from Moshi, 25 miles away, eight miles of which were under construction, with a diversion through a sisal estate. The weather was beautiful giving a beautiful view of Kilimanjaro every day. (Moris, Juliet, Boise 1998)

18. B Sr had several opportunities to meet both the old and the future king. He had been also presented to the King of England while serving in the IMC in London. Of that meeting he briefly notes that the Queen had asked, 'A missionary, what is that?' possibly thinking that England did not need any missionaries!

19. Nkrumah gave his speech on 29 December 1957. The Ghana Assembly was held 28 December 1957–8 January 1958.

20. Excerpts from letters to Ingeborg 24 May 1952, and 16 January, 5 February, 7 February and 26 February of 1954. Most of the letters have been translated by me from Swedish to English.

7

METROPOLIS AND AFRICA

Africa from a central perspective

I devote this chapter to Bengt Sundkler's scholarly work which related to Africa in the 1960s and 1970s, after *Bantu Prophets*, breaking slightly from the chronological order. His own story of the participation in the Latin African Commission was expanded on in Chapter 6. He shared with his African friends an interest in dreams; I have included their significance for the ministry in this chapter. These involvements belong chronologically to the period of B Sr's professorship. As we have seen, these deviations from his task as a teacher of Church history with missions are indicative of the difficulty he had in trying to accommodate 'field work' and practical experience with his being a 'professor among the students'.

B Sr intended the chapter 'Metropolis and Africa' to contain more than he managed to write himself. In his own autobiography he followed a chronological sequence when he included the writing of the first draft of the book on South India under the title of this chapter. He reflected that the Church of South India could become a concrete ecumenical model for the churches in Africa and elsewhere.

I interpret 'Metropolis and Africa' in two ways. Firstly, it reflects the divided identity of Bengt Sundkler. He felt strongly that he was part of the African continent and of the African people, yet at the same time he belonged to the holders of knowledge at the centre, the Metropolis, in his scholarship and in his close connections with the academic centres and with mission headquarters. As a bishop in Africa he referred to himself as 'a slightly greying man, fostered and formed by Western university life and thought,' while he also stated, 'I had much closer contact and fellowship with "the people" and with my co-workers, centrally and locally, than could ever be achieved by Western "experts" in the capital.' (See Chapter 8)

Secondly, I interpret Metropolis to mean the seat of White self-claimed superiority in relation to Africa, not only claiming political power but also power of knowledge and forms of faith over the younger churches which were born as the fruit of proclamation of the Gospel through word and service. This Centre was very different from the *omphalos*, of which Bengt Sundkler had written in his youth, the Centre from which Christ's power radiated through his cross. In the title 'Metropolis and Africa', Africa represented to Bengt Sundkler human warmth, community, creativity illustrated in the beauty of the hymns of Shembe on Ekuphakameni. 'Metropolis and Africa' indicates tension, including creative tension, between the two poles which Bengt Sundkler with his African friends, and others like them, have sought to join in a new kind of partnership.

He did not view the creativity which he found in African society as a return to tradition. Great emphasis on advancement in education was one form of evidence of it, as was the joy he received in discovering new ways of organising, new institutional possibilities and the new structures which Africa represented, not least for the universal church. He envisaged ecumenical possibilities within churches unburdened with the same kind of tradition-bound rigidity which he had met in the confessional churches of Metropolis. He saw that the churches in Africa could become bridging churches in bringing together the established church bodies which no longer had any expectation of the possibilities offered by the spiritual reality.

Challenge of independent churches

Whose Christ?[1] This question brought to Bengt Sundkler's mind a meeting with a Zulu journalist in Johannesburg of which he wrote in several contexts:

> 'There is one thing we sometimes wonder about,' he said, and hurriedly pulled his brown knitted hat down over his wrinkled forehead. He was Theofilus M., an editor of an African newspaper, an intense 30-year-old African intellectual, intelligent, quick-witted and with wide contacts among present-day Africans [i.e. 1960]. 'We wonder sometimes,' he repeated thoughtfully, 'whether we might not have got the wrong God. It might have been better if we had had our own God.'
> I thought for a moment about the Christian name he had been given in Holy Baptism – for he was a Christian and, in common with the entire modern generation of African intellectuals the continent over, had been to the mission school. It was not a Bantu name, Theofilus, – 'Loved by God'. Yes, but loved by which God? Could it be the White man's God, when the chasm between the White and Black was yawning wider and wider with every passing day, in an apartheid-ruled South Africa?
> He took me with him to the Africans' own church, a cold and draughty little shack – this was in June, winter in Johannesburg. A layman was preaching and quoted Mt. xxv:1–3. 'So shall it be with the Kingdom of Heaven, as when ten virgins took their lamps and went out to meet the bridegroom. But five were white and five were black. The whites took their lamps with them, but forgot to take any oil. But the

blacks took oil with them in their vessel ... At last they came and shouted, "Lord, open the door for us!" But he answered and said, "Verily, I say unto you, I know you not!"'

The very name of Jesus lost its power over the minds of many. The Jehovah of the Old Testament became the powerful, unifying name. Behind the shield of the name of Jehovah, the Bantu prophet who arose in their midst, was identified with Jehovah. The White man's Sunday Jesus had to make way for the Jehovah of the Sabbath – merely a covering name for the prophet in their midst – who had become the Black Messiah standing at the Gate of Heaven.

The question of White Christ leaves nobody in peace. It becomes intense on the night between Easter Eve and Easter Day. In the churches of South Africa, both in the mission churches and in the separatist groups, the command to 'Watch with Christ' is taken literally. During the course of Easter Night, 1958, I travelled from eight in the evening until eight the next morning from chapel to chapel in the Orlando district of Johannesburg, and heard there how mission churches and separatist groups struggled with the problem of White Christ. Is this Jesus really a Mediator and Saviour for Africans too?

'Whose church?' Sundkler's identification with the independent churches was authentic, but it had to be also selective:

Ever since I came to Africa 45 years ago, I have felt close to the people of Africa and I have received so much from them. But oh, what stupidity they have had to put up with from us Whites. I sympathise so much with them and can only hope that at some point there will be some genuine reconciliation, but that can come only in the name and the blood of Christ. I identified myself with Bantu prophets and saw in them an effort to break with the African slavery of the European forms, creating new forms. They made the church a home for the African soul. As I carry on reading about this history of the Church in Africa, I feel that they have intuitively grasped so much of the real thing, in their prayers and in their worship. (Letter to MLS 17 March 1982)

While B Sr was ready to see the value in the forms of worship in independent churches, at the same time he was also fully aware of the weak side in the breaking up of the universal church into small splinter groups, each with its own little tradition and freedom to experiment with any kind of belief. In an interview B Sr said that he had come from a situation in which the independent churches of South Africa had made, from one point of view, the idea of a self-governing church into a caricature. Anybody could go out of the mission-related church and form his own church. While B Sr was very careful not to judge them he believed that ecclesiastically this phenomenon was much of a caricature. (Interview with Tiina Ahonen 2 November 1990) By bringing together the local leaders of the independent churches, when he was a missionary in Zululand, to study the Bible and to discuss their commonalties and differences he did not attempt to bring them into the denomination he represented, but to give them a sense of all belonging to one and the same universal church tradition despite their differences.

Throughout his life B Sr struggled with the issue of free expression for local cultural and spiritual forms while not losing the wholeness and togetherness. His motto in Chesterton's words, 'For anything to be real it must be local', expressed part of this struggle. He defended strongly the 'flesh and blood reality' of local situations. Already in *Ung kyrka i Tanganyika,* written in 1943 but not published until 1948, B Sr emphasised the local differences found even within the same districts. According to Lars Thunberg, for B Sr episcopacy as an order of the Church offered more flexibility than the other centralised forms of church government:

> Although Sundkler is a strong defender of an episcopal structure, it is not the need for uniformity which forces him to make a special plea for it . . . it is rather the non-formal, uninstitutional character of episcopacy which, beside its being part of the catholic heritage, makes him prefer it to any other form of church government.

B Sr also saw a tendency toward some form of episcopacy in the independent churches, as well as relation with kings and generational continuity, when the churches became older. (B Sr 1948:150; Thunberg 1974:219–21)

> The strait-jacket of White worship did not suit these churches. New forms for the new faith had to be found. This was a problem for the Church everywhere, throughout the continent of Africa. There was a search for a place where the individual could 'feel at home' and where African rhythm and conviction could be expressed freely, convincingly and worthily. I have always felt that the Independent Churches have much to contribute to the treasure-house of the Church Universal, and therefore could not but try to understand and interpret their life and faith.
>
> Ama-Ziyoni they call themselves. Wherever they live and move in Southern Africa, their white garments with the green and blue sash and the wooden crozier give them away as 'the people of Zion' . . . a Black Zion, a charismatic religious movement of Africans, the beginnings of which go back to the first years of this century. Most of them are conscious of a historical link with 'Zion' in the United States, an apocalyptic healing movement formed by John Alexander Dowie.
>
> We are told that in South Africa, African Independent Churches number at least 3 million adherents. It is likely that, of these, at least 2 million are women, and it can be safely taken for granted that way over 1 million are part of the white-dressed, crozier-carrying army of Zionist women . . . I am aware of the fact that in Africa, and not least in the 'homelands' of South Africa, the Church was a women's movement. It functioned as a form of Women's Lib, long before that term was invented.[2] (B Sr 1976:5–7; 79)

What's in a name?

Bengt Sundkler was often asked to speak and lecture on the Independent Churches. One of the issues was what to call them. Early during his first stay in South Africa we recall that he was corrected by a theological student for using the word 'sect'. In the texts quoted he called them 'separatist churches'. In a letter to Professor David Bosch, in which he declined an invitation to attend a conference on 'The Challenge of the Independent Churches' and regretted that he could not take part, he took up the question of the name again, pointing out that also former mission-related churches were independent, thus a different name has to be found.[3]

> The name – 'African Independent Churches' – is generally accepted as a useful term ... If I remember rightly I had something to do with suggesting the term almost half a century ago. This is a long time. In the meantime things have changed, particularly in Africa north of the Limpopo. In my present work on the Church History of Africa I have been led to question the usefulness of this term, 'African Independent Churches,' and yet I cannot find a good substitute[4] ... but where African nations are independent and where the churches long since are as a matter of course led by Africans it increasingly becomes a problem whether one should any longer use this term at all as a distinguishing mark. So, for instance, the majority of mission-related churches in West Africa are African churches and as independent as you could wish – or not wish, as the case may be. In what sense are the Aladura in West Africa more 'independent' than their Methodist or Baptist or Lutheran neighbours? Yes, you are right, in the latter case, the historical background and present international and ecumenical fellowship with churches overseas play their part. Yet, there is at present a continent-wide effort on the part of the Independents to come together on some ecumenical basis, within Africa and beyond, and these efforts may very soon become much more important than we can at present imagine. The dividing lines which existed will thus be blurred.
>
> I have no name to suggest and must therefore continue for a while to use the term, 'African Independent Churches'. Even as I do so, it is a reminder of the provisional character of all our terms.
>
> In attempting to deal with the question of the African separatist churches, we must remember that the situation is both fluid and dramatic – a fact which was brought home to me every day in the field. We are dealing with things of the Spirit, which 'bloweth where it listeth', transcending and breaking through any wall of doctrine or organisation.

In writing on subjects relating to other peoples' faith and culture B Sr never tired of warning against water-tight definitions and fixed terminology. When he had cause to stress that even the established churches change he had much more reason to remind the readers and his audience when speaking of that fact in relation to the independent churches with which he had become intimately familiar:

The Zionist churches became a refuge, providing for an emotional outlet and, in the apartheid system, sustaining the Utopian dream. The problem with these churches was to be recognised. They sent their constitutions to the government office in order to be registered according to Article 114. In 1925–63 some were recognised when they sent reports to the state every year. Two thousand of them were in the archives. They had their own printed constitutions on the basis of which they were tolerated. They needed this to be able to build their own churches. Otherwise they met in mission churches, garages or tents. In the homelands they had their own centres. (Lecture in Helsinki 4 April 1972)

Three thousand distinct groups or one big movement?[5]

'For my own convenience I tend to regard them not as an amorphous sum of different churches but rather as a movement – with certain local and personal varieties.' 'For my own convenience' is an intriguing way of making an important statement. It could indeed be interpreted as a convenient way of getting out of the dilemma which the independent churches presented to one whose primary goal was the unity of churches. On the other hand, the truth value of that statement depends on the interpretation that is given to the concept 'movement'. Social movements do not necessarily have organisational links, they can be also ideologically linked.[6]

To take an example: the common historical roots of the Nkonyane and of the Lekganyane Zionists indicate that they are closely related and parts of a larger whole ... Yet, apart from some of these special cases, it can be held, I would suggest, that a great many of the Zionists together form one big movement rather than a number of distinct local organisations ...

The very existence of these numerous churches is indeed a challenge to the life and witness of the mission-related churches in Africa. One cannot but be impressed by the exuberance and creativity of some Zionist or Aladura or Kimbanguist churches.

Their numbers – in the thousands in Southern Africa and in West Africa – are an intriguing fact, and every new year seems to initiate hundreds of new member churches into their lively family – while it is conveniently forgotten that in the meantime quite a few among them have quietly petered out or have been absorbed by other more or less related groups. This is where I would like to question certain South African church statistics. Limiting the argument to the Zionist groups, I acknowledge a debt of gratitude to those South African scholars who have helpfully exposed the variety of tradition and expression within this group.

I realise that this generalising view cannot comprise the total sum of the charismatic churches. There are church leaders with a distinct programme of their own, very different from the other charismatics. Thus Isaiah Shembe stands out as a great creative religious personality in his own right and there are others beside him. Should a Zulu scholar come along to write a study of Shembe's hymnbook – that most surprising and marvelous poetic statement of faith and interpretation of vision – then we could expect great things.

Yet, apart from some of these special cases, it can be held, I would suggest, that a great many of the Zionists together form one big movement rather than a number of distinct organisations. (*Missionalia* 1984:3–4)

Zulu and Swazi Zionists

Bantu Prophets saw its second edition in 1961 and became a classic. The German translation was published in 1964. B Sr was told by a professor at the University of Grahamstown that he had started an 'industry', so many new scholars turned up studying the same topic, coming out with new theories and interpretations. His own reserve of field and archival material and all the data from Swaziland which he had collected during his stay in South Africa in 1958 had to wait until he made another study tour to South Africa and *Zulu Zion and some Swazi Zionists* appeared in 1976. B Sr set himself a timetable which he followed closely, sending chapters for reading to Professor Marcia Wright, my husband and myself in Dar es Salaam:

> Now July is at an end ... I have more or less been able to stick to my timetable and finish this chapter, a great and terribly interesting chapter on Swaziland before [my own] deadline. I am as always very, very pleased with myself. Because now, as from 1 August, I can turn to the first chapter in this *BZ*,[7] the one to be called 'At the Source of Living Waters'. I shall begin with something on the place names of South Africa, all these Stroom, rivier, wells and fountains: the place names reveal the ecological foundation-fact: lack of water, thirst for water, water the fundamental thing for life ... I hope to be able to finish these first two chapters in this month of August, with a gallery of preachers, prophets and healers, where I can throw them in, one and all, short sketches, the kind of thing which I always enjoy doing. (Letter to MLS 31 July 1973)

Revisiting his 'gallery of prophets, preachers and healers' gave B Sr an opportunity to elaborate on Shembe's hymnology and to introduce other individual leaders, not least women charismatics in the independent church movement.

> So today (1 July 1973) I have worked hard at my *Black Zion*. I woke up with a brilliant idea, which fortunately I can demonstrate. I begin with the chapter on Shembe and his hymnbook. It struck me that the hymnbook is really about Ekuphakameni, Shembe's own Zion, but not future eschatology as with other Zionists, rather realised eschatology, for Ekuphakameni is bliss here and now. I have worked through the 250

hymns today, all in Zulu. The whole thing is indeed really about Ekuphakameni, and life there, Ekuphakameni, and the condition of man. This will be infinitely more worthwhile than any other approach. (Letter to MLS 1 July 1973)

I can tell you I have had to struggle hard of late for the free half-hours to carry out the writing of my chapters for *BZ*. In fact, I have to steal time from others, for I should really take time to correct the manuscripts of my doctorands and carry them along! (Letter to MLS 11 September 1973)

B Sr disliked interpretations which turned poetic expressions into a dogma. He was particularly critical of the approach Professor Oosthuizen had taken and was initially much sharper in responding to Oosthuizen's criticism of *Bantu Prophets*, but softened his criticism considerably in *Zulu Zion*:

Professor G. C. Oosthuizen, of Durban, wrote a study of Shembe's hymns, entitled *The Theology of a Zulu Messiah* (1967), where the author makes this claim: 'The Izihlabelelo should be considered as the catechism of the movement.'[8] He places all of Shembe's great poetry into a terrible straight jacket of European dogmatism. We suggest that one should discard such heavy and learned Western panoply and let Shembe walk along as he used to and loved to: moving light, barefoot ... Shembe's 'Hymns of the Nazarites' ... is religious poetry of great beauty. It was born not in the dogmatician's writing desk, but in song, carried by the incessant rhythm of drums, shaped in order to be sung while dancing. (B Sr 1976:186)

I am against all the Laternaris and Barretts of this world who, lacking any knowledge of the real life of these churches, concoct any number of books and articles on them. The same applies to Bryan R. Wilson etc. I cannot even read that kind of thing any longer, I am sorry to say.
    As compared to these sweeping overviews, I claim that there is a place for the local study. Then the Laternaris can again happily carry on with their spinning of the threads of thin theory. (Letter to MLS in response to comments on the draft of ZZ 12 April 1975)

In *Zulu Zion* B Sr made an important move in no longer looking at the Independent Churches as bastions of tradition, but as a move forward: 'to those in the movement, Zion meant newness of life, health and wholeness, a new identity. If it was a bridge, it appeared to them as a bridge to the future.'(ZZ:316)

Dreams as channels of God's call[9]

Again characteristic of B Sr is that he sees as beneficial the visitations of the Latin Africa Commission to what were then French and

Portuguese colonial countries in that they gave the members the opportunity to listen.

When speaking about vocation to priesthood in his diocese, a distinguished East African bishop had remarked, 'I am glad if and when any of our candidates mention anything else but dreams when applying for ordination. They have all first seen themselves appearing in liturgical vestments in a dream.' This was probably an exaggerated account of conditions in that particular diocese and is therefore not necessarily of universal validity, but an African principal of a leading East African theological seminary also insisted that most of the candidates had been called through dreams. Similarly, the late Bishop Akinyele of Ibadan, Nigeria, told the commission members that the majority of the men who offered themselves for the ministry 'had seen themselves in a white surplice and therefore wished to be ordained'.

B Sr introduced the theme 'Dreamlife on the borderline between heathendom and Christianity' in his first book on Africa, *Ung kyrka i Tanganyika* (pp.223–8). He calls for a study of African dream life in the lives of contemporary pastors and church leaders. His thoughts on the significance of dreams for the ministry in Africa deserve to be quoted here, knowing his interest also in his own dreams which he frequently wrote down in his diaries and letters:

One misses an important aspect of what is understood as constituting a vocation to the ministry in Africa if the dream is overlooked as a channel of God's call. Generally speaking, this critical attitude to dreams is not typical of conditions in the Churches in Africa. [In] a theological school in Liberia ... students were convinced of the authority of dreams. We felt in discussion with them on this particular issue that they considered Westerners (including Westernised African pastors) unable to understand the workings of the African mind.

The close relationship of dream and vocation was succinctly expressed in the autobiography of a friend of mine, O. N., an evangelist in the Lake Victoria area. '*Mambo hutokea*,' he said, '*na mambo yatokeayo, kwanza yaotwa katika ndoto; baadaye hutokea.*' Here, in his Swahili, he has carefully formulated a psychological law, a law of dreams: 'Things happen, and things that happen have first been dreamed in a dream; then they happen.' He referred to the dreams that had preceded his own joining the ranks of the catechists.

There are certain stereotypes in the manifest contents of these vocational dreams. Some describe their dream apparitions as 'Visions of light' ... or the dreamer has seen himself in a white surplice standing in a church; or again, the dreamer has seen a deceased person, such as a missionary or the dreamer's father, in a shining heavenly robe. This motif is modified by various details.

Another stereotype is based on the experience of climbing a mountain, or struggling out of a pit. On the top of the mountain there appears a theological college, a scene of ordination or a service of baptism in which the dreamer takes a leading part, the logic of the dream being quite evident.

Many dreams seem to symbolise a struggle between dark powers and the power of the White Christ. One of the most intense African preachers whom I ever met – a strong, highly assertive personality – relates a dream which, though individually modified, is amazingly representative of many such dreams: 'I saw a mass of people divided into two groups, and they struggled about me. The one group consisted of the old ones from long ago in my clan (the spirits of the departed), and the others were strangers, clad in very shining white clothes and they had crosses in their hands. One group took one of my hands, and the other group the other and they pulled as at tug-of-war. But the strangers won and brought me with them, and they sang a joyful victory song.'

In a study of Separatist Churches in South Africa we attempted to show the importance of dreams in modern Bantu syncretistic groups, where in fact the guided dream becomes a vital factor in the life of the Church ... It would be misleading to ignore the dimension of dreams as one of the channels used by God as He calls His men and women to serve the Church in Africa. We have seen how, in certain sections and at certain levels of the churches, the authority of dreams is rejected. The actual material found for our study has convinced us that under the conventionally Westernised surface there lie deeper levels to our problem, and visions and dreams offer a key to these hidden depths.

The latent content in the hidden recesses of the mind, of which this manifest content is a symbol, remains unknown to us, as we do not sufficiently know the personalities whose moral struggles have expressed themselves in these dreams.

Only the utter rationalist would, however, fail to appreciate the importance of this dimension. For, after all, we are here dealing, not primarily with mere organisation, even less with material things; we are dealing with religion, and are trying to understand the workings of the inner being of African man as he responds to the call of the God of all men.

Dreams and visions are like dew on gossamer shining in the early morning in a clearing in the African bush. They are made of the most fine and delicate stuff, and they reveal the hidden hunger for beauty and holiness and a sacred rhythm of life. The drab and formal Western-style worship in the rough and ready chapel is not always an ideal home for the souls that have caught a glimpse of this wonderful world of vision. Those who attempt to help build the Church in Africa should not be afraid of making it, as far as possible, and in the terms of the Scripture, a 'court of heaven'.

Significantly, B Sr notes that dreams did not imply any mystified relationship between the leader and the led nor continued dependence on revelation through dreams as it might have been for a traditional practitioner whose divination depended on dreams.

With a background of vivid vision and dazzling dream one would expect, perhaps, the resultant ministry to emphasise a mystical relationship between leader and led. Generally speaking, this has never been the case, which perhaps demonstrates the great controlling influence of Western missionary organisation on the first formative generations in the life of the African Church. For the future one might possibly infer that the more missionary control is replaced by African leadership, the more scope will be found for ministry which will tend to put its particular emphasis on the relationship between the shepherd and his flock.

The last sentence refers to the possibility that, in the mission-related churches also, the same development might take place which B Sr found in the independent churches, where what he called the guided dream became a vital factor. Only dreams which fitted into the accepted dream pattern were remembered. 'They dream what their church expects them to dream.' (Sundkler, 1961:273)[10] I find no further indication in B Sr's studies that this development would have taken place in the course of indigenisation of the originally mission-related churches. On the other hand, something similar to this appeared within the revival movement in the Interlacustrine region where one could speak of 'guided confession'. Patterns of confession occurred, taking guidance from a leader or from what several others confessed; the confessing individual in his inner search began to feel that he or she had also committed that sin. As dreams remembered so also sins committed were selectively given significance.

Theology of translation

The concept 'Theology of translation' was central to B Sr's theory and practice because, as he wrote, 'mission is translation'. It did not only mean translating a message from one language to another or one culture to another. God translated his love into material and human form in his Son. The church continues this translation of the Word into poor human language, deeds of love and material form in all cultures. B Sr wrote articles and gave numerous lectures around the subject and was frequently asked to discuss the topic in terms of cultural translation with different categories of development workers and missionaries going out to Africa. The topic became the subject of heated debate within the Marxist scholarship and the media influenced by it. When the development work advanced and both the theoretical and practical aspects of translating development into the languages of other cultures became evident the critique toned down. The failures of many UN and various economic, financial and military global 'missions' have given the world community a better understanding of the difficulties in cross-cultural communication as well as of the necessity to create human bonds based on love not hate.

> The Christian church recognises being essentially and necessarily alien in every culture. Ultimately she is a 'heavenly colony' as Moffat retranslated the word in Phil. 3:20. But the Church must also trans-late her message. Mission is translation in its widest sense, translation to new ways of expressing things in language, culture, art, or in

human fellowship and working life ... African church leaders are demanding that the African heritage must be given more space in church. A leading Presbyterian pastor in Ghana ... claims for the Church the right to acknowledge and take seriously the supernatural spirit world which the Africans believe to exist.

Professor Busia in Ghana, one of Africa's great Christian laymen, professor in sociology, and African representative in the ecumenical movement, has made a serious statement about the position of the Christian church in Africa today [in 1958], which is made even more serious because of the seeming capacity of Islam to identify itself with the African: 'For all their influence, the Christian Churches are still alien institutions.' Yet within Africa we often meet the same tension in Islam between the locally adapted brotherhood groups under an African marabou and the reform movements in Egypt and concentration on scholarly Arabic in Islamic centres of high learning.

Things have changed since. Africa is often quoted as being the most Christian continent on this globe. But the Church is a young plant in the new Africa. There is little left of the earlier Roman Catholic missions in the Congo from the fifteenth and sixteenth centuries. At the beginning of the new millennium African churches are celebrating their 100- and 150-year anniversaries, many are even younger. Mission school became the throughway to Western culture and value system, the gate to Western civilisation. The clinic and hospital became the saver of lives in need of healing. [In 1958] Busia expressed this aspect in these words, 'There hardly are any African members of parliament or civil servants who have not at least at some point in their lives gone to a mission school.' (*SMT* 47,1959:23–4)

Kaija Honkala, a Finnish student doing her research for Master's degree on B Sr's mission theology, wanted to know Professor Sundkler's thoughts on the various efforts known in mission history to put into practice 'theology of translation'. The quotes below are taken from her taped interview 11 April 1972.[11]

In my ministry and theology I emphasised the urgency of the need for a theology of translation, based on experience. In the rapid change new generations of African church leaders who had studied in Europe and USA were taking over. They were suspicious of European initiatives taken in the spirit which they judged to be hollow. The time of colonialism is past. In the 1960s we said we now want Africans to use African music, drums. It was not acceptable just because it was initiated by European missionaries. 'We claim it our right to create the rhythm and tune of our worship based on our own understanding. It must be our responsibility based on our experience. Now we are going to determine how our churchlife has to be permeated.'

Missionaries have made many moves toward 'indigenisation' in their effort to translate the Gospel to other cultures. More than anybody Christian Kaiser, whom I met in Neuendettelsau, impressed me. He worked in Papua New Guinea. I think he was even better than Bruno Gutmann in Chaggaland, Kilimanjaro, who is better known for his efforts to 'tribalise' Christianity. Both had studied German Ethnology under Wilhem Wundt and were influenced by European romanticism; these background factors influence what we are trying to do. We are accused of being romanticists whatever we are trying to do. It is not only a theological question. It is perhaps shocking that I am so little oriented to theological problems. I am very pragmatic; I am not even ashamed of being pragmatic!

Gutmann's problem was that he was a loner, a unique case and was not followed by other European missionaries or by Africans. His fundamental weakness was to neglect higher theological education as he was afraid of emerging African eliticism. He depended entirely on the self-expression of a group as such. His main emphasis was good for the time. He was trying to arrive at the best possible solution. Of the British missionaries working on indigenisation, I had the privilege of meeting, in southern Tanzania, Bishop Lucas of Masasi from the UMCA. I worked with him in the Tanzanian Missionary Council which he chaired and I admired him greatly. I was present at his funeral in Johannesburg on 11 July 1945.

The Church becomes local in the line of incarnation. Potentially it is expressed when the Church follows its master in the line of incarnation. As Christ had to be incarnated in Bethlehem, the churches have to adopt a local or national form, loyal to national forms. The church is living in tension in a perspective of internationalism and change, it is important to the totality of the church.

In another interview Sundkler pointed out that cultural differences could be very local and that the churches also could adopt different practices on the basis of their different traditional accents. In Bukoba the church combined liturgical consciousness and personal revivalism which appealed to people there; they had a living and obviously functioning group movement, but because of the differences in their local backgrounds and people and historical 'accidents' which had influenced them the differences could be also locally specific within the same ethnic or even clan area. (Interview by MLS 13 January 1978)

Lars Thunberg pointed out that B Sr had already expressed this view in 1943:

Missionaries thinking in a Western way like to think that organising and uniformalising are the missionary's noblest task. A worship form or an organisational form which have grown naturally in a congregation in co-operation between an enthusiastic leader and his group often misses its freshness and its spirit when it is carried over to the whole field. The congregations have their individual character. This is a truth which cannot be stressed too much ... There is a big difference between a Kianja man and a man from Ihangiro with regard to historical background and sociological conditions. This individuality should be granted its proper space in the Church, and it will be, as long as and in so far as the Haya leaders themselves have a decisive influence in their own church, because for them the uniformity dictated from a writing desk is not the highest wisdom. They ask for what in each case and in each place is sustainable. On the other hand, in the very nature of the Haya

Church there is a tendency, not toward uniformity, but unity in plurality, toward an overarching unity of the individual congregations. (B Sr 1948:150)

Expectation and not-yet-time

In different contexts B Sr brought up the concept 'not-yet-time'. Starting from his personal experience in the Lutheran mission in South Africa and his first letter to the mission director after two months in the field, he worked up considerable personal anxiety over the attitude of 'not-yet'. His emphasis was on learning from the people wherever he was, travelling with a little note book as visible evidence that he was noting down what he learned and with whom he talked on each occasion. He encouraged these same people to trust their own knowledge, and above all, to develop their knowledge, thinking and expression. He aimed at providing people with opportunities to direct the course of their work and take over leadership positions as soon as possible. His push for the individual's advancement in education in general, and theological education in particular for the leaders of the Church, had the same goal. His engagement in the practical work of the Church offered him opportunities that mission theorists did not ordinarily have. The following quotes are from an early draft piece from his African Church History (ACH) sent to the writer.

> Two factors, closely intertwined, silently and unknowingly yet effectively determined the life of the churches and what there was of real growth in them. These factors, Time and Expectation, are always determining developments, yet their influence, positive or negative, seemed greater in the period 1920–60 than ever before and affected this continent [Africa] more than any other place. Strangely, these two intertwined factors showed their indispensable urgency even more by their absence than by their presence.
>
> 'We have time' was the confident proclamation of the Westerners. Cecil Rhodes had launched the theme in the first years of the century by his brash claim, 'I give myself four thousand years.'
>
> Half a century later a leading Belgian socialist, van Bijlsen, a radical of this period, projected the future of the Belgian colony, then called the Belgian Congo. In 1985 that country was to celebrate the centenary of Belgian rule. It was time, van Bijlsen suggested, to give the Congolese (soon to be referred as the Zaireans) their independence in that far-off year, 1985. Almost as soon as this startling and in Belgium highly unpopular, proposal got off the printing presses, the Congo became Zaire, and the revolution was on.
>
> In the churches the message with regard to time was largely 'not yet'. Henry Venn's and Rufus Anderson's programme in the 1850s was self-government and eventual 'euthanasia' of the missions, but when the matter of self-government was brought up in the councils and committees of the churches, the reaction was largely 'Not Yet'.

Not that this pusillanimity was exclusively a White view. It permeated into the African synods as well, enfeebling and debilitating. In 1946, just after the Second World War, the Basel Mission field secretary suggested to the General Synod in the Cameroon that from now on the president of the Synod must be elected from among the African leaders. This was refuted by the majority of the Synod with the assertion that the time ... had not yet arrived. The Basel Mission, however, insisted and in the General Synod of 1950, the Reverend Peter Essoka was elected. The point about this decision is that in both 1946 and 1950 the initiative ... came from the Metropolis, from Basel.

In this issue of leadership, the tension between the Metropolis and the leaders on the spot turned on its head throughout these decades. The former, informed and alarmed by the Anderson–Venn Precepts about the self-governing church were able, with their perspective of distance, to insist on 'Transfer Now'; the latter having spent a life-time in the African field and knowing Africans of yester-year, were sure that the time was not yet. [Reference to example in Ceza.]

Time, we say, was intertwined with expectation and the idea 'not yet time' was a way of implying a lack of expectation. This lack of expectation has been the most serious deficiency in the Western approach to Africa in this century, as well as in the White missions and their approach to the African church.

The two World Wars acted as effective pace-setters for the so-called Orphan Missions, i.e. ex-German missions. Suddenly they were left without their Babas and Mamas, who were safely interned elsewhere. The presumptive African successors had been given a limited theological education. Yet, in the crisis the only possible solution was a dashing step forward, in faith and hope and – expectation. The consequent story magnificently verified the rightness of this move, a blessing in disguise for the churches concerned: in Tanzania, in the Cameroon, in Togo and elsewhere.

Some denominations were more daring than others. In nineteenth-century South Africa, the Wesleyan Methodists had taken the lead and pressed on along the road into a new era ... taken as a whole the vast number of Wesleyan pastors proved through their example to be a pressure group in Southern Africa for a higher degree of optimism and decision making leading to a switch to African church structures ... the example of which was to inspire other more slow-footed bodies. (Correspondence about the ACH. n.d.)

'Expectation' and 'not-yet-time' were not only relevant concepts in relation to the churches, B Sr was aware that they pertained also to individuals. He had high expectations of individual church leaders and lay people, which also led him at times to disappointment. It is very noticeable in B Sr's diaries that he always writes down the full name of everyone he met on his travels and talked with. This becomes even more noticeable when, after becoming bishop, he writes about his church leaders and members he met, including the children's names and ages. More often than not his concern was what the person could do, or what he or she or some family should have – theology books or a lamp to brighten life in shabby parsonages – or what education should be given or encouraged. For him expectation was a conscious attitude. He made a note in his diary and told others about it several times how Stefano Moshi, the first president and bishop of the Evangelical Lutheran Church in Tanzania, had missed his chance in his youth of going to the USA in the 1930s, when he received a scholarship for his good work, because the German missionary responsible had no expectations and did not see the necessity; his next chance came 20 years later in 1952.

The antithesis of not-yet is NOW. Africa's 'now' came in 1958, as we saw in Chapter 6. The mission relinquished its independent position over, or on the side of, the mission-related churches. The churches in Africa elected the leaders they chose and the missions became servants of the independent churches, no longer their guides and managers.

Notes

1. This and the following quoted paragraphs are from an article by Bengt Sundkler, 'Bantu Messiah and White Christ' in *Frontier*, African Inland Mission Press, Kijabe, Kenya, 1960:2–7. See also Bantu – Messias und Weisser Christus. 'Die Sekten Südafrikas' in *Das Wort in der Welt*, 1961:26–32 and 'Svart Messias och Vite Kriste' in *SMT* 47, 1959:96–106.
2. B Sr did not deal with the women's movement in a generalising manner 'as a mass', but rather picked some leading individuals whom and whose churches he described in *Bantu Prophets* (1964:139–44) and especially in *Zulu Zion* (1976:79–84).
3. The letter to Professor David Bosch was published in the journal of the Southern African Missiological Society *Missionalia* 1984:3–6, vol.12:1 with papers from the conference.
4. African Initiated or Instituted Churches are other alternatives in current use. Cf. Hallencreutz, C. F. in 'Bantu Prophets'. 'After fifty years,' *SMT* 86,4 (1998):581–600.
5. The quotes in this section are from Sundkler's letter to David Bosch published in *Missionalia*.
6. In Collins Dictionary 'movement' can be 'a group of people with a common ideology' or 'the organised action of such a group', or even 'trend or tendency'.
7. Sundkler used Black Zion (BZ) as the working title and changed it to Zulu Zion (ZZ) when he discovered that the name had already been given to another publication.
8. G. C. Oosthuizen, *The Theology of a South African Messiah*, Leiden 1967, p.6.
9. B Sr elaborated on the significance of dreams in *The Christian Ministry in Africa*. The following paragraphs have been taken from the chapter 'Dreams as Channels of Gods Call' pp.25–31. Other writings of Sundkler on dreams include *Bantu Prophets, Bara Bukoba, Zulu Zion*, 'Bantu Messiah and White Christ' (1960) and *SMT* 47, 1959:96–106, 'Svarta Messias och Vite Krist'.
10. The text quoted here is from 1960 and the terms reflect that period.
11. Kaija Honkala did her Masters in Theology on 'Bengt Sundkler's Mission Theology. Main Characteristics,' (in Finnish) 1974 University of Helsinki.

Brother Folke with his big brother Bengt

Bengt's childhood home in Vindeln

The path down to the river – 'What is beyond the forests?'

Bengt after confirmation

(below): Graduating from High School in front of his Umeå home, ready for new 'beyond'

Bengt and Ingeborg with Bengt's parents and sister Ingegärd after their engagement

Bengt and his sister Ingegärd and brothers Folke and Lennart

Bengt and Ingeborg ready to leave for South Africa

As language students in South Africa

Churchwomen, *abisizikazi*, in their black uniforms of the Zulu Lutheran Church

Christians gathering at an outpost in Ceza

Baptism in Zulu Jordan river (the palm leaves are a reminder of the River Jordan)

Dressed for worship

Drums as part of worship

Swazi worship and healing service

Grace Tshabalala, of Zion
ka Baba, Father's Zion,
gave impetus to a Zionist
Union

George Nazar Khambule
with the General and the
General Clack of the Lord

Archbishop Mordochai
Sikakane in 1969

Bengt with Ingeborg on Lake Victoria

Visiting fishermen on the shore of Lake Victoria

Bengt Sundkler with pastors and evangelists in Bukoba church, 1940s

A church council meeting in a Bukoba church

Preaching to a gathering of an independent church in Durban

Visiting an independent church service in South Africa, 1958

Bengt Sundkler
being consecrated
as bishop of the
Bukoba church

Bishop Bengt
consecrating and
opening Ihangiro
church

Newly-elected Prime Minister Nyerere with Dean
Matias Lutosha and Bishop Bengt

Bishop Bengt and the Synodical Council. Future bishop Josiah Kibira to
the bishop's right

Ingeborg and Bengt back in Uppsala, 1965

Bengt Sundkler, Archbishop Sunby and Mission Director Tore Furberg
leading HRH King Carl Gustaf XVI to the celebration of the 100th
anniversary of the CSM, 1974

Bengt Sundkler as a celebrant at a folk mass in Uppsala Cathedral

Jubilee Doctor with Christopher Steed

Bengt Sundkler – favoured speaker

Moving about on an old bicycle in Uppsala

8

BISHOP ON THE EQUATOR[1]

When Paramount Chief Tomas Marealle spoke at Marangu in 1955, it was not as an outsider or as a stranger to the church. In B Sr's words:

> He was on this particular occasion eminently representative of the Lutheran Church of Tanzania. Two African pastors developed the theme of a Lutheran episcopate in Tanzania: the leading pastor among the Chagga, Stefano Moshi, and the leading pastor in Bukoba, Matia Lutosha. They consulted and strengthened each other in the conviction that their churches must now adopt episcopal leadership. Moshi said: 'This is the position not only of the paramount chief, but one that is shared by all Christians in Tanzania. If some mission does not wish this course to be adopted, at the very least it must not hinder others from following it.' Lutosha stressed a characteristic Bukoba point of view: they were surrounded on all sides by episcopal dioceses, and wanted to facilitate the fellowship with these brethren. (1980:154)

A bishop from the far north

By 1959 the Lutheran church in northwestern Tanzania, which then was often referred to as the Bukoba church, was united to accept the episcopacy. When Bengt Sundkler was a superintendent of the Bukoba church during the difficult and strenuous war years 1942–45, and with Ingeborg directed the teacher training college at Kigarama they had become indissolubly tied to a whole generation of future leaders in the church. When the question of finding a bishop arose the church leaders remembered their wartime missionary.

> I was honoured to receive their invitation to become their first bishop. They even suggested that the consecration should take place in connection with the 50-year jubilee of the Haya Church in 1960, an event at that time eagerly anticipated. (1980:157)

A diary entry elaborates on the decision process:

I had a letter from the Buhaya Synodical Council calling me to be the first bishop of the Haya Church. I am faced with the same problem which the mission board placed before me, when the CSM wanted to make me bishop of the Zulu Church. Then it was easier to say no. Now I am grateful for the possibility of the contact with my beloved Haya church and the Haya people, to be allowed to stay in contact with a living church, not as here in Sweden to live entirely on the sidelines of what happens in the Church.

But how can I give up my professor's chair and all the literary plans? Everything that I have started will be left only half done – and I have a responsibility toward my doctorands. All the same, I have to give the question serious thought. (1 January 1960)

But I had to tell them that my tasks at the University of Uppsala did not allow me to accept their invitation. Life is short, and one has to take one's present responsibilities seriously. Accordingly I sent a polite refusal. I felt this as something of a liberation, and I could return to my writings at home in Uppsala.

But Bukoba is, after all, Bukoba. At the end of August 1960 was the Haya church jubilee and in September 1960 the Lutheran World Federation arranged a conference to take place there which I had the privilege of attending. The African leaders of the Haya Church seized the opportunity. Pastors such as Andrea Kajerero, Matia Lutosha and Jonathan Karoma and leading laymen such as Sospater Zahoro and Sebastian Bishanga called me to a private deliberation. Afterwards I was told that one of the laymen, a school supervisor called Festo Kazaula, had trustfully quoted a Haya proverb: 'Agabonangaine tigatinangana.' 'When eyes see each other . . .' i.e. when people at long last meet '. . . then they will not fear one another'.

It was a slightly greying man, fostered and formed by Western university life and thought, who came to this meeting with the African pastors and laymen, whom he had not met for 15 years. In that hour he encountered a great deal of confidence and expectation. The participants at the meeting said: 'Have you not really understood? It is we, the diocese in Bukoba, who are inviting you, and not just any diocese.' Andrea Kajerero had his own way of convincing me. He had personally known Bishop Tucker in Uganda and he thought I would fit that category of people. He referred to a sermon I had preached during my first period among them about the call of God, 'Go, and he goes, and come, and he comes.' That word Bwana Sindikila should now remember when the call comes to him. Sebastian Bishanga, a hospital administrator, expressed his invitation so well and so genuinely, 'If and when you come, you must realise that your home will be our home, and our homes will be your home,' that I had to say to myself, 'What if I were to try, in spite of everything? Is this what God has in store for me?'

No official decision was taken, but Pastor Matia Lutosha felt that he could define the situation through a verbal communiqué, sent by bush telegraph: 'The child is in the womb.' In February 1961 the synod held an episcopal election. According to the constitution, three names had to be placed on the short list. This time they solved the problem by writing the same name three times.

Why did they not choose an African immediately? The Africans might perhaps prefer to answer that question themselves. In different contexts they have declared it to be consonant with the universal character of the episcopal ministry that for this, the first time, they should elect a Westerner who was well-known to them and who might conceivably convey something of the heritage and experience of the Universal Church valuable for the formation of the episcopal ministry in Bukoba. That the bishop-elect must understand that he had to find and prepare an African successor for the task was not actually spelled out. That was my problem. (1980:157–8)

Practical arrangements followed at both ends. The faculty allowed B Sr to go to Bukoba. He asked for a leave, one year at a time, from 1961 till the end of 1964. He had cultivated good relations with the rector of the University of Uppsala, Torgny Segerstedt. He had been lenient in regard to B Sr's service in Bukoba and remarked: 'It is the least we can do for the church in Africa.' (Interview 12 August 1988) In Bukoba, a house was purchased from the Williamson mines and renovated for the bishop's manse. Ingeborg had the task of packing up the household once more and selectively shipping it to East Africa. They proceeded by air to Kampala and reported home:

I beg to inform you that we have arrived at the equator. Everything is well. We stay now for two days in Kampala and fly on 5 July to Bukoba. Today I cleared all our effects through the customs. The Goan customs officer was nice and understanding. In the lists for the different boxes there were several new things we had taken along, among them a phonograph for 350 Skr. He let us pay for that in order to show that we had after all paid something, then he let me go.

For the evening I have invited the African Archdeacon Nsubuya and his wife to come for a dinner at the hotel here. Interesting people. It is exciting to come to Bukoba again, now as an elected leader for the Church. May God give His blessing for it. (Letter home 4 July 1961)

Episcopal tradition

The consecration of the bishop took place on 30 July 1961 at 10 a.m.

The whole week prior to the consecration there were heavy tropical rains. The prospects for the outdoor ceremony looked bleak indeed. Everybody was engaged in preparations for the great day. On 28 July Bishop Manikam arrived as the representative of the Lutheran Church in India. He addressed an Indian open-air meeting in Bukoba town. The consecration day began with Holy Communion, of which B Sr notes in his diary that the service gave the impression of being very European. 'Things like this must not happen again. The African clergy must feel that they are in charge and should take the initative.'

Missionaries were too visible, arranging kneeling pads and taking the collection. One of the four celebrants was an Indian pastor, Gunny, from Dar es Salaam.

The consecration was superbly directed by Bishop Bo Giertz (from Sweden). The presence of four Anglican bishops, Archbishop Brown of Uganda, Bishop Stanway of Dodoma, Bishop Shalitha of Ankole and Bishop Sabithi of Ruwenzori, was greatly encouraging, but they were forbidden by the LWF to lay hands on the bishop incumbent. This much saddened the festive day.

The fear that the apostolic continuity through the laying-on of hands might slip into the Lutheran church in Tanzania by the back door prevailed, especially among the American brethren. In this respect, greater tolerance was developed over the years.

The consecration was followed by a reception with 15–20 addresses by many good friends. There was a Swedish television interview in the afternoon and in the evening an evangelical meeting in the bishop's house, filled to overflowing with guests. Kahororo Secondary School choir provided the music.

On the two following days a conference was held in which many notable guests were invited as speakers. On the third day after the consecration the Synodical Council met at which B Sr gave his first episcopal letter in Luhaya. 'The rest of the day trying to rest – near exhaustion.'

Much later in life, when B Sr was asked about his theology by interviewers, he often referred to his two main episcopal letters, the first one at the inauguration *Ebarua y'Askofu* and the other when leaving the diocese. I quote from the festschrift *Daring in Order to Know*, in which I have elaborated on the contents of these letters and the significance of B Sr as the first bishop in the Lutheran Church in Tanzania (M. L. Swantz, 1984:38):

> [In the first letter] There were three leading themes which he (B Sr) was to repeat in a reverse order in the second letter. These themes give the key programme for Bengt Sundkler's work as the ecclesiastical leader and the Shepherd of his flock. They were 1. Inheritance of the Church, 2. Renewal of the Church, and 3. The Church as a home.
>
> A central historical significance of Bengt Sundkler's contribution to the Lutheran Church in Tanzania was to bring the African Church to the awareness of the value of belonging to the historical and Universal Church with a continuing structure, yet allowing freedom for the Church to find for herself a form in which the Christians would feel at home. The Church had to find her own modes of expression, in music, in liturgy, in Word, in service.

The Ministry of the Church was to be *Via crucis, via lucis* – the way of the cross, the way of the light. The life of the Church as worship, service, witness and fellowship of people expressed in mutual care and empathy:

The thoughtful combination of the spiritual and institutional formed the
basis of nurture given by the Bishop in his letters, messages, teachings,
personal counselling and in the innumerable discussions 'on the road'
... The Church needed to keep alive her ecumenical ties and give institutional expression to the spiritual links they had across the ecclesiastical
borders. (M. L. Swantz, 1984:39)

B Sr did not forget to remind his readers in different contexts that
the roots of the worship were also to be found in people's own tradition. Church leaders such as Ernest Lutashobya, who as a youth had
assisted his father in bringing offerings to Wamala, carried with them
an echo of the holiness of the moment to the new worship. B Sr
observed this same inbred sense of holiness in a young girl who was
carrying the bowl of baptismal water from her home to church for a
baptismal service.

The multiple roots of the Evangelical Church in Bukoba offered a
special opportunity for her bishop to exercise ecumenism and develop
the idea of a bridging church. When planning the writing of his annual
report for 1963 he remarked: 'The role of the Evangelical Church, a
bridge church [which] I have stressed in my teaching ever since writing
20 years ago about *Ung Kyrka i Tanganyika*, continued with a note
about the multiplicity of roots "Anglican – Methodist – Bethel".'

In this B Sr felt close affiliation with the Archbishop Söderblom.
When, after returning to Sweden, he wrote the book about Söderblom
B Sr made reference to Söderblom's discovery of the ancient tradition
of the Church of Sweden when walking to the cathedral of Sens in
France where the very first in the long succession of Swedish
Archbishops had been consecrated in 1164. For Söderblom the
Swedish saints from the Catholic era, the reformers, the bishops, the
pietists and nineteenth-century revival were all part of the same living
tradition. Tradition could stifle life, but there was a necessary tension
and reciprocity between tradition and renewal, between organisation
and spirit. This Church had body and soul (Sundkler 1968:255–6).

Especially valuable in analysing Bengt Sundkler's ministry and
scholarship – where theory and practice were brought together – is
Lars Thunberg's chapter 'Redemption for the Wrongs in History' in
the festschrift entitled *The Church Crossing Frontiers* in honour of
Bengt Sundkler (1969).

Lars Thunberg, whose opinions on ecumenicity B Sr particularly
respected, points out in his analysis of Sundkler's ecumenical vision
that it excludes both confessionalism and false provincialism, even
denying the claims of uniformity, also in regard to church policy.
Although Sundkler defends an episcopal structure, it was not the need
for uniformity but rather the non-formal, uninstitutional character of
episcopacy that forced him to to make a special plea for it. This fact,
besides the Catholic heritage, made him prefer episcopacy to any
other form of church government. In *Ung Kyrka i Tanganyika*,

published in 1948, Sundkler underlines strongly that what he then called the Haya Church is by its very nature pluriform rather than uniform and therefore could be regarded as a bridging-church (Thunberg 1974:221). I quote Thunberg's translation of B Sr's text from his report on the diocese on the equator in 1962.

> As long as I have had occasion to follow the Haya Church, I have regarded it, and interpreted it, as a bridging-church, uniting various types of heritage and relating to different traditions. Its history represented the confluence of different tendencies and influences: from the north (Uganda), low church Anglican tradition; from the south (South Africa), Wesleyan Methodism; from the east the Bethel Mission, German 'United' pietism – here in Africa coming from the east transmitted by missionaries and Africans from Usambara. And to that were added later contacts: Danish national church Christianity and Swedish episcopal and liturgical tradition, and all of them with a wide 'ecumenical' purpose. All these tendencies and forces are alive in the spiritual and liturgical life of the Haya Church. All this history is felt as something present. As a diocese we wish to accept this whole heritage, and we are very eager to be allowed to say yes to all this common inheritance, also within the boundaries of the united Lutheran church. Here is our problem and task, yes, more precisely, our particular calling. This calling seems to be identical with our proper ecumenical responsibility. In this respect we are integrated into a long perspective, both towards the history and tradition of the Church and towards the future, and we believe that the important task to work for a 'Church of East Africa' requires from us faithfulness to history and tradition, i.e. the age-old history and the universal tradition, not first of all the accidental traditions and customs of yesterday. This is true not least of episcopacy, which was not introduced here in a haphazard way, but because we claim the Apostolic origin and the Evangelical–Catholic purpose and intention of the Church. In the present African situation there are many things which actualise this intention and purpose to anyone who confesses 'one holy Catholic and Apostolic church'. (1974:215)

B Sr pointed to the role that the Church of Sweden played as a bridging-church in mediating between the non-episcopal Lutheran and Anglican traditions in Africa. The northwestern diocese in turn took over this bridge function. The same bridge function was later exercised in Rhodesia where even the Catholic bishop laid hands on the Lutheran bishop Jona Shiri. (Sundkler 1975:166ff)

Reading B Sr's diaries from the time he was bishop 'Bengt Bukoba', as he signed his name with a cross in the Anglican tradition, it becomes evident that he guided and taught the church to understand that it belonged to the ancient tradition expressed in liturgical forms. As often as he could he attended the Liturgical Committee of the diocese and gave lessons on liturgy in the short courses for upgrading evangelists and pastors and congregational teachers. He considered it important to hold together the liturgical tradition and the revivalist free form of prayers and meetings in the same church. He had learned that the Haya experienced continuity in worship with their own priestly tradition. There were times when he was disappointed by the opinions expressed by his dearly beloved brethren, when the inherited ecclesiological tradition was discussed. A creative tension was experienced in the search for genuinely African tradition without destroying the ancient historical connection with the age old Church of Christ. The leaders of the church came to understand the 'intention' of what the Bishop, following the line of Söderblom, called Evangelical Catholicity. It was a tradition which held fast to personal faith and spirituality while also expressing its faith in inherited signs and symbols of Biblical origin. It also accepted into the fold churches which did not hold to the tradition of the laying on of the hands as a historical continuity.

An important event which the bishop attended, together with Dean Matia Lutosha, as one of his first international duties as the leader of the diocese was the WCC Assembly in New Delhi in 1961. For this he had to prepare an important lecture for which he had limited reference sources. A god-sent blessing in the form of Dr Richey Hogg from Dallas, Texas, a friend of B Sr who had written a book entitled *Ecumenical Foundations*, happened to arrive in Bukoba at just the right time and was of tremendous help in these preparations.

There were times when Dean Matia Lutosha became doubtful about the extent of his bishop's ecumenicity. After B Sr's visit to Rome in December 1963, the bishop and his wife attended the Catholic service in Bukoba and negotiated with the Catholic priest an exchange of visits to prayer services between the local congregations during the Ecumenical Week of Prayer for Church Unity. The old German sister, Emilie Wille, had then warned Lutosha about such a move, after which Lutosha suggested that the matter should be discussed in the synod before going ahead. (Diary 15 January 1964) The rumour about the bishop attending a Catholic service spread fast and the bishop was questioned about it in one of the free discussions which the bishop had with his fold in the Lutheran Nyamirembe centre. He explained that he had indeed attended a service and had prayed there in all quietness for the unity of the church. He might not have said that he appreciated that service more than the Bible study held by an Englishman with a Plymouth Brethren background the same Sunday in the bishop's home. There were both missionaries and other Europeans from other agencies who were Brethren or had leanings in that direction. B Sr and many others found their emphasis 'Be ye separate' from sinners to be very judgemental. (5 February 1964) B Sr tried to engage the local Catholic priests in an exchange of ideas on the basis of the Vatican Council II documents, as he considered Vatican Council II to have been absolutely decisive in view of future potential for unity of the Universal Church. In local parlance the Catholics were referred to as RCs, a form also B Sr used.

Within the Lutheran context, prior to establishing the Evangelical Lutheran Church of Tanzania in October 1963, preparatory discussions were held in the Federation of Lutheran Churches of Tanzania (FLCT) executive meeting on 15–18 June 1963 in Mwika, East Kilimanjaro. It took four days for B Sr to reach Arusha where the first conference was held, in Makumira. He travelled by car via Uganda and Kenya and then flew the final stretch from Nairobi in a small plane via Musoma and Mwanza to Arusha and Makumira, where he first lectured and then the theological board of the FLCT met. The theological board, of which B Sr was chairman, voted him out of the Church Union talks, which he had chaired as the representative of the FLCT. In these talks the Anglican, Moravian and Lutheran churches were working towards greater unity. The executive of the FLCT, however, voted that he should continue as their representative, trusting him to have the highest level theological knowledge in the church at the time.

At the Mwika meeting B Sr preached in the Sunday service. The service was followed by the consecration of the Mwika Radio House as the branch of the Radio Voice of the Gospel, the headquarters of which were in Adis Abeba. I had been asked to give a lecture on the mission of the church in the same church in the preceding evening. It still at that time surprised some of the participants that a woman had been asked to speak on such a topic. Of the FLCT executive meeting B Sr reported in his diary in the following terms:

> Very good meeting. Bishop Moshi wonderfully patient chairman, handled the meeting very well. We managed to get a constitution of the Lutheran Church which preserves the Federative structure. I fought for the name Evangelical instead of Evangelical Lutheran and was attacked by Mr Shaidi, Administrative Secretary, Northern Lutheran Church, for 'wasting meeting time'. I had of course just asked the chairman whether we were now free to discuss the proposal paragraph by paragraph and had his consent. (We had spent one hour and more just correcting spelling and punctuation in the minutes from last year's meeting, Mr Shaidi taking a leading part in this exercise, so no wonder that he felt time had passed us by!) So I was in order. But our proposal was lost, and Evangelical Lutheran will be the name of the Church.
>
> In the executive I was asked to explain about the episcopacy, and I spent a day doing so, greatly helped by E. Schlink's article 'Apostolische Sukzession' in *Kerygma und Dogma*. I referred to the fact that Schlink of Heidelberg had an unassailable Lutheran position – and could therefore be accepted as an authority. The constitution became as loose and innocuous as I wanted it – so we can use it for further Church Union work.

In Mwika B Sr was asked to write a book on episcopacy, 'pleading as I did for a ministry that is acceptable by the Universal Church'. Reverend Eliwaha Mshana, the principal of the Makumira Lutheran Theological Seminary, opposed B Sr's formulation, referring to an

American authority he had studied, and pleaded for a Tanganyikan Episcopacy, '*huduma ya Ki-Tanganyika*', 'we do not care about the outside world'. As a compromise Mshana was asked to write a second book containing his views.

Theological principles of the episcopate[2]

This task of preserving the sense of historicity had to be done without offending the Lutheran sister churches for which, under considerable missionary influence, the office of the bishop was at that time not yet acceptable. When the Evangelical Lutheran Church of Tanzania (ELCT) was inaugurated in 1963 some of the member churches remained as synods and, with the exception of the Mbulu church under Norwegian mission influence, only later adopted the episcopal order. In an autobiographical letter B Sr mused what from his point of view happened when the other churches – which had become synods in the ELCT – adopted the episcopal order (Letter to MLS 27 June 1982):

> As a bishop in Bukoba ... I did probably also act in a doctrinaire manner from time to time. In this case it was a matter of a principle, of theology of the episcopate. You remember those days. Little Bukoba, tiny and inconspicuous, had on its own decided to have a bishop.
>
> Of course then Moshi had to have one, and they had the good sense of electing an incomparable man, Stefano Moshi, for the job. But then how to interpret this theologically? It was then that the official organ of the Northern Church published a lead in its official paper refuting the idea of a consecration of the Bishop. '*Hakuna maana kumbariki tena*,' they said on that occasion, 'there is no reason to consecrate again'.

By this they meant that the leader of the Church had already been consecrated as the Head of the Church, in Swahili called *Mkuu*, when the diocese was still a synod, and consequently he did not need another consecration.

> So then when Reverend Waltenberg was to be consecrated in Usambara in 1962,[3] Stefano Moshi was invited to partake in the consecration and accepted, although his diocese had officially declared that *hakuna maana*, there is no reason. I then could not go. They tried to get me and even came to fetch me with an extra plane all the way from Lushoto to Bukoba, waiting for a full day and a night and a morning, but I stuck to my view, and stayed obstinately in Bukoba.
>
> Then later, in 1964, Stefano Moshi's diocese decided that they were going to have a consecration after all. I rejoiced with them and with the whole ELCT, where, strange to say now, I did indeed have a position as a chairman of the theological board. I arranged it so that we, all of us from the theological committee, could sit in Arusha the week prior

to the consecration after all, all prepared to partake in the great consecration on the coming Sunday. But then, you know it so well, very
unfortunately the consecrating bishop in Germany got ill and was taken
into hospital. Now, over against little Bukoba, the great Moshi people
had all the time insisted on a supposingly Lutheran principle: *in casu
necesitatis* anybody, any good Christian could consecrate the bishop.
But nobody, least of all in Moshi, thought that such a *casu necesitatis*
would occur. Now it had occurred, and related to their consecration.
What to do? The Diocesan Council in Moshi sat through the whole day
and the following morning, Friday and Saturday. They sent telegrams
and, I suppose, telephoned to Germany to get a good German bishop,
but nobody could respond at that short notice.

Much later Bishop Moshi, who was embarrassed by the whole affair,
told me: They had invited a theological expert to guide them, a foreign
guest, Sigurd Aske, a radio specialist (from the Voice of the Gospel in
Adis) and therefore regarded as a really good Lutheran. He advised
them to have the whole thing postponed, and so it was. I remember
Thomas Musa, the great Singida leader, saying to me afterwards, 'They
have postponed "*bila sababu*"', (without any reason). At the very end,
the good bishop from Germany fortunately recovered. Once again, I was
as a matter of course invited to partake, but this time had to decline
owing to pressing duties in Bukoba, and I sent Dean Lutosha instead, an
old friend of Bishop Moshi's.[4]

I suppose that I was doctrinaire in that matter but I realised that
without somebody insisting on principles in a Church connection, no
structure would rise, no order, no nothing. My one leading idea through
it all was that of 'intention', a good old theological principle. The
church must demonstrate its deepest intention. In 100 or 200 years we
may be called upon to declare what our 'intention' was earlier on, say
in the 1960s. In this case the intention was Catholicity, or Evangelical
Catholicity, if you like.

But all that is past and gone and more or less forgotten now.

With a distance to active service and after a time for reflection in his
study-chamber the bishop emeritus adds:

As a free agent, as a professor and an ex-professor, nothing but an old
pensioner, I tend to become increasingly accommodating and liberal as
I get older. In fact, my theology has for years been deeply influenced
by Tillich, and I am not even ashamed of that, I am influenced by Tillich
and by existential thinking as a whole. As I listen to others preaching,
I am most often very happy and grateful, but as they bring forth those
sorts of truths, I am amazed and – saddened. I feel that the whole thing
has to be approached in a much more existential way: in the deepest of
man.

I regret that I have not taken an official stand, theologically, over this.
That is a strange Swedish reaction: one is a historian and a Church historian, and should therefore stick to that and say nothing about theology.
But this is of course a lamentable flight from responsibility, and if I get
the time I must do something about it. (Letter to MLS 27 June 1982)

The manifold tasks of the bishop

We return to the Bishop's own busy day-to-day work which followed. Immediately after the consecration the bishop began to plan his church visitations with Dean Matia Lutosha. The following day he started his work by going to the secondary school in Kahororo where he spoke and preached. 'Very good first contact.' His diaries tell of frequent visits to the secondary school. This reflects his keen interest in education and the importance he attached to keeping the educated youth informed and within the fold. The next diary note is about the need to send Standard XII graduates overseas for further education. (Diary 25 July–5 August 1961)

On this topic, a quote from *Bara Bukoba* (1980:159–60) sheds further light:

> I had an idea that at this particular time the rapid changes in Tanzanian society could best be followed in the educational sphere. And the essential contributions of the diocese to the cultural problems of the country were decided there. In a diocese which, to such a high degree, had been built up by teachers, it was important to look after the school affairs with particular care. The bishop at that time was also chairman of the board of the Kahororo Secondary School – a board which was appointed by the Tanzanian Ministry of Education – although this arrangement was later discontinued. It was instructive to follow the development of this school: the africanisation of the teaching staff, opportunities for teachers to undertake further scholarships and studies, the development of a more Africa-centred curriculum, the role of the school chapel – these were some of the questions encountered. For myself, I was altogether too curious to know the new generation of secondary youth to be able to stay away from the secondary school. It was, perhaps, not altogether unimportant that the bishop should attend its meetings and arrangements fairly often.

After the consecration, travelling around the diocese filled the days. In Kauazi he preached and baptised 13 children, walked down the mountain to William B's house and up again. He continued to Ntoma, meeting with all the Germans, and then had a general reception at Kahororo. A Church centre board meeting took place after his return to Bukoba. Kigarama was next on the programme where he met village delegations and preached in the service. It was followed by the Ruhija Bible School board meeting and a reception for the bishop in Ibura.

After the reception in Ibura B Sr left the same day for Dodoma. Travel within the country was in itself no simple matter, whatever the mode of transport. B Sr attended the Church Union Conference in Dodoma, Central Tanzania, for the East African Protestant and Anglo-Catholic churches, which he always considered very important (13–17 August 1961). He stayed with Bishop Stanway (Australian

CMS): 'Very encouraging.' Returning from there the bishop was on a three-day visit to Karagwe (near the Uganda and Rwanda border where most of the people are Nyambo, not Haya). On his way to Entebbe, he went 'all over the district, intense days: Rukajange, Nyakahanga, Kaisho, Kituntu'.

On 27 August B Sr was in Yale, USA, attending the Theological Education Fund (WCC).

From USA B Sr flew back to Uppsala where he was then bedridden for six days with the 'flu. While in Uppsala he heard the sad news of the death of Dag Hammarskjöld whom he respected enormously as one of the greatest men that Sweden had ever produced. 'Great shock to the nation and to the world.' On 22 September the bishop was back in Bukoba attending to his duties. (Diary 27 August–22 September 1961).

In *Bara Bukoba* Bengt gives credit to Ingeborg for ensuring that the Holy Communion was celebrated every Wednesday morning at 7.15, followed by agapé breakfast for those who took part. While the bishop husband was gone Ingeborg took charge of the chapel and saw to it that the services were held regularly, besides taking care of many practical matters. Reminiscing about Ingeborg's role in Bukoba B Sr wrote:

> Without Ingeborg I could never have been the Bishop in Bukoba that God wanted me to be. She gave style and strength to the whole undertaking, and I tried to live up to her expectations and demands as to what a bishop should be: that is the truth about this. (Letter to MLS 25 September 1972)

After B Sr returned home to Bukoba we find him again talking to students, now about Dag Hammarskjöld, first in Kahororo Secondary School, then in the Indian School in Bukoba town, and then to students in Kashasha Girls' Middle School, after a 'tremendous reception', all in the same week. Together with the education secretary, Joel Ngeiyamu, in his home he met with the students of his diocese who were on home leave from the East African University College in Makerere, Uganda (Diary 25 September–7 October 1961):

> [We had] lunch and a long discussion on their contacts with the church, and their questions with regard to Balokole ('the saved ones' as the revivalists called themselves and were called by others). We had prayers in the chapel [in the bishop's manse] at the end. This contact was extremely useful and we were all happy about it.

The diaries show a continual flow of visitors at meals and as overnight guests, several days' retreats in his home with the pastoral and catechetical candidates, and a constant knocking at the door in the bishop's manse. We would need to go to Ingeborg's diaries and letters to discover the burden of tasks which fell on her. The bishop and his wife not only invited the local pastors who were leaving or arriving to stay with them, but also their families, as a result often finding themselves short of space and having to give up their own beds at times. I give one week's activities as a sample:

30 January 1964. Reverend John Lutakyamilwa here in the afternoon. We had invited him and his wife to come and stay with us for a night before they leave for Dar es Salaam where he will be pastor, as representative of our diocese. Well, he and she came – with three children. We had only the one guest room, i.e. my room which I had vacated to give to them. Now we had to find new ways, put them in the guesthouse (old office building). We had a delightful evening with the family: wife Prisca (Standard VIII Kashasha), Jerome (about 5), Jane 3 and Jerrold 1 year and 2 months. The children very well behaved: eating like little bears. Jane went to sleep immediately after being well fed, but soon revived on seeing our two Lapps, man and wife, wood carvings. Then we had prayers in chapel and they had to see everything. A fine evening.

31 January 1964. Evening dinner for Festo Kiwengere, Ugandan evangelist, and ten Africans and missionaries. F. K. spoke about his experiences. Others also spoke [names given].

1 February 1964. Preparations for ordination 2 February. Sylvester Machumu and wife [earlier from the Holy Spirit Church] came and stayed with us overnight. We had a good time with them. At lunch, which took 2 hours, Sylvester went on and on, gesticulating with both hands speaking about his experiences. Jusuf Kamuzora also at lunch, grateful to get a big nice meal for once (it seemed). In the evening with Sylvester and his wife, and preparations for ordination.

2 February 1964. The day of ordination of eight pastors was full (description with all the names and texts given), starting 7.30 with the Holy Mass. Lunch at Nyamirembe. People had come by bus from Kigarama and Ihangiro. Evening to Ntoma to discuss buildings and work.

3 February 1964. Refugee Committee with two people from CCT, DSM and local people [names given]. Very important and, I think, fruitful meeting.

New missionary Sister Brogaard for Nyakahanga laboratory arrived from Denmark. Abraham Nkongo came to talk about his call to be a pastor. With Christian Lutahakana talked about the altar in Kashasha chapel.

Reverend John Lutakyamilwa with us again with his three children (out of five) before leaving tonight by ship. The children quite charming and we have lots of fun with them.

The following day the Bishop spent with the mobile clinic from early morning going to two places where Doctor Buch and his assistant treated 100 patients and the Bishop took two services:

I visited the local pastor, Reverend Felicine Kakiziba and Mrs Margaret, a fine young couple. She has no formal schooling, but intelligent and wide awake, neat and nice. Speaks Kiswahili quite acceptably. I gave them a present (personal) of an Aladdin lamp to brighten their very bad pastor's house. I was totally finished on my return to Lyamahola at 8 p.m. Had to rest a while and then returned back in Bukoba late evening.

On 5 May, Holy Communion (taken once a week on Wednesdays) was held 7 a.m. in the chapel of the bishop's manse. The Kahororo chapel committee met, followed by discussion with Lars Johansson about work. Then the Bishop had a discussion with Kirsten Steffansen about her work in Ndolage and studies in Denmark, as she was leaving for Denmark that day.

In the evening bible study in Bishop's home, some 25–30 came.

In *Bara Bukoba*, in the chapter entitled 'Bishop one degree South', B Sr described more systematically what bishop's work consisted of according to the church constitution.

What, then, does a bishop one degree South do? The constitution stipulated definitely that he was not primarily to deal with administration . . .

When trying to decide and define, in a constitution, the range and scope of the bishop's influence, a very interesting development took place within the diocese. Debating the bishop's role in the 1950s, they had tried in Bukoba, particularly on the advice of some of the sister-synods in the Lutheran Federation at that time, to limit his authority in various ways. It was not known who could be the first incumbent; it was anticipated that he could turn out to be a power-hungry autocrat – the very title of 'bishop' was supposed to lead to that kind of thing, and the hope was that a constitution might help to assert the democratic powers of the synod against such a concentration of power. But things change, even in the church. Eight months after the consecration, at a meeting of the synod of the diocese, a general concern was expressed that the constitution might be changed so as to strengthen the bishop's power and influence; this should be embodied in official documents and letters. A number of factors may have caused this change. One may suppose that they already were looking forward to the time when the diocese would have an African bishop.

The bishop had his tasks not only within the diocese but also throughout the whole of Tanzania and East Africa: a number of great and small duties day by day. Yet the most important thing was to try and keep a few essential perspectives in view, without allowing them to become obscured by thousands of details. The whole system of committees and boards, which means so much for the organisation of the diocese, is kept together in and through the diocesan council and its standing committee. The bishop was, as a matter of course, chairman of both. The diocesan council meets, on average, six to eight times a year, usually for two days at a stretch; it could delegate urgent matters to its standing committee consisting of bishop, dean, administrative secretary and educational secretary. I believe that the four of us were a well-integrated team. We met frequently and dealt continuously with the matters of business which arose.

Furthermore, the bishop was *ex officio* chairman of the mission board of the diocese; and in addition, he had the right to attend, as time permitted, all committees and boards. As most of these meetings took place in Bukoba, it was natural to keep in touch with these rather different activities in the life of the diocese. Personally I felt that the education board was particularly important. In principle there was no reason why I should have attended its meetings as persistently as I did. It was under the leadership of our excellent education secretary, Joel Ngeiyamu, which meant that we could be sure beforehand that educational questions were being looked after and managed in the best possible way ...

Ruhija means 'smithy' and the Bible School in Ruhija became a true smithy for the arsenal of fellow-workers for our diocese. The Bible School had a good staff; it was a joy to listen to or take part in the teaching. Here, too, is the music centre, which developed during the 1960s under the leadership of two brilliant German musicians, who managed to find highly gifted African co-workers. At Ruhija we met regularly for useful courses designed for different categories of workers, and we also found a quiet place for retreats. At Ruhija, but also in other centres within the diocese, I could meet catechists and congregational teachers for conferences lasting several days at a time. In Bukoba town we created a new centre, Nyamirembe, with financial support from the Swedish Church Aid Fund. There, and in the bishop's house, we could also bring together medical or educational staff for contact in conferences.

I always felt that it was my personal task to try to widen the horizons of the diocese by informing groups and interested organisations inside and outside the diocese about the situation in Africa as a whole. So I regularly lectured on the church in Africa (*Bara Bukoba*:159–60).

Political initiatives

When the Sundklers came to Bukoba at the beginning of 1961 Tanganyika was a self-governing country with internal self-rule, on its way to full independence. It was a crucial time for national political development. Tanganyika was going through the transition from a UN Trust Territory to an independent nation; with the colonial personnel still in charge of the district and provincial administration, the courts and the ministries were apprehensive, not knowing what their future held. The same anticipation, with both the missionary and indigenous personnel being aware of the impending changes, also affected the churches. It required great sensitivity from the leadership.

One of the missionaries of the Bukoba church whom B Sr had first inspired to come to Tanganyika was Barbro Johansson. She had come to Tanganyika initially as an educator in 1946. She began on a small scale like all the others, as a teacher in a teacher training college in Kigarama but was soon given the task of founding the Kashasha girls' school. The school started out with only a few students, and as the principal, Barbro had to teach many subjects, including gymnastics. She came with a considerable political awareness, a Social Democrat in Sweden, and followed with keen interest the political developments in her new country of residence. She became an ardent supporter of Julius Nyerere, won a Tanganyika Afican National Union (TANU) seat in the Legislative Council, became a citizen and later a member of the first parliament of independent Tanganyika (Johansson and Wieslander, 1989).

> Mama Barbro had a wider horizon, a braver aim than most, and she seized an opportunity when it offered itself. Mama Barbro is to be credited to a great extent for the fact that the male and female colleagues, fellow missionaries and above all the fellow African believers within the Bukoba diocese were prepared to engage in the political reorientation which took place in the country. (Sundkler 1974:113)

Barbro Johansson built a bridge not only between Sweden and Tanzania but also between the Church and the State, thus enhancing the bridging function of the northwestern diocese. [5] She also saw to it that women were not neglected, the same concern that Ingeborg had throughout her life. She started and built up the girls' middle school in Kashasha from which emerged the first generation of educated women who are still active in public life. Later, as headmistress of the Tabora Girls' Secondary School she had a nationwide influence on women's leadership in Tanzania.

Barbro Johansson held courses on adult education and community development which B Sr encouraged on his visits to congregations. The regional community development officer was first suspicious about co-operating with the church, doubting whether it could work without any bias in organising adult education classes. B Sr convinced him that the Evangelical Church was responsible for education in general, not only for Christians. In 1978 the workers' organisation, the National Union of Tanganyika Workers (NUTA), elected Barbro Johansson to represent them in parliament for another term.

In 1977 B Sr had taken it upon himself to prepare a festschrift for Dr Barbro Johansson, at that time a councillor in the Embassy of Tanzania in Stockholm, for her 65th birthday. He was about to leave for London and had to occupy himself with a host of activities:

> This morning I was inquiring about the final edition of our festschrift for B. J. (Barbro Johansson). I hope to see it on my return to Uppsala on Friday. What a joy that we could squeeze Nyerere's article into it. But as I told you: his article was delayed 2 months!!! The President's letter being mislaid in the post in Dar es Salaam, dated 19 July, received in Uppsala more than 2 months later. (Letter to MLS 3 October 1977)

B Sr had been reading the final proofs of the introduction of the festschrift in the middle of a busy schedule of visitors and travels. This made it possible to hand the festschrift, including the belatedly

received introduction by the President of Tanzania, Julius Nyerere, to
Barbro Johansson on her birthday.

As an illustration of how the Christian women entered into the political scene even when they had been left outside the formal educational
structure I quote a story about a woman leader that B Sr related in
several contexts. In his diary (19–22 December 1963) he described
one of his hundreds of visitations, this time to Minzigiro and other
congregations on the way:

> This was a tremendous experience, this congregation on an island in the
> swamps. Fine new church to be opened and blessed in February 1963
> by Archbishop Hultgren [whose visit was imminent]. Very dynamic
> people. Mrs Paskazia, leader of women's community development
> group of 18 women (2 Protestants, 16 Catholics).

Having met this dynamic woman B Sr had asked his Haya pastor
colleague to interview the woman. She was one of the many women for
whom becoming a leader both in the Church and in society was a struggle. Paskazia Mhingo's story from Bukoba illustrates the emergence of
women leaders regardless of their scant educational opportunities:[6]

> As the last child of my family and being a girl, I had no formal school-
> ing whatsoever except for one week. I was forced by my father to
> abandon the school after one week. But I tried of my own accord to
> learn to read and write. My father could not see any reason for a girl as
> I was to learn how to read and write since women were being despised
> at that time. Also it was by my own initiative that I became a Christian
> at the age of 13 years. It took one year to be baptised. I had to recite
> as many Bible verses as possible. When I got married I was chosen as
> a leader of the youth group of that time, because my first husband was
> a church leader. His Christian life influenced my life. But after ten years
> he died and left me with two children. I re-married, to my present
> husband, nine years later. He was a teacher and an evangelist before. I
> have been married to him for 35 years.
>
> During 1957 I took adult education classes and did well, so much so
> that I was chosen to teach others. I taught for two years, especially home
> economics and singing. My marriage was not accepted according to
> church standards but I continued to love the church and serve my Lord
> and worship regularly.
>
> During this time I joined TANU (CCM). Soon I was chosen to repre-
> sent my people in the District and Regional Councils, I attended many
> seminars and I have been the chairperson of UWT [*Umoja wa
> Wanawake wa Tanzania*, a national women's organisation] since 1962.
> I have written many political songs. I have tried to unite women regard-
> less of their faith. I am able to combine church and CCM activities
> because each helps the other.
>
> Nyerere means a lot to me. He advocates the emancipation of women,
> as Jesus did. Because of Nyerere I am free to speak. His philosophical
> thinking of equality of all people is wonderful. He is helping the poor
> as the Bible tells us to do.

As the head of the diocese B Sr, from his political background also a Social Democrat in Sweden, received Julius Nyerere when he was chairman of TANU, prime minister and later president of the republic. For the diocese his emphasis on national unity meant adopting Swahili as the language of church meetings and worship whenever possible and sending the missionaries to Dar es Salaam for language study.[7] The introduction of Swahili among the Haya was no simple matter. Their Haya, and in Karagwe Nyambo, identities were strong and the people were used to conversing in the vernacular, in which they also could communicate with the neighbouring Baganda of Uganda. But they had a vision, not only of the importance of unification in a national state but of the nationwide Church and the role of this Church in the new state. Bishop Bengt never ceased to use opportunities to remind the diocese of the possibility and calling to achieve Church Union.

Sharing and communicating

Sharing was a theme which B Sr brought up in many contexts when talking about the contacts in Bukoba:

> The East African revival could, in favourable cases, be a factor which helped especially the women missionaries' input. This life movement gave new possibilities and new space in the women's world.[8] Youth revolt's new simple lifestyle and blessed freedom to choose has made it natural for the young Swedish parish sisters to go to a Tanzanian extended family with African sisters – and all parties gain by it.
>
> It need not be stressed that it was a joy, in the inspections of the diocese, to visit the homes of pastors, teachers, farmers, masons and lorry drivers (the last two being especially important jobs in the new Africa) and in other houses; to sit with them eating *ebitoke* or drinking a cup of tea. There was something of a sacramental fellowship about doing so. I always learned a great deal from our talks: new perspectives on old traditions in the congregation, plans and possibilities for individuals and various organisations, associations and interests. To my host family and myself it was only natural that every such visit should lead to a short time of worship and of prayer to God, that some verses from the New Testament in Kiswahili or Luhaya should be the point of orientation and conclusion, and that the bishop should bless the house before he went on.
>
> But I was a European – not that this could be helped. Nor did it even help that I had to tell myself that I was much closer to these people in Bukoba than to any other comparable group of people with whom I had ever come into contact during my whole life. As a bishop I had, of course, my share of worries and sorrows, but never in relation to Africans. Because I was a European, there was consequently a distance which could not be overcome by even the warmest fellowship. One day, when I had been bishop for about a year, I was struck by the idea that

I must find ways to overcome this distance, and so I went to my colleague, Dean Matia Lutosha. I quote from my diary entry for 25 July 1962:

> In the evening I thought through this fact of isolation which so easily becomes the lot of the European, and obviously also in the case of the European bishop. How do I get out to the people, in order to live with them, chat with them, and pray with them? I mentioned this to Ingeborg; I also discussed it with Ronald Johnson (my American secretary) and took him with me to Matia Lutosha. We had a long talk about this until late into the night. Matia Lutosha was in his happiest mood, and really very helpful. In the following weeks I must try to arrange so that I can stay two days at a stretch at Kigarama, Kashasha and Ndolage respectively, and longer times in some other places.[9]

Of course, this was no solution even if it was well-meaning and perhaps not without some importance. It was a matter of course that as a bishop and a missionary I had much closer contact and fellowship with 'the people' and with my co-workers, centrally and locally, than could ever be achieved by Western 'experts' in the capital. That is not where the problem lies. It is to be found at another level, by which I mean that the diocese as a spiritual 'extended family in Christ's name' demanded an affinity, mobility and power of communication, which I was always conscious, as a European, of not having in sufficient measure. (*Bara Bukoba* 1980:161)

B Sr relates that he carried in his own Bible pictures of his Haya friends, Josiah, Matia, Christian, Sebastian, Joel. They were the windows through which he understood the love and compassion of Christ Jesus. Through their interpretation of the Bible he was being fed, and he was corrected by them in their frank and open relationship:

> This matter of contact and lack of contact is complicated by the fact that the norms of African society demand a certain distance being maintained between the ordinary people and their leaders. It could even be claimed that communication here presupposes a certain distance. Communication always happens with a certain ritual – for instance, with a long, ceremonial act of greeting. In order to convey a message, and particularly an important message, the African creates a ritual situation which becomes an intermediary step between the message and the receiver. So it was in older times, and this was emphasised by the traditional patterns of leadership, including those among the Hima-dominated interlacustrine peoples. When I visited Ndolage hospital for the first time a young African orderly – with Swedish contacts – said to me: 'What we need in this diocese is a person to whom people will not just say Hi!'
> It is possible that 'ordinary people' do not expect to meet the bishop face-to-face. They feel a need to look up to a spiritual authority who is, in one sense, superior. By tradition, they differentiate between office

and person. However true and important this may have been, I felt this problem as a continual vexation. It is undeniable that my African successor has much greater chances of bridging this distance and thus finding a solution to the ever-threatening isolation of office not only because he is Josiah Kibira, but simply because he is an African. I could only be conscious of the problem and try to tackle it in a limited way. (*Bara Bukoba* 1980:162)

Brotherly correction and care

[In the context of not being an African], the spiritual climate in the Bukoba diocese was a great help. According to its watchword, the revival aimed to bring everything to the light. This meant making a strenuous effort towards bringing about living fellowship at a deep level. If anyone felt that the bishop had said or done something out of place, he or she came and said so. In most cases this was a great help. I experienced this in a way which was personally decisive for me in connection with the first ordination which I carried out in the diocese. There were six young men who had received their theological education from the seminary at Makumira, and also the principal of our Bible School, Ernest Lutashobya. We had as a preparation for our diocese a three-day retreat. (I invariably led retreats in person.) It was arranged that the ordination should take place during the Sunday morning service, and on the Saturday evening we held the obligatory rehearsal.

The young candidates were told to stand in a row, and they were supposed to reply in turn: 'I, so-and-so, believe. . .' There was much to think about and much to attend to in the dimly lit church. My introductory words were too rapid and hasty, and the answers did not come immediately. I therefore entreated, possibly with a European's irritation: '*Tafadhali*!' 'Please, answer!' The following day's worship, with the ordination, was a great and unforgettable festival – but on Monday evening Matia Lutosha visited me: 'Bishop, you were in too much of a hurry on Saturday evening when you said "*Tafadhali*" to S. M. We do not want that kind of a thing here.' I never forget this poignant and necessary reminder, I was grateful for it.

About half a year later Matia Lutosha and Ernest Lutashobya came and asked for a personal interview with me for the following day. What had I said or done now? I racked my brains in vain for an answer. They came and this was what they said: 'We feel that you are working too hard. We have decided that you are going to have a month's holiday at Limuru in Kenya. Now we have divided the work between us, and determined that you are going to be free from Thursday.' And so they prayed for the bishop and diocese and the whole church of Christ on earth. (*Bara Bukoba* 1980: 162-3)

Once when interviewing B Sr I asked him whether he had been motivated by personal ambition when he was so ambitious as a bishop, scholar or writer. He formulated the answer in a manner which deserves to be quoted:

The question of personal ambition was a problem for me as a young man, a spiritual problem; it was sinful, one should not have ambitions, one should beware of it. At the time I came as a Bishop to Bukoba I faced the problem. As late as that I became reconciled with this personal problem of ambition. If you have a sufficiently big task, a job to do, you are so engaged and involved that your particular little ambition becomes a ridiculous little detail in that whole thing. If you do not have a little ambition to do a good thing the whole thing breaks down. If I may say so, it was in my pietistic time as a young student in the 1930s – because I was a pietist, not in the Swedish sense – that ambition was a spiritual problem to me. You should do good things for some other better reason. I have lived sufficiently long to be able to see personal development. There is a level of life where this problem becomes irrelevant as a problem. You come to a situation in which you must put your whole self into it and give everything. Someone will say that it is ambition. If you call it ambition, do so, but in God's eyes He will look at us with smile, God who is a forgiving God. His will be done in spite of our little ambitions. We must do this together, come, we must lift this, finish this task. (Taped interview by MLS 7 August 1985)

Bishop Kibira is consecrated

It was during a pastors' conference on 8 August 1963 that the question of having an assistant bishop was brought up for the first time. This gave the bishop the chance to declare: 'TANU has its *sabasaba* (sevenseven), we have our *nanenane* [eighteight]. We have a perspective of history, today we consider an African bishop, not an assistant bishop.' When the matter was brought to the diocesan council they wanted B Sr to carry on and have an assistant bishop but he would not have it. This was the time to start preparing for the consecration of an African bishop:

In September 1964 Josiah Kibira was consecrated bishop, exactly 100 years after the consecration of the first Evangelical African bishop, Samuel Crowther, for service 'On the River Niger'. When Kibira's Swedish predecessor had been consecrated three years earlier, an ecumenical – if that is the right word – peculiarity had occurred. Four Anglican bishops had taken part. They had walked in the procession to the altar but at the important moment of the actual consecration and laying-on of hands, they were not allowed to participate. This Lutheran resistance to full Anglican participation was particularly painful because two of these Anglican bishops, Sabiti from Fort Portal and Shalita from Mbarara, were Africans. They both belonged to the East African Revival, and Shalita at least had often visited Bukoba, invited by the diocese as a Revival preacher. These Anglican bishops were seen as brothers in the Blood, in the understanding of the Revival, and they were of course infinitely closer to the leaders of the diocese than any other church representatives who could be produced. But no, here some Lutheran edict had been promulgated from Europe and little Bukoba had to obey.

By 1964 the situation had changed. Bukoba was now part of the Evangelical Lutheran Church of Tanzania, formed in 1963. A certain ecumenical dialogue had been established between the churches of Tanzania in these decisive years. Now it was a question of an African bishop in a newly independent African nation. The diocese was now in a stronger position, some consideration had to be shown to it.

Among the participants at the consecration, besides Lutherans and Moravians, there were also two Anglican bishops – Shalita of Mbarara, who had come again unperturbed, and the bishop of Kasulu. Before the consecration we could talk over all the arrangements in detail with the presiding bishop of the Evangelical Lutheran Church of Tanzania, Bishop Stefano Moshi, from Moshi, and he approved them with evident satisfaction. The whole festival was almost swept away by rain. Since perhaps as many as 4,000 were expected to attend, the consecration had to be arranged in an open-air church. Ibura, close by, received very heavy rain, and the clouds threatened Bukoba. But now the same thing happened as at the consecration in 1961: 'God stretched out his hand and turned away the rain.' So it was said.

The ritual followed the same pattern as at the 1961 consecration, and thus followed Swedish tradition – with one exception: as the consecrating bishop I decided to omit a liturgical formula in the Swedish tradition that makes 'Our Father' the consecrating prayer. Instead, another prayer was used which followed the tradition of the ancient church, or, if you like, that of North Africa: 'O God, the Father of our Lord Jesus Christ, God of all grace and consolation; Thou whose throne is in Heaven, but Who exaltest the humble, and Who knoweth all things from the beginning: give unto this Thy servant that strength that cometh from Thee; impart to him that Holy Spirit given by Thy Son Jesus Christ to His Holy Apostles, to the end that Thy name may be glorified and men be saved, Thou who liveth and reigneth, o God, for ever and ever. Amen.' (*Bara Bukoba* 1980:174–6)

Every African diocese loves festivals and celebrations. Bukoba is no exception. But the culmination of everything was certainly this day when the first African bishop of the diocese was consecrated. The festival was in fact continued the following Sunday at Kashenye, the home village of the Kibira family, to which the whole of Hayaland – perhaps 10,000 people in all – Evangelicals, Catholics and Muslims – found their way to offer their congratulations to the new African church leader.

In time, Bishop Kibira received an Honorary Doctor's degree from the University of Uppsala in 1974, the year B Sr retired from his post. To qualify for that B Sr had urged Kibira to write a book, which he did. The book required much revision which B Sr had to do himself in the middle of many other theses which he wanted to see to the end before his retirement. Another source of great satisfaction for B Sr was the election of Bishop Kibira as the President of the Lutheran World Federation in the World Assembly held in Dar es Salaam in 1978.

The pastors and leaders of the northwestern diocese remember the lasting influence of their first bishop particularly for his wisdom in spotting the potential leaders and providing systematic theological education for them. 'What we are in this country we owe to you.' These words of Richard Mutembei, the long-time secretary of the diocese, especially reflect B Sr's educational contribution. (Interview 21 August 1988) The same point was emphasised by Reverend Byarugaba who had been baptised by Bishop Bengt and personally knew him only as a child and gave his assessment in retrospect. He also gave the first bishop credit for inducing the missionary spirit in the diocese, in his estimation more so than in other dioceses: more ELCT missionaries to other African countries came from his diocese than from any other. He also gave B Sr credit for the ecumenical orientation instilled in the church. (Interview with Reverend Byarugaba in Finland in May 1999)

Consecration of the cathedral

Five years later Bengt Sundkler was called, as the former bishop of the diocese to participate in the consecration of the cathedral which he had been planning throughout his term of service and which now had been completed, not of stones brought from Italy, but from the very region where the sanctuary was erected, the symbolism of which he brought to the attention of the gathered crowds. He continued:

> From the beginning, and from century to century, from generation to generation, a question has echoed through mankind. It is God's question to first man and woman ... God asks 'Where art thou?'
>
> But at this our time, in the twentieth century, man asks himself another question, heavy with meaning. As we look at this world, with its wars and hatred and injustice, it appears as if Almighty God had hidden himself. This time it is man who cries out, 'Our God, where art Thou?'
>
> Yet, in fact, we do not need to ask this. For God has placed his signs in the world, along the road wherever we pass. In the place where we live and wherever we move, everywhere there are in fact signs which he has placed; road signs for our safari, in order that we shall see and understand. All these superficial things in life do not satisfy. There is another meaning in life with life.
>
> We are assembled under the Sign of the Cross. The sign above all other signs is this his cross ... showing the way of the love of God, in Jesus Christ our Saviour. He who humbled himself and became obedient even unto death on the Cross. He has established fellowship and communication with us, in that he entered into our own world, with its hatred in order to remove it, and its hunger and fear and enmity in order to overcome all this. (Sermon of B Sr at the consecration, 9 August 1970)

The funeral of Bishop Kibira

Bengt Sundkler lived to attend the funeral of Bishop Kibira who died in 1988 after suffering from Parkinson's disease for some years. He praised highly the organisational capacity of Kibira's successor Bishop Mushemba. All the arrangements were well done. Thirteen of the 16 ELCT bishops had come and two Catholic bishops of Bukoba and Rulenge not only came, but spoke beautifully and simply and took part in the service with Bible readings. This was a 'fantastic' step forward from the first fears in relation to the Catholic Church, but although excellently organised the funeral was too pompous to B Sr's taste:

> The whole thing was enormously well organised. The African deaconesses had arranged the flowers beautifully. A German visiting brass band played. The funeral service lasted four-and-a-half hours. In the cathedral, the body was laid in the ecclesiastical garb with the wooden staff of the assistant bishop under a glass cover. People could come and walk by. In the service, Bishop Kweka of Moshi preached, Mama Martha, a little woman, spoke from the pulpit, followed by Sebastian Bishanga, a layman, one of the brethren. I had my chance at the grave side. About 100 pastors participated. The coffin was carried to the grave between the clock tower and the cathedral. A big cement structure had been built, an engineering job, no ordinary grave.
>
> The whole thing was a little too much. The bishops wore their robes and mitres, with the exception of myself, I had only a white robe and black stole. These signs of office are worn at the consecration of the bishop, not at a funeral, which should be done in utmost simplicity to emphasise the meaning of funeral. I talked about this with Professor Cuthbert Omari who agreed. (Interview 21 August 1988 in Meilahti hospital, in the presence of Dr Bahendwa and Lloyd Swantz)[10]

Bishop Mushemba had also arranged for B Sr to meet with all the pastors, from the oldest generation to the youngest. Attending this funeral made B Sr change his initial agreement to be buried with Ingeborg in Bukoba for two reasons. First, Bishop Kibira should be the bishop commemorated, not he. Kibira had now been given the honour due to him. B Sr's burial would be an afterthought, out of the chronological order – the people would no longer have the same contact with him as they had while he was serving them. The second reason was the elaborate funeral. He felt he would not have wanted anything like that for himself. (Interview 21 August 1988 in Meilahti hospital) When the time for B Sr's funeral came, the leaders and people in Bukoba felt disappointed. Bishop Mushemba and the leading deaconess came to represent the diocese at Bishop Bengt's funeral. It was not easy to explain why their first bishop had wished to change the initial arrangement.

Notes

1. Parts of this chapter are reprints from *Bara Bukoba, Church and Community in Tanzania* by Bengt Sundkler, C. Hurst & Company, London, 1980.
2. Autobiographical notes in a letter 27 June 1982.
3. The Usambara synod of the Evangelical Lutheran Church, later to be called northeastern diocese, was to become a diocese and have Reverend Waltenberg as its first bishop.
4. In writing this account, B Sr did not make any direct reference to the fact that he would have been the obvious candidate for consecrating Bishop Moshi. Here then came the theological difference which the American and Norwegian Lutherans insisted on and which had influenced African opinion on the matter. The Apostolic Succession had to be avoided by all means – on that occasion. It had of course already been passed on through Bishop Bo Giertz.
5. *Hem till Tanzania*. Boken om Barbro Johansson berättad för Anna Wieslander, Rabén & Sjögren, 1989. (Home to Tanzania. A Book About Barbro Johansson narrated to Anna Wieslander.) Festschrift: *Vision and Service*. Papers in honour of Barbo Johansson September 25, 1977. Eds. B. Sundkler and P.Å. Wahlström Uppsala 1977.
6. Paskazia Mhingo was interviewed by Hesekiel Balira at B Sr's request when she was 60 years old. B Sr received Balira's report on 20 March 1980 in response to detailed questions he sent out to numerous people in order to get concrete information about women's participation and leadership in the church.
7. I was one of the three teachers in the language school for Swahili in Dar es Salaam, with Elizabeth Bernander and Fanueli Kiwao, education inspector from Usangi, North Pare.
8. B Sr encouraged and showed great interest in Birgitta Larsson's PhD thesis *Conversion to Greater Freedom? Women, Church and Social Change in North-Western Tanzania under Colonial Rule*, Studia Historica Academica Uppsala 1991. The book elaborates on the liberating effect of the revival for women who joined the movement.
9. B Sr had two other American assistants consecutively, Joel Wiberg and Paul Borg, who took care of the English correspondence and had to take hold of many practical details. B Sr always praised them highly.
10. Mama Martha was Bishop Kibira's wife.

9

'GOOD TIMES IN UPPSALA'

Introduction

The year 1964 ended with moving events for Bengt and Ingeborg Sundkler. They were leaving the continent behind where, in the heart of Africa, they had participated with people in their struggle for Life and in their search for meaning. The handing over of the leadership of the diocese to Bishop Josiah Kibira took place only four days before their departure from Bukoba, a few days before Christmas. They left with a sentiment, 'God has been very good to us here in Buhaya and Karagwe.'

From here on the resigning bishop would, in faith, keep the continent alive in his heart and in his mind's eyes, with disciplined thought, imagination and dreams, and interpret it in spoken and written word to people prepared to listen and respond.

After his return to Sweden at the beginning of 1965, Bengt Sundkler had to take on his teaching duties and see to the supervision of the doctoral candidates for whom he was responsible. In his work as professor and teacher he cared for his students but was troubled that, due to a narrowness of insight into the history and theology of the Church, the subject he represented did not have a greater general respect in the faculty.

Having gone through a 'personality transforming' period as the bishop of a new diocese in Africa his interest was now directed toward the Church of Sweden and its episcopacy. He became involved in the ongoing debates in the church, including the ministry of the church and women's ordination, on which his views had altered.

After the episcopal years he found salvation in his writing. With his keen ecumenical concern for the Universal Church he was attracted to the personality of the great ecumenical leader, former archbishop of the Church of Sweden, Nathan Söderblom, whom he had met in his youth and with whom he identified closely. Soon after returning he began to contemplate writing an extensive study of Söderblom for the Swedish public. Instead of starting to write in Swedish he was entrusted with the writing of Söderblom's biography in English. For personal therapy B Sr required tasks which engaged him fully. Writing on Söderblom offered him the second 'personality transforming' experience, as he himself described it. (Letter to MLS 2 March 1973)

At the end of the decade, in the midst of his busiest time with the students and practical chores while moving house, Ingeborg suffered a serious illness from which she did not recover. After Ingeborg's death Bengt had to reorganise his personal life and to find his bearings without the spiritual and domestic support of his wife. In the last four years of professorship he divided his time between the doctoral candidates, writing and continuing international engagements, which meant also considerable time spent in travel.

To accommodate the above aspects into this chapter I divide the last ten years, which remained for Bengt Sundkler to work in the university, into eight sections: Transition from Africa to the North; Back to Church of Sweden; Professor among students; Nathan Söderblom – a liberating experience; Teaching and travels; Ingeborg at rest; Back to the students; Bengt Sundkler's theology in a nutshell.

Transition from Africa to the north

Assessing the past

While in transition from their beloved Bukoba home to the cold north Ingeborg and Bengt Sundkler gave themselves a breather in their favourite retreat at St Julian's, in Limuru near Nairobi. On the way, they drove around to Queen Elizabeth Park in Uganda to greet herds of elephants and 'thousands' of hippos and flamingos in Nakuru Kenya. They spent Christmas on the road with a shattered windscreen, rain approaching, no help in sight, but after a great deal of trouble, seasoned travellers as they were, they managed to attract the necessary assistance. They lingered in Nairobi making many contacts as usual, among them Dr Audrey Wipper, who had come to see B Sr the day before they left Bukoba and now had more time to exchange notes on independent churches and groups in Kenya and South Africa.

The resigning Bishop of the northwestern diocese of the ELCT felt a need to reflect on his work that had now come to a close. Before leaving Bukoba he wrote in his diary:

> How wonderfully we have been upheld, helped, encouraged by all we have experienced in one corner of this great continent of Africa. What a joy, what a privilege it has been to be allowed, at this time, this hour of Africa, to serve this our beloved diocese, this our family which has been so kind to us. 'God is a good God,' this saying of Nicholas Bhengu

of South Africa, a great evangelist and leader, comes to my mind, as I
go into our chapel the last evening of my Episcopal service in Africa.
(Diary 22 December 1964)

In the quietness of St Julian's B Sr looked back over his years in
Bukoba and Karagwe, assessing the positive and negative sides of his
service as bishop in those three-and-a-half years during which he
had taken leave of absence from his professor's post in Uppsala. He
felt deep gratitude for the experience, but considered also his own
failures.

B Sr was happy that Bishop Kibira could now contribute much more
than he had been allowed to give or do in the Church Union talks,
while he regretted that he had been replaced in them by three solid
Lutherans. Kibira would also represent an important voice in the
Lutheran Church in Tanzania. B Sr was happy that the internal relationships within the synodal council were good and potential crises
had been avoided. In reminiscing, he went through the relationships
with the main church leaders and was able to identify ways in which
conflicts had been dealt with. Also the missionary relations had been
good in general, with the exception of three 'problem children'. As
was characteristic of B Sr he always remembered people by name,
missionaries as well, making a few generally positive remarks on
each. Cardinal Rugambwa and other RC connections and fellowship
with the Save the Children personnel, they all were remembered with
gratitude: 'It is this enriching fellowship with them that is all one
remembers in looking back.'

On the negative side, B Sr regrets that the cathedral was not built
in his time. They encountered problems in acquiring a good site. They
did not manage to build the girls' secondary school nor the homecraft
school. His illness contributed to a degree of inactivity in 1964 with
fewer visits to parishes than he would have wished. He also felt that
he had concentrated too much on day-to-day jobs and not planned
sufficiently for the future. More contacts could have been established
with pastors, more frequent visits to their homes, and the bishop's
house could have been even more open. For lack of research and
writing he would make amends on his return to Sweden.

B Sr recognised his failure to maintain living contacts with the
Mission organisations in Sweden, Denmark and Germany, which co-
operated in the work in the northwestern diocese. His relationship
with the Church of Sweden Mission had been less positive than the
relationship with the African church. He felt that the CSM on its part
had given him little support while he served one of the main mission
partners of the Church of Sweden. Against his own wishes, he felt an
outsider in his relations with the Church of Sweden:

I dislike mission secretaries, as such. This is very unreasonable of me,
but I confess I do. I feel the CSM secretaries have let me down by lack

of contact, communication and encouragement. I was completely surprised to receive a positive and appreciative letter from H. Benettsson yesterday.

However, it is my fault not to have managed to write for the mission papers and Swedish newspapers, or papers in Denmark and Germany. But with my temperament I need some little prodding and encouragement for this kind of a thing; it never came.

However, all this is transitory and of little avail as compared with the great enriching experience which we have been through ... My remaining years must be devoted to thanks to God for such an honour, privilege, joy and all His mercy throughout the episcopal service in the diocese on the equator. (Diary 31 December 1964)

Backtracking

The homeward flight was not yet on the programme. B Sr backtracked still for five days to Kampala and even to Bukoba. His American assistant, Paul Borg, came to Nairobi and took Ingeborg with their Peugot to the Mombasa beaches while Bengt flew to Entebbe. Once more he was with the Anglican archbishops, Beecher of East Africa and Leslie Brown of Uganda, but this time also with many other religious leaders, a Pakistani and African sheikh, Indian Brahman, a Jewish Rabbi, RC priest and one woman. They all met under the chairmanship of B Sr's good friend, Professor N. Q. King, for the Council for Higher Studies in Religion for the University of East Africa at Makerere. For the following day the Association of Theological Colleges in East Africa was scheduled, which B Sr had chaired for the period 1963–64, in 1965 being replaced by Reverend John Gatu, General Secretary of the Presbyterian Church of Kenya. The evening was spent with 'a young Danish Church historian Holger Hansen and his charming wife Inge, a biochemist'. Also on the way back from Bukoba they were accommodating. Professor Holger Hansen was later of great help when B Sr worked on his African Church History.

B Sr returned to Bukoba once more, even if only for two days. Families and children had a prime place in his diary notes (6–7 January 1965):

> 6 January. In the evening went to Richard Mutembei's shamba and had a nice time there: 8 children. They sang and danced and twisted for me and Bishop Kibira. With Lars and Birgitta Johansson and then on to Dean Lutosha ... 7 January. Coffee in Benedict Nyamwihila's house. Very nice family of five children. The youngest daughter, Flora, 3 months, very beautiful, looked at me with calm, big eyes ... At Kibira's home, (B Sr observing) little Namala, 6 yrs old, Bishop K.: 'She is a most gifted child, very observant.'

B Sr had a little premonition of what the newly gained freedom from White tutelage might mean when Bishop Kibira told him that one preacher had played a drum and twisted while preaching on the rejoicing of the woman who found the lost silver coin in Luk. 15, and Reverend Karumuna's two choirs had twisted while singing hymns! This kind of freedom of expression was something B Sr would have anticipated.

After returning to Nairobi Ingeborg and Bengt still spent some days in St Julian's and Nairobi before finally taking off for Sweden. They arrived in Arlanda on 12 January in the evening and were met by Dr Diehl and wife, Holger Benettsson and N. L. Holmström. They moved into their small flat at Odensgatan 5 that same night, with no means to manage with for the first few days. Journalists from three major papers and the radio were soon there to interview B Sr and in less than a week the seminars and lectures began.

B Sr had behind him his first 'personality transforming experience'. As bishop, he had communed with Christian brothers and sisters who were deeply influenced by the East African Revival Movement, he had practised 'ecumenics in the banana groves', and also cultivated relationships with the Evangelical and Low-Church Anglicans. All this had changed his High-Church spirituality and ecclesiology, in relation to the office of the church and episcopacy too.

Back to the Church of Sweden

Debates on the ministry of the Church

Having been so deeply involved in the birth of a Church in Africa it was not easy for B Sr to rejoin the faculty of theologians for whom theological formulas remained untested in practice. For many in academia the vision that Church History comprised a history of Christianity throughout the whole world and was a history of the Universal Church on all continents was still a distant idea. They hardly felt the same need to share this history in a spiritual partnership with the sister churches in Africa. Sundkler did not look for acceptance in the sense of recognition of his accomplishments – which also would have been welcomed – he looked for a deeper recognition of the human and spiritual unity within the Universal Church and common humanity, sharing and responding. Theory for him was linked with and growing out of practice and remained rooted in experience and lived history.

When B Sr returned to the Church of Sweden he found that the controversial issue of the office of the church, specifically related to the ordination of women, was still the subject of heated debate. In Sweden, the ministry in charge of education and ecclesiastical matters, after assessing the outcome of the review which it had made of diocesan opinions on women's ordination, had presented the issue for approval to the synod of the Church in 1957. The reaction of the majority of the bishops was negative, and after substantial discussions the majority of the synod rejected the proposal. In 1958 there was a new government and new minister, and the synod was called to reconvene. The issue was again discussed and this time the bishops' opinions were divided three ways. A few accepted the proposal, possibly with reference to the explicit preferences of the new government, a few opposed it on biblical–theological grounds, and a few held the same view they had the year before that the issue would have to be decided in a broader ecumenical context. A decision was taken in favour of women's ordination which meant that the first three women were ordained to the priesthood in the Church of Sweden in 1959.

In the 1950s B Sr had opposed the ordination of women on biblical and ecumenical grounds. His High-Church leanings and views of men who had been important to his spiritual and intellectual growth had influenced his opinions.[1] During his episcopal years he had changed his views and his own ecclesiological orientation and moved to a more open and inclusive position. This he also knew to have been the position of the former archbishop, Nathan Söderblom, whose views he valued in more ways than one, even if, in Söderblom's time, neither the Church nor society were yet ready to act on the issue of women's ordination.

The greater tolerance of differences in the practices of other churches, which B Sr had experienced in Africa, had helped him to change his opinion about women's ordination. He saw that the biblical interpretation had been based on conditions of its time and it was no longer necessary to argue against it on ecumenical grounds. He had realised that the adoption of the new position in the Church of Sweden did not prevent the Anglican archbishops in Africa from inviting him to take part in several bishops' consecrations nor him from helping out the local Anglican church in the absence of their own priests in Bukoba. The Church of Sweden had also been given to understand by the archbishop of the Church of England, Geoffrey Fisher, that the issue of women's ordination was an internal one for the Church.

In the autumn of 1965 B Sr was drawn into public discussion of the issue. The question was also discussed in one of Sundkler's seminars on Church History. As a teacher he expected more variation of opinion on the subject than the students were prepared to consider, not simply arguments for or against women's ordination. B Sr, characteristically, looked for more conciliatory views at a time when the Church was divided on the issue of the office of the Church. He heard the fine church leader, Bishop Bo Giertz, of Gothenburg diocese, who had consecrated B Sr as bishop, give a lecture in which he turned his subject 'The Future of the Church' almost solely to the issue of women pastors. B Sr found the lecture very unsatisfactory, but he was sorry that this man who, despite his position on this issue, was giving spiritual inspiration to the church, did not then appear to receive the public recognition he deserved, owing to his negative position on women's ordination. (Diary 9 February 1965)[2]

B Sr responded to an article 'The Church narrows its front', '*Kyrklig front förkortning*', which his colleague and friend, Professor Harald Riesenfeld, published in *Svenska Dagbladet*. Riesenfeld seemed to be suggesting that because of women's ordination the Church of Sweden, stripped from the signs of office, would build on a common narrowed basis with the free churches. He was of the opinion that the bishops should have started their own church, committed to the ancient tradition, when the government, according to him, pressed the Church to decide for women's ordination.[3] B Sr assumed that this position would make those of the High-Church tradition decide to become Roman Catholic, as Riesenfeld himself, in fact, did when he retired from the faculty. (Diary 4 September and 14–18 October 1965)

B Sr's response in the same newspaper, 'Not narrowing, but widening the perspective', pointed to the need for a broader ecumenical perspective. The Church of Sweden cannot limit itself to the Swedish scene but must consider the issue in the scope of wide-ranging international dialogue with other churches. It cannot forget its bridging function, to give and to receive, assuming the widened responsibility is God's way to renewal, to a deeper, broader understanding of the apostolic heritage of the Universal Church. The problem relates to the visible unity of the Church of Christ and the capacity of the different churches to change, as well as the versatility of the established churches, which was B Sr's message after Vatican Council II and his own African experience. B Sr pointed to a changing view within the Anglican Church, which was anticipated, (and took, in fact a decisive turn in 1975) and to Jesuit professor Jean Daniélou's declaration in the context of the Vatican Council; he saw no 'fundamental theological objections' against women priests. (*Frontförkortning i ekumeniken*, Sundkler 1965:68–70)[4]

When B Sr returned to the issue in 1975 he noted that Riesenfeld had, in fact, already broadened his views at an important point in 1965. He had questioned the former biblical–theological position based on Paul's word in the Corinthians, i.e. that women should keep silence in the churches. Moving away from Fridrichsen's 'biblical realism' Riesenfeld had come to see a hermeneutic task to interpret the word for 'the people of *our* time and in *our* situation'. 'Faith can no longer live on without taking risks' were Riesenfeld's words. (Sundkler 1975:165)

Candidate for episcopacy in Sweden

Living close to Uppsala Cathedral, in fact, having his office in the gatehouse of the cathedral for many years, B Sr was in close contact with the church leaders and loved to preach in the cathedral when asked to do so. Having been consecrated as a bishop in a sister church, yet feeling that his episcopal position was given little recognition within the Church of Sweden, increased his feeling of being an outsider. He represented the faculty in the Archdiocese Chapter (*Domkapitel*) for many years, but found the meetings during Archbishop Hultgren's time long-winded and inconsequential. He had good relations with Hultgren, yet he remarked at times that Hultgren did not use his position either in preaching or in other meetings to say anything significant.

When serving as a bishop, Bengt Sundkler had placed great importance on his relationship with future pastors. He gave them extra teaching about the church order, liturgy and key message and mission of the church and took them into a retreat for several days before ordination. When he then heard Archbishop Hultgren saying a few superficial words to the diocesan council in leaving his service as the archbishop he lamented about lost opportunities at key moments when prophetic words were called for more than ever. (Diary 27 September 1967)

In a pastors' conference on 8 June 1965 four pastors from the Luleå diocese approached B Sr asking him to stand as a candidate for election as bishop in Luleå. He refused and did not even contemplate the proposition: 'They are nice – but they do not understand how foreign the thought is for me, to disappear in the snow and ice in the north and to be directed by a certain faction regarding certain opinions.'

Then, when Archbishop Hultgren's retirement was approaching, representatives of the Lund diocese sent a letter to B Sr at the end of 1966 asking whether he would set himself forward as a candidate in election for the archbishop. The matter was also discussed in the archdiocese pastors' conference where B Sr seemed to get support. He thought he should not refuse without further consideration, but he questioned how general the support was. He doubted his own qualifications for the great task, but on the other hand, he felt he should leave the possibility open. His identification with the great archbishop, Nathan Söderblom, was perhaps one incentive toward accepting the candidacy. He was afraid that those with High-Church leanings would vote for him on the erroneous assumption that he would be sympathetic to their position toward women's ordination. He made his views clear to his potential supporters.

B Sr was influenced by his wife whom he naturally consulted about the matter. Ingeborg was in Rättvik and wrote a letter from there urging Bengt to think carefully what his calling was, how competent he was for the task which would require also good administrative abilities. She pleaded him to consider that as the archbishop Bengt would not be free to do what he wanted, he would be restricted in his international contacts and he would not be able to write: 'THINK! What is your calling?' (Letter n.d.)

Later B Sr was approached once more from the archdiocese. After a great deal of persuasion he finally allowed his name to be put forward. (Diary 8 June; 31 October; 13 December and 26 December 1966)

Bengt Sundkler's name was not one of the three among whom the election was carried out. They were Gert Borgenstierna, Ruben Josefson and Krister Stendahl. He could not attend the archdiocese chapter meeting, where the preliminary election was done. He was left guessing for the rest of his life which one of the representatives failed to give the one additional vote he would have needed, to have his name among the final three.[5] One can detect a faint sadness at missing the great challenge:

> It was a sad personal weakness from my side to give in to pressure from the diocesan secretary Morén and vicar Sven Holmström, and a whole lot of my doctoral students and docents, to set myself up as a candidate. I have my task and my line and I must be faithful to it: 8 or 7 years of professorship still left ... Then, I hope, we move to England. I have the hope of being able to get hold of a total view of England's or Great Britain's input in missions during the colonial time, a general inventory of the mission archives. Then we can build something down in Sussex and have a wonderful existence in a generous milieu. Since 1938 (St Augustine, Zululand) Ingeborg and I have lost our hearts to what is Anglican and English. It is a line to be faithful to. (Diary 15 March 1967)

At this point B Sr also mentions his political alignment with the Christian Social Democrats, a reference to this appeared in the popular press in the context of the bishop's election process. It gave him a reason to elaborate on the reasons why he had chosen that line:

> But even this relates to my English heritage. In the Tanzanian time 1942–45, and in London 1946–49 I took up membership of the Fabian Society;[6] because of the impact of the Labour government's contribution to the abolition of imperialism (Attlee, Cripps, Creech-Jones); contact with the Foreign Office (A. B. Cohen) – and the Anglican bishops' (Gore, Temple) engagement on the left gave direction to me. Why could I not continue this also in Sweden? (Diary 15 March 1967)

B Sr thought that at least for some he had been politically suspect. He was known to have been on the Social Democrat ticket in the local parish council.[7] B Sr also suspected that his political connection was the reason why he time and again had difficulty getting his entries correctly reported in the conservative newspaper *Svenska Dagbladet*. (Diary 22 October 1967)

Professor among students

Guiding doctoral candidates

Bengt Sundkler had timed his return from Africa so that he was ready to start a new year and new term of work in the theological faculty in January 1965. He had been absent for three-and-a-half years, but not totally away from his academic duties. During the first faculty meeting he participated in he learned that he would be the promoter for the theological faculty in the customary solemn promotion of doctors in May.

During his absence the acting director of the Institute of Mission Research was Tore Furberg, one of the doctoral students he guided in thesis writing while he was in Africa. The assistant professor of Church History, Allan Sandevall, was acting professor in Sundkler's absence and it was agreed that B Sr could carry on supervising the doctoral students.

Soon after leaving B Sr had written a letter (1 July 1961) to his three doctoral candidates, Tore Furberg, Per Beskow and Rolf Sjölinder, giving them his address in Bukoba and promising to keep in contact with them. He also informed them that he would be back in Uppsala in mid-September 1961 and would have several seminars with them about the chapters in their dissertations. Good chapters required well-formulated introductions and conclusions. The correspondence shows that B Sr indeed read and made suggestions on the parts that were sent to him by Tore Furberg. (Letter to Furberg 27 December 1961) Professor Riesenfeld stepped in as an assistant supervisor for Per Beskow. B Sr promised to make last minute suggestions and to be present at Per Beskow's defence. (Letter 25 January 1962) B Sr was present when Sjölinder and Furberg defended their theses in April 1962. His four-month-long illness meant that he was in Uppsala for several weeks in 1963, and he made one or two additional visits while he attended conferences in Europe, in order to maintain contact with his doctoral students.

B Sr was quite demanding in his requests for assistance from his substitutes in the institute in gathering material for lectures he had to give, or papers he had to write while he was out of reach of resource materials. Allan Sandevall had health problems and was not fully able to carry his part in relation to the students, but in B Sr's absence he supervised C. F. Hallencreutz and Eric Sharpe who had started to work on their dissertations before B Sr left for Africa. Sharpe defended on 8 May 1965, getting his docentship also. B Sr had encouraged the active Christian Social Democrat Stiv Jacobson to take up doctoral studies, as well as David Lagergren, the principal of the Baptist Theological Seminary in Stockholm. Both of them were helped by Sandevall, but B Sr continued to work with them when he returned.

Hallencreutz defended in December 1966, which meant that B Sr could read his work and discuss it on several sessions, as he faithfully reported in his diary:

> I had also the joy of receiving the first part of Hallencreutz's thesis on Kraemer. Totally surprising, with new content and good flow of material. Not surprising if one thinks of the outstanding author, but surprising that it has been possible to get as much out of the topic as he has done.

After B Sr came back to his students, the number of doctoral students grew year by year. It is likely that the 18 doctoral degrees taken in Mission History in Bengt Sundkler's time exceeded the number of corresponding degrees in any other theological subject in those years. In 1960 Sigbert and Marianne Axelson had returned from missionwork under the Mission Covenant Church in the Congo, where Sigbert had been teaching at a theological seminary. Sigbert decided to take his doctoral degree in Uppsala because of B Sr's and Stig Lagerqvist's expertise on Africa. He started writing his doctoral thesis when B Sr was back in Uppsala. Seminars were held with Sigbert Axelson, who was writing his thesis on Culture Confrontation in the Lower Congo in reference to Swedish missionwork by the Mission Covenant Church there. He defended his dissertation in 1970. In the diary there are several references to the excellent seminars they had in relation to Sigbert Axelson's thesis. To give just one example:

> 29 April 1968. Seminar with Sigbert Axelson and Stiv Jacobson. Dr Lars Sundström present. Sigbert Axelson gave a very remarkable introduction, a chapter from his thesis. What a brilliant talented person he is with a fine knowledge of Africa's history.

David Lagergren's thesis on the Mission and State also dealt with the Lower Congo. Sigbert Axelson and David Lagergren were the first doctoral students from a Free-Church background. At the end of 1970 Lagergren defended his dissertation, as did Sigbert Axelson and myself. Several days were spent with David Lagergren and Stiv Jacobson, at times in their homes, in a mutual learning process. Stiv Jacobson was working on the British missions and the abolition of the slave trade and slavery both in West Africa and in the West Indies with valuable material from both sides. He defended with a final volume of 660 pages in 1972.[8]

Sigvard von Sicard wrote his thesis on the history of the Lutheran Church on the Coast of Tanzania during the years of Berlin Mission Society in 1887–1914. He served as the President of the Uzaramo-Uluguru Synod of the ELCT for part of the time when my husband and I also worked there. Sigvard's father, Harald von Sicard, had been a missionary in South Rhodesia, Zimbabwe, and was sent by the mission to visit the orphaned fields in Tanzania when B Sr was in Bukoba in the 1940s. Sigvard von Sicard also disputed in 1970 and then studied at the American University in Cairo for a year. He became an expert on Islam and has made his career as a lecturer in Selly Oak College in Birmingham.

For B Sr the teaching was not entirely satisfying. I move ahead in time by citing what B Sr wrote on leaving the university about his discomfort in the setting in which Mission History was taught. After the last faculty meeting on 2 May 1974, he described his teaching situation in the following terms:

> Yesterday after the faculty meeting I handed my Bukoba book to each one of the colleagues. I did so with gratitude that I have experienced such a good time with this crew. We have never had any quarrel. Mostly this is because of my tremendous meekness, which goes too far. I think of the fact that because I could not give extra points in Missions for the lower exam, only Pass, or *godkänd* (approved) ... I have all the time largely ignored my teaching of the subject, I am sorry to say. I have given them written tests, which I can correct and mark in less than half an hour and have thereby not had any trouble with drawn-out long oral exams. This has saved time for me and from that point of view it has been all to the good, but I am afraid that for generations of young people I have hardly existed, apart from the short course of Missions which they have followed. Then of course I have had them in Church History and this has been helpful. All the more I have given my attention to the doctorands.
>
> In spite of all these shortcomings I have of course had exceptionally good contacts with the young students. But I wish I would have been in a position to credit their results better. That would have inspired them more, to greater efforts, I think. I should have protested about this, but have not done it, and just let the years go by, for the sake of peace and quiet. Very bad. (Letter to MLS 3 May 1974)

B Sr was an attentive listener at sermons and was very disturbed when he discovered how weak the Biblical and New Testament foundation of the preaching was in the Church of Sweden. The lack of understanding of the centrality of mission in the New Testament message was particularly disturbing to him, when not even the mission Sundays gave a clear message of the Gospel. This affected his teaching. He felt that for his own sake and for the sake of the theological students he had to include more New Testament theology in his lectures, mission and baptism as potential themes. He felt his speciality was to be exposition of the Bible. (Diary 17 December 1967)

He tried to bring his concerns about theological teaching, especially the significance of the changes taking place in the churches to ecumenicity, into the discussions at practical theology conferences:

> In the Church History and Practical Theology Conference I spoke a couple of times and pointed out that one subject we should consider is the capacity of the churches to change; the churches do change. This is so in our own church ... and in the churches in the USA, but is seen

in a sharper relief in Asia and Africa ... it is significant for the ecumenical aspect in the Church. Are the churches not different aspects of the same Church? I spoke also about the sociological aspects ... I emphasised that we would need to think of the church in large cities as single units ... and that sociology would be of great importance (for such themes). My statements raised opposition from my colleague in Church history, although my intention was not to oppose the historical method, as he (Professor Göransson) for some reason assumed. (Diary 27 September 1965)[9]

B Sr was concerned for the students' personal well-being and culti- vated good contacts with them by inviting them as a class and as individuals to his home. He became inspired by the students' response when he related to the future of the students in the church. He was then also better able to express his views:

12 October 1965. I had a seminar for theological students on India and Ceylon, and a lecture on 'Mission and Ecumenics' with an introduction of a few words about the Riesenfeld issue, including the Faith and Order debate. It is an exceptionally nice group. I had 4–5 students here at home afterwards. We discussed the situation in the Church.

Ingeborg also notes such visits in her menu diary (1965): '20 young people from Bengt's seminar were invited, 15 came. In a hurry, [we managed] bites of roast beef and potato salad.'

Excerpts from diaries of the immediate reactions to meeting with the doctorands and the teaching events in the 1960s and 1970s tell of the mutual enjoyment that these contacts gave them. They tell also of engagements outside the university and of the inconvenience which teaching could be for someone who, besides teaching, devoted his time to writing and conducted his research in the field. There was also a constant stream of international visitors. I cite a few diary notes for some fragments of the story:

13 August 1967. As usual, incredibly fruitful discussion, full of rich viewpoints, with C. F. Htz; this time perhaps also as profitable for Hallencreutz as for me. Otherwise I am usually always on the receiving side in these discussions with this striking young man.

14 September 1968. A seminar for theological students with Joseph Öhreman about Mission and Church in the Congo, about 25 people were present. A very valuable and charming person and lecturer. Afterwards ... 20–30 theological students waiting at the Dekanhuset [Theological Faculty building] ... I went to give a lecture on Ecumenics ... A very interesting and pleasant, engaged group of students to whom it was a joy to speak. Met one of these students who expressed enthusiastic thanks for yesterday's lecture and I was quite touched to hear that they could follow my thoughts.

16 September 1968. Dr Edward Mondlane was here.[10] I had a talk with him in his hotel room and also interviewed him for *Svenska Missions-tidskrift*. He gave a lecture about 'Strategy for the Liberation of Southern Africa'. Lively debate followed about Portugal's colonial policy.

21 September 1968. Seminar for theological students on 'World Mission 1945–65' in which they showed interest. Gustav Bernander was at the licentiate seminar talking about 'Orphaned missions'.[11] I had a lecture on the Faith and Order movement. Could not unfortunately get out anything significant of the subject.

24 September 1968. I spoke at the Meeting of the Archdiocese on 'A Holy, Universal and Apostolic Church'. I myself had the impression that it was a decent lecture . . . I had good contact with Archbishop Hultgren. In the evening Ingeborg and I flew to Oslo, Lyseby.

25 September 1968. [In Oslo] I spoke on 'Our position in the meeting of Christian and Non-Christian religions'. It was a fine group. There were [in attendance] a psychologist, Professor Frohm from Copenhagen, an intelligent and fine person; Johan Galtung from the Peace Research Institute, fine as always; Carl Fredrik Engelstad, in whose home we stayed and who was a great joy to meet again; Mrs Segerstedt-Wiberg, a very generous person; Gr. Bauer-Hansen, an ideal Chair for the Academy, and Anne Thunberg, the Chairperson for our group, very skillful in chair.

B Sr had nothing but praise for many of his brilliant students he worked with. He did not think that he was the great guru who performed miracles with students, but he knew that his main gift was encouragement and it is perhaps what aspiring candidates need most.

Nathan Söderblom – a liberating experience

Commissioned to write the biography

When B Sr returned from Bukoba he contemplated writing a 3-volume book on Archbishop Nathan Söderblom in Swedish. He started gradually collecting material but was hesitant to take on the job on his own initiative. He wondered whether it was not too presumptuous of him to take it on and who was he to do it? B Sr was hesitant but felt he had good reason to take on the task. Not only had he had personal contact with Archbishop Söderblom, he had also gained a new view on ecclesiology and ecumenicity and the writing on the great ecumenic would present him with the opportunity to deal with the central issues of the universal church:

I was one of those who had been under the direct influence of the magic of his personality [having been called to meet him in person as a student]. Not only that; in those last weeks of his life [he died on 12 July 1931], he found time to dictate long letters to that Swedish student in Strasbourg and Paris, planning his future, as he had done for thousands of others more worthy of his exertions and expectations. (1968:10–11)

B Sr had already discussed with Staffan Runestam, Söderblom's grandson, the possibility of writing the first volume in Swedish in the summer of 1965 (Diary 12 July 1965) and also returned occasionally to the idea later on:

> Staffan Runestam, Sm's daughter's son, was here, splendid. He illuminated Nathan and Anna Söderblom's and their family relations and Uppsala milieu. It was very valuable. We discussed the potential Söderblom books I–III in Swedish. I suggested that S. R. would take on the editing of the letters, diaries, visitation reports ... he was quite agreeable to this. He could give them as a series of different volumes. We went to Carolina and looked at the papers with Gösta Timon. I should not postpone this task but to take it on as soon as possible. (Diary 15 August 1967)

The Swedish volumes got pushed to the background. At the time of a Nordic Ecumenical Mission Conference in Sigtuna in August 1965 B Sr was invited for a dinner at Archbishop Hultgren's house with Visser 't Hooft (the General Secretary of the WCC), Bishop Dibelius and Nils Ehrenström.[12] He was approached by these eminent people and asked to write the book on Söderblom in English and to have it ready for the forthcoming WCC World Assembly in Uppsala in 1968. He was delighted, now he need no longer hesitate. He recorded in his diary (20 August 1965):

> Visser 't Hooft and Hultgren decided during the dinner that I should write a book on Nathan Söderblom. It was Visser 't Hooft's idea to which Hultgren agreed, as is his custom. After dinner Visser 't Hooft came over to me, followed by Hultgren and Mrs Brillioth, Söderblom's daughter. The latter raised her finger, telling me to listen and take on the task.
>   It is wonderful that now the idea and the task came from outside, from the World Council of Churches and our Archbishop. I answered right away – from my side I would be ready to take up the work. They indicated also that it would be a modern English biography ready for June 1968, in time for the WCC Assembly in Uppsala, and two volumes should come out in the same context in Swedish. Visser 't Hooft said that he would retire in August 1966 and would then write his memoirs and could perhaps work with me in relation to Nathan Söderblom and see to it that I received various kinds of help.
>   I try now to weigh how much time I should set aside for South Africa: I should reduce the time from three to two months and fully concentrate

on this task. I should take leave for the academic year 1966–67 and
devote myself fully to this great Swedish-international cultural deed.

Bengt Sundkler used superlatives in talking about the privilege he
had been given to write about the great Swede, Archbishop Nathan
Söderblom:

> For me it was an immense joy getting to know Söderblom . . . Meeting
> with the African Church and the personality of Söderblom were liber-
> ating and joy giving influences for me. (Letter 2 March 1973)

> Walking with N Sm for 2–3 years transformed me. Generous person that
> he was, he overcame all the criticism, all the pettiness of people of his
> generation. This presented a challenge for me. I asked, 'Where does one
> receive such strength, to live such a life as Nathan Soderblom?'
> (Interview 31 October 1985)

The process of writing

From Bengt Sundkler's diaries we learn that he organised his seminars with Professor Göransson around the Söderblom theme. In this
way he was getting material collected by 25 students for their own
essays. He also got invaluable help from his teaching assistant
Hallencreutz (Diary 5 October and 29 October 1965).

B Sr recorded in his diary the first ideas for an outline which he
credited to Hallencreutz. He would first frame an 'image' of
Söderblom which was prevalent in Scandinavia, then cover the image
he held of himself and that which was being developed during his
active years. Secondly he would answer the question, 'Who was
Nathan Söderblom?' and describe his personality: 'I set these in their
functional context, before the ecumenical meeting in 1925. Who was
that man whom they were 'used' to seeing in 1925, how did he
appear, what went on in his mind?'

The first outline reflected the Swedish edition which B Sr had been
planning to write for a longer period. Its emphasis on personality and
the image others had of that personality is characteristic of B Sr.
Earlier works on Söderblom had been written in Swedish, thus the
prevalent Scandinavian picture would have been formed on the basis
of them. An important treatment of Söderblom's youth, him as a
scholar, and his years in Paris had been written by Professor Tor
Andrae, Söderblom's most brilliant student, in Sundkler's words. The
book gave leads to B Sr when he was acquainting himself with
Söderblom's background, how he grew to be the multifaceted man he
was. Another book by Nils Karlström – Sm's personal secretary for
the last five years, was written on his ecumenical activity. B Sr had
to reshape his initial plan to take into account the international reading
public.

The October 1965 diary notes tell of contacts he made with people who could provide information on themes relating to Söderblom. Archbishop Hultgren promised to approach the WCC in order to get some support for the work. B Sr also discussed with Hultgren a questionnaire which he sent to people who were knowledgeable about Söderblom. In his customary way, B Sr made use of any opportunities that came his way. While attending a conference in Lund he consulted Professor Anders Nygren about his personal views on, and contacts with, Söderblom. Professor Nygren had been elected the first president of the Lutheran World Federation at the inaugural meeting of the LWF in Lund in 1947. He, along with Archbishop Erling Eidem, had been the main initiators of the assembly.

B Sr started systematically acquainting himself with the Nathan Söderblom library and partly restricted archives. Anna Söderblom (1870–1970), Archbishop's wife and life-time critic and support, had over long years meticulously organised the archives in the archbishop's manse. The collections were placed in Carolina University Library in 1956 as Anna Söderblom had planned. The work on them was continued by the grandson, Staffan Runestam, and later also by library assistant Gösta Timon, both of whom were of great help to B Sr during the years he was writing, or planning to write, on Söderblom (Sundkler, 1970). B Sr gave a speech to the Söderblom society on the remarkable woman that Anna Söderblom was and subsequently expanded it to a published essay. Her husband never ceased to emphasise her significance on his career and person.[13]

B Sr contacted Söderblom's long-time secretary Gerda Rodling, a most resourceful and interesting personality, and went to see her on two different occasions, in 1965 and in 1989:

21 October 1965. To Stockholm for a long discussion with Gerda Rodling, N Sm's secretary from 1919 until his death. An alive and interesting person, whom it was a joy to meet. She gave a lot of good information. Now I know also 1. There is no N Sm's letter diary so that one would know which letters went out; 2. Often he did not take copies of the letters written with a typewriter!

I cannot but think that this lady has made a laudable contribution to church history. In 1908 13-year-old Gerda had visited the vicarage in Staby. After the visit she had written home to his father, a medical doctor in Fritsla: 'Now I know what I would like to be when I grow up, although I know it cannot ever happen. I would like to become a private secretary to Professor Söderblom.'[14]

In 1989 B Sr found this lady in Fritsla in south Sweden, 94 years old, blind and toothless, but brilliant and still in very good form:

I was with her 15 February evening and the whole day 16 February. She went on and on, never stopped. I had to ask her to give me 5 minutes for a little rest and she kindly allowed this – but then was at it again. I am deeply impressed by her and think of the service she gave over twelve years, 1919–31, together with Archbishop Nathan Söderblom. (Letter to MLS 17 February 1989)

Gerda Rodling had the 'distinction' of being a niece of S. A. Fries.[15] She was given a flat in the archbishop's house in order to be available at all times. The working day started after breakfast when the incoming letters were opened and answers dictated. In the evenings she sometimes found a bag of chocolates on her working table. It was a sign that there would be an extra long night session. Gerda Rodling related as follows:

> Söderblom dictated quickly without any doubt. He paged the floor rattling his keys. He never dictated in a monotonous voice or even rhythm. He always spoke as if he had had the whole auditorium in front of him and his words were accompanied by characteristic gestures. I have taken shorthand notes in cars and trains, in restaurants and by the chairman's chair in ecumenical meetings, church meetings and bishops' meetings, usually while he was chairing the meetings. At a streetcorner where the archbishop by chance met me I had to take notes on the back of a bill which I happened to have with me.

For B Sr the process of writing was strenuous. He had the spring term 1967 free for writing and C. F. Hallencreutz took over as acting professor. From the diaries one gets the impression that the writing did not get started seriously during the first part of that year. B Sr was suffering from low blood pressure which caused him to experience dizzy spells. The doctor advised him to take a long rest in a warm climate which he decided to do. He spent three weeks in the Canary Islands, Ingeborg joined him for two of those weeks. B Sr's blood pressure went up and he returned to gather materials and writing small parts for the book with some help from Byron Swanson from the USA. Some quotes give an idea how the work progressed:

> What an incredible person he was, this Nathan Söderblom. (First reaction in Diary 8 October 1965)

> I started the work of writing the book on Söderblom alongside my regular job in January 1966 and gathered my material single-handed for 18 months. Then I wrote and finished the book from 1 July 1967 to 15 February the following year, 1968. There was inhibition in the months of the first half of 1967, in order to strike the right note for the book. But then I was gripped by this frenzy which knows no fear nor obstacle. (Letter to MLS 21 January 1972)

Bengt's friend and contemporary Öyvind Sjöholm was a constant listener to B Sr's evolving thoughts as also Carl Fredrik Hallencreutz.

A good and valuable discussion with Ö. Sjöholm and C. F. Htz. I am so immensely grateful for the effective help, sustained encouragement and really admirable ability to penetrate into my work which C. F. Htz shows. What a gift it is for me. (Diary 23 October 1967)

Was not the archbishop perhaps an actor? So they asked, some of these north Europeans, overlooking the fact that they themselves were acting out a role; a role less obvious because more stereotyped than his, tin soldiers in uniform, immobile, snowmen in high places.

Kierkegaard says that each man's life is to be a poem, as if we are each to write or compose ourselves. But a Christian allows God to write his life's poem ... The means and the method will be a combination of two things: The free and spontaneous impulse of faith and discipline ... a saint is he who reveals God's might. Saints are such as show clearly and plainly in their lives and deeds and in their very being that God lives.[16]

I cite at length mainly from the book *Nathan Söderblom* but also from the Swedish book on *Söderblom and his meetings* (*Söderblom och hans möten*) with the intention of showing how, in my view, Bengt's own personality and thoughts had an affinity with the great person he characterised and whose evolving line of thought he followed. I suggest that B Sr's choice of significant events and experiences with an inner impact on Söderblom's life was not self-evident, but rather reflects the writer's personal insight. I have earlier pointed out similarities in their two lives. B Sr also had a special interest in many of the issues with which Söderblom struggled, among them the relation between 'body' and 'spirit', institution and spirituality, and naturally the emphasis on ecumenicity. Here also, as we shall see, the contact with French culture, which B Sr had since his student years and stay in that country, provides another point of contact, as does the significance of Bach, of Handel's Messiah, and N Sm's experience in Westminster Abbey, the heart of the Anglican tradition:

The Swedish pastor in Paris also acted as chaplain to Swedish seamen in Calais and was expected to work in Calais during the summer. Söderblom liked it that way ... One of Söderblom's experiences in his first years there was never forgotten. It may be that it determined some of his fundamental theological views at this time. A young Swedish artist had committed suicide. The little group of friends, together with the pastor, walked slowly behind the coffin through the endless streets, to a cemetery. What, in fact, could he tell these men, on that occasion, at that grave?

There were the solemn words of the church's ritual to be read, and hymns to be sung, and there was the helpful human fellowship and solidarity. Was there anything more to it than that?

Then, there were those few, confident notes welling up from his heart, a jubilant conviction, in Handel's 'I know that my Redeemer liveth'. This became his message. He had heard those notes in Stockholm in 1888. He also remembered his visit to London in 1895, when together with a group of Swedish singers he had stood in the choir of Westminster Abbey below Jenny Lind's memorial plaque, 'the greatest memory of Swedish song'. Round the portrait those words were chiselled in English: 'I know ... that my Redeemer liveth'. And above Jenny Lind's portrait: a picture of Father Handel himself. In front of him lie note pages: 'Now I discovered the two first notes of the Resurrection aria in the Messiah, these two notes which pronounce the firm and clear assurance of faith that the Lord and Master lives.'

The Swedish pastor was in via ... on his way to a personal, more existential understanding of faith. He wrote to his parents: 'It is not enough to make of Christ the best of all men, and our example. This produces moral goodness, the highest. And this we must seek. But it is not religion, and it cannot satisfy the soul. For that, Jesus must be unto us a Saviour, so that through him we can receive God's grace and forgiveness. That is my standpoint ...

It was that interpretation of Handel's, that had given him conviction about the victory of Christ. On an existential level of religious experience, the music of Handel and, of course, of Bach, expressed the conviction of his heart. But he now needed new intellectual tools, new categories to interpret that religious, or mystical dimension. (Sundkler 1968:43)

Söderblom got such tools from A. Sabatier whose book on St Paul made clear to him 'the importance in religion of the mystical relationship with God. He underlies the importance of the innermost, the heart, that life of feelings least attainable by reason ... Symbol was a living organism, with a body and soul ... The function of symbols was to express the invisible and the spiritual through the visible and material.' They would permit veneration for traditional symbols and the independence of the spirit. (1968:45)

In his book *The Religion of Revelation*, 1903, Söderblom had warned against a dichotomy 'spirit–body'. In 1915, he published a book called *The Body and the Soul of the Swedish Church*. B Sr points out that the body–soul concept in the Church was not just Sabatier's influence on Söderblom; it appears also in Luther.

B Sr shows how, after the existential experience of war, Söderblom saw the need to show the Churches in his generation an ecumenical way, but he had to use the concepts and frame of reference known to him and his generation. B Sr points out that no attention had so far been given to the ecumenical implications of the concept Söderblom used in *Oud Wassenar*, when he proposed 'an ecumenical council representing Christendom in a spiritual way'.[17] (1968:40–7; 232)

N Sm's summarising statements in his book on the ecumenical Stockholm Conference in 1925 emphasised two principles which were brought about by 'the awakening which has taken unanimous expression in the World Conference of the Churches in Stockholm'. The inner life is essential, institutions remain a shell without soul and life, but love, the inner life must be mobilised for its own sake.[18]

This concentration on the Spirit, 'the inner', 'innermost'

(*innerligheten*), must not lead to quietism, inimical to the world. It must be kept in creative tension between the spirit and body, spirit and institution. It should take expression in service, in Life and Work. (1976:135)

Ministry of the Church

I have already written at some length about the debate on the ministry of the Church. In Söderblom's time the question had arisen in 1919 with the rise of the modern ecumenical thought. An official committee had then recommended that women be allowed entry to the ministry. When Söderblom made a statement on this in the Diocese Chapter 1923 he did not even mention the biblical–theological question. He based his view on the wishes of the congregations and the disposition of women which to his mind was 'not very suitable to the responsible and leading positions for the congregations' (Sundkler 1975:162–9).

> Söderblom considered the office, like everything else in the Church, in relation to 'Spirit' . . . For Söderblom the depth dimension of the Old Testament, the prophetic message, and later also ancient Christendom's spiritual character were essential . . . One can recognise the religio-historical school's 'enthusiastic' interpretation. This characterised Söderblom's view of the Spirit as a critical instance over against institution.

This emphasis on the spirit and ecstasy was criticised by Fridrichsen and the growing High-Church movement in the Church of Sweden (Sundkler 1975:160ff., Fridrichsen 1942[19]). B Sr himself wanted to keep the balance between the *pneuma* and institution in his church leadership. He reminded those involved that the High Church also had its spiritual dimension of soul care, as he himself had experienced:

> In propaganda against the High Church it is often forgotten that its charisma is soulcare tradition . . . without which the Church cannot live. It is fine to have congregational councils, legislation and collected church taxes, and other rules and non-rules. But the question in a Negro Spiritual can be unpleasantly penetrating in the midst of welfare, and there only a church which practices personal, individual soul care helps:
>   'Doctor, state and county doctor, suh,
> Can you heal some sin-sick soul, suh?
> Oh no, oh no, dat's a question
> he could not answer.' (B Sr 1975:163–8)

At the Jubilee of the Church of Sweden in 1993 Bengt Sundkler gave a talk on Nathan Söderblom, who besides his other work was bishop of three Swedish provinces, including the city of Stockholm and its environs. In 1916 he had visited 40 parishes:

The task was overwhelming. How did he manage it all? 'Time is elastic,' he said, 'almost anything can find place in it.' And he would tell the pastors: 'Work yourselves to death – but please do it slowly.'

Another emphasis familiar from Bengt Sundkler's own fundamental orientation is the combination of international and local, in Chesterton's words which B Sr had taken as his motto, 'For anything to be real it must be local.'

He was, of course, a complex personality. There was in him a combination of perseverance and flexibility. He contemplated an international horizon, and yet his focus was on the local province, the genuineness of the local province, its language, music and crafts. This relation to the local province could give a person a 'distinction'. He had an international horizon but at the same time an emphasis on his Lutheran heritage. There was in him both an ascetic self-control and an artistic talent with his innate musicality. There was his amazing vitality, courage and iridescent joy, covering and hiding a whole personal history of increasing illness.

I have not attempted to give a review of the Söderblom book as such, but rather looked for points which illustrate the personality of Söderblom and at the same time give an insight into Bengt Sundkler's own personality, his innermost ambitions and humanity and the 'office of encouragement', which he said he had inherited from Söderblom.

Office of encouragement

Concentration on personality was in line with B Sr's theory on the significance of personalities in history. It was no accident that Söderblom had also had the same interest in writing a study of Eric Gustaf Geijer, the authority on the Swedish philosophy of personality, 'the personality is the greatest thing in history'. The way B Sr described Söderblom is an echo of his own personality which obviously contributed to his enthralment in writing the biography:

Communication, the urge of this expansive, outgoing, generous personality ... He needed people in order himself to function fully ... Life in its essence is nothing less than the will of the living God who wills us truly alive ... Being at home in existence.[20]

These were some of his enthused words I have recorded at different times when he was talking of the person about whom he was entrusted to write.

Let me go on, naively, lavishing encouragement on everybody: I consider myself to have discovered Nathan Söderblom's 'office of encouragement': That I must take upon myself and carry out further, as far as I can reach. (Diary 17 September 1968)

In a speech, B Sr sketched briefly Söderblom's 'office of encouragement' and his character. I cite a portion from the speech to give a taste of the charismatic personality, as the high and the lowly experienced him:

> He developed his generous contacts with people: 'I congratulate you'. There is nobody in Swedish culture and in the history of Swedish culture who has used the verb '*lyckönska*', congratulate, as Nathan Söderblom. He showed charismatic encouragement and concern for all, from royalty and aristocracy to ordinary and very ordinary workers, all belonging to the same family of God. In February 1966 I had an audience with His Majesty the King, Gustav VI Adolf, in order to ask him about Söderblom's influence on his life. 'First, he was the greatest moral influence in my life. Secondly, he taught me to speak, how to give public addresses, not to slur over the words, but to take hold of the word and lift it forward so that it could be heard by everybody in the hall.'
> I remember Anton Jönsson, an 80-year-old pensioner and former building-worker living at Börjegatan in Uppsala. What did Söderblom mean to him: 'There was never anybody who was *så bra, så bra*, so good, so good, as the archbishop.'[21]

B Sr took this 'office of encouragement' as a heritage from Söderblom who exercised it especially through the some 30,000 letters he personally wrote, in the Söderblom collection of 80–90,000 letters archived in the Uppsala University Carolina Library.

> It seems that for Söderblom a letter was more than a letter: it was an out-stretched hand, an opportunity to do what his contemporary existentialists declared impossible, to create communication between people ... We shall regard letters as the means of communication. We have never had in this country such a genius for creating communication as Archbishop Söderblom. ... An actively creative, positive, and generous person has created these letters. (Sundkler, *Nathan Söderblom as a letter-writer*, 1971:7)

The reception of the book

B Sr finished writing the book on Nathan Söderblom in mid-February, in time for the World Council of Churches Assembly in Uppsala 1968. On 15 February he left it with the printers and on 16 February he flew with Ingeborg for a week's holiday of sun and exercise to Gran Canaria. The rounds of proof-reading were still to be done. Uncertainty as to how the book would be received caused restlessness in the meantime.

B Sr had initially feared taking on the writing of a biography of

Söderblom on his own initiative. The fear was not perhaps so unreasonable, judging from some of the reviews written in Swedish newspapers after *Söderblom och hans möten* (Söderblom and his meetings) had appeared in 1975. The reception was excellent, but one or two reviewers warned that the subject was too big for any one person to tackle, referring also to the English book: 'Every time one picks up a new work about Nathan Söderblom and his world embracing contribution, one must think: THE book about this man will never be written. He was too multi-faceted, shifting, too difficult to have an overview of.' (Erik Hj. Linder in *Göteborg Posten* 14 November 1975) To the writer even the English biography of Söderblom was only a good attempt at sketching the life story of a man like Söderblom. B Sr had anticipated such a reaction.

At the time of the Uppsala Assembly, Söderblom was not the topic of the day, but for Bengt Sundkler the writing of the biography of the man he so highly respected and with whom he so closely identified was one of the great achievements of his life. Visser 't Hooft gave recognition to the book at the time of opening of the assembly and B Sr noted in his diary that this was probably the only attention that was going to be given to this input.

In the book *Nathan Söderblom* B Sr wrote, 'I have not personally taken the initiative for this book, but was commissioned to do so.' The word 'commissioned' became an issue when the WCC later did not acknowledge the commitment made by its former general secretary, Visser 't Hooft. WCC had a new general secretary, E. Carson Blake, who perhaps did not even know of his predecessor's initiative, and also the archbishop of Sweden had changed. Visser 't Hooft himself praised the book as the best ecumenical biography he knew, but B Sr remarked afterwards that the *Ecumenical Review* never reviewed his book, nor was it given the publicity by the WCC it would have deserved (personal communication from B Sr). This caused him some disappointment.

Before leaving the fate of the Söderblom book I jump ahead a few days to 5 August after the assembly guests had departed. We find B Sr in the Dag Hammarskjöld Institute attending a lecture delivered by Gunnar Myrdal, one of the great Swedes, nearing Hammarskjöld himself, in B Sr's estimation, to whom he had sent a copy of his book. Myrdal's lecture was on the United Nations and B Sr judged it to be brilliant. As the speaker was ushered to the podium by the director of the institute, Sven Hamrell, he saw B Sr and stopped to exchange a few words:

> He said to me that he was grateful for the Söderblom book: 'He was a fascinating man. He was like – ? Yes, do you know whom he resembled? He was like me, of course. But he was also like a certain Asian leader: Nehru. The same tactical communication as J. Nehru's!!

The question of writing the Swedish volumes on Söderblom crops up from time to time, but the second edition of the *World of Mission* and the books on the African materials were given precedence at the time. B Sr expressly mentioned that he did so because he thought the Söderblom book had not received the recognition it would have deserved. However, he returned to writing on Söderblom in Swedish and the book was very well received. He described the way the book got its name in a letter:

> While sun-bathing on Söder-Manskär the title for the book came to me: *Nathan Söderblom och hans möten.* So far I think it is a good title, and I am pleased with it. It is a tremendous help to have the title and so carry on in writing out the book. (Letter to MLS 27 June 1975)

After the assembly and after the great volume was completed seminars, examinations, lectures did not seem like 'work', yet the usual self-chastisement fills the pages for not accomplishing enough.

Teaching and travels

The year of 1969

The Sundklers had been looking for a house on the outskirts of Uppsala in the hope of finding a bigger house and garden. They found one in Malma Ringvägen 32, to which they moved soon after returning from Bukoba. Their first impressions were of a wonderful and refreshing villa. When the spring came Bengt spent some afternoons and weekends working in the garden and the two of them enjoyed bicycle trips into the surrounding beautiful parks. In the long run, they did not find living outside the centre satisfactory. They would have needed two cars which Ingeborg thought they could not afford.[22] Bengt's travels and speaking engagements took up time, even if Ingeborg quite often accompanied Bengt, on travels abroad as well. The location of the house added to Ingeborg's problems in keeping touch with people when her husband was away. When Bengt was frenziedly writing the Söderblom book he would spend long days and even nights in the Dekanhuset or in the institute, at times returning only in the early hours, in time to bring morning coffee to Ingeborg in bed.

Writing the book on Söderblom interrupted B Sr's teaching and other academic work in the faculty. When the new term started in 1969 B Sr intended to devote more uninterrupted time than before to his students and doctorands. He now faced the big challenge of bringing to completion the doctoral theses which he had agreed to supervise.

Regular teaching duties brought the teacher into invigorating contact with young people. B Sr referred to the students on his Missiology course, 80–90 of them, as 'unbelievably cheerful and nice young people' with whom he 'had an excellent fellowship' and who 'received teaching with charming response and friendliness'. What more could he have desired from his teaching experience. (Diary 14 April 1969)

At the beginning of February 1969 Ingeborg wanted to make another visit to her beloved Tanzania and travelled alone to East Africa. In his turn, Bengt now felt lonely having been left alone at home to manage. While Ingeborg was in Africa her nephew, Cecil Morén, informed Bengt that there was a chance that they could acquire a bigger flat in their old house in Odensgatan 5 B. The decision was made quickly although they had been making inquiries about the flat since Christmas. Bengt records in his diary 8 March 1969: 'I sent a cable to Ingeborg: 'Lindell proposes exchange your flat with hers. You agree? Bengt.' The answer came 4 p.m. from Ingeborg: 'Accepted.'

The agreement was finalised the following day. The papers were signed on 29 March 1969 after which Bengt writes: 'This should now be our place where we stay until our dying days, whenever they are ahead of us.' Little did they know that after Ingeborg came home and began to make arrangements to move she would never have the chance to move into their new home – moving back to Odensgatan 5 B came at the time of her approaching death.

Directly after Ingeborg left for Africa B Sr had been invited to lecture and preach in Turku (Åbo) by the theological faculty of Åbo Academy:

8–10 February 1969. At dinner in G. Lindskog's home I met the whole faculty, all together 35–40 guests. I made valuable contacts. The following day I preached in Turku cathedral on 1 Peter 3.12: 'Exposed and Loved', and then gave a talk on 'The Church on the Equator'. On the 10 February I gave two lectures in the Theological Faculty: '1945–1969–2000' and 'The Church and Syncretism in Africa', and a talk about Nordic co-operation. It was bitter arctic weather.

I was interviewed by a charming woman, Mrs M. Torvald from the *Åbo Underrättelser* newspaper; her husband is a poet. I talked with Docent Martola, a young assistant specialising in Judaism. It was also of interest for me to meet Professor Gotthard Nygren and his new student wife. I returned home in the evening.

The struggle with passing time was a constant worry for B Sr. Many visitors interrupted his teaching duties and writing:

14 March 1969. How on earth have the days come this far. Where have two and half months gone? I must be engrossed and take hold of the tasks I have: concentrate totally on them, devote myself fully to them and carry them through. It is no more complicated than that.

'The years like great black oxen tread and work
and God the herdsman guards them from behind
and I am broken by their passing feet' . . .
God save me from meaninglessness and despair. Renew in me a spirit:
Let me live for Thee and receive new meaning and life in and through
that service. If I had such will, fire, enthusiasm, devotion, then I could
give important direction, new lines to the Swedish mission situation.

20 March 1969. J. H. M. Beattie from Oxford, a Bunyoro specialist and
an old, good friend from Africa, turned up unannounced. I took him for
lunch, to the castle and Old Uppsala. Heard masses of gossip from
Africa, Evans-Pritchard and social anthropology. What is he (Beattie)
doing? Yes, the same old song: Various books on Bunyoro on which he
has been working for 20 years or so. What a misery! Why not finally
do something more talented, more results. I was thinking of myself of
course at the same time: I should not give in, show no results, month
after month, year after year.

On 28 March 1969 a telegram came from Ingeborg that she was
coming home in two days. Ingeborg had spent her last ten days in
Tanzania with us, the Swantzes, at Mbezi beach outside Dar es
Salaam, in fact in Barbro Johansson's house, which we were renting.
She told us that she was anxious to get back home to participate in the
Easter celebration with Bengt. 'I feel responsible for Bengt', were her
words. She felt above all a spiritual responsibility toward Bengt but
took care of the domestic side as well.

Ingeborg arrived home in time to celebrate Easter resurrection with
Bengt (5–6 April 1969) on Sala hills in Östanbäck, where Bishop
Bengt was to spend most of his Easters and where he later became the
visiting bishop to the non-Catholic Brotherhood of the Holy Cross.
The Easter drama, celebrated with action, singing and word, sounded
an echo of the experience in Ceza, Zululand, in the hearts of Ingeborg
and Bishop Bengt. The wonderful celebration started from the dark
hill where the Gospel text was read by a young boy, the congregation
continued in procession to the church where the light was shining.
B Sr preached on a theme taken from C. S. Lewis's book entitled
Surprised by Joy. On the second day of Easter they were back in their
villa cleaning inside and out in the garden.

This was the last celebration of Easter with Ingeborg. Moving
ahead in time, I add here a few words about Bengt and Ingeborg
Sundkler's connection with Östanbäck. When Bishop Bengt in 1975
assisted in 'professing' the first four novices into the celibate Order
of monks – the first time since the Reformation – he wrote that he was
motivated to do so because of the keen interest that Ingeborg had
taken in the community (Letter to MLS 21 July 1975):

I have returned from three days with my very wonderful friends, the
monks at Östanbäck. We made history or at least Swedish Church

history ... I suppose I have not really thought through fully the implications of all this nor the role that I was to play in it, but the fact is
there now ... I was there for three days and I needed the two days of
preparation as I had to do everything almost, in view of the circumstances that I am, in bishop's orders, their bishop. That I ever agreed to
so become has much to do with the memory of Ingeborg. She was their
mother and she took much trouble over them. So when asked some years
ago, I did say 'yes' with a reference to Ingeborg. It has all developed
from there.

I almost need to make this clear to myself, for only a few minutes
before leaving for Östanbäck on Friday last, I had of course finished this
book in Swedish which may cause my young brothers many questions
and some worry. But for me, as I am constructed, I refuse to admit this
compartmentalisation in the Church and see them all as part of the same
Church of Christ in Sweden and in the world.[23]

The event had its consequences: the press was after the archbishop
to know what had happened in Östanbäck. Did it mean a return to
Rome? What had happened was apparently illegal, for the Swedish
law did not allow monasteries. The discussion between B Sr and the
archbishop was cordial, but I cannot resist quoting here Bengt's
humour in regard to the event, even if it obviously shows a degree of
irresponsibility, in that he had not clarified the legal aspects beforehand. My husband and I were supposed to come to Sweden and Bengt
was to meet us at the airport. Together we were to go to Märtha and
Bengt Simonsson, mutual friends from the time they were in Kitwe,
Zambia (then Northern Rhodesia) and Dar es Salaam, and now living
in Sollentuna, not far from Arlanda:

It may happen that I cannot come to meet you at Arlanda and I shall be
in prison instead for this terrible thing. Could not you and Märtha come
along with a basket of coffee and some bisquits then? I shall try to
inform you the number of the cell. It would be such a joy to see you
under such circumstances. But perhaps one should not be too facetious
about these things. Anyway, the newspapers will have something other
than bathing and revolutions in Portugal to write about.

In my old age I thus become interesting for a whole afternoon it
seems, but this will soon pass and the world and Sweden will soon forget
about me and things will return to normal again.

Very welcome to Arlanda. If you do not find me there you will know
the reason. You have been warned. (Letter to MLS 21 July 1975)

Back to the spring 1969. Life continued with visitors and visits as
well as attention to the students.

Bishop Emeritus Leslie Brown (the Anglican Archbishop of Uganda
1960–65) and his wife Winnifred, good friends of Ingeborg and Bengt
from their time in Bukoba, came for a four-day visit in April. The
Sundklers met them and took them around in Stockholm and then to
Västerås, Buskarö and the usual tour of old Uppsala. From Uppsala

they also paid a visit to Sigtuna, meeting many important people. Brown gave a lecture on '100 Years of Church History in Uganda' in Dekanhuset and in the evening the Sundklers had dinner for them in their home with a few friends. A lunch with Archbishop Hultgren was part of the programme. On Sunday Bishop Brown and B Sr celebrated a mass in St Ansgar together. The following day Ingeborg took the visitors to Arlanda for their departure. The visit brought back many good memories which made it enjoyable for both couples.

Between 22 and 28 April 1969 Ingeborg and Bengt Sundkler were in Leiden as guests of Hans Holleman's Africa Studies Centre. They made contacts with several other Africanists and took a car trip through southern Holland up to Rotterdam and then to Leiden in preparation for Bengt's South Africa visit.

Jonas Jonson, now Bishop of Strägnäs, who had become a doctoral candidate working on China for his dissertation, was also a mission secretary in CSM. A positive response from him in relation to the coming centenary celebrations of the CSM inspired B Sr greatly:

> 30 April 1969. Had a friendly letter from Jonas Jonson concerning my proposal for the CSM centenary celebration, that it should not be a festival issue no one reads but a study programme 1972–74 with 3–6 written productions per year, culminating in an illustrated publication which would reflect the content of the 18 books.

It gave B Sr satisfaction that the committee for the CSM centenary celebration accepted his proposal with acclamation and discussed it in detail. He continued to preach and lecture, 'Ecumenics after Uppsala' being one of his topics.

> 6 May 1969. In the evening Ingeborg and I went to Stockholm where we spent the evening with Job Kaijunga, the rector of Katoke school in Bukoba. He had been invited by Tage Erlander for a visit with five others for three weeks. We were both fascinated to listen to J. K. a very promising 30-year-old rector judging from what he had to say about Tanzania. A charming representative of his diocese whom I was very glad to meet just that day.
>
> The following day, 7 May, Ingeborg and I wandered around Stockholm. We visited the new State archives among other things. Returned to Uppsala in the evening. I was 60 years old; it was my birthday. What a serious step to take, into the unknown – or known?

B Sr had advised the press that he did not wish the day to be written up, but coming home he could not avoid the usual delegations, flowers and telegrams.

> On 11 May family members came: Folke, tax official in Östersund, Ingegärd Hellsten, bishop's wife in Luleå, Lennart, provincial assessor in Växsjö, they all came to us first for coffee and they then invited us for dinner in Flustret. We had a very joyful and happy day together. We

talked about the past times and yesteryears. Elizabeth, Folke's daughter was with us for the dinner.

Between engagements both Bengt and Ingeborg worked on the new flat. On two days B Sr spoke to 25 Swedish International Development Authority (SIDA) teachers and port consultants due to go out to Tanzania in the summer. As usual, he remarked that he had made fine contacts and the time with them was very stimulating. (Diary 17–18 May 1969)

The crowning glory of the sixtieth-birthday celebrations was the wonderful festschrift *The Church Crossing Frontiers, Essays on the Nature of Mission, In Honour of Bengt Sundkler* which had been prepared and was presented to him on the 21 May, a date when one of the editors, Carl Frederik Hallencreutz, had returned from Birmingham where he was a lecturer at the time. The second editor was initially B Sr's first doctoral student Peter Beyerhaus, and in the absence of the two from Uppsala the nitty-gritty editing work was left to Tore Furberg and Sigbert Axelson. Many of B Sr's eminent international friends, including Professors J. F. Ade Ajayi and E. A. Ayandele, Daniel T. Niles, Josiah Kibira, Monica Wilson, John Taylor, David Bosch, Stephen Neill, Leslie Newbegin, Hans-Werner Gensichen and Philip Potter, as well as friends and former students closer to home, had written their contributions for the volume. B Sr appreciated enormously the work which his former students and colleagues had done and he often referred to the articles in the volume for a better understanding of his work. (Diary 21 May 1969)[24]

Many visitors, particulary those from the Third World, are given space in the diaries. There was a minister from Adis Abeba, a Papuan Christian doctor from the Biak Islands in New Guinea, Buddhist mission representatives and Barbro Johansson who was always invited to report the latest from the government and diplomatic circles in Tanzania when she was on a visit to Uppsala.

31 May 1969. Perhaps the last such promotion in Uppsala university.[25] I was not there. I sat and worked on the second edition of the *Missionens värld* [*World of Mission*]. In any case, I went to listen to the Student Union's celebration afterwards, outside the university building. It was cold, only a few people. The chairman of the Student Union spoke using the most worn-out clichés that there are in the language. One could not take this to be anything other than conscious mockery of these old grey-haired jubilee doctors whom he pretended to celebrate. The son of one of the jubilee doctors, Dr Höijer, spoke, stiff and cliché-filled language, had difficulty in reading his manuscript. The whole thing was horrible, I was glad to return immediately to my *Missionens värld*. [The Student Union Chairman's speech was printed as it was delivered in the Uppsala newspaper the following Monday.]

In his diary B Sr remarks that the reception of his work on Söderblom, or rather the lack of it, justified leaving further work on Söderblom aside and concentrating on South Africa. (12 June 1969) The first week in June was spent on the *World of Mission*, 2nd edition, which he managed to leave with the printers before he left for Africa. The rest of the time was spent in preparation for a fresh journey to South and East Africa, reading notes and viewing films from earlier visits. 'It is wonderful that I am now free to devote myself to my South Africa problem.'

South Africa once more

From Arlanda the flight took B Sr via Brussels to Johannesburg. Everywhere he met old friends and made new acquaintances, renewing his contacts, giving lectures and updating information. In Johannesburg, B Sr had useful visits with Peter Mkize, who in his younger years had been B Sr's assistant in gathering material for the Independent Churches and who as a bank supervisor in Johannesburg still continued to facilitate contacts and material for B Sr throughout (Sundkler 1976:332).[26] He visited the Christian Institute on several occasions, meeting Drs Beyers Naudé and v. Wyk, and met in Pretoria with the former chief of the Native Affairs Department.

While in the Durban and Dundee areas, B Sr visited the evangelist Nicolas Bhengu in Entumeni (Eshowe) and renewed his fellowship with Reverend Johannes Galilee Shembe, the great Isaiah Shembe's son, with whom he stayed for two days. He had the opportunity to attend the great Sabbath in the annual July Festival and to hear Johannes Galilee Shembe to review his father's life and message. (1976:169) While in Durban, B Sr twice visited the well-organised church of Reverend Paulo Nzuza, led by his son Petro Nzuza, in Camperdown. He was also taken to Himeville to Cekwane headquarters, similarly under the leadership of the second generation Frederick T. Cekwane, the son of the founder Reverend Timothy Cekwane.

B Sr had an appointment made to meet Reverend Henry Nkonyane, the leader of the Nkonyane Church and the grandson of the well-known Church Father, disciple of Reverend Le Roux, Reverend Daniel Nkonyane. The day before B Sr was to meet him, Henry Nkonyane was killed in a car accident. He could only attend his funeral in Charlestown two weeks later. B Sr had this funeral in mind years later, when writing ACH he came to realise the significance of death and burial in the churchlife in Africa (see Chapter 11).

The academic contacts were significant as well. In Pretoria B Sr stayed with Professor Johannes Lombard on his bee farm and met his whole faculty. In Umtata, Transkei, he met Dr David Bosch and made good contacts with the faculty of the Anglican Theological School. In Cape Town B Sr had the opportunity to meet Professor Monica Wilson, whom he held in high esteem and counted as a great friend, and also lunched with her son, Francis Wilson. B Sr had also a chance to hear a lecture delivered by Lady Barbara Ward (Jackson) in Pretoria. Another woman who gets a special mention in the diary notes is Mrs Mdiniso, a senator and the wife of the Lutheran Dean, Reverend Mdiniso, whom he met outside Mbabane, Swaziland, where B Sr stayed for a week. The contacts were many, I have given only a sample here.

During his time in South Africa B Sr also went to Tanzania in mid-July, where he lectured on 'Historical Factors in the Development of Ministry in Africa' in Makumira Theological College, at a Conference of African Theologians organised by the LWF, Geneva. I flew from Dar es Salaam to meet him there to discuss my doctoral thesis on *Symbol and ritual of the Zaramo, with special emphasis on women.*

After a week in Makumira B Sr flew back to Johannesburg to continue his visits. On his return to South Africa, he received news of Ingeborg's illness but was advised by her to finish his programme. On 19 September B Sr flew to Entebbe and from there to Bukoba. In the evening, a great reception was held for him at Bishop Kibira's home. He spoke, reflecting on memories from 1942–45 and 1961–65. When Joel Wiberg, his former American assistant, took him via Karagwe to Kampala, he had spent ten days in the diocese.[27]

Ingeborg at rest

Serious illness

We follow here the events and reflections during the two months of Ingeborg's illness, when Ingeborg and Bengt rather unexpectedly faced Ingeborg's approaching death. I invite the readers to spend some quiet moments with them in Samariterhemmet where Ingeborg was hospitalised and where Bengt went to see her in any moments free from the many duties which were at that time crowding in on him. He was busy with students and he was left with the responsibility for moving their home back to the city centre. Before the year ended Bengt had to go through Ingeborg's irrevocable departure.

Ingeborg informed Bengt in a letter, which reached him on 12 September in Johannesburg, that she was seriously ill and had been admitted to hospital, but not knowing yet that she had a cancer of the pancreas. Bengt phoned her then and asked if he should return immediately home, but Ingeborg, in her usual brave way, wanted him to finish his programme. He phoned the hospital again from Capetown on 16 September and then from Bukoba where he stopped on the return journey, but the message was the same, 'continue'. On 25 September he flew from Entebbe via London to Uppsala where their good friend Gunnar Johansson met him at Arlanda.[28]

25 September 1969. I was allowed to return healthy and spry, but with restless and sad heart. Ingeborg was ill in Samariterhemmet [the Deaconess hospital in Uppsala]. Dr Wallden talked with me about the nature of the illness.

In between the visits to the hospital and attending his teaching duties B Sr arranged his South Africa papers. On 5 October he attended the dinner which the Swedish government organised in honour of President Nyerere of Tanzania.

9 October. I spend much time at the bedside of Ingeborg. Much of the time I go there three times a day. Some nights I am in the hospital, but it does not seem necessary.

During his visits to Ingeborg's bedside Bengt learned from Dr Wallden that Ingeborg's pancreatic cancer was incurable and all the doctors could do was to give her medicine for the pain. Ingeborg wanted to know what exactly the doctor had said.

11 October. Ingeborg understood more than what was said. She said to me afterwards, 'Life is harsh [*bistert*], Bengt, very, very harsh.' The seriousness of her state became quite clear to her. She wanted to clear up everything, big and small things. She is unbelievably brave. These doctors cannot do anything except to relieve the pain.

The time concept became, if possible, even more pressing for B Sr:

12 October. Thanksgiving Day – Ingeborg – 'I want to thank God for a disciplined life and devoted life.'
   My life must be concentrated on the two or three tasks that are left for me to do, if I am still given more time. Time! – 'I had the time.' (J. B. Priestley). I 'have' the time, but only if I extremely systematically and strictly discipline myself and seek to plan my years and days. [The tasks are listed.] I get my joy from conceptualising and writing, and I can leave the result in God's hands. Thanks and praise!
18 October. I stayed with Ingeborg. She was very serious, 'What would I do without you, Bengt? But what will come out of you now? I am grateful for every moment you can stay here with me.' I am very happy to write down these words. The time of illness has brought us nearer to each other than ever.
With Ingeborg, [apart from necessary tasks and visits]²⁹ from morning till evening.
21 October. Far too disjointed to be able to start writing.
22 October. Ingeborg: 'May all the care and goodness and love which has come to me stream out to those who think of me.'
23 October. 'To be saved: to come through, not to be lost.'
24 October. 'What a rich life I have had. I have seen so much beautiful, met so many good loving people.' We read the Swedish hymn 575.³⁰
25 October. I thought I should ring Jarl Agne, which I did. [A long

discussion on the phone reported.][31] The upshot was that he sent flowers and promised to come and see Ingeborg.

26 October. Ingeborg: 'In eternity I shall do one thing in relation to this world. In eternity I shall thank for all this goodness which has come to me from so many people and pray that what they have so generously given me would stream back to them.'

Communion service in the evening in Holy Trinity church ... The text John 10:28. had this valuable word: 'I give them eternal life, and they shall never perish, and no one shall snatch them out of my hand.'

27 October. Ingeborg: 'One does not have strength to pray.' I answered her, 'You have prayed so much in your life that you can let Him take over now.' Ingeborg smiled gladly and happily.

29 October. Cecil and Margareta Morén with Ingeborg. Jan Agne was also there.

With Ingeborg: 'I am only thankful for everything I have experienced. I am most grateful for the nights I have been able to sleep.' 'Now I can only think of God, my Father, and the Son, my Saviour, and the Spirit.' 'In my Swedish Bible, the date of the great breakthrough, 8 July 1928, is written on the first page, in Birkeland, Norway, in the evening of Holy Communion.' [Hallesby meeting, although Ingeborg was not wholeheartedly impressed by Hallesby himself.]

Ingeborg is an incredibly moving [*oerhört gripande*] and magnificent person, not least now with full knowledge and full wisdom – in death's waiting room.

Margit Österberg was with her today: 'Indescribably wonderful,' said Ingeborg afterwards.

31 October. Ingeborg to Margit Byegård: 'This All Saints Day – my last one here on earth. Next All Saints Day I will be dead and in Heaven.'[32]

2 November. Barbro Nordberg-Leimdörfer with Ingeborg. 'Because she is so wonderful, she sees these good things in me. There hardly is anything good in me.'

3 November. Ingeborg: 'You must say it just as it is to our friends. I might still live longer, but people cannot any longer keep on praying for me. I have no strength any longer either to pray or to look up.' 'When that day comes and it will be too difficult for me and I cannot manage, remember that I thank you for everything you have meant for me throughout life and now.'

7 November. Ingeborg is most grateful about the nights. She is able to sleep, has a right to rest. 'Keep yourself close to God, Bengt.'

Ingeborg sits up in her chair, extremely tired. Can say hardly anything. Time rushes its way, while people wait for eternity. The latter is assumed to be something eternally lasting peaceful quietness, 'rest in peace,' etc.[33] I study the death announcements in *Svenska Dagbladet*. They reveal often a very strange mentality and belief world. What do I myself believe, really, about this? Yes, the following: God is the living Lord over life and death, the Mighty Creator and Re-Creator [*Nyskaparen*]. People are born and work and suffer and die: Then we belong to God's, the Almighty's and the Merciful's communion and thought [*Sen är vi till Gud's, den Väldige's och Barmhärtige's gemenskap och tanke*]; and this we understand for the sake of Jesus Christ. That's all, and that's enough. [The last sentence written in English.]

Ingeborg: 'I am not in need of anything. I am not dead – yet. In regard
to my burial: Very simple. Let a man's voice sing Ida Granqvist-
Merikanto: "Det gäller".'

For Bengt, the weekends in between examinations, seminars and
meetings were devoted to moving from Malma Ringväg 32 to
Odensgatan 5 B (Diary 9–10 November).

Most of the time Ingeborg was very tired, her condition varied from
day to day. After only brief activity she became totally exhausted
(12–14 November):

'Now I resign and wait only that God will soon let me go home.'

We read the Holy Scriptures and hymns again, as usual, two three
times a day.

As part of the diocese meeting, a Harvest Mass, created by Ingmar
Milweden and Martin Lönnebo, was celebrated by me and seven other
pastors. A historical heavenly experience, strikingly beautiful, gripping,
fully wonderful, not least the biblical drama groups. Öyvind Sjöholm
sang wonderfully.

I phoned Ingmar Milweden and thanked him for the yesterday's
historical experience. It must have been the greatest day in his life.

16 November. Morning with Ingeborg: 'God presses me deep down.'
'Write to St Julians that I go slowly toward the gate of death. They
should not continue to pray that I would regain health.'

17 November. With Ingeborg. She had a good night and had rested well,
but had pains. She repeated Jesus prayer: 'Jesus Christ, the Son of God,
have mercy upon me, a sinner. Let all the goodness shown on me stream
as blessings.'

Going home

18 November – the day of her death

9 a.m. Ingeborg was in deep sleep on her back. The sisters said that she
only sleeps for hours. I organised a room for myself in the
Samariterhemmet hospice from the following night as it seemed that
Ingeborg had taken a turn for the worse. 11 a.m. she was still sleeping.

I chaired a meeting in CSM 1–2.30 and at 2.30 came to
Samariterhemmet. Sister Kerttu: 'It can be near the end now but it can
still take time. No one can tell.'

I sat down with Ingeborg. She opened her eyes. I asked if she was
cold and she said she wanted a blanket. I covered her and asked whether
she wanted a hot water bottle. No. I held her hand. Read hymn 555 and
the blessing and made the sign of the cross on her forehead.[34]

Outside the door the sisters said it might still take time, she feels only
very weak. I drove home via the Institute. Felt a migraine coming and
took a taxi home to take some medicine. Came home, took some tablets,
and telephone rang. It was sister Kerttu. They had taken Ingeborg for

an x-ray, why? 'It is best that you come right away!' I rushed to the street, waved down a car which went by on Odensgatan (I had left my car by the cathedral because of the migraine.) It was engineer Bengt Eriksson, a builder in Björklinge. He took me directly to Samariterhemmet.

I ran and ran in order to get there in time.

But it was finished, irreversibly, irrevocably [*oåterkalleligt, ouppnåeligt*] finished. Ingeborg lay there quietly, beloved, high and pure and good – with closed eyes. But now she was dead. She looked so alive, as if she would open her eyes and smile any moment.

It was finished, irrevocably. I was alone with her and cried.

Later Dr Wallden, Sister Margit Byegård and Sister Kerttu gathered in the room. I read two texts from this week's texts. I gave the blessing and made the sign of the cross. 'Ingeborg loved the sign of the cross,' I said. Leif Gustavsson was called to take a picture. Margit Byegård helped me, gave me something to eat in her home. I then went home to the flat. The 18 November came slowly to its end, as everything goes toward its end.

Ingeborg is dead. She was a noble Christian, an intensively living person, with an unusual personality, my wife and friend. If I should try here to reccount what she has done for me, this book would not have space for it.

19 November. To Samariterhemmet again 9 a.m. Ingeborg lay still there in her bed, so quiet, my beloved, the same as always. But the forehead was cold. She was taken to the Samariterhemmet's '*crypta*'.

At home, in Odensgatan 5 B, Ingegärd Hellstén, my sister, Sigbert Axelson, Sigvard v. Sicard, Per Hellstén and his fiancée worked to put the home into order. In the evening Britt Brundin and Gunnar Johansson helped in the house.

20 November. Telegrams, telephone calls. Bishop Kibira, the eternal optimist, tried to call from Bukoba!!! The only thing I heard were sounds of waves, probably from Lake Victoria or some other sea. In the end they said: 'The call is over, your call is finished.' I tried to say that it never started, but it was in vain. But the thought was good. I got then later a fine telegram from Kibira and the diocese.

The loneliness which Bengt experienced after Ingeborg's death was different from anything he had ever gone through before. They both had recognised the basic difference in their expectations toward life but during the last weeks of Ingeborg's illness they realised how much they had shared and had in common during their 32 years of marriage. They had taken for granted the spiritual unity which they shared and the expressions of piety and devotion in which they found togetherness.

When the new year began in 1970, Bengt wrote in his diary (27 January):

Ingeborg's death has been a traumatic experience. One can show and put up an unconcerned face, as one tries to, but I have found that particularly the dreams take out their revenge, and one cannot help crying in one's sleep at least. Then it is also all the musical associations to

Ingeborg: some of these are altogether overpowering, particularly for the tragic reason that Ingeborg felt that she missed her real calling in not being able to spend more time and energy on working on her piano. It has all been difficult. I have, however, been greatly blessed by many friends, old and new, old and young, who have taken care of me.

Back to the students

Support of friends

The external and internal emptiness left behind with the loss of the union Bengt had with Ingeborg became a new kind of receptiveness. B Sr was grateful for the friendship and support he got from his former students and old and young colleagues, and he made new acquaintances and close friends. He needed close relationships and he was generous towards friends who responded to him. Communication was perhaps the most frequently used word in his vocabulary. He was tenderhearted and had much to give to his friends and relatives; those mentioned here in no way exhaust the list of even of those closest to him. Because of his overpowering urge to devote himself to his literary task, friends were there to support him in this.

C. F. Hallencreutz, who had been in Birmingham, came home and gave again time to B Sr's continuing work on Söderblom:

> My dear friend and co-worker, Carl Fredrik Hallencreutz, here with me for three wonderful hours in which I got an opportunity to discuss again my lecture [on Söderblom] with him: a great listener and great talent, quick associations, great ability to bring together what is being discussed. I thank God that Carl Fredrik Hallencreutz devotes himself to my subject – pure grace. A talent like his should really devote itself to some other subject [discipline], but now that he gives himself to Mission History, a bit shamefully I say to him 'You must not throw away your youth by becoming a missionary after you have disputed. You must stay here and become a docent in the university.' (Diary 29 December 1969)

Tore Furberg, who became the mission director of CSM and later the Bishop of Visby, provided steady support throughout the years.

> Then again before I was going to retire, I had that enormously valuable contact and co-operation with the mission director, Tore Furberg, who had taken his doctorate under me, as had Hallencreutz. Their encouragement and kindness is of very great importance and helped me and healed me. (Interview 31 October 1985)

Tore Furberg was also Bengt's choice for conducting his funeral when the time came for that, shared with Jonas Jonson, Bishop of Strängnäs, who was the celebrant at the Holy Communion.

Gunnar Johansson had been a friend from the Bukoba times on and the visits of Bukoba friends were always very welcome, Joel Ngeiyamu being perhaps the most frequent. Jonas Jonson brought China 1944–52 into the wide spectrum of topics. His work made B Sr regret that he had not earlier devoted more time and interest to China, but he had to concede that time after all had its limits.[35] Jonas Jonson defended his thesis in 1972. His significance in B Sr's life grew as the years went by. He and his wife Birgitta invited Bengt to their home for several of the last Christmases of his life where Bengt greatly enjoyed their delightful little daughter Karin Rebekka and meeting Birgitta's parents, Professor Sven Rubenson and his wife.

Whenever B Sr's student and friend, Axel-Ivar Berglund, was in Uppsala he was called for help, whether he was needed for transporting Bengt or his visitors to or from Arlanda, or most importantly, to provide the expertise in matters relating to South Africa, Zulu culture and language. This was much needed when B Sr was writing *Zulu Zion:*

> We have had Axel-Ivar Berglund and family here this week and I had them all for dinner here. Then long talks with Axel-Ivar about his great book and about my own BZ. It was a real heaven-send to have him here. I have profited enormously from my talks with him. (13 July 1974)

Axel-Ivar Berglund presented his doctoral thesis to Professor Monica Wilson, the best possible authority on South Africa, getting high praise from both teachers. He was a friend who perhaps more than anyone else could understand B Sr's love and devotion to Africa and think in African terms. From this background we can appreciate that B Sr has words of high praise about Kerstin and Axel-Ivar Berglund's daughter Ingrid's wedding to Sören Jonsson in 1980; and that after the funeral of their son Erik's sad early death B Sr had said it was the kind he would want his own funeral to be.[36]

In his diaries and letters Bengt Sundkler repeatedly exhorts himself to devote himself totally to what he saw as his main calling in life, writing based on his experience and scholarship. He never ceased to repeat, 'This One Thing Only.' To this he from time to time added, 'Everything else is a mistake.' First it referred to his literary work with *Bara Bukoba* and *Zulu Zion*. After he retired he wrote that he was starting on a new career, as a full-time writer. After he started work on the African Church History, everything focussed on that. But before he could devote himself fully to writing there were still five years of teaching, guiding doctoral students and taking care of other academic duties.

Back to his students

After returning from South Africa, B Sr introduced his most recent findings in South Africa into his teaching topics. Many student sessions with doctoral candidates had coincided with Ingeborg's illness which caused a lot of pressure at that time. The diary records the various seminar sessions faithfully and meeting with the students and doctoral candidates. The travels continued to interrupt teaching duties, as we learn in other parts of this book.

> 6 November 1969. [We took a trip] with my church history seminar of 30–40 students to Stockholm Statehouse and City archives, *EFS (Evangeliska Fosterland Stiftelse)* archives and state archives from the Middle Ages, etc. Rector David Lagergren introduced the Betel seminary school and archives. We visited home economics school which prayed for Ingeborg and I greeted them for her. Fine singing with guitar, very moving. In the Lidingö Mission school for the SMF (Swedish Free Mission) Sigbert talked in his brilliant way about archives from Congo. Then to the Baptist church, baptismal grave, etc. Everyone in good spirits coming home. A successful trip.

The attention B Sr gave to individual doctorands was uneven, depending on his other duties, but probably also on the level of scholarship, the amount of assistance the candidate required, and on inspiration in their relations. In the words of one of the prominent former students, 'Sundkler had a lot of good ideas to suggest but he did not always follow them up.' The diaries tell, however, that much time was taken in small doctoral seminars for discussing chapters of the various theses, allowing the candidates to thus support one another with ideas and offer mutual guidance. Inevitably, some of the hardest students to guide took up time. With several of the candidates B Sr spent days making sure that the standard of the work did not fall below the requirements.

Some of the doctoral candidates never finished; some failed to get a good enough grade for their docentship. With the passing years time was getting short:

> 3 July 1973. I have seven doctorands at present, and I do sincerely hope to take all seven of them through to their doctorates before I leave the chair in 330 days time. I have asked them to send me Progress Reports prior to 1 July, 1 September and 1 November of this year so that I know exactly where they are. I had two such this morning, one on Reichelt [Håkan Eilert], and one on the Swedish seamen's mission [Ingemar Bergmark]. It is a very satisfying thing to follow their development, and I shall try to inspire each and every one in such a way that we can together achieve some good results.

To encourage his candidates B Sr sent three or four circular letters to remind them that the time was passing.

Doctors' theses: I am reading them, lots of them, correcting, suggesting and doing my best and having a fine family fellowship with them: Bergmark, Säverås, Zetterquist, Eilert, Gnanabaranam. I also have the Kibira volume to work on for his honorary doctorate from the Uppsala university. All must be ready in May 1974. You can see that I am not left unemployed. (Letter to MLS 23 August 1973)

Had a wonderful evening with some 40 students last night. I spoke on 'being a student'. First I spoke what it is to be a professor and then what it was to be a student in the 1930s, finally 'engagement and openness', as a model for a life in service. We became great friends all of us and had a fine open fellowship. These are all freshmen and second year students. Splendid young generation. I am so glad to have had this contact with them right from the beginning. (Letter to MLS 5 November 1973)

I am in the midst of this very demanding and exciting week totally devoted to my doctorands. We spent the whole day yesterday on Säverås from Norway and his thesis on the Mekane Yesu Church 1940-58. We used all the time on two chapters, and I feel that he received very effective and necessary help. It is very satisfying also for me. I am also giving much time to the others, in so far as I can feel that it is at all worth while. The most gifted is Håkan Zetterquist who writes a sociological study of the beginnings of the Diocese of Stockholm 1941-51. I derive much joy from discussing with him. And all these men are so encouraging to me that I am quite moved and of course very grateful.

There was a written test with five questions yesterday for 51 youngsters. The average result poor, I feel, but at least I get the sense that I have not turned them into enemies of Missions. (Letter to MLS 21 November 1973)

I have spent four full days with my doctorands, from Monday till Thursday p.m. We have been together 5-6 hours a day. I believe it was worth while. Yesterday we met here in my home. They had brought food for a luxurious lunch, each contributing food, wine, cakes and everything. We had a glorious time together. Jon Nilsson [a long time missionary in Tanzania] also turned up, moving in and out, as he is wont to do, as you know. (Letter to MLS 23 November 1973)

I have just returned at 15.30 from my seminar. I have never in my life had such a lively and relevant seminar: two young people, Fryxelius and Vallby, had an essay on Bangkok 1973, and this gave me an occasion to say something that they will never forget: about the need for a real theological position, let it be liberal or High-Church or pietistic or modern in some way ... only that it is thought through and relevant to them, and then let each one fight for it and give arguments for it, and believe in the position ... I invited them to come to me next Wednesday, 19 December, to the flat here, where I can give them something to eat and where we can meditate on the Christian message together. I am better all the time, but unfortunately with less theology than before, but they express themselves better than before, and there are a few very good ones among them. (Letter to MLS 13 December 1973)

In the spring term of 1974 B Sr was pressed to have all the doctoral theses and disputations finished before he left the university at the end of May: Bergmark, Eilert, Flodell, Zetterquist. The last defence was, in fact, after all the farewell celebrations were over. By the time B Sr left his post he had seen through 18 doctoral dissertations in his subject. Later, reminiscing on the final years at the university, B Sr felt special gratitude to his former students who continued to support him.

Farewell to the university

Bengt Sundkler greatly rejoiced that his leaving the faculty coincided with the celebration of the centenary of the Church of Sweden Mission. It meant that he could give his farewell lecture in the presence of a distinguished international audience on 14 May 1974, when many foreign guests were in Uppsala by invitiation, particularly friends from different parts of Africa and Asia, including Bishop Kibira from Bukoba and Bishop Mhlungu from Zululand, both with their wives. He had also the joy and privilege of participating in the organisation of the festive commemorating service on 18 May 1974 on the island of Birka, where St Ansgar stepped onto Swedish soil bringing the message of Christ:

> That service is being prepared now. There is on that little island a little, more or less open chapel which only can hold some 50 people. It was built at the instigation of Söderblom of course, and consecrated in the Name of the Father, Son and the Holy Ghost by him in that great year 1930, great for him, for he was awarded then the Noble Peace Prize. (Letter to MLS 7 May 1974)

> I am working on my sermon . . . We have prepared a very rich service with the participation of all the leaders . . . The weather is still very beautiful to the despair of all the farmers, but to the joy of us who can still hope that it will be fine tomorrow on that little historic island. I have discussed this all with Henry Weman who will take care of the singing. We shall sing Laudamus in Zulu, all of us singing responses, and then a sequence to St Ansgar in Latin and the texts read in Tamil, Sotho and Haya, with English translation for all, and a Malay lady taking one of the prayers. (Letter to MLS 17 July 1974)

> Sunday 19 May (the actual centenary day). Great service in the Aula of the University . . . At 11 a.m. the king arrived and Archbishop Sundby, Tore Furberg and I received him outside and took him in. I then sat with the king and directed him during the service. He took Holy Communion

from the hands of Reverend Ngema, of Zululand, assisted by Biörn Fjärstedt ... a remarkable fact.[37]

After the service I took the king to the Archbishop's House and there we had tea and coffee. At our little table were seated the king, Kibira, Sundby, Lukumbuzya and myself ... The Bukoba choir came and sang. They have been amazingly good. Full of life and fun and beauty.

Then to Riksalen, state hall, to have a dinner ... greetings ... Then we went to the cathedral and there was a final liturgical service with wonderful singing. After everything the Sundbys invited me to come to their kitchen: there were the Sundbys, Stig Hellsten and my sister Ingegärd, the Svenungssons [Sundby's secretary] and myself. We reviewed the whole thing and felt that, on the whole, it had been very good. We have had some glorious days and I have been so glad to be able to play a part in it all. (Letter to MLS 21 May 1974)

This all coincided with B Sr's 75th-birthday celebration on 7 May and his farewell dinner by the Faculty on 14 May which he describes in the same letter. In closing his story, he quoted Ingeborg's words about how she felt in Bukoba, 'This kind of life fits me to perfection.' Only a few days before he had described his feelings about the comparatively insignificant role he had been given in teaching. On a day like this he had forgotten his feelings of not belonging:

About my farewell lecture, 14 May ... The Room IX where you defended your thesis was overfull, to much more than capacity, the two or three first rows of the faculty and all the foreign guests from Africa and Asia – and then students and the whole of Uppsala, the Free Church as well. The lecture went very well indeed, and I had a real message about dialogue, I think. The lecture was listened to with great attention and sympathy. Harry Daniels said to me afterwards, 'You are not a northerner, are you, you seem to be different from all these Swedes.' I think it was meant as a compliment. Then Sigbert Axelson spoke on behalf of the doctorands. Then an applause mightier than anything heard in this university for a long time, and perhaps never on an occasion like this. It was overwhelming. I could never believe it.

Then dinner at Gillet. Dean Ringgren spoke and at the end I responded. I gave my whole life, *Min stora tid i Fakulteten*, My great times in the faculty, my difficult times in the faculty and my good times. I went on and on, and they laughed and cried and had a good time altogether as did I. Ingegärd, my sister was there and Kibira. (Letter to MLS 17 May 1974)

After an occasion like this B Sr did not lament, as usual, that in fact he had gone on for too long. He enjoyed the occasion himself, and his audience could afford to give him that joy.

Bengt Sundkler's theology in a nutshell

Christ and the religions

The lecture 'Christ and the Religions' was B Sr's farewell message delivered when leaving the missiological teaching post in the university. In his view, both Karl Barth and Hendrik Kraemer had with their message widened the gap between the Gospel and the religions. 'my eminent Indian friends D. G. Moses, Paul Devanandan, M. M. Thomas ... paved the way for the new approach in the 1960s'. In his lecture B Sr elaborated on two schools of thought: the radical Catholic theologians of Vatican Council II and the 'dialogue approach in the non-Roman world of missions'. The Catholic radical theologians queried the statement that outside the Church there is no salvation. For them the Cosmic Christ was already there in the world of religions prior to the arrival of the missionary caravan or ship of which the speaker gave first a caricatured picture.

The religions have their necessary place in God's plan of salvation. This is stated in a surprising re-evaluation of the old values:

> While the Church represents the extraordinary way of salvation, world religions – Hinduism, Buddhism, and the others – rightly understood, are the ordinary ways of salvation for non-Christian humanity. Any other view is an expression of intolerable conceit on the part of the Christian missionary.

Daniélou pointed to the Old Testament figures prior to Abraham:

> [They were] 'saints' of the 'cosmic religion', as he calls the universal search for the God of all men. They were outside Israel's religion; yet walking with God, (God's covenant with Noah and Melkisedek) and receiving salvation. This does not mean ... that Daniélou assumes the religions as ways of salvation. (Sundkler, SMT 1974:63–72)

Here then B Sr brings his additional point *ante* and *post*, before and after. After the leap of faith, the mystery of Christ can be grasped and his presence recognised, having already been there before the 'leap'. Dialogue is rare and difficult, but it takes both parties out of their security and challenges them. B Sr comes to his recurring understanding that dialogue does not take place between religions but between individual Hindus and Christians, each professing his own faith.

> Dialogue stems, in other words, from a profound recognition of the mutuality of a common life. The new scope of our International Age thus provides the new frame of reference for theology and mission in our own day and in the future ... Christian missions can no longer make

that happy but facile claim that, slowly but surely, the world's population was being won from its religions, and ir-religion, to and for Christ. Mission today hesitates to make such triumphalistic claims. It is as if it perceived Christ even today in a world of religions, asking the Church that question recorded in John 6: 'Will ye also go away?' Then there is something in the living experience of missions which induces the answer as that of the apostle in the Gospel. And with that answer, my friends, I take leave of the task which it has been my privilege to attempt for a quarter of the century: 'To whom should we go? Thou hast the words of life eternal.'

In an interview in 1990 B Sr had viewed his theology in a meaningful way, briefly summarising the points he felt were important to him as he was getting older:[38]

My High-Church background in Sweden informed the way I behaved as a bishop and my work as a bishop. One must study my episcopal letters to the diocese, from 1961 in Luhaya and English, and from 1965 in Swahili, later translated into English, in order to understand my theology. My theology is related to practical work. It was worked out in practice. It strikes me that whatever theology or research has been written out in theory it does not determine the facts that make history in relation to a living church. My theology changed when serving a living church.

The great sweeps and themes in a particular time in which the person exists are of great importance. I have been living in a time of the ecumenical movement, this has been an overarching theme in my situation, but also history, Church history. In Bukoba I had to fight with 'ecumenics in banana groves' (cf. *Bara Bukoba*), not the ecumenics in Geneva or Oxford, but really in the village. My theology was to try to give foundation for an ecumenical attitude between the churches. When I came to Bukoba as bishop some Lutherans were sceptical and nervous. We had close contacts with Moravians on one side, Anglicans on the other. There was not much more difference between these than between the different Lutheran synods and dioceses which joined in the Evangelical Lutheran Church of Tanzania.

The great thing about history as a whole is the problem of change. This is where the person of this poor old Sundkler, my theory, my hypothesis, comes into being. In a certain crisis the Church takes a decision, in one direction or another, because of a personality or a group of personalities who worked together in order together to achieve this change in that direction. This is what I call the role of persons/personalities in the sweeps and streams of history. History changed and history changes, not as such but because of the intention and the action of certain personalities. So you have to know those personalities and try to explain that change in terms of that personality or those personalities. I am perhaps more intent on that than anybody else. I see that I am very strange from that point of view.

What then is my own theology? I have no close theological system, but for me the cross of Golgotha is the centre of the world. From that the influence goes out, light from his blood shed for the whole world.

More and more I am oriented toward the Fourth Gospel, to John, 'I am the Light of the World' (John 8:12). 'Light shines over all the world' (John 1:6). I would like to spend the rest of my life on that word, to have it as the centre of our whole missiology. To take hold of that as the central thing, as a positive approach to other cultures. Syncretism is not our danger. The other pole is the self-imposed ghetto. 'We have achieved, we have arrived.' It is all wrong. The outgoing glow, light at the centre shines from the cross, the radiant cross.

I have theology there: Where two or three are gathered together there Christ is amidst them. Christ in us, instead of us, in place of us. This is also redemption. I return to this in every sermon. This is the congregation in his name . . . the unseen Lord in amidst us. The Church in the World.

In the New Delhi WCC Assembly of 1961 the idea of cosmic Christ came through as an important issue in evangelical missiology. Christ is in a non-Christian world and a secular world, not on the basis of creation, but on the basis of salvation. He is there as an unseen Lord. Church, the new pilgrim people of God in the world and the Lord, as I try to say in *The World of Mission*. He is in other religions and in the social conditions of the West, in a latent way. I refer to Tillich. Tillich has meant much to me in the last ten years. When I went to the Marangu All-Africa Lutheran Conference in 1955 to lecture, a fellow Scandinavian missionary found out that I had Tillich's book with me. I could see from his face that it was a terrible thing to happen. Tillich's idea of latent presence of Christ is very important to me. I see it more paradoxically than others who have learned it from Tillich.

I am trying to say that Christ, who is present in an unseen way, comes to the fore when the missionary comes and claims his presence. 'Before' and 'after', *ante* and *post*, are my categories. After the event we see that Christ was there already before. When a Hindu takes the step (toward Christ) he says Christ was there already drawing me, beckoning me to come, in many things of my life, in my family. What was happening? You cannot say it in an uncluttered way before the event, you can say it after the event. You cannot say it in a theoretical way before.

The teaching about latent Christ and manifest Christ is a very important teaching. If I had the courage, energy and time to express this I would do it, to drive it through. I never have the time to do it. So to the question on what basis, the answer is on the basis of salvation, not on creation.

I am open to critical questions. I have become more open on getting older. A missiologist should be open to other religions in his approach, not to weaken his own base, but going humbly in the footsteps of the humble servant Jesus Christ. There are no unbelievers, only human spirits struggling with problems of life and death, seeking contact with powers which have victory over death. Dialogue is important to me.

My ecclesiology is hidden in the Church of South India. The Church of Christ is a Universal Church. I learned much from E. J. Palmer, Bishop of Bombay, who was the theologian behind the Church of South India. I interviewed him in Oxford in 1947. God's Universal Church, in categories that they tried to do in South India. I am never satisfied with confessional limitations. We have to see beyond borders, crossing those borders. I say I want one Church in my life time. I know it is unrealistic, but we have to see beyond borders. I feel sorry for those theologians who do not see this, the Universal Church which yet is at the same time local.[39]

Theory and practice

B Sr had stressed the significance of practice and experience in formulating theory already when he came back from his first term in Africa in 1945: to teach or study Mission History one should have experienced mission service (see p. 119). For him there was no theory without practice. Theory came alive when he articulated it in his way of doing research, in his teaching of theology or history, and in his churchmanship: as a bishop, an ordinary missionary, a pastor giving pastoral services to specific families,[40] a celebrant of Holy Communion or when invited to preach.

Theory linked with practice was a consequence of his need to view life as an integrated whole. We shall see this in his choice of models for his Church History of Africa, when he wanted to produce what he called a total view of Africa. It was also his desire on a personal level, to live an integrated life, knowledge permeated by practical experience was what he taught and preached. It was not enough for him to study in the archives and have the 'material' on his desk available for him. He hesitated to write about the Church history of Namibia or Ethiopia, countries of which he did not have a better feel through any concrete contact. (Letter sent to Namibia to MLS 28 November 1991) Naturally this did not mean that one would have to experience and see everything before one could fathom theory, but it is indicative of a desire to be concrete. This is also in line with B Sr's motto from Chesterton, 'For anything to be real, it must be local.' This desire for the concrete and for relating theory to practice also became evident in his rejection of the theories of Laternari and the statistical approach of David Barrett in the study of African churches (see p. 314).

B Sr became conscious of the need to study the ongoing practice and changes taking place in the Church, and to base decisions on his study, when he got acquainted with the Church in South India. He saw how the joining churches changed when the former denominational churches learned new interpretations from one another, while they lived them out in practice. With the revival in Bukoba B Sr had experienced that a church changes when new life comes into it through living Christian congregations and individuals. He had also seen that a church can become rigid and immobile, and above all, less expectant of change through ecumenical connections, if it is guided by theoretical theological positions more than by a way of life anchored in biblical understanding. He returned to the concept 'expectation' in different contexts and found that too rigid or normative an adherence to 'body', institution, precluded expectation for the movement by the Spirit. The significance of both the Pulpit and the Altar had to be honoured equally, proclamation of the word and the sacramental communion and symbolic piety of liturgy evoked sending for mission, 'service for all men and whole man' (or rather, all humans and the whole human being).

Notes

1. In particular, Professor Fridrichsen and Reverend Ingmar Hector from the Hjälmseryd retreat centre.
2. It is interesting to note that as I write this I read the news from Sweden that the Swedes have chosen Bo Giertz as the most influential churchman of the century in Sweden while Nathan Söderblom was given second place.
3. This would mean that the Low-Church part of the Church of Sweden would have closer relations with the so-called free churches, while those who hold to the ancient tradition of the Established Church with Apostolic Succession would either have to start their own church based on that tradition or choose to join the Roman Catholic Church. For B Sr ecumenical unity was the foremost consideration.
4. The article was published in *SMT* 53,1965:129–34. Later in the 1970s B Sr referred to his book *Söderblom och hans möten*, 1975:129–34 as his public pronouncement of his position. He was afraid that it would cause some friction between him and the Östanbäck community for which he offered episcopal services, but in fact, the brothers took a generous view toward his right to his position.
5. Ruben Josefson was appointed. Stendahl, professor in Harvard, became later Bishop of Stockholm. He had also been one of the students favoured by Professor Fridrichsen.
6. The Fabian Society, with a Leftist reputation, was active in the British politics in carrying out the decolonisation of the colonies, protectorates and trust territories of the UK.
7. Because of the close relationship between the State and the Church the council members could be listed as candidates for political parties.
8. *Am I Not a Man and a Brother? British Missions and the Abolition of the Slave Trade and Slavery in West Africa and the West Indies 1786–1838.* SMU 1972.
9. I would like to point out that the language of the diary is more 'colourful' than the text I include in the quotes.
10. The political leader of Mozambique and Frelimo who was murdered with a letterbomb in Dar es Salaam before the independence of Mozambique. He took his doctorate at Syracuse University, NY, USA.
11. Gustaf Bernander was a long-time missionary in (South Rhodesia), Zimbabwe and (Tanganyika), Tanzania. He wrote a book about the wartime missionwork in Tanzania. The missions and churches, which were left without missionaries when the German missionaries were interned, were called orphaned missions (see Chapter 5).
12. Nils Ehrenström was sent by Söderblom to the Geneva Ecumenical Institute to represent the Church of Sweden where he worked for 25 years. According to B Sr 'I can observe a tendency in the Church of Sweden to forget such ecumenical Swedes who have been engaged for longer periods in international work. Their efforts to tie themselves again with Sweden have not always been successful. They made their choice, and can blame themselves. Nils Ehrenström, Bengt Hoffman and Krister Stendahl come to mind.' Ehrenström ended up abroad, as a professor of ecumenics in Boston where he served 1955–72. (*Söderblom och*

hans möten, 1975:149) Sundkler no doubt thought of himself also in writing these succinct words, being better known abroad than at home, as he often had a cause to remark.

13. Sundkler, Bengt 1970. *Anna Söderblom 1870–1970*, Uppsala. Reprint from Nathan Söderblom Society Yearbook *Religion och Bibel* XXIX.

14. From a letter written by Gerda Rodling to B Sr and quoted in his lecture on 'Nathan Söderblom as a Letter Writer' delivered at the Nathan Söderblom Society on 15 January 1971. B Sr faithfully attended the meetings of this society and was often asked to lecture on Söderblom. Information on how Söderblom worked was based on his visit to Gerda Rodling and the letters he later received from her in answer to specific questions. Gerda Rodling died just before she reached the age of 98, on 8 March 1993 and B Sr wrote *In Memoriam* in a couple of Swedish newspapers. (Letter to MLS 22 March 1993)

15. A close friend of N Sm with whom the latter corresponded during his time in Paris; 'distinction' was a favourite expression of N Sm to which B Sr returns in several contexts, e.g. in *Nathan Söderblom och hans möten*, 1975:145, in relation to whoever would take up N Sm's great ecumenical task in the Church of Sweden after his death, he must be someone with 'distinction'.

16. Discussion with MLS 13 January 1978 with quotes from the book on Söderblom 1968. B Sr's sense of self identity in writing on Söderblom was not only alluded to, it found expression in different interviews. The significance of Handel's Messiah to B Sr and Ingeborg was referred to in the chapter 'To the Equator' and the significance of music for writing in Chapter 12. B Sr struggled with the problem of 'spirit and institution' in his practical work as a bishop and intensely when writing the Church History of Africa, his last major work.

17. A meeting of the World Alliance in 1919 which Söderblom attended and at which he presented a memorandum outlining his thoughts for an ecumenical conference which resulted in Stockholm 1925: 'Our task is not to bring organisations together, but to unite hearts and minds and endeavours.'

18. Nathan Söderblom 'Parisårens inflytande på hans ekumeniska insats,' *Svenska Sofiaförsamlingen* I Paris, Jubileumsskrift 1626–1976.

19. Fridrichsen, 1942. *En bok om kyrkan*.

20. Excerpts I noted down from conversations about Söderblom and included in an illustrated hand-written book I presented to B Sr on one of his birthdays.

21. Diary 20 October. '4.30 with a carpenter Anton Jönsson, 82 years old, who was around in the great strike in 1909 and remembers Söderblom well. N Sm had buried his father in September 1907 and used to talk with Anton often when he as a young carpenter working on Vasa street. He was a fine, sweet old man.' Cf. Sundkler 1975:47)

22. I stayed with them in August 1968 when I went to get advice on my thesis and found them discussing the location and the problem of transportation. Bengt had the Söderblom book fresh out in his hands but he was aware it did not give the same joy to Ingeborg as it did to him, after the loneliness it had cost her.

23. The letter continues to describe the event, the visitors – a Benedictine Abbot and a Prior from Germany and a Fransiscan from Bornholm, the four monks Johannes, Bengt, Caesarius and Ingemar 'professed,' etc. The book he refers to was *Nathan Söderblom och hans möten* and the concern related to the differing views that the community held on the office of the Church.

24. The book project had been initiated by Axel-Ivar Berglund and besides those mentioned Eric Sharpe and Stiv Jacobsson also assisted in editing.

25. B Sr, as many others, thought that with the revolutionary spirit, formalities would be done away with before long. This did not happen.

26. The reader finds the personalities mentioned here in *Zulu Zion and Some Swazi Zionists* 1976.

27. The stay in Africa is reported in the diary 'Resa till Sydafrika (Zululand–Swaziland) June–September 1969' and in letters to Ingeborg.

28. In this section I have left out all the references relating to activities with the students. The busy schedule B Sr had at the time of Ingeborg's illness can be seen if the dates of the students seminars etc. are compared with the activities going on in between visits to the hospital.
29. 'Professor Torsten Christensen (Church historian from Copenhagen) was here this afternoon: A splendid scholar, 48 years old, full of ideas and joy of work. Fully for complete integration of Church History and Mission History. It was fascinating to meet him again. He gets something done and of the highest quality.'
30. *En dalande dag, en flyktig stund, Är människans levnad i tiden ... Och dock är mitt hjärta oförskräckt. Min ande bidar förskoning mig räckt, Som bjuder frid och försoning.* (A dying day, a fleeing moment, is human life in time ... Yet my heart is not afraid. My spirit waits upon mercy bestowed on me, Which offers peace and reconciliation.)
31. Ingeborg had two brothers, Cecil and Jarl Agne Morén. Ingeborg was closest to Cecil. Jarl Agne was bitter about some wrong he felt he had suffered in dividing the father's estate, towards his brother as well. He had kept no contact, had treated Ingeborg with bitterness and not wanted any reconciliation. This had caused the good and noble Ingeborg much sorrow.
32. 31 October. Evening meal with the Wemans, Henry and Birgitta. What a wonderful home they have and what good and living people they are.
33. Docent Thure Stenström, later professor of literature, came to see B Sr now and later in his times of anxiety. Bengt much appreciated the opportunities to discuss literature with him. They had in their school time, far apart in time and space, had the same literature teacher who had brought them together.
34. *Min kropp här såddes dödelig, Men skall stå upp odödelig, I härlighet förklarad.* (My body is sown in mortality, But it will rise immortal, Glorified.)
35. (Diary 11 December 1969) A list of doctoral theses supervised by Bengt Sundkler is given in the end of the book.
36. We owe this information to Katharina Hallencreutz, Carl Fredrik's wife. Holy Communion was celebrated at Bengt's funeral because of this.
37. Biörn Fjärstedt succeeded Tore Furberg as general secretary of the CSM and later as Bishop of Visby.
38. Interview with Tiina Ahonen 1990. See also Sundkler 1965:41, 247.
39. I thank Tiina Ahonen for the permission to use this interview which is available on tape. I have rearranged some of the thoughts, but have kept them as close to the original oral presentation as possible.
40. Bengt Sundkler was a family pastor to the families of K. B. Westman, Docent Gun Björkman, Professor Carl-Gösta Widstrand, Professor Harry Tegneus and their daughter Elizabeth, and Bengt's and Ingeborg's families.

10

INTERNATIONALE OF MISSIONS

International before popular internationalism

Bengt Sundkler was a true internationale, long before the time of popular internationalism. He had an inherent desire for *beyond* which started, as we have seen, when he wanted to penetrate through and beyond his home forests, remaining rooted locally, but constantly looking beyond, until he reached the ultimate. His mission had an eschatological perspective, beyond time.

B Sr often felt that he was better appreciated outside than within his home country, a fate of many internationales, and above all, of many visionaries. Individuals, movements, groups with a view to beyond the present will have to wait until a discovery, a way of viewing issues, fits better into its environment, until the environment has attained the conditions in which a new way of experiencing has become possible. With other path-breakers B Sr watched as time and again new generations 're-invented the wheel'.

In this chapter I have collected those of Bengt Sundkler's international commitments which have not been included in other chapters, summarising his international work. I also include some of his international political involvements and reflections. Two features stand out in all his internationally oriented work. One is his unremitting insistence on an ecumenical approach, seeing denominations as different faces of the same faith. His emphasis was on the universal, catholic, one Church of Christ in the world, regardless of its many facets, and on its historical continuity. The other is his willingness to learn and listen in all situations and as a learner to allow practice to inform his theory and theology.

Sundkler's international engagements were too many to recount their extent. The richness of the articles written and edited by Bengt Sundkler (or B. S.) throughout the years in *SMT* is amazing, to apply the adjective frequently used by himself. He followed closely major developments within the ecumenical and even confessional movements and brought them into readers' consciousness. As one of the subscribers to the journal since 1959 I realise how inadequately I made use of the opportunity to learn what was happening in the universal Church and the world for which the Church was charged with responsibility.

As a development studies researcher I am astonished how closely and how early B Sr followed the secular international scene in relation to developing countries. He followed closely Gunnar Myrdal's research, was theoretically influenced by development sociology and in the last 20 years followed keenly the history writings of Africa. His interest was directed to Third World issues rather than political issues in Europe, even in its years of Nazism or Communism. He was absent from Europe in the years in which 'Hitler's war', as he called it, raged there and for this reason, and as a Swede, did not have the same personal contact with it as many others of us. On the other hand, he was in Sweden during the years of Cold War and was fed with Solshenitsyn's books to develop an abhorrence of Communism. He never visited the Soviet Union or Russia, nor even the Baltic States, in the churches of which he had an interest through Söderblom.

B Sr voted for European Union, based on his own close relations with the central countries in the Union, also considering it a good choice for security reasons for the Nordic countries. He also saw in it possibilities for a greater unity within the Church. Having been on different sides with him on that issue I found it impossible even to try to open a debate with him about the negative sides of joining the EU. For him, as for many other colleagues and friends, the threat of Communism, or being lumped together with unknown future forces and not counted as part of the West, overrode any other considerations. For him it was not an economic issue, nor did he engage in debates which would have required any knowledge of economic theory. In the 1970s he accepted the need for radical change in international relations in regard to the Third World countries, but did not always appreciate the narrow theoretical perspective of the revolutionary radical writers. He saw the need for the Church to respond to the challenge of China, but resisted the materialistic and anti-religious slant of that challenge. This also prevented him from starting a serious dialogue with people who, in one way or another, seemed to be siding with aggressive anti-religious forces or who with their arguments seemed to play into their hands. He was refused a visa for South Africa at least once in July 1968, but received it after applying again the following year. It seems he was not in any major way hindered from doing his research of the independent churches, in spite of his clear, yet not publicly polemic statements against apartheid while in South Africa.

B Sr was a Social Democrat. In later years, he lost confidence in the party leadership and changed his voting pattern. He sided publicly with the Biafra issue and took sides with those who settled in Scandinavia to escape service in the Vietnam War. He did not in general enter into open political polemics. He defended himself with the weakness in his psychological make-up, which made public debating difficult for him. Perhaps it would not be wrong to conclude by saying that he appreciated conciliatory rather than judgmental views in most issues and stayed out of the public eye in those in which he could not express a conciliatory view. This did not prevent him from expressing harsh views, particularly on issues which touched on the Third World.

In 1990 B Sr was invited to spend Christmas in France with the noble family of Count Gilles du Gauze de Nazelle and his Swedish wife Elizabeth, daughter of Professor Harry Tegneus, for which families he was a family priest or pastor, (he used both terms). In the French context priest was a more familiar term. He had baptised Elizabeth, had seen her grow up and graduate with a doctorate in law from the Sorbonne, and he had assisted at her wedding ceremony in Paris in March 1975. After returning from France on New Year's Eve Bengt went on to express general political views, leaving the story of his visit to France to be told by phone. His concern was the Gulf War which was waging at that time:

> Coming back to Sweden ... one returns to this terrible world getting used to the idea of war, a devastating war. I cannot accept it and I dislike Mr Bush intensely having forced the Western and Third World countries to accept his views. This war will also very soon affect him and all he stands for and all of the American way of life.
> What then is the alternative, people will shout at you? The alternative is peace. Anything but peace in this world situation is madness. It is strange that a whole world will have to line up to defend a Kuwaiti emir's family. Do they deserve it? (Letter to MLS January 1991)

At least from the time of the painful struggle in South Africa and then Martin Luther King's death on 4 April 1968 B Sr had taken part in peace issues and formed a small peace committee in Uppsala:

> The great apostle of non-violence has been assassinated. Twenty years after Gandhi. The world has lost one of its best. 'I have a dream: a dream of love, conciliatory spirit and reconciliation.' (Diary 5 April 1968)

The Director of the Christian Institute of South Africa, Beyers Naudé, a Christian radical, was a close friend, and his visits to Uppsala were occasions for the peace committee to meet, even if some of B Sr's close South African friends held the view that South Africa could not emerge from the struggle without bloodshed. (Diary 30 April and 2 May 1968)

During the General Assembly of the WCC in Uppsala 1968 a peace train of young pilgrims came to Uppsala from Stockholm and held a communion service in which two Bengts assisted, Bengt Sundkler and Bengt Hoffman (who, with his wife, was a guest of the Sundklers at the time). The service was taken by brother Hans Cavallin of the Östanbäck community of the Brothers of the Holy Cross.

International conferences

On reading the history of the international ecumenical conferences, one is impressed how the issues which half a century later were taken up as great innovations in development circles, were even then being seriously tackled. In the Jerusalem Conference of 1928 the social issues of the day in industrialising societies, in Central Africa among others, attracted great attention. In the 1950s and 1960s the relationship between the younger churches and the missions was brought into focus. Some concepts which decades later have gained currency were already being introduced in the 1940s, one such concept being 'partnership'. The motto of the ecumenical conference of the International Missionary Council in Whitby in 1947 was 'Partnership in Obedience', meaning partnership between the older 'sending churches' and the younger churches.

The concept of 'participation', which became fashionable in development circles in the 1990s, was often part of the Christian workers' presence in communities in which they served, at times being conscious of the necessity to participate as close to being equals as was possible under the circumstances. B Sr himself used the participatory approach to research from the beginning of his work in Africa and found in his old age that it was gradually being approved of in mainstream scholarship and development practice. (*SMT* 40, 1952:93–100)

In the International Missionary Council (IMC) conference in Willingen in 1952, Germany, five years after Whitby, the concepts of partnership and being united in practice had been developed much further. The conference was first planned only for the mission bodies of the older churches, but was broadened to include the younger churches. Even the concept 'partnership' was there found to be inadequate, the need was to be united, to belong together. Partnership was not enough. In the conference both older and younger churches were considered to be 'sending churches', all with the same task, all belonging to the same universal church and participating in its mission. The IMC moved from mission strategy to mission theology. The Indian representatives in Willingen, Dr R. B. Manikam and Dr D. G. Moses, were particularly vocal about this. The same issues related to Africa as to Asia, even if there was a tendency to think that things were moving more slowly in Africa. This was then a step toward integration. B Sr points out this development when, in his Swedish Journal of Mission Research (*SMT*), he reported on important international and ecumenical events in which he took part. He compared the themes, the key messages and results from the progression of conferences, including also the LWF and Faith and Order conferences. (*SMT* 40, 1952:69–72, 133–49; 50, 1962:98–102)

This process within the churches and mission agents is of special interest for someone who has followed the slow progress in development circles towards a closer and more balanced relationship between the so-called 'recipients' and 'donor agencies', including the UN and World Bank 'missions'. Development, which within the churches was envisaged as early as 1947 in Whitby and clearly articulated in 1952 in Willingen, is only now being adopted in development discourse. The 'recipients' are not readily trusted as equal partners. There is much to learn in all quarters, but it seems that the church agents have not become aware of the lessons they could have promoted from their history. They have rather subjected themselves to the position of other non-governmental organisations (NGOs) and adopted project-based strategies dictated to them by 'donor' government policies. Within the mission debates, B Sr pointed to the common divine authority which both partners shared, subjecting both parties equally, with no exception, to the same rules and above all the same love for and commitment to service. One could suggest that within the intergovernmental relations one such external referent could be a commonly agreed code of ethics with the mediation of the UN.

The following examples of B Sr's impressions give glimpses of his estimation of the significance of the IMC conference in Willingen, in which he played an important role (*SMT* 40, 1952:133–44):

> The Anglo-Catholic newspaper *Church Times* described Willingen as the greatest conference the IMC had organised, while also being the humblest and most realistic. This assessment came from a man who was the most irritating speaker in Willingen [personally I considered him one of the most stimulating speakers]. The assessment has points in common with Professor K. S. Latourette's summary ... Willingen 1952 was 'most realistic and fruitful'. The opinions will vary ... but in any case Willingen will form an important milestone in the international mission movements' history.
>
> For me personally it gave much. In my evaluation the six Bible studies on the theme I Cor. 1. under the leadership of Hendrik Kraemer take first place. It gave an idea of the depth of the Word which is not yet in its richness reflected upon ... With the passage 1. Cor.1:13: 'Is Christ then divided?' the speaker brought into sharp focus the perforated ecumenism: Only in Christ do the churches come truly close to each other. The main problem the conference had to struggle with was the biblical–theological problem, the Missionary Obligation of the Church. (*SMT* 40, 1952:133–44)

When B Sr was interviewed in 1990 by Tiina Ahonen, he elaborated on his own role at Willingen:

> For the Asian, African and Latin American church leaders, the meeting at Willingen in 1952 was important. There I played a small role. It is

there that I used the term 'christonomy', not independence of the churches but Christ-dependency. The self-centred idea (of self-governing, self-supporting and self-propagating churches) came right from the 1850s, from Henry Venn of the Church of England and the American Congregationalist Rufus Anderson, and was later taken up by the German theologian and missiologist Gustav Warneck. Because of my background with the church in Bukoba and African independent churches I questioned too strong an emphasis being placed on the 'three selves' which dominated the mission thinking.

Instead of autonomous churches I had thrown out the idea of 'christonomous', Christ centred church. People have returned to it, more than I myself have done.

The church is never rooted in any place, it is on move, the church is rooted in Christ and related to the soil, to society and nation. (*SMT* 40, 1952:140)

I have earlier quoted B Sr's thoughts on the South African independent churches which he, in this context, called 'caricatures' of churches, to emphasise the necessity of belonging to the historical One Church, to have the sense of being One.

The Theological Education Fund

Of the numerous international commitments B Sr was asked to undertake, and often felt privileged to take on, he considered presiding over the Theological Education Fund for some years to be highly important. It deserves special mention here. B Sr always considered the emphasis on theological education to be of great significance and was very happy to be able to influence it universally and ecumenically. One of the commitments to theological education in Africa was the participation in the Latin Africa Commission (see Chapter 6 p. 133) and consequently the task of gathering together the results of all the missions on the ministry in Africa. As we have seen, this resulted in *The Christian Ministry in Africa*, published in 1960, and revised in 1962.

Another Theological Education Fund meeting was held in Edinburgh directly before the 50-year commemoration of the famous Edinburgh conference of 1910 in which, under the leadership of John R. Mott, the great lines of Protestant missions had been drawn. B Sr wrote to his brother-in-law, Bishop Hellsten, a letter on St Olof's Day (29 July) 1960 from St Colombia in Edinburgh. While others more interested in the financial matters were clearing them, Bengt was busy writing letters:

Here we are now for a Theological Education Fund meeting in Edinburgh, as beautiful as always, which is saying a lot. We number 15–20 persons: Dr Franklin Clark Fry, Van Dusen, Liston Pope, John

Mackay, etc. and from Japan, India, Indonesia, Africa and the 'Continent' of Europe, one representative from each, and ten Americans. We have 4 million US dollars for theological education in the younger churches for five years, 1958–63. It is quite interesting and instructive to follow. Tomorrow I shall travel to St Andrews for a joint Committee of the WCC and the IMC. Then comes the administrative meeting of the IMC. I have never been to St Andrews and am very glad to be able to see the town and to make these contacts.

I then return to Edinburgh for the 50-year jubilee 'Edinburgh 1910'. I hope that the old noble 87-year-old J. H. Oldham comes along ... he was the incomparable secretary of the 1910 conference. John R. Mott, the chairman, died in 1955, and others also like him. But the movement which Edinburgh set going is in full swing [referring to the missionising movement in the churches which got their inspiration from Edinburgh 1910].

The Christian movement was 'in full swing' in the world, but the terminology, and strangely looking back to the world of the nineteenth century, did not accord with B Sr's thought pattern or language.[1] Even then the conference challenged the churches to be the Church in the world and was in Richard Hogg's words, 'a lens catching diffused beams of light from a century's attempts at missionary co-operation, focussing them, and projecting them for the future in a unified, meaningful and determinative pattern'. (Edinburgh 1910; Ghana Assembly 1958:192) B Sr regarded J. H. Oldham very highly and never uttered his name without some epithet of great praise. The book *Edinburgh 1910* is of one opinion about the general secretary of the conference:

> J. H. Oldham contrasted strangely with the chairman (John R. Mott who hammered 'the sentences with careful, scientific deliberateness'). Small in stature, and of unassuming face and mien, he slipped in and out of his place at the table, as one not merely unnoticed but not meriting notice ... The secretary never opened his lips from beginning to end, save to give out formal notices. Why then was it that the first time he rose to give out a notice, the whole conference applauded as though it would never cease? ... those that knew were aware that, more than any one other, the spirit that was in this very unobtrusive exterior had been behind the great conference, not merely in respect of its organisation and its methods, but also of its ideals, its aspirations and its hopes.

Soon after becoming bishop of the northwestern Evangelical Church in Bukoba, Bengt Sundkler had to attend the Theological Education Fund meeting in Yale, USA. Two years later he again attended a Theological Education Fund meeting in North America, this time in Montreal.

He made use of this opportunity to meet and stay overnight with Josiah Kibira for whom he had made it possible to continue his studies in Boston under the Swedish professor, Nils Ehrenström. The latter had come there from the Geneva Ecumenical Institute where he had been sent by Nathan Söderblom. B Sr remembered this visit with joy. He had wanted Kibira to get into contact with the African–American community, which Kibira had done. Kibira took B Sr to the common room of the University cafeteria, ordered food for him and then went around saying, 'Let me introduce my Bishop from Bukoba to you.' The bishop's remark was that Kibira had picked up quickly the American ways. To him it was 'a thing that only Americans could do'.

While in the USA B Sr was attacked by a virus which then kept him ailing for four months. He managed to fly to Sweden to be treated there and have time to convalesce.

New Delhi 1961

The New Delhi Assembly of the World Council of Churches in November 1961 followed Amsterdam and Evanston, Illinois. It was a turning point in international mission scholarship and theology. In it the vote for the integration of the International Missionary Council into the World Council of Churches was taken by the representatives of the young and old member churches. It was the first appearance of the Asian, African and Latin American churches in full force. New Delhi was also a turning point ecumenically with the Orthodox churches being represented.

Having worked so closely with the IMC organisation B Sr had been elected to the office of vice president of the IMC. In that capacity and as one of the representatives from the northwestern diocese in Tanzania he attended the historic assembly in New Delhi. B Sr had also been asked to review the past work of the IMC in its conference which preceded the WCC assembly. I quote a few of the key thoughts from the summing up of 50 years of IMC work which B Sr delivered at that conference:[2]

> The call and the task for the IMC was nothing more and nothing less than to strengthen and to serve the Church of Christ in the world ... Dealing with the organisational problems within the 'young churches', which were fortunately discovered during this period, seemed to result in a retreat to an ecclesiastical ghetto. There has even been theological uncertainty regarding the understanding and interpretation of the claim and gift of the Gospel in relation to other religions, and at times an accompanying lack of dynamic witness on the borderline between Christian confession and another faith. It is at this fundamental level that the ecumenical discussion concerning the mission task of the Church has given new direction and new conviction during recent years. An understanding of the Church has matured not as a self-sufficient, self-preserving ecclesiastic piece of machinery, but as new God's people, God's pilgrims, sent to the world. It consists an interpretation of the Church as a happening more than an institution, the Church as functioning, in herself a sign and the first fruits of God's kingdom ...

This integration [of the International Mission Council and the World Council of Churches] marks a new beginning of an utmost significance for the witness, unity and service of the Church.

The assembly was addressed by the prime minister of India, Jawaharlal Nehru, which gave it status in a country dominated by the Hindu and Muslim religions. I quote some excerpts from B Sr's impressions from New Delhi as a place for a world conference and from the assembly itself:

There are important positive points to having had the conference in Asia. Compared with the earlier assemblies of the WCC, in Amsterdam 1948 and Evanston, IL 1954, one can clearly see that for the first time this meeting projected Asia–Africa to a different degree from what earlier was possible. The Indian milieu dominated the impression that one was left with. Visits in Indian homes, in Indian Christian churches in New Delhi, contact with the noble Indian social and political leaders have remained as the finest memories from the conference. One night I visited Dr D. G. Moses in his home; this Indian churchman and educator became one of the six vice presidents and played an important role in managing the conference.

Others as well as the Indians contributed to the memorable conference. One night I was with others invited to the home of the Swiss ambassador, Dr Cuttat. He had penetrated Hindu religion to the point that he was ready to convert to Hinduism, but just by studying Vedanta he had discovered Christ anew. I remember gratefully this Catholic diplomat and his intensive, intellectual struggle with spiritual problems. It is valuable that in the religious Indian milieu the West is represented by people who are aware of the spiritual values.

In general, the personal contacts with church and mission leaders from other countries were incredibly rich. I was able to attend a meeting in a YMCA in New Delhi where both the Archbishop of Canterbury and Billy Graham spoke. In one of the main lectures by Professor Joseph Sittler from Chicago, complicated by its difficult theological jargon, the idea of cosmic Christ came through as an important issue in evangelical missiology.

Outside the conference programme proper, the Asian, African and Latin American church leaders had gathered in an improvised and intensely interesting evening meeting just to get to know one another and each others' groups. The brilliant theologian and fiery evangelist, D. T. Niles, a Methodist from [what was then] Ceylon, was clearly the chairman but African and Indonesian leaders talked as readily. We were a handful of adopted Whites who were invited to join, and indeed, we felt very much at home with this group of different colour shades.

The important event was the joining of the Orthodox and African churches in the WCC, and of course the integration of the IMC with the WCC. The IMC had come to its last conference, two days before the assembly. The conference was chaired by the chairman of IMC, Dr C. Baëta while Bishop Lesslie Newbigin was its last general secretary. (*SMT* 50, 1962:98–9)

I became member of Central Committee and Josiah Kibira member of Faith and Order commission on my proposal. (Diary 13 November 1961).

Apart from being a great event, the stay in Delhi became memorable to B Sr also because of a disastrous food poisoning attack he suffered there and was forever grateful to a fellow participant of the assembly, Dr Ruth Rosvere, who saved him from near death. Having to spend some days in bed and suffering from the day's heat and the night chill left an impression that for him Delhi was not the most ideal of places.

Uppsala 1968

In 1968 the General Assembly of the World Council of Churches was held in Uppsala. B Sr, together with Professor Riesenfeld from the theological faculty, was a member of the official delegation of the Church of Sweden. B Sr's involvement in the conference and his views on it deserve a few paragraphs in the chapter on him as an internationale.

We have seen that for B Sr the greatest event was his book on the great internationale, Archbishop Nathan Söderblom, which was published just in time for the assembly. On 2 July the Nathan Söderblom exhibition was opened by Visser 't Hooft in the building of Carolina Library. Visser 't Hooft also mentioned Bengt Sundkler's book *Nathan Söderblom* in his speech at the opening of the assembly which was broadcast on television on 5 July.

The opening of the assembly was in the Fyrishall where Prime Minister Olof Palme spoke and the president of Zambia, Kenneth Kaunda, delivered a keynote speech. Olof Palme and the government of Sweden gave a festive dinner in Kaunda's honour on 2 July. The former prime minister, Tage Erlander also attended. Kaunda returned the honour giving a dinner in Stockholm where Tage Erlander in turn gave a friendly speech. Ingeborg and Bengt Sundkler were also invited to attend these occasions.

In the University Aula James Baldwin gave an unforgettable speech to a full auditorium. While there, Archbishop Ramsey of Canterbury used the opportunity to invite B Sr to Lambeth, to which he remarked that he would accept the invitation if he were not granted a visa to go to South Africa. B Sr also met the Archbishops of York and Melbourne. Other meaningful contacts were with Kimbanguists from Zaire and Pentecostals from Latin America from whom he heard of the plan to prepare a manifesto to be sent to Pope Pius VI, admonishing him to further a secular revolution in Latin America!

In Section II of the official conference B Sr spoke and presented the Scandinavian alternative version of the draft paper on the mission of the church to the draft prepared in Geneva. He had been present in a group in Sigtuna preparing the document. In his intervention he took a generally positive view with the Geneva document and the world-wide agenda in it. The intention was to stay together with Geneva, 'to walk, work and pray together', but they were not ready to sociologise the mission to the same extent, wanting rather a more central grip on mission. Apparently the alternative proposal did not get a good reception. B Sr was dissatisfied with his own performance and felt miserable afterwards at not having been sufficiently collected and positive. His somewhat depressed mood was further aggravated when two young men from Lund got hold of him claiming to be reporters for *Hot News*. They deemed that the Scandinavian draft was shameful and treated B Sr as the culprit.

The missiologists managed to have two refreshing afternoon meetings in SIM amidst an otherwise rather trying conference, giving the host useful new contacts. He was encouraged to hear later from Professor Charles Forman from Yale that these two meetings were the best part of the entire Uppsala 1968 conference. Others who took part were Gerald Anderson (Manila), Douglas Webster, H. J. Margull (Hamburg), G. C. Oosthuizen (South Africa), A. van Leeuwen, Deminger, Furberg and Axelson. Kenneth Cragg merited the epithets 'wonderful, incredibly valuable contributions, quick, quiet, brilliant'.

B Sr was interviewed for television about 'Poor and Rich Lands' together with two others. He was able to see the interview since it was shown late at night but as so often, he was not pleased with his own performance, he had been tense and sad, not relaxed. The other two had done well!

The worship services at the beginning and end of the assembly, with their colourful processions and the participation of representatives of different churches, continents and colours, impressed B Sr as usual. In particular, the Mass for Christian Unity, held on the anniversary of Nathan Söderblom's death, touched those who partook very deeply. B Sr worked hard to make it as inclusive as possible, with Catholic representation as well. Even then, there were complaints afterwards from free-church quarters and from Krister Stendahl, who had not participated and thought it had been a Church of Sweden high mass, and as such a mistake.

In preparing for the Uppsala 1968 conference B Sr had had a dream that this would be an assembly to which the Pope himself would be invited and he would recant the bull on Martin Luther. He had intended to present the thought in one of his sermons in the cathedral in the spring of 1968 but was told that it was not really his concern to take such an initiative. The thought was not totally spurned, but B Sr himself did not return to the matter in his diaries later.

The assembly was a disappointment to B Sr from many points of view, but provided many sideline opportunities. A joyful part of it was meeting with many friends and colleagues from different parts of the world. Bengt and Ingeborg Sundkler were delighted that they could entertain personal guests from Bukoba, above all Bishop Josiah Kibira, who stayed with them throughout the conference. They enjoyed getting personal news and contact with the situation in their beloved diocese from Kibira and the diocesan secretary Richard Mutembei. Among the visitors whom the Sundklers entertained was Dr Francis Wilson of Cape Town, then an editor of *South African Outlook*. The couple served several lunches and dinners for a number of other guests. Reverend Else Orstadius, a friend from their Bukoba days, was frequently in their home with foreign guests, as she was at this time. Other guests specially mentioned were F. Michaëli. (Paris); B. Anagnostopaulos (Halki); D. G. Moses (New Delhi); Ruprecht (Göttingen); Althausen (the two Germanys); Douglas Webster (London); Oosthuizen (South Africa).

Apart from official functions Uppsala 1968 is remembered as the 'revolutionary' assembly, held in the year of the student revolutions and upheavals in different parts of the world. These affected the gathered representatives of whom many came from very troubled parts of the world. B Sr later wrote on this in his book *Söderblom och hans möten*. Expectation, breaking up the old, revolution, were the words at the end of the 1960s, in Africa and Asia as well as in Europe. Within the Universal Church the Vatican Council II heralded a new era. It was a call for a new relationship with other churches and a reaching out to the world with new concern. The churches were gaining a new vision of their task in the world:

'Can a military dictatorship be saved?' asked Sigbert Axelson. The concept itself, 'saved', had in the course of the years gone through a substantial semantic change in the Swedish language of preaching, especially on the free-church side. Uppsala 1968 and Bangkok 1973 took the concept from an individualistic prayer-meeting milieu to barricades and structures in a revolutionary world.

The Christian Student Movement in its modern form KRISS interpreted salvation in new dimensions, clearly aware of the relation between salvation and social justice. (1975:170)

B Sr continued the chapter by singling out the ecumenical U-week[3] for social responsibility for the Third World as a response to the new interpretation. This had great ecumenical significance especially at the grassroots level, but also in its contacts with the social departments in Geneva and Rome, and with Swedish Christianity on a broad front. B Sr pointed out specifically that women were in leadership in interpreting the socio-ethical debate with ecumenical emphasis, mentioning Anne-Marie Thunberg's contribution in particular.

In the 1970s a new song was born which carried through society with words not necessarily in tune with the Catechism, but with a clear echo within people:

Guds kärlek är som stranden och som gräset,
är vind och vidd och ett oändligt hem.
(God's love is like a shore and like a grass,
it is wind and width and an unending home.)

Half the human race and more than half the Church

The year 1975, which was declared the 'International Year of
Women' by the United Nations, gave the churches and mission organisations more reasons than any other to consider the above theme. It
reminded people in Africa as well as in other continents that one half
of the human race had been sorely neglected. Interestingly, B Sr was
invited to speak on women's role in the missions in a series of
Women's Lib meetings during 1975. The meetings were organised by
his close friend, a recognised pioneer of women's studies in Sweden,
Professor Karin Westman-Berg, daughter of his respected teacher,
K. B. Westman. (Letter to MLS 13 October 1975)

B Sr had seen the significance of women in missionwork and in the
churches of Africa much earlier and was ready to write on the theme
and also give speeches on it. In the independent churches the record
of women was even more striking:[4]

Missions and churches came in contact with the problems of women in
developing countries earlier than others. Yet from handbooks and
reviews one can easily get the impression that missionwork has mainly
been carried out by men, in William Carey's and David Livingstone's
footsteps. This is especially so when the mission in question is of the
Church with its priestly character. Just in relation to the Church of
Sweden mission this does not correspond to the actual situation.

In 100 years 813 missionaries had been sent out from the Church of
Sweden Mission. Of them 283 were men, 530 were women. These
numbers in themselves give us reason to stop to consider women's
contribution. During the first period 108 were sent, out of them 39 men
and 69 women ... Close to 400 women missionaries have been sent
since 1950, and many among them have been significantly creative
personalities. Thirty of them are still [1974] active after having gone out
between 1950 and 1965, 17 have served from 11 to 20 years, many
serve three years, some less.

The situation of women in developing countries has been one and the
same. Woman was subordinate and had to show her submission. She
was considered a developing human being in a developing country. Into
this kind of a situation mission entered ...

What have the churches and missions meant for the great majority
in their organisations? It is not easy to give a fair and univocal answer
to this question. When we here regard as the most important social
contribution of missions just this giving of right, voice and self-aware-
ness to all these women, I am at the same time aware that in many
places they have to face strong traditional resistance from the men's
side and that these attitudes also influence the young churches' deci-

sion-makers. It would be false to give the impression here that the situation was ideal.

Even then it is justifiable to be reminded of the contribution of the churches for China's women before Mao and for India's muted women's world among the casteless – and in Africa through their schools and their rural educational programmes.

For the whole of South Africa the church women's movement has become a decisive power factor. Abasizikazi is a Lutheran branch of the great Manyano tree. It started with the active 'Wesleyan' Methodists and spread to other churches . . . Together they form a large women's army. In their colourful uniforms – white, red and special blue, and for the Lutherans black and white – they appear everywhere. On Thursday afternoons all African working women have their free afternoon in South Africa. The women dress themselves in uniforms and gather in their meetings. They colour the whole district with their clothes, songs and togetherness. Also Sunday is a Manyano day. In Swaziland . . . it happens that a *umsizikazi,* a Lutheran pastor's wife, is also a senator, the only woman among twelve senators . . . Women's Year draws attention to the missionising churches' significance in the developing countries.

Among thousands of independent churches women are in some cases church presidents, with hundreds of pastors and a couple of bishops subject to them. MaNku in Evaton, Johannesburg is perhaps the most important example of this. She has special healing gifts and thousands of people claim to have been healed by her . . . Grace Tshabalala is one among a million Zulu Zionist women . . . The more one studies her life, the more she stands out as a paradigm of the history of the Christian Church among the Zulus in the twentieth century. She is representative also because she belongs to the dominant Nkonyane Zion Church.

B Sr had seen the central role of women both in missionwork and in young and independent churches throughout the years. He saw it already in their time in South Africa and was aware that women's services were overlooked when, as IMC commissions, they were reporting only on Christian ministry based on ordination. The central role of women in the churches contributed to his conviction that the theological position against women in ministry was indefensible.

Being an 'internationale of missions' meant keeping one's horizons wide. Bengt Sundkler's retirement opened up a different kind of freedom for him to make his own choices of travel and rhythm of life in general. He did not hesitate to accept invitations and found homes, communities and monasteries to stay in wherever he went. He was an internationale rooted on two continents.

Notes

1.   We only need to read the treatment of the non-Christian world in terms of 'occu-
     pied' and 'non-occupied' countries and fields in the world to recognise the need
     for change. The meaning of the words in the context in which they were used

was not in the sense 'taking hold of' or 'taking possesion', but rather 'to live, stay or work in', which is the first meaning given in *Collins Dictionary*.

2. Diary 1961. The lecture is reported in *SMT* 49,1961:193–201 in Swedish. The name of the address 'Daring in Order to Know, International Missionary Council – from Edinburgh 1910 to New Delhi 1961', In German in *Weltmission Heute*, 'Die Missionierende Kirche 1962' vol. 21/22:5–11. In International Review of Missions 1962:1. B Sr stayed in N. Delhi from 17 November till 4 December.

3. U from *utveckling* meaning development. U-week is an annual nationwide ecumenical event to promote development in developing countries.

4. *SMT* 63, 1975:1–4; 1976:74–5. Descriptions of leading women in independent churches in South Africa and Swaziland are in B Skr's books *Bantu Prophets* and *Zulu Zion* as also in *Bara Bukoba*. I have taken some excerpts more extensively than the biography would merit, to illustrate the fact that the author was always sensitive to women's lot in life, long before general attention was drawn to the question – from the Catholic sisters he received detailed answers to equally detailed questions to which we return in the chapter on ACH.

11

A CONTINENT THROUGH
NINETEEN-HUNDRED YEARS

Getting started

During his active academic years Bengt Sundkler had included in the literary plans, which he sketched for himself from time to time in his diary, a book on Africa and Christianity as one of the tasks he should undertake. Life being as full of duties as it was he never got as far as making a concrete plan or starting to write it in earnest while he was a university professor. One thing was clear to him. The history of the church in Africa must no longer be written as a history of missions.

In 1963 B Sr wrote an article about history-writing on Africa in which he made it clear that Africa as a continent demands her own history, not a history of what others have done to her. *The Planting of Christianity in Africa*, the 4-volume book written by his good friend C. P. Groves, and published in 1948–58, was in itself a fine work, but it was mainly a history about the contribution of the Whites. Why not our history, what the first Christians, first catechists, first evangelists, pastors and church leaders did and what they struggled for or against? This was the silent question of the Africans to the writer. B Sr was determined to respond to that plea and to reverse the viewpoint. (Sundkler *SMT* 50, 1963:98–102).

Earlier in 1968 B Sr had been planning to write 'a total interpretation of Africa', an African *Orm og Tyr* (Snake and Beast). This Danish book by Martin A. Hansen fascinated him immensely and served for him as a model of how the book could be conceived. Hansen's book dealt with Nordic religious scene in two parts, the old beliefs and how they worked themselves into Christian practice. He had also been thinking of Johannes Pedersen's comprehensive 2-volume *Israel, Sjaeleliv og samfundsliv* (Soul Life and Social Life), the knowledge of which had distinguished him from other students during his theological studies and earned the attention of Professor Fridrichsen in Uppsala. The way the work dealt with the religious dimension of the nation and secular society holistically, in an integrated manner, had impressed him throughout his life. This for him was what one should aim at and what one could be inspired by. He thought of the images of 'a circle' and 'a cross' as appropriate metaphors which would capture the whole, the circle symbolising oneness, unity, togetherness and the cross the centre of Christianity. He wrote:

> I am no Hansen, I know it very well, but that does not hinder me from trying ... something corresponding to that I should try to create about Africa. Crossing from African religion to Christian church, an interpretation of African Christianity, Evangelical and Catholic and the separate groups. (Last pages of the diary book 1968–69; probably written at the time of the next note)

> The name could be 'The Circle and the Cross'. An interpretation of African milieu in its most compact situations which I have met: Swaziland and Dahomey, and Cameroon, in meeting with the West and with culture. *Gemenskap*, community, in the religious meaning in Africa and the place of the church.
>   My *Christian Ministry in Africa* never became what I had hoped for. What was required was a solution to the recruitment of pastors [its prescriptive purpose] was never fulfilled. But it was a mass of material and I put much work into it ... The only good thing is that a number of African theologians got hold of the book and it came to the fore in that way. (Diary 7 August 1968)

The final chapter, 'Toward Christian Theology in Africa' had been criticised by a Sierra Leonine theologian Harry Sawyerr. B Sr was in many ways sensitive to criticism directed at him, but when it was on points which he himself could also see and agree with, or which came from those concerned, he had the humility to accept it and even be grateful for it. Such was the case with *The Christian Ministry in Africa*.
    In his diary for 1968 B Sr returns from time to time to the thought of writing a more comprehensive book on Africa and Christianity:

> How can I get time to tackle this task: Christian Church in Africa, an overarching total vision? Well, a passionate writer does not set the question in that manner ... he (or she) only writes because he (or she) must! (Diary 7 August 1968)

The writing of the Swedish version of *Bara Bukoba* was a prelude to tackling the whole continent. On 10 November 1968 B Sr notes in his diary:

> I took a mass in St Ansgars. I felt myself liberated because I finally had got started my composition which I have been intending to write for such a long time. So far I have not had an opportunity to start writing, i.e. I never have created the time and space for it. I am reminded of J. B. Priestley: 'I had the Time'. What it means is that one has to make

that time, to devote oneself uninterrupted, unswervingly, to what is most important. In my case it is writing, especially because for me it is psychologically the greatest therapy.

The name *Bara Bukoba* is a play on words: in Swahili *bara* means 'upcountry' or 'continent', in Swedish the meaning is 'only', thus Bara Bukoba could be interpreted as 'Upcountry Bukoba' or 'Only Bukoba'. It had given B Sr the opportunity to do what he had envisioned: 'An interpretation of an African milieu in its most compact situation', not yet conceived historically but as 'the heart of Africa' in transition, which he most closely associated with 'the vitality and resilience of Africa'. (Diary 18 December 1964, phrases used when resigning as the bishop of the northwestern diocese)

The task was once more interrupted. After four months he utters a cry of regret that he did not yet get the uninterrupted writing going: 'Two months [of the year] have flown by. I need new challenge, being captivated by a great demanding task, a great meaningful book [as the book on Söderblom had been]. (Diary 3 March 1969)

B Sr had a substantial book in mind and at the end of 1969 he mentions that while he was finishing the second edition of *The World of Mission* he had also started with an introduction to the larger book on Africa.

Both *Bara Bukoba* (1974) and *Zulu Zion* (1976) were in themselves significant and expressed the '*inlevelse*', living in and with the interior of Africa, which was the inspirational source for the larger Church History of Africa. They prepared the way to what B Sr had in mind, the great book on Africa:

For me, among the Zulu, relatedness under duress, segregation, as apartheid was then called, in Bukoba, relatedness under the cross, revival, openness, were not only material for Church history, but relatedness, living people, not the Western impersonal system of knowledge. Africa saved me from this approach. This engaged approach I try to mediate to the 'Academy' in the African Church History (ACH).[1]

ACH is an ecumenical mandate. Catholic and Protestant Missions working among the same people with the same language and same problems, but never met, before the beginning of the 1960s (Vatican II), separated by geography, a knob of a rock, and history with different traditions.

My relatedness, a Swede, a Lutheran expanded by my relations to Anglicans, Catholics, Methodists and Baptist churches. This relatedness to people also concerns the archives and the archivists with whom I have had the privilege to work, who opened up their incomparable sources and spread them out for my gaze. I shared with them personal relatedness: Lamay – Lavigerie; Per Noël – Dupuquet. This relatedness shared with those who have meant most for this book: Inspiration, sustained enthusiasm for this task. (Hand-written draft on ACH process 1974–90, n.d.)

In 1975 B Sr started the search for materials, not yet knowing the shape of what was to come. He was in Rome in December beginning to think what the book should be like. He was sketching the potential headings for the chapters, so that he would know what material he would need to collect (Letters 7 and 14 December 1975).[2] In 1976 he had thought that the book could be called 'Christian Movement in Africa', having discovered the movements that the church consisted of – the church as a youth movement, women's movement and refugee or returnee movements. (Letter 9 April 1976)

In his own story B Sr describes how the great work on Africa finally developed. He wanted to recruit African scholars for a team of writers, but in the end took on the work himself following the advice of Roland Oliver and also Terrence Ranger. Even if he, a European, ended up writing it by himself instead of a team of historians as he first had envisaged, he corresponded with a large number of Africanists, historians, archivists, scholars in different fields and with the common people of the great continent. He made extensive visits to Africa to attend conferences and to visit archives, libraries and study chambers of numerous scholars. In his most active writing years he was one of the most intense users of the Carolina Rediviva University Library in Uppsala.

In connection with the quintennial celebration of the University of Uppsala, in August 1977, Bengt Sundkler invited a group of scholars to Uppsala to think through what the volume on African Church history should consist of. Of this B Sr wrote:

Twenty-five historians, Africans and Westerners, met for three very constructive days in Uppsala. We had the privilege of listening to unforgettable statements by Reverend Dr Ethelbert Mveng of Cameroon, Jacob Ajayi of Nigeria, Elizabeth Isichei, Terrence Ranger, Marcia Wright, Richard Gray and Reverend Father Adrian Hastings – to mention but a few.

He prepared a paper which he started with the following statements:

A bitter pill which the majority of writers on Christianity and missionary activities in Africa should swallow is that they have not been writing African church history.

This statement by Professors Ajayi and Ayandele (who contributed to B Sr's festscrhift) must serve as a challenging departure for an introduction to discussion of a project: a One-volume church history of Africa. The two West African scholars develop their point by claiming that hitherto church history has been written 'as if the Christian church were in Africa but not of Africa.

The time they were experiencing was revolutionary from many points of view which they were to grasp. For the church history of Africa it meant above all an African initiative.

Sources of inspiration

B Sr read early mission history and made an important observation which relates in a deep way to the change that the period of Rationalism and Enlightenment caused in European religious thought and its effects globally.

In the sixteenth and seventeenth centuries the Catholic missionaries somehow shared the essentially mythological thought world of the Africans, but Europe after 1789 and the Enlightenment was something else. So the missionaries that came after 1800 were essentially different from those that had gone before. (Letter 23 March 1977)

B Sr was fascinated by an idea he got from some late-nineteenth-century manuscripts, handed to him by his Bukoba friend Leoniadus Kalugila, Old Testament scholar and resident pastor in Aarhus, Denmark, continuing his studies. The Haya wise men and women had expressed fears when they heard the first Catholic missionaries' preaching of Christianity:

> 'Will not then our rivers believe and our forests read (or believe)', meaning of course that there would be a catastrophe: it would mean the secularisation of whole life instead of the greening of Buhaya. It is very moving indeed. This was about 1879–1900 as a reaction to the first preaching of the RC missionaries coming from Buganda. One could feel the very pulse of the first reaction to this new Christian religion.

As one of the great inspirational sources B Sr returned again to the book by Hansen, gaining insight from it, studying again particularly the contents of the book:

> Instead of Cosmology of Africa, 'Towards the Interior of Africa'. I have returned to the most inspiring book I know: Martin A. Hansen's *Orm og Tyr*. It consists of two parts: Nordic Religion and Faith in the White Christ. I have allowed the chapter headings of the first part to penetrate my mind and soul and spirit and body while thinking of my own task and material. (Letter 5 May 1977)

The chapter titles for part one were: *Vejdefolkets vier* (Hunters' holy places), *Fraendernes alter* (Altar of the kinsmen) *Aettens sal* (Ancestors' hall), *Solens folk* (People of the sun), *Taagernes aartusind* (Foggy millennium) and *Gudens fald* (Fall of the God).

In a French review, B Sr read of a book on the theme of death and burial which he realised was quite central for the meeting of Africans with Christianity:

> I meditated on Pierre Chaunu's book *La Mort à Paris*, 1978, by that great French historian, a study of the 300,000 testaments in Paris 1500–1700 ... I suddenly saw a new dimension for my book, La Mort en Afrique, Death in Africa, the ecological fact of Sickness and Death,

so important in the crises of life for so many people ... It is a wide
general dimension to the book, but I would not have seen it as such, nor
dared to launch it in a big way, without the help of a French historical
review of Chaunu's book, and I hope to get his books from the library
tomorrow. (Letter 12 October 1980)

After reading Chaunu, B Sr addressed a letter to Mr Peter Mkize,
a friend from his time in South Africa now working in Johannesburg,
telling of the interest that had been aroused in him in the problem of
sickness and death throughout Africa. He refers to his readings also
of other authors on:

death in America, France and in Paris ... by highly stimulating historians, and whatever I read I immediately apply to my own problem, so I
must ask about development of attitudes to Death in Africa, and now
particularly in the cities ...

The two-page letter gives detailed references to facts known to them
both, but also information on why the problem is interesting, not only
in South Africa, but elsewhere in Africa, and at this time, especially
in cities. He refers to the burial of their friend Henry Nkonyane,
which they had attended together at Charlestown when B Sr was doing
additional fieldwork in South Africa in 1969.

It lasted a day and a full night and a day, 5,000 people assembled in a
tent all this time, and you remember the infinitely moving plaintive
singing of the whole congregation. [The recording is in his tape collection.] I am trying to find out what are and what have been the corporate
expressions of sorrow and solidarity in these cases, in the various
churches, and what changes have taken places and why.
    In Africa, the burial of the deceased had to take place most of the time
the day after the death of the person, and this meant that in many cases
the officials of the church or the congregation could not be reached ...
There may thus have developed certain customs ... There must have
been going on a certain development, a 'history', in burial customs on
the Rand in the period 1900–80. (Letter 15 October 1980)

Soon after being inspired by the issue of death another impulse from
a lecture on Dostoyevsky was on the way which again illustrates the
way B Sr worked. How the lecture on Dostoyevsky relates to the
outline which followed is anyone's guess, but this illustrates the associative mind of the writer at work. Perhaps if one had heard the
lecture, the connection would be more obvious:

Over the phone I told you of the Dostoyevsky lecture yesterday, by
Stewart Sutherland from King's College, London; one of the very best
lectures I have ever listened to. It gave me a vision for my own writing:
    To see that the theme of the book is the church as an alien institution,
or a home. That must also lead to a real *auseinendersetzung* [taking one

another's' place] with the White, more or less Christian population in Southern Africa, to whom the Christianisation of the Bantu was an embarrassment.

Further the theme of Death. Nineteenth century up to the 'Influenza' in 1918–19, cf. Europe in the Middle Ages, the Pest 1350, and the Church. Death, burial, adaptation.

Folk religion, the Christian church as a folk religion. I have received Jakob Rod, *Dansk Folkreligiositet i nyere tid,* and I shall write to Hermansburg and to Berlin to ask them to help me within a year's time. (Letter 21 October 1980)

Inspiration also came from music and art and was directly related to the writing. We return to this theme in Chapter 12 where the examples serve a somewhat wider purpose.

Consulting scholars, archives, artists

Writing the African Church History was an exacting, but communicative process. Many scholars visited Uppsala and B Sr was eager to see them in his home in order to gain the maximum benefit from meeting them. Gathering material also meant an enormous amount of travelling, but it gave the writer rich international contacts and kept him going in spite of advancing age and illnesses hiding in his body. His sense of getting more recognition outside Sweden than within the country started of course before the writing of the ACH but it was strengthened by the fine response he received everywhere where he went abroad:

I know only too well that because of my international connections I get much more than I deserve of the academic game, being that a theologian, and especially one who has anything to do with missions, does not deserve to be accepted as in any way 'belonging'. If it were not for my necessary contacts with SOAS in London and with academics elsewhere in the world, I believe that I would feel this to be trying. But now I feel that in fact I get much more than I deserve of confidence and helpful expectations. (Letter 23 November 1973)

I rejoice in the privilege which is mine, given to me by the expectation and trust by my British friends and co-workers, all professors of Modern History or African History – and what a paradox in the eyes of the academic establishment here in this country that I should have such connections. This infinite job of mine puts me on a diet of asceticism as far as publication etc. is concerned.

If my life is spared so that I shall be able to conclude this infinite work, that would indeed be the one great recognition which I yearn for. (Letter 31 October 1980)

Quotations from letters give glimpses of the kinds of activities that the writing brought with it but which also interrupted it. In a letter from London B Sr thinks back of the events before leaving:

> Last week: I had a good time with Professor Henri Desroche: we discussed each other's literary ideas. His idea of Open University, with connections with Canada, Brazil, Mali, France (and elsewhere) impresses me. He has the right kind of daring personality to take on a job of such magnitude. Impatient, absolutely concentrated on his one and only interest . . the one upon which he is just working . . . never smiling, yet enjoying himself a great deal. Most charming wife, ex-pianist, ex-Dominican nun, just as he used to be a Dominican monk as a young man. Now 64 years of age.

During the same night when B Sr was reading proofs of the B. Johansson Festschrift, he had also started translating from French into Swedish 13 tightly hand-written pages of Professor Desroche's lecture, to be handed out to the audience who otherwise would not have understood a word of the complicated French in which the learned scholar lectured. B Sr invited the speaker and his wife with a group of French-speaking guests to his home for dinner after the lecture. B Sr's close friend Kaarina Drynjeva, fluent in French, was of great help to him on such occasions.[3]

The trip to London was short:

> Leaving for London in a few minutes. I hope to be back on Thursday or Friday sharing the Birgitta Mass Saturday evening.[4] After that nothing for the rest of the year except 'this one thing'. I have much to recapture. These weeks have passed so quickly . . . and without trace as far as written new chapters, alas. But I shall try again, and with renewed strength. (Letter 3 October 1977)

B Sr flew to London in order to assist in the making of a television programme on the South African independent churches:

> I hope this visit to BBC and London will be fruitful. I understand that Harold Turner will also be at the BBC TV programme called 'Zulu Zion', in a 'Long Search' series on the Religions of the World, and I shall be glad to work with him. [After arriving in London]: Had a nice flight; prepared to meet all the excitement of London. (Letter 3 October 1977)

This time the visit had only this one purpose. When we find B Sr again in London in December, the television programme had been broadcast:

> The 'Zulu Zion' TV programme has had very good press and people have all been very much impressed by it. Unfortunately I did not see it, although I did of course earlier see bits and pieces, but I shall ask the makers to show it to me privately, if they can afford the time to do that. (1 December 1977)

I add here another appreciation of the programme on 'Zulu Zion', which B Sr received the following year from an African historian whose opinions he both trusted and highly appreciated, Professor Marcia Wright of Colombia University, New York. She wrote:

> Last night I watched 'Zulu Zion' on TV and came away convinced that it was the very best treatment of African religion (modern) I have ever seen on film. The variety of characters, the restraint in narrative and excellent selectivity made it really remarkable. You must be pleased. (Letter from Marcia Wright to B Sr 19 November 1978)

The recipient's response to Professor Wright's letter gives more details how the programme was produced:

> To me it was a fine experience to work with the organisers of the film, particularly with that very remarkable man Ronald Ayre who was the interviewer not only in 'Zulu Zion' but also in all the other 12 films in the TV series. A couple of days ago I had a letter from my old friend Grace Tshabalala (73–74) whose face comes through so very well and beautifully on the film. She writes to say that she is sorry that the film is not shown on South African TV, and I have written to her to tell her how much her contribution was appreciated by people such as you and Roland Oliver. (27 November 1978)

On leaving for London in October B Sr envisaged that, after returning, he would have an uninterrupted period of writing ahead of him for the rest of the year. Instead, the letters relate of a visit to Tanzania and another stay in England in November and December 1977. He had agreed to serve as an external examiner for the Bachelor of Divinity degree students in Makumira Theological College in Tanzania and on his way home from there, stopped for an extended stay in England to make contacts in various academic centres. He relates the events prior to his arrival in London in an interesting way, again showing how he seizes every opportunity that offers itself for communication, and in relating, flavours his narration with irony and humour:

> I left [Makumira] Sunday morning. [In the service] 10 a.m. .... [I was] glad to say a few words about Advent. Then the great Principal was going to take me in the College van. We put in my things and, pious as he is, he prayed before the journey. Then he remembered: he needed water for the car. Well, got it and poured it in. Then switched on – the car was dead and remained such. I suggested we borrow Festo's car and we got it.[5] We were in time at the airport but the plane was 2 hours late. There I found Elimu Njau and family going to New York via London. We had a very grand time together in the Airport and on the plane. Decided to settle all about addresses in London Airport. His great idea: In connection with the Refugee Conference in Arusha in September to make a Refugee Festival, their own art, music, etc. I invited him to

come to Uppsala in December to discuss this further. In London airport we were in different queues for passport etc. - and I lost them.[6]

Took a taxi to London. We came too late for St Edward's who rise early. I was in the city only about midnight. Got into a small hotel and got by grace a room 2m x 3m. At breakfast this morning, only one English lady there. I spoke to her. She came there from Saudi Arabia, where her husband works as an accountant. She was going to New York at noon; the same BA plane as the Njaus. I described them and sent a letter with her for them on the plane, so I can have his New York - London addresses. A very small world or - big! God's world!

I feel well and refreshed, or a little manic over this E. Njau business!! Now have settled in my room at St Edward's. I am [writing this] at the Methodist Mission Society [MSS] ... Also here I meet so many good friends. (30 November 1977)

While in England B Sr wanted to follow up particularly two nine-teenth-century themes, the Chief and Missionary especially in South Africa, and what he called the King's Way, in the interlacustrine region:

I am surprised by my own resilience. I feel very well indeed and very happy to be alive and about. There was a sudden change of climate and all that, yet I manage very well, it seems. I have spent two days in MSS, looking through Yearly Reports from 1820–50, referring to S. Africa. Very fortunately their archive papers, letters, etc. are packed in boxes, now waiting to be handed over in a year's time to SOAS Library. But really, this is a blessing in disguise to me, for there are long extracts from the letters in these reports, and I get what I want and need about the theme Chief and Missionary. These Wesleyan missionaries were – like all others – waiting upon the chiefs all the time, hoping against hope that they would see light. But this is only to say that they had to work through the structures of that particular period. Some scholars now think that it was bad and are critical of the motives of the missionaries to work through the chiefs. But what else could they have done!!? The MSS people are very nice to me as usual.

Last night I went and saw Douglas Webster, Canon of St Paul's, my old friend, and had a good talk with him. I shall take him out for dinner next Monday. Today, I have lunch at SOAS with Richard Gray and hope to plan my stay further. I have to get out of St Edward's Friday morning because of a retreat they will have here. I may go to York, or to Cambridge or Oxford for the weekend, but hope to be back on Monday p.m. I shall be ... leaving late that evening and taking the plane back home following morning. So everything works out just fine, it seems, don't you agree?

Later the same day:

I am carried by angels, softly, softly. They are so kind to me, helping me along. I went along to the Institute of Commonwealth Studies, next door to SOAS, wanting to see Shula Marks. Yes, she would come down for me but had no time just then. She came – and in the same moment Roland Oliver and Richard Gray came over in the passage from SOAS. The three of them were to attend Oliver's seminar just then; so I joined them. Dr David Cohen, a young man from the US speaking on 'Oral traditions' and how to define time in Busoga. Highly sophisticated debate. I did not understand a thing. Afterwards he came to me, knew me and my *Bantu Prophets*, that amazing key to the hearts of men; I am surprised every time; cannot believe it.

Discussed time for an interview with Shula, and a historian, Cory Haines, from Howard, Washington, wanted my advice on his ms. on Martin Luther King and Albert Luthuli – a comparison. I gave him half an hour. He knew all about *Bantu Prophets* and was very appreciative of what I tried to tell him about Alb. Luthuli and his background in Natal Congregationalism and the American Board tradition. Then lunch with Richard Gray who fixed for me – over the phone – visits with Chris Hill at York, and the Rangers in Manchester, December 8–9, speaking to his seminar and sharing in Sheilagh's (Ranger's wife) birthday. Chris Hill, as you know, has a Southern Africa Institute ... Oliver invited me to eat at their flat today at 6 p.m. and Richard for lunch on Sunday. Sounds mighty good.

I am amazed at the goodness and generosity of all these people I meet.

Evening: I have just come back from the visit to the Olivers. They are my great friends here – very generous. She is amazing; reduced by pain to a little bundle of a person, but very bright and with perfect memory of people and places and so interested in everything. Back here at St Edward's I met three Anglicans, two priests and one psychiatrist, a committee on exorcism. One of them, a quintessential Anglican priest with an enormous laugh at nothing at all. (1 December 1977)

Another letter written on 13 December recounts the events and meetings of the two first weeks of the month:

May I now continue my travel report. I believe I stopped 1 December, in the afternoon. Just as I had finished that last letter of mine, I met the most unlikely and interesting person one can at all meet. I was reading papers of the LMS [London Missionary Society] in SOAS, and as I collected a new batch, the Librarian said: There is a young man who has ordered almost the same papers as you, and he sits over there. I went and saw him, Alistair Sutherland, young anthropologist, working on the Yeye tribe in the swamps of Northern Botswana. Yes, he had these papers, and then his fiancée had some other papers and she would be back in a short while. This was this extraordinary little creature, absolutely original and totally surprising and great fun. We went out in their car, a very euphemistic term for the contraption which they used for transport. But somehow miraculously it held together. 'We can park outside my editor's,' she said. Oh, so you have published books? Yes, I think she said she had already published two or three. And they are real best-sellers at that. We went into a café and had a cup of tea, and I was given her latest creation, Babette Cole's, Promise Solves the Problem? She is from Jersey, and all people in Jersey are, as is well known, somehow strange and funny, and she is, but above all very charming and a really creative little creature, totally unaware of any difficulties in life, just trusting and carrying on.

2 December. I had some time with Dr Douglas Jones, a specialist on Senegal, and then I went and saw my old friend (since 1941) Professor I. Schapera. He is about 72, spry and active, but he has lost his voice after an operation on his vocal cords. He was very helpful indeed about the chief and missionary theme in nineteenth-century S. Africa.

6 December to York. Met the South African specialist Christopher Hill, a nice and good man ... He had arranged a seminar for me and I spoke on the African Church History, which raised much interest; then a dinner for me with six or seven members of the staff.

7 December. Saw York Minster, taken round by Reverend Sister Alison, OHP (Whitby): it was a very great experience to see the Minster and the crypt. From there to Archbishop Blanch at Bishopthorpe, a great charmer, and very nice. He took me around in the Palace and we had a very good talk. Then taken to the station and on to Manchester; met by Ranger who drove me to their home some 12 miles outside the city of Manchester. Three nice daughters. Long talks with Terry about ACH, and interviews with the most impressive young S. African Jewish couple, John and Jean Comaroff, social anthropologists, specialists on S. African nineteenth century. One hour with them was worth months of study, very helpful indeed. Then Dr Nehemia Levitzion, specialist on Islam in Africa, rather good, and very friendly. Thursday evening meeting on Zimbabwe; the Rangers are of course in the forefront of this struggle.

Evening back in London and stayed again with the brothers in St Edward's House. I was late for dinner but they had put something aside for me, and then to bed. But at about midnight I had an attack, I thought it was malaria, but of course it was food poisoning. I was sick the whole night and in the morning did not know whether I could risk to take the car and the plane. But I did and barely managed to keep standing or sitting.

Somehow I came through and was met by Stellan and Lena Morén [Ingeborg's nephew and his wife] at Arlanda. I was taken to their home in Stockholm and then to the place where I took the baptism of their child. Quite a crowd there and very nice contacts.

Sunday 11 December. A service in St Michael's, with sending out by the Archbishop of three [missionaries] for Tanzania, and one for South Africa. First ordinary High Mass and Holy Communion, and then the sending off.

In the evening I was fetched to go to Enköping, not very far from Uppsala. Precisely ten years ago I opened a church hall there, 'Lillsidan' [Smallside], and we now celebrated the 10-year Jubilee. I spoke first on the theme of 'Lillsidan', the importance of small groups, cells in the church. Also 'Small is beautiful' and then a new address on Tanzania, all greatly appreciated. We had great fun in fact. Then back to Uppsala, and to bed, preparing for the new week. (Letter 13 December 1977)

The reader must be as exhausted by reading about the pace of this programme as I am in writing it all down! He had indeed reason to be 'amazed by his resilience'.

The visits to Britain were quite frequent. In September 1982 we find B Sr again in Birmingham. As many other times, his beloved England did not serve him well when it concerned 'modern' facilities. This time he had problems shaving. Perhaps there was a good reason to go back to razor blades!

The great Edison did his best, but failed as far as this benighted country is concerned. I have been looking the whole morning for somewhere to plug in my electrical shaver but with no success. Scotland was modern enough to adapt itself to the possibilities of electrical appliances, so I had no problem there – but here I am nonplussed.

While waiting for the house to wake up B Sr related the events in Scotland:

I had a great time with Andrew Walls in Aberdeen and then in Edinburgh with George Shepperson, Kenneth Little, Andrew Ross and Mrs Dr Brock. Walls and Shepperson gave me much of their time, so did Andrew Ross, and the group he called together for a Sunday afternoon tea. I looked through fine PhD theses and was greatly helped by that. George Shepperson, the great man, is now my great new friend, very encouraging and helpful. Mrs Sheila Brock, wife of an Edinburgh geneticist, wrote a thesis on James Stewart of Lovedale and I could read that in the small hours of the night before getting up Monday morning at 4.30 for the plane from Edinburgh to Birmingham. She has a splendid grasp of South African matters.

Kenneth Little I knew in the 1950s, an impressive gentleman ... His last years in the chair he was kept on and got his salary, but did not teach ... 'What are you writing yourself?' 'My autobiography.' Title? 'Walking through the night,' meaning his illness. He had an illness, the same as that of Goethe, I think he said, and my literary–medical education does not rise to that.

Monday morning left at 4.30 from the University Club. Pitch dark when coming down with the lift into the Lodge. I do not know how I managed to get through and find the door and some light.

Now at Selly Oak, staying at Kingsmead, where as a student I stayed 45 years ago in 1937. Great numbers of the Third World people here for a course on British social life or something. The day begins with a chapel service according to the programme at 8 a.m., so I went there. Sitting there were three Black women and three Black gentlemen and me, looking at our books. I suggested a hymn and said a prayer and we said Our Father together and joined our hands for 'May the Grace ...' No staff at all to be seen: this is a utilitarian country devoted to speedy progress. The weather fortunately quite good, not cold or wet, but heavy fog now in the morning.

I find some great books in Selly Oak Colleges Library, including Leslie Paul's *First love, A Journey*. Very remarkable.

Now I shall again make an effort to find somebody, the staff should be there now at 9 a.m. to show me somewhere I can plug in my electric shaver. I shall rejoice with Edison, if that thing could be found ...

Yes, I found the Principal, Peter Russell. He has been at Epworth, Harare, so he could provide a shaving contraption. I now hear hymn singing, so there is a more general prayer meeting. I was too early as usual!

I contacted Harold Turner and spent the whole day, most profitably, with him and was received by the Turner couple. He has over the years built up an impressive collection of papers on the independent churches throughout the whole world, with the possible exception of southwestern Finland. An enormous collection and now he is getting the whole thing on microfiches, made into sets of 50 x 50 copies for the Third World and for the rich countries to buy a similar set, at a higher price.

I also met an RC Father from Malawi who is doing his doctorate in Oxford on independent churches in Malawi, Father Joseph Chakauza, obviously a very gifted and able young man, and we had a good time together. The whole day very much worth while, giving me useful perspectives on my own work and a renewed contact with Harold Turner, a scholar who has really taken this thing about independent churches seriously, much more seriously than I ever could do, and a practical person who finds ways and means of all sorts. (Letter 14 September 1982)

B Sr's contacts with the Catholic Church made it possible for him to pay equal attention to the history of the Catholic and Protestant churches. B Sr was always extremely appreciative of the reception he had during his recurrent visits to the archives of the Catholic orders: of the Holy Ghost Fathers in Paris, of the White Fathers in Rome, the Jesuits at Heverlee, Belgium, as well as those of the Franciscans, the Capuchins and the Palatines. With the help of the archivists he learned of the role of the French Catholic missions, in the footsteps of Libermann, Lavigerie and others in the nineteenth century. No church history in the future should in his opinion be written without including both sides of the picture.

B Sr never ceased to stress the significance of Vatican II, which led up to the 'African Synod' in the spring of 1994, for the history of the Universal Church in the twentieth century, and to the Church in Africa. We have seen that on his part he made an effort to work out its promise with contacts with the Catholic Church at the local level while serving as the bishop of the northwestern diocese in Tanzania. He had the honour of having been sent off with the blessing of Cardinal Rugambwa in Bishopthorpe's private chapel when the Cardinal had sent his envoy to bid farewell on his behalf at the time of the first Lutheran bishop's departure from Bukoba.

B Sr was particularly grateful for the help he received from Father Noël at the Holy Ghost Fathers where he was also able to interview many experienced Africa missionaries:

I spent two weeks with the Fathers and did not see anything of Paris!! Yes, in the first four days at rue Lhomond I could walk down to Boulevard Michele once or twice, just in order to revive old memories

from my time in Paris as a young man in 1932. But for most of the time
I have been in the archives, and I have profited from this very greatly.
Also from three or four important interviews with Fathers Pierre,
Coulon, de Mare and Rolland – excellent help given by these men with
great generosity.

I am more struck than ever by the wide difference between Catholics
and Protestants: the enormous contact and direction given to everything
in the Catholic fold, and the spontaneity, soon to turn into form, in the
Protestant way of life. And the immense numbers of missionaries, men
and women in RC, in so many of these African countries. It is all very
impressive. I have specialised on Angola, Brazzaville, Eastern Nigeria
and some East Africa, with all kinds of extras along the way...

RC have done more research than the Protestants – I think – in the
form of studies, surveys, statistics, reviews of every kind – yet they do
not have them gathered into a survey of the whole work – very little of
that, in fact. Another observation from the point of view of Congo-
Brazzaville, a very interesting country, is the impossibility of dividing
the whole canvas into Established churches and Independent churches.
The latter are part of a much larger and more common development and
must be interpreted in that light. This applies also to some of the South
African groups. (Letter 25 November 1983)

The work continued with Eastern Africa and brought the topics to
interlacustrine regions. The 'Lake line' formed there another theme,
suggested by Professor Richard Gray, in addition to that of the Kings'
Way:

I make this lake line ... one of brief sketches of each community and
then comparisons as to response, reaction, result. (1 February 1979)

I have been pressing on with my ACH. After Ethiopia, Egypt and
Northern Africa, I have had to reshape certain things about 'The Church
at the Kings' Way', that is, from Buganda to Fipa and Bemba, and now
some concerning South Africa. I am still working on the latter: Hard
work but rewarding in the end.

Simple clarity, clear solid paragraphs is what I am after. In the choice
between high fluting brilliance, so called, and real clarity, I am happily
skipping the former and keeping to the latter, and this is a real gain. (21
August 1982)

When the work progressed and B Sr made the acquaintance of
specialists from various regions he hoped that some parts of the book
could be written by them, some of whom were Catholic fathers. It was
not as easy as he had wished since he found their style very different
from his own, but after some rewriting was able to make use of some
of the material. He benefitted greatly from the writings of Fathers
Francois Bontnick and John Baur, as also from the contributions of
his friend C. F. Hallencreutz, Holger Hansen and review work of
Gustav Arén to mention but a few. Apart from some shorter sections,

only Christopher Steed, his long-time assistant, learned to work in a style that satisfied him and ended up writing several sections and putting the finishing touches to the vast book:

> I had a letter from Father Bontnick in Kinshasha and I have just written a long letter of four pages (enclosed) suggesting boldly that he write Part II of my book, the period 1500–1750. I suggest that he write in French which makes it easier for him and then this could be translated in English, and this as I tell him would bring it closer to the French translation of the whole book. (Letter 15 March 1982)

In the enclosed letter B Sr tells of his meeting with Father Bontnick in Brussels and recognises his great expertise in the period in question, suggesting that he write a summary text of 50 or more pages. He also tells Father Bontnick about his own 'old – but sadly neglected penchant for Patristics' and his wish to return to that first amour for the writing of the chapter on the period 1100–1250.

Texts were received and modified also from Father John Baur who spent some time with B Sr staying with him in his flat and later sent texts to him.

It is evident that B Sr did not work chronologically. He had started from what he considered to be the most important and interesting part, 1800–80, and then continued to the end of the century and beyond to 1914. He came to the earlier periods after effectively finishing the nineteenth century, but of course had to start preparing for the work on them if he wanted others to contribute.

> The day before yesterday I had a fine paper from Holger B. Hansen, helping me immensely with my own Uganda chapter, and yesterday I had a splendid criticism of John Baur written with incisive energy by Gustav Arén in Adis Abeba. So I am after all surrounded by good and fine and generous friends: Is that not anything to thank God for! (Letter 17 March 1982)

Friends close by, who tirelessly discussed and reviewed written texts and wrote new ones, were constant supporters. Their names are frequently mentioned in diaries and letters. Lloyd Swantz had been training pastors in urban work for the churches from different denominations in Africa and served as a resource person for the later history in which urban Africa formed an important theme in every region:

> Just returned from the station to where I took Lloyd [Swantz] by my bicycle. I am again on my own. We have had a lovely time together and to me very profitable. We had yesterday afternoon two hours discussing comparison of the church conditions in the three East African capitals 1920–60. This is an exercise I would like to be repeated with others on other comparable problems. Then a little dinner for Lloyd with Hallencreutz and Christopher. This dinner was followed by a really helpful discussion again on the general plan, my fifth or so tentative plan

for the period 1920–60. It has been the nicest privilege to have Lloyd here. Yesterday morning after he had left for the Simonssons, I phoned Märta Simonsson to ask whether he had left, and she and I had a good talk about our guest and we decided that he is the most helpful and generous person one can meet.

In the night now I have had good and great ideas about replanning and rearranging my Uganda chapter, making it tighter and not chopped as hitherto. Should prove to be very helpful. Christopher is coming along all the time and is increasingly useful for the general study,

I had a visit from a Glasgow historian Nicholas Hope, writing a Cambridge volume on the Church History of Germany and the Lutheran North 1700–1918. We had a good time together. (Letter 6 August 1982)

There was no end to material, and finding new sources at times brought on real states of frustration. One could not imagine anyone covering the vast continent and 2,000 years flawlessly:

Just at present I am in fact in good form and somehow in charge of this task of mine. Often I am otherwise tossed about between despair and hope over every new chapter, but just now I am hopeful and am having a good time with my problems. I had finished Ethiopia – Chris is working on it now – and had to turn to some bits and pieces in the chapter on Uganda ...

Just in the middle of it all, I come across a new book edited by my new friend Donald Crummey, Ethiopia specialist, and somewhat Marxist. The book is called *Modes of Production in Africa, The Precolonial Era* and includes some heavy criticism of my people: Oliver, Gray, Curtin. I am very much impressed by the argument, not least the emphasis on inequality. I had in the last few days been writing on the Uganda Agreement of 1900 and had myself in half a sentence said that it certainly was not a democratic arrangement. But I see now so very sharply that this was inequality manipulated by governor and bishops together – the Catholic and Anglican bishop and the others, these Saza chiefs. Anyway it is a very helpful criticism, and I shall spend a day or two at Urbana University, Washington DC, at the end of November. (Letter 7 July 1982)

In Britain Bengt Sundkler had become known for his book *Bantu Prophets* which, as a pioneering book in the field, had become a classic. It was not all that easy to break new ground. There were many who considered it a pity that he had left his prophets:

The trouble with me over here is that wherever I go I am known as 'Mr Bantu Prophets', while in Sweden I would have to be known as 'Mr Bara Bukoba'! In any case, this play on book titles shows the importance of finding a good title for a book: it is about all that people read and remember. One should give them at least that to bite on. (Letter 14 September 1982)

In Sweden Bukoba had become familiar currency to the point that

when Matia Lutosha was visiting Uppsala and the pastor less familiar
with missions than the audience announced a meeting informing them
that a Dean Matia Lutosha from the church in 'Hagalund' was going
to speak, the congregation corrected him out loud: 'Hayaland' [not
Hagalund].

In October 1982 B Sr had been invited to lecture in the United
States and he wanted to make the most of his visit. He asked Lloyd
Swantz to help to arrange for his arrival in New York and later
reported to us extensively the eventful travels across the North
American continent. He carried out the journey according to the
following plan:

> November 1–3 New York meetings with the Lutheran and Ecumenical
> church and mission leaders
> NY University, C. Beidelman. Stay at the Seamen's International House
> 4–7 Washington c/o Bishop James K. Mathews [address etc. given]
> 7–9 c/o Mac Gaffeys, Haverford, Pa
> 10 Yale University, Professor Leonard Thompson
> 11–13 Divinity School, University of Boston, Professor J. Robert
> Nelson
> 15–19 Ventnor, NJ, Overseas Ministries Study Center, on whose invi-
> tation to lecture in US
> 22 Bloomington University, IN, Professor Phyllis Martin
> 23 Urbana Champaign, African Studies, Professor Donald Crummey
> 25–29 St Augustino, Protestant Monastery Order, Oxford, MI.
> November 30–December 5 via Aili Tripp [daughter of the Swantzes]
> family Chicago;[7]
> to Minneapolis – c/o Reverend Ronald Johnson, former assistant in
> Bukoba, Holy Trinity Church
> December 6–7 Professor Robert Hill. History Department, UCLA Los
> Angeles
> Father Arthur Kreinheber, [Orlando, Florida was cancelled; B Sr met
> him in Oxford]
> (Letter to LS and MLS 30 October 1982)

The tour of so many states was exhausting but B Sr found many
good friends in Minneapolis from the time of his work in Tanzania,
our daughter's family in Chicago, and his Protestant brotherhood
connections in St Augustine's, Oxford, Michigan, rather different
from those in Östanbäck in Sweden. He greatly enjoyed the visits to
academic centres and scholars but also took rather a positive stand on
the USA in general. He took part in the annual event of the African
Studies Association in Washington, DC, where he stayed with the son-
in-law of Stanley Jones (*Christ of the Indian Road*), (Methodist)
Bishop James Matthews and his wife Eunice, 'lovely and generous
people', 'in a luxurious quiet villa outside the city'. It was a stimulating opportunity to meet new scholars and old friends and colleagues
who specialised in African history and societies. He gave lectures
in Boston (Robert Nelson) and Harvard Universities (William

Hutchinson and Krister Stendahl and wife), visited Yale staying with Richard Elphick and family (Professors Leonard Thompson, John Middleton and Leonard Doob) and taught at the Ventnor Centre for five days (Gerald Anderson) finding the contacts as encouraging as in Britain and in places on the continent, 'I found so many who really thought that what I had set out to do was worthwhile.' The letters with vivid detailed reports from every part of this trip and all the people he met would deserve a whole chapter of its own which I must forego here. I feel that privileging some would do injustice to others.

Contacts through letters

From time to time B Sr sent out circular letters to friends and potential interested parties from whom he hoped for some response. These letters shed light on how the book gradually evolved and grew in volume. In 1982, he claimed to glimpse some faint light at the end of a long dark tunnel after seven solid years of work. He felt relatively confident of having completed the third part, covering the period 1800–1880–1914, of his African Church History, which he first thought of calling 'The Christian Movement in Africa'.

With the exception of some months of serious illnesses, one in 1980 caused by a tropical virus, he had devoted all these years exclusively to what he constantly referred to as 'This One Thing'. In a circular letter the author was now asking for help from the friends who had helped him for the period 1914–60, and he included a Tentative Plan for that period, requesting their reactions, suggestions, comments and criticism:

> There has been no rest, only sheer exhilarating toil, studded with some insights and discoveries – whether these are relevant or not will be for others to say.
>
> I was eventually led to organise this period 1800–1914 by way of regions and if I did not know it beforehand I understand now that these regions are very different. Moving from one to the other sometimes seemed like going from one planet to another.
>
> During these years I have had very valuable help from you and other friends, including admirable, long-suffering archivists, Catholic and Protestant: I have pestered these people because I know that this kind of work can only be done through co-operation, in sharing views and perspectives. (Letter 20 August 1982)

A small conference was held in London on 28 April 1983, to the participants of which he wrote another letter explaining how he had approached his study:

> The presentation of the nineteenth century will, I hope, be of some value as it deals with the Catholic, Protestant and Orthodox-Coptic develop-

284 Africa in his Heart
284 Africa in his Heart

ments to the same extent. I there stress the role of the African 'agency' and the African group initiative and deal with certain 'movements' in nineteenth-century African society ... Nineteenth-century church history is set in a fluid situation (thus so very different from the ordinary view of it, as being some solid, immobile tribal situation). The approach to the nineteenth century is thus taken by way of different regions. The twentieth-century survey (of some 200 pages) is carried out by way of Themes, cf. Plan enclosed. [The writer remarked that it was the fourteenth plan!]

I shall have a brief survey of the regions in the new twentieth-century situation – what kind of broad shifts have taken place in each region ... Particularly dramatic changes a) in the social and political conditions – b) in the Western staff and the African leadership and staff.

The book deals with African church history and my concern is to underline as much as possible the contributions of local African churchmen and -women. And more than just the name: the personality, the creative role, if any, of this person.[8]

A letter dated 28 April 1982 reports what happened in the little seminar:

I had that conference or seminar on the Church History of Africa 1900–60, helped by excellent people: the ex-Archbishop of Malawi, Dr Arden, Father Stubbs, CR, Tom Beetham and Elliot Kendall. They all responded most generously and most helpfully. Already the fact that they came and were willing to set aside this day for my sake was something to be grateful for. The notes I took from the seminar are all very valuable and exciting. I may have felt weak physically at the time but never felt it or thought of it as long as the debate continued.[9]

We get interesting glimpses into the way B Sr made his contacts and how he sought to make use of all the opportunities that came to his notice. One Saturday morning, 23 April 1983, which he notes down to be Shakespeare's birthday, he opened his daily newspaper and learned that a Catholic lady from South Africa, Dr Bernadette Mosala, was visiting Uppsala, where she was attending a Life and Peace Conference. He immediately took his pen and writing paper and addressed a letter to this lady, adding to the above description of the date, 'hopefully the day of meeting you' I quote:

It is very good to have you here now in Uppsala. I very much appreciated your statement in this morning's newspaper, *Uppsala Nya Tidning*. Just right now I am very anxious to receive from you a gift of half an hour's interview some time for you to decide, either today or tomorrow (or later if you stay on). Kindly phone.

This old writer is well-known to your colleagues in the Council of Churches, particularly my friend Bishop Desmond Tutu. [An explanation of present writing follows.]

Likewise, twentieth-century church history in Africa is a women's movement. For South Africa this is very easy to show with regard to

Manyano of every kind and I am in constant contact with Debbie Gaitskell, etc. But now, dear lady, I plead with you to give me half an hour to show how this African women's initiative proves itself in the Catholic Church. I am otherwise in danger – very much against my own will – of saying too little about the RC women and leaving the impression of an enormous silent mass of pious women in the queue for the confessional.

Kindly help me here and now, and then, follow this up, please, sending me rich and free material from your office. I hope that I will find you in the crowd this morning: you are the only person I care to meet among all these metropolitans and archbishops.

Yours in His service.

Bengt Sundkler

Another general letter was written on 9 September 1986 in which B Sr again draws his readers' attention to 'a literary enterprise of some magnitude'. Now he has been working on the book for twelve years 'non-stop of unremitting labour' and thinks he is coming to the end of the work of some 800 pages. He again refers to the great number of Church leaders, archivists and scholars, who generously have given of their time and experience to his enterprise. This time his interest is the central problem in the development of the Church after the Second World War, the transfer of leadership from European church leader to African bishop or president. Rather than dealing with the formal side, it had to do with the very substance of the Church's life. He refers to his own experience and in that light is interested in knowing what others have done and how they experienced it, on both sides:

> How did the last Western bishop in a certain diocese conceive of his task and what did he actually do? Then, again, how did the African successor conceive of his task, perhaps along new lines altogether? What did he emphasise in the work which his predecessor had not seen or done and perhaps, as a foreigner, never would have been able to do? Co-operation with co-workers, Diocesan Council, Synod? Inspiration toward renewal of the spiritual life etc.
>
> I claim that the problem I am raising is very much part of the life of the Church's history in the last generation, and only you can help me to make this special inquiry worthwhile. I am sending this letter to you and a few select Church leaders, Catholic and Protestant . . . I shall be grateful for your comments. (Attached to letter 22 September 1986)

Developing themes and approaches

B Sr continued to keep two crucial approaches to writing African church history: He emphasised the interrelation of social history and church history, and he continued his personalised way of looking at history, through the actors who made history. As part of social history he looked for common structures and repeated themes over time and inter-regionally, while recognising the differences even within small distances. He narrated different social histories even in close-lying communities. He planned to organise the material for the ninteenth century by regions and then from 1914 on to deal with cross-cutting themes, as we have already learned from the letters he wrote.

What B Sr had already learned as a young man from Professor Hans Larson about the significance of the detail also followed him when writing on ACH:

> One feature in my presentation of Africa has struck quite a few people. It is to emphasise what others would call details, personal or local details which lead up to generalisations. (Interview 31 October 1985)

> It has followed me when writing about that unknown continent of Africa, not to be ashamed or afraid of detail. I have come across church leaders who were looking for the grand lines and thought disparagely of details. I have written details as part of a much bigger whole, put the detail into a much bigger whole where it has a role to play.[10]

A letter to Marcia Wright gives an overview of how the themes in the South Africa chapter were being shaped. I trust that writing out some of these processes gives a good insight into B Sr's workshop (27 November 1978):

> This year has been a difficult one for me as I have been trying to write on South Africa 1800–70 and 1870–1919 . . . I had a bad beginning with the chapter. In order to take part in a conference in Manchester in February 1978, I made a first quick attempt, and have since had to change that altogether. At long last I got Legassick's thesis in microfilm form and that has been a tremendous challenge to me. It meant that I had to make a clear break between the Khoi-Khoi-Griqua-Coloured chapter and the rest, [in] the following way: S. Nguni, N. Nguni, S. Sotho, N. Sotho and a chapter entitled 'Tswana'. It seems and looks very simple but to me it took a long time to break through to that simplicity, and then follow one main theme Chief and Missionary.
>
> That theme – Chief and Missionary – I can follow for the first part, until 1870/75, and then have of course to carry on with another total conception. There are other continuous themes, particularly the importance of the Refugee factor: all these little refugee groups within the established Xhosa or Zulu communities to which the new religion did appeal, while the established peoples, particularly Xhosa and Zulu, and comparable did not need it, until tragically, at the end of the century their strength had been broken by European guns.
>
> Some of these themes I hope I shall also find in the East African situation when I go over to that part of the continent.
>
> As I think of the splendid and unique group of scholars gathered here in August 1977, discussing my thing for two unforgettable days, I feel really embarrassed now when thinking of my ignorance at the time. But there is nothing else to do than to go through all the basic material available.

Some of the old German volumes are very helpful, even if they take an enormous time to go through. Those old Germans were Pietists and therefore interested in more than statistics, namely in the soul and the yearnings of the soul, and in individuals whom they follow for a while. It is all very helpful. Well, these are some of my problems as I continue my exacting but exciting and rewarding work.

But, in any case, I have totally given up the missionary society and the missionary as the leading parts and instead concentrated on the African community and the African initiative.

If one needs proofs to show that a new approach to the Church History of Africa is needed, it is sufficient to look at Peter Hinchliff. *The Anglican Church in South Africa,* 1963. There is not one African name in the book, except a little of B. Mizeki for Rhodesia. The whole thing is only a projection of English struggles and squabbles, transported to Africa.

The observations of the Mfengu had led the writer first to the *refugee theme*. He made a decisive discovery of the role of social history for the reception of the new religion while spending some weeks in Rhodes University, Grahamstown, South Africa in 1980. It made the movements, with which he had already been working, more specific. Of this he wrote:

> The discussions there opened my eyes more than ever to the interrelation of social history and church history, more particularly with regard to Mfengu refugees and their reception of the new religion: a drastic sociological change created in this group an openness for new values. This should be compared with the Gqunukwebe Xhosa who, in the nineteenth century, had their own ethnological reasons for accepting the new creed; they felt apart from other Xhosa and took this apartness with them into the church. The role of the Griqua is another parallel showing a group reacting not as individuals but as a well-knit community in their approach to the new religion. (Letter to Marcia Wright 1978)

The role of the refugees for the acceptance of Christianity became one general theme in the book throughout the continent for the nineteenth century. It also gave B Sr the idea to start the whole church history book with the quote about the first refugees to the continent of Africa, 'It was as refugees, according to St Matthew, that the Holy Family came from Bethlehem to Egypt.'

In Uganda – Buganda and Ankole – the refugee theme was supplemented with the role of *returnees*. Above all in the case of the returned liberated slaves in West Africa B Sr found a parallel returnee-concept on the southeastern islands of the Indian Ocean, when he decided to include Madagascar in his history of Africa, as he explains in his own story. The returnee theme in turn led to numerous migrant situations, and to movements of people in general, which then gave the whole history the sense of movement and change.

I recall that when, at the beginning of the 1980s, I was going on a

Finnish government mission to Ouagadougou, Burkina Faso, B Sr wanted me to deliver a letter to Professor Laburthe-Torra in person, with whose work on the Beti of Yaounde he was familiar. He wrote to me:

> This immense work of his on the Beti of Yaoundé, in three volumes, also opened my eyes to a methodological problem of a wider importance: I have been speaking of refugee movements, but there are also the immense migration movements over vast territories and over time and Laburthe interprets the significance of this particular movement in a way which helps me to a very great degree. (Letter 16 February 1989)

Another letter was sent to me while I was in Nairobi asking me to contact Reverend John Gatu of the Presbyterian Church in relation to the same questions of *migration*. He had discussed these questions with Reverend Gatu in Uppsala and had later written to him but had not had an answer. He was interested in finding out whether the proto-migrant labourers brought religion back home and what its importance to evangelisation was. As usual, he wanted to get information about specific names, dates, circumstances and possible results of this development. The church was not to be thought of a static institution but as a movement within societies in flux. (Letter 23 February 1982) I see from my own notes that I did phone the reverend and he promised to send answers later in April.

As we have seen, there were two further themes which B Sr followed in the nineteenth century, the 'Chief and Missionary' and the 'King's Way'. The latter he took up particularly in South Africa and in the interlacustrine region.

The process of writing

The writing process was strenuous and became B Sr's last major work, taking 20 years. He got some financial and technical assistance from the Nordic Institute of African Studies and for a period also a room for his assistants. The year 1977 was a fruitful and important year in the writing of ACH. I return to the travels and crucial meetings with African scholars in that year further below, here I follow first the actual process of writing and then refer to some of the inspirational sources that B Sr benefitted from. After three years of planning, collecting material and sketching, the letters begin to express the urge to get on with the writing:

> Now I feel strongly, desperately almost, that I need to concentrate. Nothing must come between me and this great task. (Letter 8 January 1977)

> Everything is all right here except that I do not yet start to write my

great book, only flitted here and there with this immense material. (Letter 25 January 1977)

I hope to write – as a machine – according to the clock and the calendar. It suits my strange temperament, so hungry for result and achievement. (Letter 21 May 1977)

There are certain times of the day when I am really productive: I need the morning for one thing, the long and real perspectives; to jot down on a big piece of paper the plans of each chapter and part of the chapter. It is in the morning that I see this clearly and strongly, and in the evening I now feel best at ease for writing. I have at present no other history, nothing else that happens. (Letter 28 October 1978)

B Sr started by writing the period 1800–1914 first following the regions: South Africa, West Africa, Central Africa, East Africa and Madagascar. North Africa and Ethiopia were treated with the early history at the beginning of the 1980s. The period after the First World War to the modern day started with themes. Naturally it was not possible to follow the plans systematically when new material often unexpectedly became available in the middle of writing something totally different from what was underway.

His mood changed from day to day, despairing, then again comforting himself with the thought that there is no other way than to press on, and writing letters seeking encouragement, response and ideas:

I cannot manage this infinity of papers that I have to command for this book. (Letter 3 October 1978)

Over here I struggle along, happy to be at work with a really worth while study, yet irritated that it should take such an enormously long time. But this book and each chapter thereof must take its time to mature and let the presentation come through with something of that richness and simplicity which I see as the ideal for this kind of a book. I have of course too much material, yet need it all in order to discover the real issues, beneath the apparent ones. I am amazed at what has been printed by my predecessors in this field, amazed that these people should have thought it possible to approach the matter in that very strange way. And then I am looking at my own 'First Draft' of the chapter on South Africa, produced in February 1978, and I am really ashamed at the unworthy statements which I then allowed to come through. (Letter 28 October 1978)

Towards the end of 1978 B Sr felt that he had inspiration and wanted to concentrate fully, not taking invitations for Christmas or other events, in order not to interrupt the flow of thoughts before he had finished the South African part:

I feel that I am in a period of creative writing now and must work at it all the time. So easily one can be thrown from the saddle and then it takes an enormous effort to get back on again. This kind of a job is a hard one. It demands total discipline and absolute devotion. But then one gets results also in sleep. I am amazed how the generalisations and clearer outlines come in the sleep and then have to be written down immediately.

Strange to say I do not get nervous by the sad fact that my writing takes a long time. Time is needed for a creative breakthrough, time of incubation and growth and final clarity. It simply must take the time, and yet I am aware that even if I never get to bed before midnight the days are much too short and pass so very rapidly. (Letter 23 November 1978)

After 1978 15 long years were still spent before the reviewed, revised and shortened manuscript was in the author's hand. It required perseverance, physical strength and willingness to make new plans and endless reworking of paragraphs and pages:

I am carrying on with my book. My intention is to finish North Africa and Egypt in the main before 1 August [1982]. I have had good days of study and writing, and I have again discovered that it all boils down to taking the trouble to write down the little things, the individual bricks to be placed into the main building. '*Plocka småsten medan ni vilar Er*', pick up small stones while you rest, was the injunction of my maternal grandfather, as he worked with his 12 children, and I have to make these bricks and form them and then bring them together by some kind of cement. We shall see. (30 July 1982)

During the night between yesterday and this morning I solved a real problem which I had not seen before. I am not going to have a special chapter on independent churches but integrate these various bits and pieces and persons into the regions: the Rand etc. and treat these preachers and prophets as if they were as decent and self-governing as any nice old Pentecostal or Plymouth Brother or Lutheran. What, after all is Independent? I don't know. My great competitor in the field and my friend, Adrian Hastings, in his book on 1950–75 has a tripartite division throughout the book: church and state, historic churches, and – the independents. I don't need that kind of a thing. I shall have a short thing on the changing conditions for 'Independents, so-called' but the presentation of the men and women, those leaders, will come – surprisingly – together with the other Baptists and Lutherans and Catholics. It has taken me a lifetime to see that, but then in the night I had a vision and I believe in it just as much as your Jonathan Livingston Seagull. (Letter 23 June 1985)

In fact, B Sr had seen that the so-called independent churches belong to the same family of churches as the more established churches while writing *Zulu Zion*, but it took time before he was ready to include them among other churches. In Zulu Zion he wrote: 'there are number of Zionist churches which in intention and confession are as loyal to Jesus Christ as Mission-related churches ... The Church of Christ is not uniform but Universal.'(Sundkler 1976:317)

January 1989: I have had a good time here on my own. Christopher in England and you in Asia somewhere, and only my task here to attend to. I have been working on the last period 1960–90 and have not managed too badly. All the time one has the same problem: To say something substantial, yet in the shortest possible form. (Letter 22 January 1989)

B Sr had set out to write a one-volume book. For a while the publisher thought the material could not be compressed into one volume, but in the end, the book has been published as such. This the author thought would make it easier for students to read and use as a reference book.

There had been tentative contacts with the Cambridge University Press for having the important book published. Some difficulties were caused by the great delay in getting the writing finished. It was being reviewed and B Sr was able to make substantial revisions before his death, even if the final editing was left to his faithful assistant, Christopher Steed. The last years of writing were made easier by the knowledge that the publishers had accepted the work in principle:

I have just had a letter from John Lonsdale, enormously helpful as everything from this excellent man: he is an adviser for Cambridge UP and tells me they have now decided to take this book of mine and he does not see any hindrances in the way, except of course the little detail of mine, in trying to come towards a full stop. Oh, how I long for that day. (Letter 8 October 1987)

Health problems

Bengt Sundkler regularly reported on the condition of his health when he occasionally had quite serious health problems and then felt well again. It gave him reason to be grateful for all the good days and times. One is surprised that his deteriorating health did not deter him from continuing unabated with his writing and the travelling necessary for acquiring the material:

My health is fine just now and I told myself a moment ago that it is perhaps better than ever just now. I can only hope and pray that it will last like that. Sometimes I feel little signals from the inside of the ear, and it is worrying, at least for a little moment. But I cannot spend much time nowadays on worries as my task is too big and too precious and too important for that. (Letter 21 October 1980)

You must congratulate me. I have just survived a fall from on high. Had to return a couple of books high up on my bookshelf and climbed a chair, and then fell from there, backwards, headlong, on to the floor. Fortunately I did not hurt the head. I felt pain in a wrist for 36 hours but this is also over. It was pure grace that I managed so well. If I had

had to decide myself how I would wish to fall, I could never have figured out this elegant way in which I now preferred to tumble down. I was obviously carried by angels and it proves that they too want me to carry on with this task of mine. And I owe it to them to make this book as good as possible. Just now I am working on Egypt and the North and shall soon be finished with it. Just now the work proceeds well I think I can truthfully say. (Letter 26 July 1982)

Serious health problems forced B Sr to take time off for health checks, stays in hospital and recuperation periods, while he was working on the ACH. He had to take several months off after his visit to South Africa having caught a very serious ear infection which required a very exacting operation. It left him deaf in his right ear which consequently hampered his hearing in larger gatherings. His kidney trouble stemmed from the first period in South Africa but miraculously he was able to continue beyond all the doctors' predictions. The third ailment during the writing of the ACH was the hip operation from which recovery was harder because of the rigorous '40 gr. protein-reduced' diet he was on which weakened his general condition. He pulled through all of these and at times reported feeling better than ever. He did not succumb to the common problem in old age of paying major attention to inevitable health problems and thereby reducing capacity for creative work (quotes from letters to MLS):

What date is it today: over there, outside, among the world of healthy people? Oh — the 23rd of June 1983, and today is the day when I go home, after almost two full weeks at the Samariter Hospital: days full of examinations and explorations, day after day.

It was a difficult time, and a blessed time. End result: All this high *sänka* (sedimentation; now 100 and 115) goes back to kidney trouble and this again possibly connected with illness decades ago (from) amoebic dysentery with emetine [?] injections twice in Zululand. I am now on the whole happy and reassured. Once again they send me from here to the Kidney Specialists at Akademiska Sjukhuset, Uppsala, later this summer, and routine return here 19 September. But I feel I am on the right road back to, or forward to, strength and health and courage.

I saw it in a dream: no longer negative dreams, but a positive, reassuring one, giving me the feeling that now I shall be able to manage. [A drawing of a curved edge of a table going up, with places marked A, B and C.] This is what I saw in the dream: as you discover, an academic crowd, after a procession sitting down along a table. I walk in and there is no place among them at A for me. Well, then, yes, I discover a chair at B and I walk up, but I take a place at C, and feel very comfortable! I take this dream as a good and clear omen that I am on the right track and thank God for it.

I should be terribly worried over the fact that I have lost so much time – but I cannot feel worry, only a hunger to get back now, to keep on writing without feeling that tiredness overmuch. At least they seemed to have localised the trouble now and I hope they will press on and have me restored to something of my original strength and determination.

The letter continues giving the programme for the summer, full of visits of people and B Sr to go to Umeå brother-in-law Bishop Hellsten's seventieth birthday (a letter dated 25 July 1983 records the celebration), a visit to Helsinki and a sermon in the cathedral, Uppsala, 8 August. All this besides the main work: writing. In August he was in hospital again for what he thought would be a routine check-up stay but was extended for four weeks. Letters dated 23, 25, 26 August are written from hospital where, after the regular tests, a kidney biopsy remained to be done, but a pierced blood vessel led to unnecessary and time-consuming complications. A letter dated 2 September reports that the stay in hospital had lasted for four weeks, yet after that the travels continued unabated. B Sr went to Paris in November of the same year to work for two weeks in the archives of the Holy Spirit Fathers and had considerable difficulty with his special protein-reduced diet, but he did not want to put any blame on his hosts:

In Paris: I am writing this in the morning of my departure from Paris. I wish I could say that my health is very good, but I have been having a bad cold these last few days and as I am not allowed to catch a cold on account of my kidneys, I am a little worried, yet I am glad, after all, that I am on my way back to Uppsala and my flat and my strict diet. (Letter 25 November 1983)

Uppsala after return: I can begin by reporting that I am getting over my cold. I know how I got it and from whom, but I was also sure that it had nothing to do with the arrangements for my food with the Fathers (Spiritain). They were all very nice and very friendly, but in the kitchen there was a man and a woman who could not think of doing anything extra [B Sr had a strict protein-reduced diet and would have required diet food.] I got a little container sometimes for the meals but it never had anything but some watery boiled carrots, sometimes a boiled egg. They never managed to make an omelette ... then there were difficulties with my special bread ... No, the food was something of a joke, a sad joke in fact. (Letter 28 November 1983)

Time flew but more and more information was needed. The more one studies a subject the more it opens up new avenues. We find B Sr in Louvain in 1987 with Jesuit fathers, still having the same problems with diet. This time he had brought along his meal ingredients and had meals satisfactorily organised:

Father Edw. Parein looks after me, sees to it that I get toasted bread once a day, and that my food which I have brought along – 10 meals, I think – is arranged day by day. He represents a great tradition of learning here, having served as secretary to both Father Pierre Charles S.J. and to Father Van Wing, both great names in RC missiology and anthropology. (Letter 12 September 1987)

The energy of the ageing man is admirable, in spite of the weakened health.

But there is one problem which overshadows all the others: The speed with which Time is running out. From every point of view, I have no extra time, every new day is precious loan which must not be wasted. (Letter 22 January 1989)

Here in Uppsala, at this desk on Odensgatan, things come and go and change all the time. Billions and milliards are the number of cells in the human brain. How then to influence this multitude? It happens that in some segment of the brain, some cells fall out or loose their strength – or die. It is all the more remarkable to see and feel how they can be recharged as is the case with me. I have got new medicine, Madopark, (of Roche Ltd. Basel) which has sent waves of freshness and joy through my brain, ever increasing each week. It will go on until the fifth week. Isn't that a good miracle. I am so grateful for this help. Before I felt that something was wrong, loss of life and joy. I feel that the routine of taking the medicine gives me a new gust of life and joy, happiness and light. (Letters 4–20 April 1993)

At B Sr's death bed his trusted doctor Wikström told us that he had expected Bengt Sundkler to die 12 years before the time of his actual death and he felt that Bengt had lived on a miracle, even without the dialysis which the doctors thought was at that time the only solution. At a suggestion of one of the younger doctors he opted for a diet to which he kept strictly until his hip operation. He would not have recovered from that had he continued the diet. Bengt felt that the miracle happened because of his important book on African Church History.

Impulses from the environment

Bengt Sundkler did not only respond to people, his moods and impulses also drew elixir from the beauty surrounding him, weather, nature, music, art, movement. Descriptions of these abound in letters and diaries:

You kindly ask about my African Church History: well I am building up my material and should perhaps not rush into writing too soon. On the other hand, I need something else on the side with which to be concerned and where I can all the time try to be creative and formulate new things. So I am brought back to your great concern: my autobiography and the preparations for that. Please do not allow me to leave that aside. I need your help. (Letter 21 June 1976)

I have now discovered what I have known all the time and preached to others all the time. This writing business – conceiving and writing an article or book – depends, in my case, on minute index cards and references. I was sure that this time and for this simple little task I would not need this – and hereby unfortunately I cheated myself.

Yet, the bitter experience has been worthwhile. For now I know that this iron rule applies even more necessarily in the case of my Church History of Africa. I must there be prepared to write tens of thousands of index cards and very often repeating the same fact on different little cards, in order to create that peaceful feeling of mastering a very large body of items. I had been worrying about this for some weeks now and wondered whether I had perhaps lost my ability to write at all and I got afraid. But now today I have finished this thing in one go, and I hope that it will be worth while. (Letter 16 June 1976)

To grow old, to grow older. How does one manage it? 'One loses one's powers' – they all say. I can get very tired and I wonder why? I should have more exercise with my exercise-bicycle. Walk more. I must take time for this. Now I only lift hand weights, 101 times every morning. But it is not enough. I have to watch my weight [he was in no danger of getting too fat] ... I must be directed only to This One Thing which is my African Church History. Just now it means Baltimore lectures which must be ready right away. Now it is 12 October. They must be in Baltimore 20 October. It means that I must be ready with them right away. (Free Associations 12 October 1978)

To dare to read through my South African chapter which has been typed out for me by Timothy Davies. To dare to face facts. To dare to face facts. To dare to face facts. To know exactly where I am. To have a definite plan and to follow it and finish this whole South African part of the ACH and to go further: to keep on: I get tired because I do not follow my own plan. (Free Associations 1 October 1978 English)

The most insidious, usual temptation of all: to give up, to fear, to be afraid of the failure ... I must go right through with it, and be able to manage. Time presses on; flies; difficult to keep up with it. Then, I give away. But no, I must be filled with This One Thing. This One Thing only must fill me, ACH chapter by chapter, consisting in finishing each small part, one after the other. (Free Associations 2 April 1979)

The change in weather, over to something very close to spring, inspires me greatly. I now discover that in 1980 I lost more than I have understood myself. Not only was I sick and had an operation, but I was ill in the very months which to me are the best working months, the spring, so I was really put back. But thank God, I feel better now than ever, and full of joy and hope. (Letter 17 March 1982)

Today is a very great day: I have started to go by bicycle again, and I enjoy it very much indeed. Also had a long letter from Père Noël in

Paris about the whole study of the Holy Ghost fathers as they approached Mandera and the rest in Bagamoyo hinterland, and Kilimanjaro, so that I can see it in perfect detail. (Letter 23 March 1982)

We all know, the Frenchmen Michaux and the German Fischer belong to the great benefactors of mankind. By inventing the bicycle, they added immeasurably to the enjoyment of life to masses and millions of poor little individuals like myself. You go out in the late afternoon. It is sunshine and bright and warm and green and fine wherever you turn. You move along fast and then slowly, meditatively. And you ruminate over your next section of your chapter. Then suddenly, there it is, of course I shall change it all around like that, and there, thanks to the revolving movement of the wheels and the peace of the landscape and of the inner landscape of your soul, you have the solution. I had been worrying how to present the mission history of Swaziland, and how to get all the factors and figures. This is much more difficult than I at first realised. But here, being carried on wheels through the landscape, I realise that I can change it all around: I give the bare outline and then say in a nasal tone that of course that kind of objective chronology is not the concern of these people, and that there is a process of constant re-interpretation of the history of missions in the minds of these Swazis, and that is the only interesting thing. And there I can get closer to the real process in the historical development.

I am so pleased with this that I must look up 'velociped' and cycle in the dictionary, and I send grateful thought to our old friends Michaux and Fischer who first thought of the thing. (Letter 31 July 1973)

I have mislaid my fur cap – how can I dare go out? It is so cold that one has to be careful – and then I discover that it is June 21 and soon Midsummer! A strange world indeed, I cannot believe that it is true ... I am plodding along. Planning to begin my part on the period 1914–60 soon ... I am now back in Uganda and should be able to bring the chapter on the Church at the Kings' Way to a conclusion before too long. (Letter 21 June 1982)

Over here we are pressing on with the African Church History. Once or twice lately I have felt a little sorry for myself, as I think of all that I could have done if I had not been tied like this, chained like this, to this desk: one could have gone to all kinds of nice islands, Spanish, Greek, Swedish islands, and had a nice time. But here I am voluntarily chained to this table, trying to produce one page after another, and I am once again too ambitious, of course trying to manage this enormous job of mine. Sometimes, too, I get a fright that my eye-sight may not last. But then, a prayer to Almighty God imploring Him to help me through it all, to the end. (Letter 27 June 1982)

Of all the months of the year July is the very best. This is also so this year. We have now at long last a very sunny and warm time and I enjoy it very much. It is also the perfect time for work and writing. Everybody is away. This long apartment building with sixteen apartments in four stories, I own it all, and the others have all paid for the rent of their various parts but in fact I own the whole place. Nobody to disturb me – where I leave the lift when I go away for some time, there I find it when I return for nobody else has used it. Then the wonderful routine: half an hour or more on my Tenerife of my balcony, and a few minutes of it after lunch. Then I take my bicycle tour about 4.30 or 5 p.m. and I again own the road, hardly any cars on the little road I take from Husbyborg towards Brobygård, day after day. There I am on my own and can, while cycling along, meditate on the problems of Uganda or, as now, on Egypt ... Then back to the second shower of the day and some hard work again. In fact, it can be too much of that kind of thing. For once I have found it difficult to sleep, overwork, as I try to accommodate myself to the chapter on the Church in Egypt 1800–1914. I shall take the warning. (Letter 14 July 1982)

To me this summer is the perfect time. The climate is perfect and adorable, perpetual sunshine and I give it my devotion twice in the day: about half an hour in the morning (one hour this morning) and half an hour after lunch, both spent on my high Tenerife, looking at the same old and ever new sun as the Canary Islands tourists – and cheaper. The half an hour or more on my bicycle about 5.30 p.m. My health has never been better, thank God for ever and for ever, and no headache at all this whole year. (Letter 2 August 1982)

This sun which shines over my little balcony must be the nicest and kindest sun in the universe. I take it that there are many other suns recklessly thrown about in space somewhere shining and shining, but this one which is so close to me is particularly good. No cloud at all today and then I suppose about 28–30 degrees Celsius. If it were not for this eternal book of mine I could lie on the balcony all the day but the book bids me to leave after some 45 minutes of priceless enjoyment. (Letter 30 July 1982)

Sometimes extra great joys invade my rooms here in this apartment of mine. Years ago I saw a programme with the great Canadian pianist and musical theoretician Glen Gould. Now I saw that he is coming again, and that was yesterday evening, a programme on Bach which is his whole world. He was interviewed by another specialist and he played piano not cembalo, which seemed to give him an extra opportunity to re-create every new note and make the utmost of every new note, and then make this part of a great whole and totality. And then I cannot help it, but apply this to my own situation. I wrote in my diary on 13 January 1981:

'Glen Gould playing Bach fugues, with commentary.
    A pure vision of genius ... The concentrated passionate disciplined genius, altogether devoted to the high task of performance and interpreting the great and incomparable Master in Leipzig and what he once had created.
    It was a very wonderful experience and as always with me these days, very challenging: This masterly knowledge of Bach, moving from one fugue to another and then comparing it with Beethoven right

down to Schönberg, with infinite knowledge and feeling: Why, why, why, am I so small and mean, so half-hearted, why – as with my ACH task – do I not know and see and comprehend this theme of mine, Africa's church history, and know it in and out and in depth and why can I not bring it out in a great and compelling way and in a really beautiful way.

God deliver me from my mean hesitation. Lead me with great assurance so that I can do something worth-while of this task of mine. I am in danger now missing this whole thing. But I must come back to a great grasp and to great clear lines and beautiful architecture. So be it. Amen.'

So you see my situation? I hope to live up to the challenge. So be it. Amen. (Letter 14 January 1982)

I never knew that the Uppsala autumn could be so exhilarating and beautiful: I have walked all the way from the Academic Hospital to my home and I have looked at all these trees and seen how the leaves, changing colour, try to hold fast to the branch, and hesitate, and then fall and in the end one sees the whole architecture of the tree and the glory of the tree itself. It is about 10–12 degrees and soft and warm in fact. I enjoy it so much because it is the very last of these days of autumn and all this glory before it will all give away to snow and ice and the terrifying danger of men falling from their branches. (Letter 8 October 1987)

Irreplaceable Christopher

Numerous people contributed to the birth of the African Church History over the 20 years it was in the making. They are given credit in the Acknowledgements of the book itself. There were, however, people who need to be mentioned here very specially. The key person in the writing process of the ACH was Christopher Steed:

I am having a very good time with Christopher, my young assistant, sent to me by his great teacher, Roland Oliver. He is determined to see this through with me, to the end, and oh, how very much I hope and pray that I shall be privileged to finish this book. In a way it will be of some honour to my good friends here in life: Marja Liisa and Carl Fredrik. (Diary 17 March 1982)

I have had Carl Fredrik here today and we have discussed the strategy of my book-writing. I had written to Geneva and the WCC for help with my next big part of the book, 1920–60, and the Librarian van der Bent suggests that I come there myself. It is possible that I send Christopher in my place while I go to Selly Oak and its fine Library for a week or so. The Selly Oak Library I know of course very well since the years 1946 and 1947 when I worked there with great joy. It was my old friend Groves who built up the Africa section of that library, and should be helpful to me now. We shall see. (1 July 1982)

To start with, Christopher Steed and some of the other assistants provided whatever assistance they could. Receiving visitors in the Odensgatan 5 B meant some household duties in Bengt Sundkler's one man household in addition to writing. Sometimes it meant using the basement facilities for washing clothes, many other times cooking and serving dinners to the visitors. Bengt Sundkler's personality drew people to do things for him, or with him, without that they would have felt such chores to be outside their contracts!

Christopher was irreplaceable in innumerable practical things, whether it meant entertaining visitors or taking care of practical arrangements:

> This morning my young friends left and went to Stockholm (i.e. Eva Swantz-Rydberg, Lea Swantz-Mäkelä, daughters of L and ML Swantz, and Warren Tripp, husband of the eldest Swantz daughter, Professor Aili Mari Tripp) ... I so enjoyed having them here, and I am so glad that they could come. It was my first time to meet Warren. I liked him very much. He is a very charming young man, but much more than that: mature, vocal, generous and helpful, and full of joy. My assistant Christopher took charge of them as they saw Uppsala, and I hope something of that was of interest to them. (Letter 1 July 1982)

The following quote from a letter might give a humorous insight into the practical side of life of the widower who had previously been able to leave most of the home duties to his wife:

> The young generation: In order to welcome my visitors worthily I have been busy with the Hoover in the flat this morning, but then there is in the middle of it an unfamiliar sound. Probably the bag is full of dust and I leave it, until Christopher comes here. I meet him at the Church House and tell him about it. 'Have you got extra bags?' No, that is just the problem, I do not know whether there are extra bags in the house. But he is unperturbed. 'Don't worry. We take out the bag and empty it and place it back again.' I had not even been able to imagine such a thing, but the young generation of today have another attitude to technical problems! (Letter 29 July 1982)

The same letter tells the reader also of the most important side of Christopher's contribution:

> Christopher has been asked by me to take care of the chapter on Southern Sudan for the African Church History. He will do very well I think. He has also added a couple of good pages on Islam to be incorporated into my chapter on Ethiopia; this should be very valuable and very much needed of course. (Letter 29 July 1982)

Christopher Steed also wrote several sections on Islam and of the part on West Africa. After Bengt Sundkler's death he ended up doing the tedious work of finalising the vast bibliography and checking the references.

Perhaps more than anything else Bengt Sundkler had tremendous assistance from Christopher Steed in getting books from the libraries and giving information about published materials he came to hear of. Christopher was a real wizard in discovering new publications concerning Africa and its history and he kept on carrying them to Odensgatan 5 B to B Sr's study. Letters and the drafts of the manuscript tell of Christopher's multiple contributions:

> We are struggling along with this impossible and fascinating task of ours. The book will be too long, much too long, but it will be a solid piece of work. As we are reading the manuscript one sees that it has been worthwhile. (Letter 12 September 1987 or 14 June 1985)

Other co-workers

Bengt Sundkler was very grateful to the many co-workers who saw to it that his sketches became solidly typed chapters and parts of chapters, especially since he himself did not start using a computer. His English-speaking assistants could also see to it that the English texts were polished, but the language remained a problem. There were times when corrections became so unsatisfactory to him that whole sections had to be reworked. How to balance between keeping to one's own style, yet succumbing to necessary corrections in order to make English true English? This was an especially delicate question to someone who was very conscious of the style he recognised as his own.

Jocelyn Murray, herself an accomplished author and experienced editor, arrived in summer 1977 by ship from Aberdeen, got a SIDA (Swedish International Development Authority) flat for accommodation, and a room where to work in Nordic Africa Institute. She spent long months in Uppsala and came for a second period to assist in writing in 1985. She was an efficient and devoted co-worker who made very valuable contributions to ACH, as she had also done to some of Bengt Sundkler's earlier work. Krista Hertie and Aina Abrahamson, both from the USA, were also helpful and devoted assistants for some parts of the work.

A colleague who influenced much also the writing of ACH was Carl Fredrik Hallencreutz. He used endless time in discussions with B Sr about the different stages of ACH, until he became a teacher in the University of Zimbabwe.

My own contribution was to act as a kind of sounding board, making observations here and there and providing a correspondent who responded to the writer who required communication to keep up his inspiration.

Notes

1. African Church History is abbreviated ACH which B Sr also used.
2. Unless otherwise stated, the letters quoted in this and the following chapter were addressed to myself, elsewhere noted as MLS.
3. B Sr received some help in translation the following day from a young Swede, Kennet Ritzén.
4. The St Brigit Mass was a historical commemoration of the Swedish woman saint from mediaeval times at which B Sr was the chief celebrant and preacher. Detailed reporting of the Birgitta mass and the television programme is given in the letters 27 September; 1 and 7 October 1977.
5. Dr Festo Bahendwa from Bukoba, teacher in Makumira with a doctorate from Helsinki University.
6. Elimu Njau is a well-known Tanzanian artist with galleries in Nairobi and Kilimanjaro.
7. In letters addressed to my husband and myself there are detailed accounts of all the visits in US, some of which we helped to organise for him. He ate his Thanksgiving Day dinner with our daughter, now Professor Aili Mari Tripp, Madison, and her husband Dr Warren Tripp, then living in Hammond, IN.
8. The plans which were enclosed changed constantly, thus they are not included in the text. After the thirteenth plan B Sr sent another one in a letter 12 December 1981: 'I send you the "Plan" of ACH, fourteenth edition. The Plan itself is by now not bad, the question is only how to fill it with good and important writing, equivalent to the splendid theme itself.'
9. The report contains interesting details about the visit to Professor Roland Oliver's and his wife Caroline's country place and Oliver's church connections, a stay at St Julians in Sussex for a rest, and contacts with Christopher Steed's parents, Professor Gray and Andrew Roberts in SOAS.
10. Interview by Tiina Ahonen 1990.

12

TO WRITE IS TO LIVE AND CREATE
SKRIVA FÖR ATT LEVA

Writing is creating

To write is to live. Writing for me is creating. It is a healing process. I am unhappy that I am not seriously active and creative literally. Personality runs the risk of being dissipated. When writing dissipated personality is brought together, sharpened into focus. Writing is a similar process as prayer for a Christian, prayer holds the person together. I am consciously aware of this. Thoughts become formulated while writing. Paragraphs are bricks in the building process. Architecture of paragraphs, chapters and finally the book are my great secret joys, secret between God and myself.

The act of writing gives me immense joy ... I should like to write of that which now fills my heart: a yearning for clear expression. I am eager for one thing, the clear beautiful form, forming the thought, forming everything around me, perhaps also with hands. I feel I need years to try to arrive at something beautiful, the simple, clear form.

(Interview 28 December 1982)

In reading the numerous letters and diaries, as the author of this biography, I have come to realise that B Sr had one great ambition throughout his life: to write and to do so well. From B Sr's diaries, Free Associations and letters it is possible to have a view into his study, his walks, his meetings with people, selectively following the process of creating. Some of this ground was covered already in the previous chapter when it related specifically to ACH.

After B Sr no longer had his teaching duties he felt free to take up writing as a full-time career, he became in his own words a 'free-lancer'. The urge to write was an urge to create. In a letter he quoted words of Vera Stravinskij to a friend, a quotation from the diary of Jules Renard:

What is left is to take the pen, make the lines on the paper and then patiently fill the paper. The strong ones do not hesitate. They sit down, they sweat, they continue until the end. They squeeze out the ink, finish the paper. They are nothing but oxen. The greatest ones are nothing but oxen. The greatest ones are geniuses, those who can toil for 18 hours a day without being tired.

B Sr himself continued from there: 'It certainly is just the medicine I need now. The strong ones do not hesitate!' (23 August 1975)

In this chapter we see what inspired Bengt Sundkler, what made it possible for him to write, and what 'pains and woes' he suffered in the process of creating. I start with the way he gathered his material while 'in the field', in actual contact with the people and places he wrote of. I then cite thoughts which express the central significance of writing for him. Other creative people provided models for his writing. Whether they were composers, musicians, artists or writers, he could identify himself with their creative moments.

Bengt Sundkler needed creative people around him, responsive and warm people because he created in response to what the people he met and lived with gave him. I have never met anyone else who so faithfully recorded any thought of another person, which gave him associations and put his thoughts into motion. There was always a notebook and pen at hand whenever he met people or moved around making observations. He left behind a big box full of small notebooks covering half a century, notebooks of a size that fitted easily into his coat or shirt pocket.

Gathering material

Whatever B Sr was working on at the time, he gathered material for it with rare intensity, whether directly from people, from books and archives, or through observations which even remotely reminded him of the topics he had in mind and which gave him new associations. He wrote most readily on topics with which he had had a concrete connection.

I quote from Professor Åke Holmberg's review of *Bara Bukoba* which to my mind not only gives us an idea how he gathered his materials, but also summarises the essence of his life's work and him as a person, and shows what made Bengt Sundkler the writer he was:

Characteristic to Bengt Sundkler in his whole life work was to combine theory and practice, scientific contribution and practical mission work, and concentrating this wide register totally to capture and understand whole human reality. Anyone who has seen Sundkler in action among people and events knows that his was not just a scientific programme, it comprised his whole life. He would be speedily making notes in a small notebook, having the same enormous appetite for a new word in a local dialect, for a glimpse of a human lot, a flower's name and a new insight into some social context. (*Göteborg Post* 14 May 1974)

B Sr described his approach of interviewing people in the Preface to the *Christian Ministry in Africa*:

> As to the method of soliciting fresh material I can limit myself to one observation. In my visits to Africa I found that interviews with individuals or small groups of three to five were much more rewarding than discussions in big conferences.[1] The African pastor or evangelist is like most of us also on that point: He is much more ready to talk freely when in his own home or office than if the interview is to take place in the form of an officious statement in a big conference. Being more interested in overtones and unsolicited reactions than in polished reports, I found that such reactions were more likely to appear in the intimate group in the pastor's own home. To arrange this kind of ideal meeting was, however, more difficult than is sometimes realised. Even when I prepared my own travel routes myself, I was up against what I describe as a 'wall of whiteness'.
>
> In all parts of the continent, not only in the South, there is at work a machinery of social control that gears the visitor into ... 'white' channels – if I may say so, without appearing too ungrateful to my Western friends in Africa, who went out of their way to make my studies profitable. In order to overcome this wall of being Western I held before my eyes throughout the years an unwritten rule, 'A day without a visit to an African pastor – in his home or in his office – is a lost day.'
>
> There were many such lost days, but perhaps not as many as the case might have been without this golden rule. I was enriched personally by these meetings and am grateful for having been given an excuse for enjoying what I regard as the most rewarding and refreshing occupations, making personal contacts with African churchmen. (Sundkler, 1960:11–12)[2]

B Sr took copious notes and he also read those notes afterwards, underlining important points to remember and at times crossing off the things he had already made use of. Before leaving on a new study tour he studied what he had gathered on previous tours. The following was written before B Sr's new fieldwork in South Africa in 1969. Not only biographers, even he himself had difficulties with his own handwriting:

> I have gone through 15–20 notebooks of my interview notes from South Africa. They are incredibly rich in contents, but very tiresome to go through. To write, to compose, is not at all tiring, thereby one gathers new strength and I am naive enough to obtain great satisfaction from my work. I think it is good. But to read old notes is very tiring ... I have great treasures in my notes from 1958, which I must make use of and carry further. I also tried out my new foolproof camera and a tape recorder, which I bought for the trip. (Diary 11 June 1969)

Visions for living and creating

The quotations below from various sources give glimpses of the process of creative writing. They have to be read with the kind of associative mind which B Sr himself had:

> Why do I write these pages of diary? Why do I not go out to fresh air and look at the hippos, which graze below the window – in fact all vegetables except parsley, which would be so healthy, as the doctors say? Do I write diary in order to live in memories? Have I also now become so blind that I believe that a person lives in memory through a book?
>
> I need a diary for the sake of my soul, I must see to it that I unravel what is happening with me when years pass by so incomprehensibly fast ... Concentrating, that is life and happiness [*salighet*] for me. I have grown much since the 1950s ... more peace, more inner depth; quiet, and more persistent joy. (Notebook in Bukoba 1961)[3]

In the spring of 1969, after Ingeborg had gone to Tanzania and B Sr was advising a number of doctoral candidates, his anxiety grew about not writing. He had finished the English volume on Nathan Söderblom and had been thinking of writing three Swedish volumes. The lack of response to the English book discouraged him and he was turning to other tasks. Besides the second volume of the *World of Mission* he listed a book on Bukoba, an article on K. B. Westman for *SMT*, and the second book as a continuation of *Bantu Prophets* as his tasks. He was encouraging his 'brilliant students', who would not perhaps have needed encouragement as much as he himself was in need of a little push from somebody. He exhorts himself day after day in his diaries realising that if one wants to write there must be an inner necessity to write:

> It must come from within, as an inner force, unavoidably, something that must be said, that I must say. It is a question of concentration and courage, courage that checks everything else, lay everything else on the side, whatever the world (or the University) says, and to give oneself totally to this only thing: This one thing I do. (Diary 16 February 1969)

> I live and struggle and exist for writing, for outlining [in Swedish *dispo-sition*], for creating. It means that I must make room and prepare opportunity for myself to devote myself to it. Very gratifyingly I have had a good contact with the younger generations of my students. But even that is a sideline for me who has to write in order to live; I try to give form to what is living. No one else knows about this, it is my little secret, on my level. Perhaps I fail so completely in my effort for form giving that no one could imagine me to gain joy from such a thing. So it remains my little secret. Joy, at times gained from chaos, and at times from creating order, a simple and good form in presentation. More important than such things is of course that one has something to say,

wants to say something and to fight for some cause – with clear intention and will – will! (Diary 2 May 1969)

To write, to compose, is not at all tiring; thereby one gathers new strength and I am naive enough to obtain great satisfaction from my work. I think it is good. (Diary 11 June 1969)

I am glad to have my music and reading, reading English poetry and French prose: Eliot, Auden and Valery. And all the while and all the time I am after nobler form, finer expressions, higher level of expressing myself. (Letter 31 March 1973)

When advising his students B Sr made the point that one should not start from the beginning and never to start from writing first the introduction. It was sure to change in the course of writing. You start from what is clear in your mind and let other parts take shape as the writing evolves. He himself had to find the right note on which to start in order to get started and get the inspiration to continue:

I always feel that in order to start to write I must feel in myself what note to strike, what kind of level on which to write, and then visualise the plan of the whole book – although ever prepared to change this as one goes along.
But it is only life, Life itself, which can give fire and cause fire. The more of real life you can give in the book, in its brutality and beauty, the more the book will itself live and be felt as really alive. The important thing is to have good notebooks or other means, which you can use in order to preserve your daily observations and ideas. I have not even mentioned the language. That comes as one writes, to the one who has something to say. (Letter 22 May 1973)

I fetch my inspiration from architectural sketches, the more modern the better: these clear, pure pillars symbolise for me striving for clarity and wholeness, total grip over the thing I am trying to formulate at each time. This is a peculiar feature in me, but I must make use of it and develop it further, play it out fully – in all secrecy, of course. For me it [writing] means shaping *dispositions* [outlines or plans for the book] all the time. What does an architect do as a form giver, a building: He sketches without ceasing new plans, uses masses of papers for one version and plan [Eero Saarinen]. This, my building, must be built and taken down and built again in the same way. Outline, make new versions till it is a *disposition*. The problem is psychological, to decide that just this is the one I shall carry through. (Free Associations 25 February 1979)

I had to phone in order to share my deep emotions after having seen a Finnish television film on Helen Schjerfbeck [a remarkable Finnish artist]. I was very deeply moved by it. I think it struck me right to the core at a time when I was singularly receptive and responsive ... This singularly dedicated woman was doing This One Thing and Only This

One Thing. She had this incredible concentration in spite of constant weakness and illness and being harassed all the time right and left, yet she kept on and at it because whatever people said she knew that she had something to say, a message to convey. Living in that utter isolation of hers yet seeing the vast horizons and the unseen beauties. Gotthard Johansson wrote at an exhibition in Stockholm about 1938: This is '*Den stora konsten. Detta är heligt rum*'. [This is great art. This is a holy room.] ... I was deeply moved by this experience and it helped me to go into myself much more definitely, to an inner world of dedication and dependence upon God my Saviour, my only refuge. (Letter 11 May 1981)

The following reflection was written some time in 1974 after B Sr had finished writing *Bara Bukoba* and was moving on to *Zulu Zion*. B Sr often played with the idea that the posterity might find something in his works which the present ignored. B Sr's self-effacing attitude reflects the prevailing Marxist critique, which made theological viewpoints sound hopelessly bourgeois. In Free Associations B Sr wrote about *Bara Bukoba*:

That this book was created in an attempt to make a good and beautiful book, will for ever remain a secret between you and me. No, I think in 90–100 years, 2064–74, some bright Swedish or Danish social anthropologist will discover it and say, 'Ah, that was an interesting old book by somebody who knew something about Tanzania.' But then he will be taken to task by one of the ruling clique: 'Did the reviewer not know that the author was a theologian, and a bishop at that?' ... We are not supposed to mention works of such intellectuals.

The question remains, how could people like that go on publishing. The secret is, when publishing one book that old man was already far ahead with the next one. He had almost lost all interest in the one just published and was altogether concentrated on his next book. This funny method actually saved him from total despair. He was even known to have given the impression of being content, glad and happy. Very strange – it must be the result of naiveté.

After *Bara Bukoba* B Sr started to write *Zulu Zion* in earnest. He kept on revising it, which caused an extra expense since the proofs were read over and over again. He made substantial changes each time the suggestions for corrections reached him from his readers, of which the present writer is one. Our correspondence followed closely the process of writing *Zulu Zion*. When he had left the final version with the printers he joked about it:

The printer said he would come 7.30 in the morning for it but Swedish precision is not what it used to be, so he came only at 7.40. I was glad to hand it all over to him, and thankful to God that I have had this opportunity of writing this and concluding it. Right through the night one came up on new names and institutions which somehow should be squeezed in, but then I wrote a general apologia at the end so that people will have to try to understand. Anyway it has been a joy to do this.

This is the ideal form of existence for me, being thus stretched in order to do one's utmost. And miraculously it also keeps one happy and healthy, it seems at least. I have had to use the bicycle a lot, running about in town and to archives and libraries. So I had my little exercise after all which I fully realise I need. I always take some strenuous exercises in the mornings and enjoy this immensely. (Letter 17 July 1975)

Zulu Zion did not become as well known as *Bantu Prophets*, but it has been read and appreciated by the Zionists themselves who have drawn inspiration for their church life from it.[4] This would give the writer of it fullest satisfaction as he even when writing it was trying to find a note which would have been non-Western and non-academic. (Typed notes on 1970–90, n.d.)

It was important for B Sr to stay close to reality when he was writing, being real, true to one's own belief and thought-world and to make use of the moments which were at hand. He was reminded from time to time about the uncertainty of life and necessity to live out the reality of today:

The being or not being real is a fundamental question ... I am pragmatic enough to deal with it this way: fundamentally to carry on, to deal with the task given to me, to thank and praise God continuously for it. But more deeply to know at the same time that one day this task can be suddenly taken out of my hands, by illness or some sudden ailment, and yet, yet, I must be real. What then is the uniting factor in both kinds of existence? ... I think it is the knowledge that I am in God's hands. My religion is this, as simple as that. It is as simple as that of a pious old hewer of wood in the forests of Norrland, very uncomplicated. Yet, I know that my faith is very different from his, he would be shocked at the unconventionality and undogmatic way in which I look at the ultimate things in life and existence. But I know that this trust and acceptance help me to carry on and to make me real.

Urge to live real life. How? To plan as if that were ordered by God, but on a deeper level to live now as if ambitious planning were not necessary.

This minute that comes to me
Over the past decillions
There is no better than it – and now.

That is Walt Whitman, and it is his word, which has been close to my writing desk for 50 years. It is at the same time the NUN, 'now' of the New Testament, not flirting with life in daydreams, dreaming about something else, but living to celebrate that life which is given to me now: this sun-set, this snow, this walk, this letter, this day, this hour, this minute that comes to me now.

I should not forget that I belong to that infinitely small minority, that privileged group of people who can do something creative. At least I would like to call it that. Then life is all the more responsible, requires of me all the more responsibility. Having this kind of a chance and this kind of existence, which gives me a chance at creativity, is infinitely much more fun and gives much more joy than the existence of narrow routine with which most people have to try to manage and be satisfied.

But then, if only I could have constant courage, constantly being disciplined to carry on with writing, that is my frontier of personal struggle. What is needed is a total kind of abandon to the task and that helps one to forget tiredness and any little ailment. (Letter 14 January 1982)

The pains and woes of creative writing

The diaries are full of self-blame for not accomplishing, not being creative. I cite some of them here as they also express self-analysis and an inner search for committed study and a striving for well-formulated artistic expression. For B Sr there did not seem to be any distinction between the two:

> Must I show to myself and others that I cannot manage this? I should instead show that I love to keep at writing, that putting the pen on paper and formulating pregnant sentences is therapy. I have no time to loose. I ought to get much and important [things] done every day. I only read and make notes. But in my innermost I am afraid to start now writing all of this. State which I know so well. (Free Associations, n.d.)

> If I may dwell on the plane of psychological well-being and health for a while, I feel in my own recent experience that there is an immense difference between creating an ambitious book and turning out the little articles which in the nature of one's job one has also to produce. I enjoy the former so very much but have come to dislike the latter more and more. This latter reaction is bad: I wish I could teach myself to be a good journalist who likes to turn out well-rounded articles, fitting the situation and being useful in the kind of world we live in. But no, it seems the older I become, it is for the really worthwhile, lasting thing that I am hankering.

> I am always far too interested in the effect on other people, always with my tentacles in all directions trying to register reactions. I need to be much more resting in myself. Last Sunday in my sermon I made the distinction between the bad being *instängd i sig själv* and the good *vilande i sig själv* ('closed within oneself' or 'resting in oneself'). The latter knows that he or she has value and thanks God for it. The latter tries to develop it, and foster these things, which have been given to one, bent on doing the One Thing which is right, and which must be done, not looking right or the left, but pursuing it whatever the consequences. This I must try to learn before it is too late. (Letter 12 September 1973)

> My spirit will sing and give expression to what is in my innermost self. Why then am I hampered and cannot really take hold of my writing? Where from comes this fear in my innermost self? Why not ordered, clear, determined? 'Let our ordered lives confess the beauty of Thy

peace.' (Whittier) All these papers on my desk! It is too bad: I must be determined, strong, clear and frank. (Free Associations 3 October 1974)

The interruptions were not always unpleasant. Social life and being included with the 'high and mighty' also took its time, but in its aftermath it tended to turn to a regretful mood:

The Swedish scene has been dominated by the king's wedding, and I was invited to attend in the Storkyrkan together with Kekkonen and kings and others. It was a very fine day, a historic day for Sweden. This is the very best that this young king ever did: she, our Queen Silvia, behaved so very well and endeared herself to everybody in a way that no one could have believed possible ...

But let us now for a moment leave kings and queens and presidents aside and turn to something even more interesting: myself. I am in a little bit of a quandary. Just at present I do not fully believe in my ability to write and therefore fool around with all sorts of chores and tasks, which in any case have to be done and dealt with. I am spending far too much time with this Söderblom in Paris article, yet, not yet seeing how I am going to do it in order to make it worth while.

I really do not have the time, which I now so generously give to this. Yet I do not face this problem squarely – my old pernicious tendency to avoid and evade. I really would need to take a week off. Ideally I should be walking quite on my own in the forests of Dalecarlia, or some such place, walking and meditating, absolutely alone, receiving new strength and new visions. I may try to do that when I return from London on 4 July. (Letter 21 June 1976)

I have crossed Rubicon. After a tortuous climb I have jumped over Kibo and have found that it looks just fine and nice and sunny on the other side: One can see out over free and long vistas. I feel like doing what Rebmann did on 11 May 1848, at having 'discovered' Kilimanjaro.

Oh, I agree, it is very childish of me to react this way ... But this preparation for writing an innocent little article on 'Söderblom in Paris' and the consequences for his ecumenical vision, this article has taken much too long time from me and even made me really worried as to whether I could at all write anything any longer. (Letter 16 July 1976)

I am today and I am for the millionth time ordering my papers. I must cry, shout to myself: to face facts. But I am well: no headache, no migraine equivalent, 'no nothing.' Let me finish this job now while I still manage, still have got the strength to do it! Give me courage, joy, persistence, perseverance, God my God. Time will come when I shall be unable ... then I shall regret these wasted days and months. 'Time is irreplaceable, waste it not' (Freeman Richmond) That is my motto ... or should be my motto. I have no time to waste. Let me revise my time schedule and make one, which I can follow ... and then follow it: keep at it. What system shall I follow? Large papers and small cards: necessary. (Free Associations 1 October 1978)[5]

Jonathan Seagull has not been quietened within me or threatened to do so. It is stretching out and wishes to fly free and higher . . . I am reread-ing it again and again, and I need it all the time, and shall never be tired of it. (Letters 22 July 1975 and 14 June 1985) 'To fly as fast as thought, to anywhere that is, you must begin by knowing that you have already arrived.'6

Here in Uppsala just now, I am unhappy, I am only plodding along, reading all the time while I should be <u>writing</u> . . . But . . . within a day or two, I shall be back in writing and then therefore the happiest person around. I am totally alone here, these days, and that is very good. In a way, being basically and fundamentally a very communicative person – something which I have only discovered late in life – I need somebody to speak to and be inspired by, and therefore the visits to Helsinki are so very very helpful and really godsent. They are basic and fundamental to me... But writing, I must try to do that on my own and by the flickering light of my own understanding. We shall see. (Letter 25 January 1982)

Autobiography in letters

Bengt Sundkler intended to write his autobiography and finish it together with the ACH. Writing letters was one way of writing an autobiography. He also read of other people who had written autobi-ographies and who gave him inspiration for ideas or the way of doing things. I pick quotes from Bengt's reference to other autobiographies and cite what he himself referred to as role models for himself:

I have just come across a great word of *Max Weber*: 'No thing is of value to man as man, if he cannot pursue it with passion' with his whole heart . . . I must get the German original from that genius, called Max Weber. I translate it to my own situation, my own life situation just now: There are a few things, only a few really worth-while things to be done, and these I must pursue with passion, with determination, This One Thing. It is when I forget this that I get distraught. It is when I live up to this ideal that I am integrated and whole and healthy. It means to surrender oneself to This One Thing and pursue it with a whole will. (Letter 12 September 1973)

You will be gladdened by the news that your persistent emphasis on my duty to write on that strange little person called BGMS [Bengt Gustaf Malcolm Sundkler] seems to bear fruit. I have got a real grasp of how to do it. I think it was reading something by Heinrich Böll that I saw my first two chapters and this night I have got an idea of the third one. Above all I see that it is not a question of writing a big tome with heavy chapters but little light chapters centred around a dramatic event which illuminates the whole procedure, one at 7 years, one at 12, one again about 16–17. Those three take me right through to coming to Uppsala, when of course I find it easier to write. I have phoned to my old friends at Vindeln, my birth place, and I shall go there on 3 August to spend two days with them and then I hope to pass some time, a couple of days at Umeå in order to read old newspapers from about 1913–19. I have also phoned to the newspaper up there. (Letter 22 July 1975)

An interview this morning with Magnus K. Lindberg, Uppsala, translator to Swedish of *Patrick White*, who got the Nobel Price in literature last year, in *Uppsala Nya Tidningen*. ... White had told M. L. that he had been so downhearted when he did not first get the prize that he felt tempted to regard himself as passé. In the end, the prize gave him a new boost or something. Now, it is interesting to notice how people on that level react and function. He needs as much encouragement as anybody else, and in the end he got it in the form of some money which in fact he did not need or use, he gave it to other Australian authors.

I, of course, react personally to all that happens and all that I read. And I have to say to myself that I thank God for the continuous encouragement, which I receive through the fellowship with my friends. This transcends all prizes in this poor world of ours. (Letter 27 December 1974)

I complained about the fact that I had not been informed about Edv. Westermark's Autobiography. But in reading more of it, I come to the conclusion that the fellow was very conceited, surprisingly so. I am of course impressed by his contacts in England and Morocco and his imaginative effort on behalf of his country, then under the Russian heel, but one would have wished this gentleman a little more balance in the view of his own achievements. (Letter 28 September 1987)

You have encouraged me more than anybody else to make a try at an autobiographical book. Astonishingly you are not the only one ... I have recently come across a few others who have suggested as much, Sigbert Axelson being one. (Letter 12 June 1982)

As a Finn you will be interested that there is a note from 14 December 1958 in my diary. I was listening to poetry in the Swedish radio and a programme called '*Röster från Öster*', 'Voices from the East'. I cannot forget a note from Gunnar Björling, in the dark evening:
'*Det blir glömt*
som en sång jag ej bar.'
(I will be forgotten like a song, which I did not sing.)
My notes are brief [in Swedish]: I sat and listened to the radio programme 'Voices from the East,' the wonderful series with better poetry readers, Finnish, than one can ever hear elsewhere. In Björling's poem I can remember this word about oblivion and essential want. Like a song, which I did not sing out.
God, how many songs I have not sung. Outbursting songs of joy, which never could reach the consciousness. Deep tone of gratitude, which never has found voice, other than through constant awareness that I can be healthy and may work. Let me not vanish in stinginess, narrow-mindedness and pettiness. Give me courage, give me voice, give me the grace to carry out the song about you. (Letter 14 December 1985)

You will be glad to know that as I have started in earnest with my autobi-ography I have been greatly helped by dipping into Mircea Eliade's <u>two</u> autobiographical volumes . . . I find him very exciting: a young Romanian who at 20 years of age decides to go to Calcutta and the whole of India and becomes a world expert on Yoga and whose real yearning is to write novels. Dipping into this gives me a boost for trying my own thing so <u>very</u> different. I am on my way and am glad that you are pushing me along. My ambition (I am still young enough to count with ambitions!!!) is to produce this autobiography now so that it can be published <u>together</u> with the African History. The tone of the African Church History is stern and correct, thus there is a need for a complementary volume which is more personal as this 'Beyond the Forest Range' necessarily must be. I have found that I get tired and sleepy from failing to write, and the writing itself – as this autobiography inspires me strongly and strangely. (Letter 2 July 1992)

My autobiography: I have written out by hand a number of chapters, but . . . to get somebody who could take down the typing, steno and typing or computer. I could spend some 10,000 kronas on this to get it finished as the final ms. (Letter 13 December 1992)

I am taking as much time as possible with my autobiography. This works well, the ACH has to be neat and proper in tone while this auto-biography can be much more personal and must be so. I am trying to find out the reasons why I came to live for Africa. Africa became my fate, and I am so grateful I could come to the real Africa while we still could enjoy hope for the continent and its peoples.

After a cold week, we are again having most beautiful spring and early summer day. I cannot appreciate this enough. I am amazed by its beauty and clarity. Next Thursday – 8 April 1993 – I go to Östanbäck in order to speak at the Easter preparation and on the Easter Day there, as has been my custom for years. We Northerners do appreciate the change from winter to spring: it is a wonderful drama, this change, much more dramatic than the change in the equator – it seems to me. (Letter 3 April 1993)

Autobiography through dreams

B Sr was not only interested in the role of the dreams in the life of the African Christians, he gave significance to them also in his own life. He kept a pen and notebook by his bedside and after having an interesting dream he would take up the pen and record the dream. He has recorded numerous dreams in his diary and letters. He gave them biographical significance. Here are two samples of them:

1974: This last night I had a most remarkable dream. I had made some additional notes in Bantu Zion [later *Zulu Zion*], saying that I had not gone into the matter of the colour schemes of white-blue/green vs.

red/black ... Well, I gave much thought to this colour scheme question and then went to bed.

I woke up about 5 in the morning after a seemingly long and exceptionally clear and comprehensive dream experience. I dreamt that I joined the brotherhood of monks at Östanbäck (where I am of course a Visitor). I joined them in putting on their white long habit – in fact they do not use white but being Benedictines they have a black habit. I joined them on trial. They seemed to be proud over their new acquisition.

But I felt a conflict inside, How do I dare to appear publicly, <u>outside</u> the monastery, in that white habit of mine? We were going to attend a lecture at the university. I put on my habit, but with a few qualms, wondering what my university colleagues would say. I went out, to go to the university. There was a steep hill, and I recognised the place clearly, in Africa or Europe, but I did not know which. It might also have been the steep descent near the Vindeln river, but that guess is more to satisfy your constructive urge, binding it with childhood. In any case, it was too steep, so I decided to go down some less steep hill. I had to run in order to get there in time. I found that I ran competing with a woman whom I recognised as Märta Dahl (now Gissler). She was a mission candidate in England at the same time as Ingeborg and I in 1937. I spent 14 days and 13 nights at the same infamous place, an Oxford Group centre with extreme control of the souls and hearts and minds and lives of the CSM mission candidates, and I revolted strongly against this. Märta Dahl was the spider in that control net which the Mission had at that time, in its effort to turn all the future missionaries into nice little Oxford groupers ... I left the place and went to Birmingham. Strange that this experience should have been such a violent one to me.

So here I was running competing with this woman, and trying to come in time to the lecture. About there the dream ended, and I woke up with a feeling that this dream experience had been altogether satisfactory, a total dream and totally satisfying. That is what I told myself after jotting down these notes from the dream ...

Some obvious things are to be found in the dream: I am glad to be in contact with my brethren at Östanbäck, [a non-Catholic brotherhood] and yet feel theologically increasingly estranged from them. I am preparing to say something radical in this general chapter of mine on the Church of Sweden, in the little Söderblom book to appear shortly. That conflict is obviously in the dream. The competitive race against a self-appointed Moral Constraint and Ultimate Law is an expression of an effort to achieve personal freedom, freedom from *Zwang*, straightjacket (I had been reading C. P. Scott's chapter on Einstein, struggling constantly against what he called *Zwang*). The Oxford group experience must have caused a deep chasm in me, judging from my notes which apart from returning to the London experience from time to time also indicate reaction to finding active groupers in Dundee. A camp of 200 young people was impressive, yet too much 'Come forward!' 'I was a sinner but was changed.' There was too little speaking of Christ, too little food for intellect and no upbringing for Christian life.

The most remarkable thing which I experienced from the dream was that it was not tiring. It did not leave fatigue or headache but rather a feeling of satisfaction and clarity, related to the whiteness of that habit which I had put on, and which yet I hesitated to be seen with outside the monastery. Anyway ... here is a real dream: clear in sharp outline, not blurred at all.

Another dream 31 July–1 August 1979: A piece from a more comprehensive dream which I did not grasp: A child, a son, in a small bundle was laid on my arms and I stroked quietly the cloth on the stomach and he smiled and chuckled very pleased [*förtjust*]. I wrote this down right away: 'the most loveable dream I have ever had'. I felt fully relaxed and fully satisfied. Perhaps this happened after the evening television show on 'Communication' a deep, existential and essential, satisfying. In it these brilliant Frenchmen presented the idea that in a conversation, in a real communication between the two, the word creates a third one, a child. (Free Associations 1 August 1979)

Responding to the work of others

B Sr's forum for reviews and criticism was his journal *SMT*. The reviews were written mainly to inform the Swedish-speaking readers who did not always follow the international journals or events, rather than to criticise the works. With some scholarship close to his own field he disagreed thoroughly, both in style and content. One such case was Oosthuizen's interpretation of Shembe's hymns, another was David Barret's concentration on statistics which to him did not reflect reality.

There are warnings against conceiving and writing of things in this particular field. Yesterday Christopher and I were looking at certain pages in David Barret's majestic *World Christian Encyclopaedia*. We had to laugh and laugh and laugh, and I had to say, 'That kind of mania for completeness, how do we avoid that and do we dare to be really selective. Well, we try.' (Letter 14 June 1985)

In the case of David Barret the laugh was about the author's belief in predictions based on detailed statistics of churches, including the Independent Churches. Their friendly laugh concerned a mistaken conceptualisation of the African churches.

A creative writer also admired the work of other people who created, whether it was beautiful architecture or well-produced television programmes. It was B Sr's custom to praise, and on other occasions also criticise, what he read, heard or saw:

It is ironic. People do not take seriously what they consider my exaggerated need to give encouragement. I am a bit different in that from most people. When I like a person I like very much indeed and I use also high praise. It is nothing I have concocted. I feel very deeply, for me it is not being insincere. I am trying to be sincere and say these nice things. In twentieth-century Sweden such things are [said by] strange actors, maniacs and drunks. Positive expressions will be misunderstood or derided. I have felt I am carrying on the inheritance from N Sm. People need a bit encouragement, even in 1985. (Interview 31 October 1985)

B Sr exercised the office of encouragement often by sending comments on programmes to people who produced them, be it a fine television programme, a newspaper article, a sermon or a well-conducted worship service. The following letter to a television producer, Ethel Karström, is an illustration of how he expressed his admiration. The recipient responded saying it was the finest praise she ever had received:

> This must be Ethel Karström, I thought. It must be Ethel Karström who produces in this way … It must be the producer who lifts out what is beautiful and great and true for us human children. Yes, we got it confirmed at the end of the programme.
> I never wrote to thank you for the wonderful service in Uppsala Cathedral in September last year. The same producer did it, someone who could let the great worship service drama come forth in its full beauty, liveliness and power, and let lights up there under the great vault shine and uplift.
> And now in this small church of Ingarö there were only few things to capture photographically but she could picture it in an unforgettable style, beautiful scenes from nature outside, people, choir, fine quick portraits. There were fine old ladies in folk costume, and a few other women added, and the two men with their collection hoops, and the very remarkable preacher and pastor Marianne Sautermeister. It was all so real and so good. With all this the producer could lift forth a great and beautiful message, also this time. Thank you.
> Yours truly, B Sr.
> (Midsummer 1986)

B Sr often grabbed the phone after listening to a sermon or a touching liturgical singing and thanked those concerned for offering such an experience. He also noted down disappointments in his diary, and at times sent notes to those concerned, when he felt the preachers lost their chance to interpret the liberating message they potentially had to deliver to listeners.

Does the language matter?

The language mattered enormously to B Sr and it had a profound influence on his work. Language related to style and B Sr was very particular about his style. He generally wrote his diaries in Swedish, his *SMT* journal was edited in Swedish and many of his books were written in Swedish, some of which were later rewritten in English. As we have seen, he felt more of himself writing in Swedish. The style of his language was highly praised, especially in the Swedish edition of *Bara Bukoba* and in *Söderblom och hans möten*. He himself was not pleased with the language in the second edition of the *Missionens värld*.

In writing both Swedish and English B Sr was conscious of style: 'Passion for form giving becomes in me stronger and stronger.' (Letter 25 January 1982)

He would say, '*Stilen är människan*', style is person, a person is known from his/her style. In finalising *Zulu Zion* B Sr described the way he strove for finesse in style:

> I have gone through the text very carefully and lifted out any unnecessary word. Amazing how the adverb weakens the sentence: in lifting the adverbs out in most cases, the noun and adjective stand out in bare and clear strength. (Letter 27 July 1975)

> Simple clarity, clear solid paragraphs is what I am after. In the choice between highfalutin brilliance, so called, and real clarity, I am happily skipping the former and keeping to the latter, and this is a real gain. (Letter 21 August 1982)

B Sr wrote about Nathan Söderblom's style in letter writing. After describing Sm's readiness to recognise the changes that were taking place in the writing of Swedish prose, he goes on to say that Söderblom in his correspondence consciously took up this modernising tendency. He expressed in writing that it was his concern both in the style of living and in letter writing to overcome the conventional. This was also Bengt's own ambition. (1971)

To find the right style B Sr fetched his inspiration from other writers but also from artists and musicians. It was not difficult for him to transfer his artistic and musical impressions to his own style of writing:

> Last night I listened to Grieg's A-minor Piano concerto, op. 16 where John Ogdon played the piano ... It was a great experience just to see this concentrated, totally concentrated huge pianist. Now I could listen to him again, over the radio. I sat in the dark, with my head in my hands, taking in all this beauty of form, all this daring in finding new form. While listening I was deciding to try to find time to go through my Bukoba ms again, in order to make the style finer, clearer, lighter!! We shall see. (Letter 31 March 1973)

The style related to choice of words, expressions and phrases. On the one hand it was a question of discovering the special qualities in the ordinary, self-evident, obvious, on the other hand finding new ways of expression, expanding the language:

> I must admit that one of my own great secret ambitions is to try to discover the obvious matters, those fundamental things which are so

'*självklara*' – as we say in Swedish with a dangerous term, self-evident, – that one does not ordinarily see them. But there again ... certainly for me, the remedy is writing ... and when writing trying to widen and extend one's language all the time. It is therefore that I enjoy books by Per Wästberg and by Ingmar Bergman, because of their capacity to expand their Swedish all the time ... (Free Associations 5 March 1978)

I meditate on the mystery of translation. I often read quite modern Finnish Lyrics in Swedish translation. And I must say that if these expressions can be so brilliant in Swedish what must they be in their original, in Finnish ... Translation is such a mystery. Daily and all the time I struggle with the English language trying to find the lively, peculiar term and word, not the worn-out, conventional term ...

In our common language – the international means of communication, English – one has to try to extend and expand one's language all the time. How can we help one another in being more ambitious for better English writing and speaking? This is my constant concern, as I am now since 13 and a half years writing on this book of mine. One would like to attain to a level of English, which is both lively and related to 'life' and placed on a certain level of 'excellence'. But oh, how terribly one falls short of such an ideal, so I should not even use the term at all, obviously not being worthy of it. There is no way out of this dilemma, it would seem. In order to reach out to the world and to posterity one has to write in an international language. Yet how to do it so that the best of English writers could recognise it as a worthy effort? ... I am struggling with my chapters, in the hope of some day coming to the end. (Letter 5 January 1988)

B Sr's eternal regret was that he was not born with English as his first language. It was a real problem for him, as he said, 'at the foundation of his personality'. I see it, from the way he expressed it, to be related to his close hereditary and spiritual identification with the British. There were also things to tell to the Swedish friends, but the international Bengt Sundkler concluded, 'the world is my parish':

I feel a deeper problem [than that of 'form'], that of language. It is a deep problem at the foundation and in the structure of my personality, in my whole attempt at communication. I am of course ever oscillating between Swedish and English, but also some Bantu and even French expressions or terms. Therefore I think, it is because of this fundamental problem it was such a liberating and therapeutic experience to me to write on Söderblom, and write for my English friends. The book deals with Swedish material, mainly, and of course a tremendous lot of other material, but I am all the time interpreting, trying to translate this person on to an international scene. That was such a joy and such fun for me to try to do it like that. I could not have written that book in Swedish, I would have lacked the impetus, the inspiration for it. But I remember how I ached and suffered all the six first months of 1967 in trying to find the right note on which I wanted to write that book. Then I made a break-through, a little chapter on Sm and Riga or the Baltic States, and then I knew that this was the kind of style that I would like to attempt, and that style fitted me precisely. You will see that I am on the same track in this little contribution on the Nordic Missions Council.

Then it was very satisfying to me for a time to write in Swedish, in this book on Bukoba. Again I felt that it was interpreting to some friends in this country who might take an interest in what we had been doing. But more and more I must tell myself that the world is my parish. (Letter 14 April 1973)

We have already seen that B Sr recognised that he expressed his inner self when, on his return from Tanzania, he switched from English to Swedish, yet the oscillation between languages was inevitable and caused additional anxiety in writing:

Why do I write sometimes in Swedish? I have done so in my diary now for many years. But I should not do it. I do not belong here. I must use English only and write and think in English which will serve this One Thing: My task which is the only thing with which I am now concerned. Of course the language is a problem and it has been brought home to me very forcibly this summer by the translation and correction work of Tim Davies who lifted up my English in *Bara Bukoba* and ACH to a new level.

I must work and act through English. There is nothing else, yet I feel ashamed that I do not do better and that after all these years, I do not write more fluent English, a more natural English. Why is this? Why do I have to struggle all the time, and be defeated on this central point?

Zulu Zion was not good from the English point of view. I must not allow everything to slip through my fingers without having had my English really corrected. Yet there is a danger of being too correct and editing the life out of one's writing. God, keep me, now and ever. (Free Associations 5 November 1978)

Language held a general interest for B Sr, also in relation to other modes of expression. He was good at classical languages, which gave him the foundation for the Romance languages. He lamented that he never tried to learn Finnish seriously. It was easy for him to learn languages in Africa. The following quote demonstrates another dimension of the interest in language, the 'language of angels':

I am now leaving for Carolina Library in order to pick up a few books on the philosophy of language and psychology of language; I shall need them in order to deepen my thoughts on that incomparable prophet of mine Khambule. Just think, he must have come through Dundee many times in those years 1938 and to 1940. I must have seen him, could have invited him, but no, there did not occur any opportunity. Now I get to know him more intimately than anybody else through that diary of his and the liturgies of his which are really some kind of extended diaries. But how is it that this man, illiterate only a few years earlier, can sit down and write a diary, having that inner monologue or inner dialogue with himself?? Here is a man language-obsessed, obsessed with the beauty and wonder of his Zulu language, and yet sometimes it was not enough, then he had to pass the borderline. He could so easily pass that borderline and receive the language of angels and he himself could speak it, and he writes it down *mm rrfXPL*, etc. In fact there is a concern of his that is universal: the religious experience cannot be reduced to ordinary speech. It must break through those barriers of language. (Letter 31 July 1973)

The language as an intentionally adopted barrier was a strange thought to B Sr. This he found to be the case in Louvain, but even there he himself found a way to break through the language barrier with his ability to speak Afrikaans:

It is very strange to find here in Louvain quite a few of these Jesuit fathers, who do not speak a word of French: They insist on Flemish, and I try to accommodate myself with a few odd Afrikaans phrases, and this is very acceptable. I am surprised at seeing how deeply divided the Belgian nation is, from top to bottom, because of this language issue – and one reflects on the attitude of Africans with regard to the imposition of European languages: they manage without much protest and enjoy speaking all our strange lingoes. I understand now that it is altogether an exception and privilege for me to be let in here, speaking French. I think in fact that fewer speak French in this house now than a few years ago when I was here last. That is what the sociologists call 'development', I suppose ...

The weather is marvellous ... The books are plentiful in Jesuit library, the Librarian as nice as one could expect ... Only time goes, rushes ahead. Seven days seem a lot – but they are just like a wind, a gust of wind. I try to catch this element of time, but it is also here, as always, elusive, uncompromising. I hope that I manage to dispose of it in a right manner. (Letter 12 September 1987)

The final 20 years of writing had been in many ways a joyous experience. Bengt had felt strongly that every day and every moment were as if borrowed time from God for the one purpose of writing his last great work on the Church History of Africa. For that reason they gave him, in his own words, 'immense joy'. Many letters were written in the 1980s and 1990s to assure himself that in spite of the enormous task ahead, he could do it:

There is one problem, which overshadows all the others: The speed with which Time is running out. From every point of view, I have no extra time, every new day is precious loan which must not be wasted.

'Beyond our fellowship'

Bengt Sundkler's 'passed beyond our fellowship' on 5 April 1995. The funeral service with a Holy Communion was held in Uppsala

Cathedral immediately after Easter. His good friends and former students, Bishop Emeritus Tore Furberg and Bishop Jonas Jonson were the celebrants, Östanbäck brothers sang and the large congregation of family and friends communed with the departed. Bengt and Ingeborg's ashes were buried near the Chapel in the back of the 'Bishops' Corridor' in the Old Graveyard of Uppsala. The gravestone bears an inscription 'Jesus Christ, God's only Son, have mercy upon us now and in life eternal,' the Jesus prayer Bengt Sundkler had repeated in his later life more often than any other prayer.

The *Journal of African Religions* published an editorial and included Richard Gray's article commemorating Bengt Sundkler. It is fitting to close his biography quoting them:

> For many years Bengt Sundkler has been unquestionably the 'bishop' of everyone in African Christian studies: An ecumenical bridge builder between prophet and pastor, Protestant and Catholic, African theologian and missionary strategist, south and east. Now that in death he has passed beyond our fellowship, it is fitting that this journal honour the exceptionally distinguished personal contribution that he has made over many decades to our understanding of the subject. It was always scholarly, but still more was it one of spiritual and humane intuition into the minds of individuals, their callings, dreams, rituals and heavenly telephones. I don't think Bengt ever wrote an article for the Journal, yet it has lived within his presence throughout its thirty years. I doubt whether anyone else has been referred as often in its footnotes and bibliographies. (Editorial)

Richard Gray gives credit to B Sr's vivid style of writing in *Bantu Prophets*:

> In a hundred years' time *Bantu Prophets* will still be consulted for its information concerning some of the pioneer leaders of these churches. Typically he claimed that the splendid, close-up photographs 'contribute to the fuller understanding of the personalities' discussed in the book; but these impressive photographs are totally eclipsed by his word portraits, the fruit of brilliant observation, perceptions and descriptions. Mainly on account of these descriptions, the book was a decisive landmark in the study of Christianity in Africa. It opened up to the wider, previously hostile audience, the motivations, aspirations and something of the potential of the profoundly significant movement and phenomenon represented by these leaders. (*Journal of Religion in Africa* XXV, 4: 342–6).

Notes

1. This was the case long before B Sr had an ear infection and had his hearing organ removed from his right ear, a very exacting operation. After the operation it was hard for him to hear people in big groups. He contracted the infection on his trip to South Africa in 1980.
2. B Sr seldom forgot to mention women. In this case he really meant men since

there were no female pastors yet at that time in the established churches: they were many in the independent churches. The quote is from the *Christian Ministry in Africa* in which the concentration is on the ministry in the established churches.

3. The first diary of B Sr which I have seen was started in 1927 with six pages, but not continued: 'God, you will be the first and the last in my diary and in my daily doings. Give me courage, light and strength. *Ora et labora. Vouloir c'est pouvoir*. That you cannot, it may be so, but never because you do not want.'

4. Information from A.-I. Berglund.

5. Here he refers to his small card system, but he also loved to have large lined papers on which he could write with big letters. He said often: 'Sweden is a paper-producing country, let us use paper profusely!'

6. Reference is made to the named book in which B Sr has double-underlined the quoted sentence, p.58. Bach, Richard, *Jonathan Livingston Seagull, a story*. 1973. London: Pan Books Ltd.

DISSERTATIONS SUPERVISED BY PROFESSOR BENGT SUNDKLER

Published in the series of *Studia Missionalia Uppsaliensia*, Uppsala.

Beyerhaus, Peter. 1956. 'Die Selbständigkeit der jungen Kirchen als missionarisches Problem', *SMU* I.

Furberg, Tore. 1962. 'Kyrka och mission i Sverige 1868–1901', *SMU* IV.

Sharpe, Eric J. 1965. 'Not to Destroy but to Fulfil: The Contribution of J. N. Farquhar to Protestant Mission Thought in India before 1914', *SMU* V.

Hallencreutz, Carl F. 1966. 'Kraemer Towards Tambaram', *SMU* VII.

Aagaard, Johannes. 1967. 'Mission, Konfession, Kirche. Die problematik ihrer Integration im 19. Jahrhundert in Deutschland. I–II', *SMU* 1967.

Estborn, Sigfrid. 1968. 'Johannes Sandegren och hans insats i Indien kristenhet', *SMU* X.

Sicard, S. von. 1970. 'The Lutheran Church on the Coast of Tanzania 1887–1914 with special reference to the evangelical Lutheran Church in Tanzania, Synod of Uzaramo Uluguru', *SMU* XII.

Axelson, Sigbert. 1970. 'Culture Confrontation in the Lower Congo. From the Old Congo Kingdom to the Congo Independent State with special reference to the Swedish Missionaries in the 1880s and 1890s', *SMU* XIV.

Swantz, M. L. 1970 (2nd edn. 1986). 'Ritual and Symbol in transitional Zaramo society, with special reference to women', *SMU* XVI.

Jakobsson, Stiv. 1975. 'Am I Not a Man and a Brother? British Missions and the Abolition of the Slave Trade and Slavery in West Africa and the West Indies 1786–1838', *SMU* XVII.

Jonson, Jonas. 1972. 'Lutheran Mission in a Time of Revolution. The China Experience 1944–1951', *SMU* XVIII.

Harlin, Tord. 1973. 'Spirit and Truth. Religious Attitudes and life Involvements of 2,200 African Students', *SMU* XIX.

Bergmark, Ingemar. 1974. 'Kyrka och sjöfolk – en studie i Svenska kyrkans sjömansvård 1911–1933', *SMU* XXIII.

Eilert, Hakan. 1974. 'Boundlessness. Studies in Karl Ludvig Reichelt's Missionary thinking with special regard to the Buddhist–Christian Encounter', *SMU* XXIV.

Flodell, Sven Arne. 1974. 'Tierra Nueva', *SMU* XXV.

Zetterquist, Håkan. 1974. 'Stad och Stift', *SMU* XXVI.

BENGT SUNDKLER'S
MAIN PUBLICATIONS

Articles and lesser publications are not included. A full bibliography up to 1974 has been published in *The Church Crossing Frontiers*; an addition to the bibliography up to 1984 has been published in *Daring in Order to Know*.

Svenska missionsällskapet 1835–1876. Stockholm 1937.
Bantu Prophets in South Africa. London 1948. 2nd edn 1961.
Bantu Propheten in Südafrika. Stuttgart 1964.
Ung kyrka i Tanganjika. Stockholm 1948.
The Church of South India: The Movement Towards Union 1900–1947. London 1954.
Svensk Missionsatlas. Stockholm 1957.
The Christian Ministry in Africa. Uppsala 1960. Abridged edition London 1962.
Missionens värld. Stockholm 1963. 2nd edn rev. 1970.
Maailmanlähetys. Helsinki 1965 (Finnish translation)
The World of Mission, London 1965.
Nathan Söderblom. His Life and Work. Lund and London 1968.
Bara Bukoba. Stockholm 1974.
Bara Bukoba. Church and Community in Tanzania. London 1980.
Nathan Söderblom och hans möten. Stockholm 1975.
Zulu Zion and some Swazi Zionists. Lund 1976.
A History of the Church in Africa. Cambridge 2000.

BIBLIOGRAPHY

Abbreviations

CCT	Christian Council of Tanzania
CSM	Church of Sweden Mission, cf. SKM
EFS	Evangeliska Fosterland Stiftelse
IMC	International Missionary Council
IRM	International Review of Missions
LWF	Lutheran World Federation
NIME	Nordic Institute for Missionary and Ecumenical Research
SIMR	Swedish Institute for Missionary Research
SIM	Svenska Institutet för Missionsforskning
SKM	Svenska kyrkans mission, cf. CSM
SMT	Swedish Missiological Themes, also Svensk Missionstidskrift
SMU	Studia Missionalia Upsaliensia
WCC	World Council of Churches

Adolfson, M. and A. Berntsson. 1984. *Ceza, a Roundabout Way to the Goal. Three Decades of Medical Missionary Work in South Africa*, Käppan.

Ahonen, T. *Bengt Sundklerin käsitys kirkon lähetyksestä* (Bengt Sundkler's conception of the Mission of the Church). Unpublished thesis, April 1992, University of Helsinki.

Berglund, Axel-Ivar, 1969. 'Servant of the Frontier Church' in *The Church Crossing Frontiers, Essays on the Nature of Mission In Honour of Bengt Sundkler*, eds Beyerhaus, P. and C. F. Hallencreutz, *SMU* XI, pp.161–70. Uppsala.

Berglund, A. I. 1984. 'Bengt Sundkler, Prophet among Prophets', in *'Daring in Order to Know'. Studies in Bengt Sundkler's contribution as Africanist and Missionary Scholar*. ed. Hallencreutz, C. F. *SMU* XXXIX, pp.25–7. Uppsala.

Berglund, A. I. 1976. Zulu Thought Patterns and Symbolism. *SMU* XXII. SIMR. Uppsala and Cape Town.

Bernander, Gustav. 1968. *The Lutheran Wartime Assistance to the Tanzanian Churches 1940–1945. SMU* IX. Uppsala.

Culwick, A. T. and G. M. Culwick. 1935. *Ubena of the Rivers.* London.

Erixon, P.-O. 1994. *Ett spann över svarta ingentinget: linjer i Thorsten Jonssons författarskap.* Stockholm.

Fridrichsen, Anton, 1942. 'Nytestamentlig församling,' *En bok om kyrkan.* Uppsala.

Groves, C. P. 1948–1958. *The Planting of Christianity in Africa,* Vol. I to 1840; Vol. II 1840–1878; Vol. III 1878–1914; Vol. IV 1914–1954. London.

Grubb, K. 1971. *Crypts of Power: An Autobiography.* London.

Hallencreutz, C. F. 1998. '"Bantu Prophets" – After Fifty Years', *Swedish Missiological Themes, SMT. Annual NIME Papers for 1998.* Vol.86:4, pp.581–600.

Hallencreutz, Carl Fredrik. 1984. 'Doctor Missiologiae Upsaliensis', *'Daring in Order to Know', Studies in Bengt Sundkler's contribution as Africanist and Missionary Scholar.* ed. Hallencreutz, C. F. *SMU* XXXIX, pp.5–23. Uppsala.

Hansen, M. A. 1978. *Orm og Tyr.* Copenhagen.

Hellsten, Ingegärd, 1993. *Erinringar från ett liv.* Unpublished, Umeå.

Hunter, M. 1936. *Reaction to Conquest: Effects of Contact with Europeans on the Pondo of South Africa.* London.

Jakobsson, Stiv. 1975. *Am I Not a Man and a Brother? British Missions and the Abolition of the Slave Trade and Slavery in West Africa and the West Indies 1786–1838, SMU* XVII. Uppsala.

Knak, S. 1928. *Zwischen Nil und Tafelbai: Eine Studie über Evangelium, Volkstum, und Zivilisation.* Berlin.

Larsson, B. 1991. *Conversion to Greater Freedom? Women, Church and Social Change in North-Western Tanzania under Colonial Rule. Studia Historica Academica,* Uppsala 1991.

Mason, A. 1993. *History of the Society of the Sacred Mission.* Norwich, UK.

Missionalia 1984. '"The Challenge of the Independent Churches." A letter from Bengt Sundkler,' pp.3–6. *Journal of the Southern African Missiological Society,* Vol.12:1. Pretoria.

Myrdal, G. 1970. *Objectivity in Social Research.* London.

Oosthuizen, G. C. 1967. *The Theology of a South African Messiah,* Leiden.

Pedersen, J. 1934. *Israel, Sjaeleliv og samsfundsliv* (2 vols). Köbenhavn.

Preiswerk, R. and D. Perrot. 1978. *Ethnocentrism and History. Africa, Asia and Indian America in Western Textbooks.* New York, London, Lagos.

Riesenfeld, H. 1965. 'Kyrklig front förkortning', *Svenska Dagbladet* 14 October 1965.

Sandström, J. 1935. *Bland svarta kristna.* Stockholm.

Sandström, J. 1944. *Från den första kärlekens tid.* Stockholm.

Söderblom, N. 1932. *The Living God.* Stockholm.

Söderblom, N. 1903. *The Religion of Revelation. Tiele's Compendium,* 3rd edn, Leiden.

Söderblom, N. 1916. *Svenska Kyrkans kropp och själ.* Stockholm.

Sundkler. B. 1933. *Huru gammalt är barndopets sakrament?* Stockholm.

Sundkler, B. 1936. 'Jésus et les païens: Contributions à l'étude de la pensée missionaire dans le Nouveau Testament. *Révue d'Histoire et de Philosophie Religieuses* pp. 462–99. Also in *Strasbourg Theological Review* 1937, 6, pp.1–38; in seminar reports in German 'Arbeiten und Mitteilungen aus dem Neutestamentlichen Seminar zu Uppsala herausgegeben von Anton Friedrichsen'.

Sundkler, B. 1937. *Svenska missionssällskapet 1835–76: Missionstankens genombrott och tidigare historia i Sverige.* (The Swedish Mission Society 1835–76. Breakthrough of mission thinking and its early history in Sweden.) Stockholm.

Sundkler, B. 1939. *'En Ljushärd', Makitika i Zululand.* Uppsala.

Sundkler, B. 1948. *Ung kyrka i Tanganyika.* Stockholm.

Sundkler, B. 1956. (rev. edn) *The Church of South India: The Movement Towards Union 1900–1947.* London.

Sundkler, B. 1959. 'Response and Resistance to the Gospel in a Zulu Congregation', *Basileia, Tribute to Walter Freytag,* eds J. H. and H. J. Margull. Stuttgart.

Sundkler, B. 1959. 'Svart Messias och Vite Kriste', p.47, *SMT* 2.

Sundkler, B. 1960. 'Bantu Messiah and White Christ', *Frontier,* Kijabe, Kenya.

Sundkler, B. G. M. 1961 (rev. edn). *Bantu Prophets.* London.

Sundkler, B. 1961. 'Bantu-Messias und Weisser Christus. Die Sekten Südafrikas', *Das Wort in der Welt,* pp.26–32. Hamburg.

Sundkler, B. 1962. 'The IMC from Edinburgh 1910 to New Delhi 1961.' *Daring in Order to Know, IRM,* I:51, pp.4–11. In German 'Von Edinburgh nach Neu-Delhi',*Weltmission Heute. Die Missionierende Kirche.* Heft 21/2.

Sundkler, B. 1962. *The Christian Ministry in Africa.* SMU II. Uppsala.

Sundkler, B. 1962. *The Christian Ministry in Africa.* abridged edn, London.

Sundkler, B. 1963. *Missionens värld.* Stockholm.

Sundkler, B. 1965. 'Frontförkortning i ekumeniken', *SMT,* 53.

Sundkler, B. 1970. *Anna Söderblom 1870–1970,* Nathan Söderblom Society Yearbook *Religion och Bibel,* Uppsala.

Sundkler, B. 1974. *Bara Bukoba. Kyrka och miljö i Tanzania.* Stockholm.

Sundkler, Bengt, 'Alla dessa kvinnor' Kvinnogärning genom SKM 1874–1974.' ('All these women' Womens work through CSM

1874–1974). *Mission 100, Svenska kyrkans missions årsbok* 1974, pp.71–118.

Sundkler, B. 1975. *Nathan Söderblom och hans möten*. Stockholm.

Sundkler, B. 1975. 'Halva mänskligheten och mycket mer än halva kyrkan' (Half of humankind and much more than half of the Church), *SMT* 63, pp.46–55.

Sundkler, B. 1976. 'Nathan Söderblom – Parisårens inflytande på hans ekumeniska insats', *Jubileumsskrift 1626–1976*. Paris.

Sundkler, B. 1976. *Zulu Zion and some Swazi Zionists. SMU* XXIX. London and Uppsala.

Sundkler, B. 1980. *Bara Bukoba, Church and Community in Tanzania*. London.

Sundkler, B. and C. Steed. 2000. *A History of the Church in Africa*. Cambridge, UK.

Swantz, M. L. 1970 (2nd edn 1986). *Ritual and Symbol in transitional Zaramo society, with special reference to women*. Uppsala.

Swantz, M.L. 1974. '+ Bengt Bukoba.' *Daring in Order to Know*, *SMU* XXXIX, pp.35–44.

Swantz, M. L. 1998. *Paths for Change*. Helsinki.

Thunberg, Lars. 1974. 'Redemption for the Wrongs of History' in *The Church Crossing Frontiers, Essays on the Nature of Mission In Honour of Bengt Sundkler*, eds Beyerhaus, P. and C. F. Hallencreutz, *SMU* XI, pp.57–66. Uppsala.

Webster, D. 1954. *What is Spiritual Healing?* London.

Webster, D. 1955, (1953). *What is a Missionary?* London.

Webster, D. 1956. *What is Evangelism?* London.

Webster, D. 1953. *What is this Church of South India?* London.

Wieslander, Anna, 1989. *Hem till Tanzania. Boken om Barbro Johansson berättad för Anna Wieslander*. Stockholm.

INDEX OF SUBJECTS

Society for the Propegation of Christian
  Knowledge (SPCK) 71
Society for the Propegation of the Gospel
  (SPG) 32
Society of the Sacred Mission (SSM) 31
Nathan Söderblom: his life and work 12
Nathan Söderblom och hans möten 219, 224,
  225, 248 n.23, 261, 317
Strasbourg xxiv, 11, 12, 53
Strasbourg Theological Review 11
Student Christian Movement in Schools 8–9,
  49
Svensk Missions Atlas 142
Svenska Dagbladet 48, 207, 209
Svenska Missionsällskapet see Swedish
  Mission Society
Svenska Missionstidskrift, SMT xx, xxiii,
  xxiv, 128, 131, 214, 250, 253, 305
Swedish Institute of Mission Research xxiv,
  122
Swedish Mission Society 56, 59, 60, 61

Tanganyika xv, 69, 74, 90, 102–3, 110, 112,
  134, 151, 190, 191
Tanzania ix, xiv, xxv, 24, 91, 78, 103, 143,
  176, 189. 211, 273, 282, 319
teaching 127–9, 130–1, 135–7, 141–3,
  149–51, 210–14, 225–6, 239–41
Tenerife *(see also* Canary Islands) ix, xxii
  n.3
theology x, 8, 21, 51, 55, 56, 63, 89, 90,
  101, 128, 138–9, 154, 155, 161–2, 179,
  180, 185, 198, 205, 212–13, 220–1,
  240–1, 243–7
theological education 35, 55, 89
Theological Education Fund 255–6
theology of episcopacy 179
theology, lay 6
theology of mission 153, 171
theology of translation 138, 170–3

Umeå 5, 7–8, 10, 21, 47–50, 63
  Minerva Library 7, 48
Umeåbladet 64
Ung Kyrka i Tanganyika (Young Church in
  Tanganyika) xv, 28, 112, 116–17, 163,
  168, 180

Vatican II 39, 182, 207, 261, 278

White Fathers 39
White Frocks 21–22, 101
women 79, 93, 140, 158 n.17, 163, 183,
  191, 192, 221, 232, 262–3, 264 n.4,
  284, 285
  abasizikazi see women, *umsizikazi*
  Haya 79, 112–13
  manyano 26, 263, 285
  missionaries 97–99, 193
  ordination of 154, 201, 205–7
  umsizikazi (pl. *abasizikazi*) 26, 93, 94, 95,
    105 n.9, 263
  Zulu 26, 93
World Christian Handbook 33
World Council of Churches (WCC) xxiv,
  133, 215, 217, 224, 252, 256, 258
  Faith and Order 130, 213, 214, 254
  New Delhi 1961 182, 245, 257–9
  Uppsala 1968 215, 223–4, 252, 259–61
World of Mission, The xxv, 225, 231, 245,
  267, 305
writing and publishing x, 11, 44, 54, 116,
  128–9, 131, 134, 135, 153, 157, 201–2,
  208, 216, 218, 223–4, 226–7, 238,
  265–301, 302–22
  handwriting xxi, 75, 304–5,
  sources of inspiration x, xiv, 48, 49, 128,
    163, 220, 222, 223, 231, 245, 265,
    269–71, 286–7, 294, 295–7, 303,
    305, 306, 307, 311–13, 318
  style xiii–xv, 49, 103, 105 n.13, 130, 146,
    153–4, 279–80, 285–6, 290, 296,
    300, 302, 306, 317–21

Zionists 17, 21–22, 23, 91, 163, 165–6
Zulu xiii, 14, 16–17, 18, 22, 72–73, 91–99,
  117, 144, 238
  Zulu Church 21, 26, 177
Zulu Zion and some Swazi Zionists xvii, xxv,
  23, 32, 94, 166–7, 307, 267, 290, 307,
  308, 309, 313, 317, 319
Zululand 13, 14, 16, 21, 48, 73, 84, 86, 87,
  90, 91–99, 143–4

INDEX OF NAMES

STUDIA MISSIONALIA SVECANA

Formerly Studia Missionalia Uppsaliensia (No. I-LXXX)
Editors: I-XXVII Bengt Sundkler, XXVIII-LXIX Carl F. Hallencreutz,
LXX-LXXX Alf Tergel, LXXXI- Alf Tergel and Aasulv Lande

Congo from the Old Congo Kingdom to the Congo
Independent State with special reference to the Swedish
Missionaries in 1880s. 1970

XV   *Peter Oesterbye*. The Church in Israel. A report on the
Work and Position of the Christian Churches in Israel
with special reference to the Protestant Churches and
Communities. 1970

XVI   *Marja-Lisa Swantz*. Ritual and Symbol in transitional
Zaramo society with special reference to women. 1970

XVII   *Stiv Jakobsson*. Am I not a Man and Brother? 1972

XVIII   *Jonas Jonsson*. Lutheran Missions in a Time of
Revolution. The China experience 1944–1951. 1972

XIX   *Tord Harlin*. Spirit and Truth. Religious Attitudes and
Life Involvement of 2 200 African Students. 1973

XX   *Carl F. Hallencreutz, Johannes Aagaard and Nils E.
Bloch-Hoell (eds)*. Missions from the North, Nordic
Missionary Council 50 Years. 1974

XXI   *Josiah Kibira*. Church, Clan and the World. 1974

XXII   *Axel-Ivar Berglund*. Zulu Thought-Patterns and
Symbolism. 1975

XXIII   *Ingemar Bergmark*. Kyrka och sjöfolk. En studie i
Svenska kyrkans sjömansvård 1911–1933. 1974

XXIV   *Håkan Eilert*. Boundlessness. Studies in Karl Ludvig
Reichelt's Missionary Thinking with special Regard to the
Buddhist-Christian Encounter. 1974

XXV   *Sven Arne Flodell*. Tierra Nueva. Svensk grupputvandring
till Latinamerika. Integration och församlingsbildning.
1974

XXVI   *Håkan Zetterquist*. Stad och stift. Stiftsbildning och
församlingsdelningar i Stockholm 1940–1956. Ett bidrag
till stadens missiologi. 1974

XXVII   *Olav Saeveraas*. On Church-Mission Relations in Ethiopia
1944–1969 with special reference to the Evangelical
Church Mekane Yesus and Lutheran Missions. 1974

XXVIII   *Ingvar Kalm*. Mission i Linköpings stift. Biträdets-
missionssällskapets verksamhet 1841–1875. 1977

XXIX   *Bengt Sundkler*. Zulu Zion and some Swazi Zionists. 1976

XXX   *Herman Schlyter*. Der China-Missionar Karl Gützlaff und
seine Heimatbasis. Studien über das Interesse des
Abendlandes an der Mission des China-Pioniers Karl
Gützlaff und über seinen Einstaz als Missionerwecker.
1976

XXXI   *Carl F. Hallencreutz*. Dialogue and Community.
Ecumenical Issues in Interreligious Relationships. 1977

XXXII   *Gustav Arén*. Evangelical Pioneers in Ethiopia. 1978

XXXIII   *Timothy Yates*. Venn and Victorian Bishops Abroad. 1978

XXXIV   *Carl-Johan Hellberg*. A Voice of the Voiceless. The

examples de dialogue entre spiritualités après le concile Vatican II. 1998

LXXI *Veronica Melander*. The Hour of God in Guatemala. A people Confronting political Evangelicalism and Counterinsurgency (1976–1990). 1999

LXXII *Ngwabi Bhebe*. ZAPU and ZANU guerilla Warfare and the Evangelical Lutheran Church. 1998

LXXIII *Carl Frederik Hallencreutz*. Religion and Politics in Harare 1890–1980. 1998

LXXIV *Bengt Sundkler & Christopher Steed*. A History of the Church in Africa. 2000

LXXV *Gustav Arén*. Envoys of the Gospel in Ethiopia. In the Steps of Evangelical Pioneers 1898–1936. 1999

LXXVI *Oddbiörn Leirvik*. Images of Jesus Christ in Islam. Introduction, Survey of Research, Issues of Dialogue.

LXXVII *Oscar Stenström*. Proverbes des Bakongo. 1999

LXXVIII *Lars Berge*. The Bambatha Watershed. Swedish Missionaries, African Christians and an evolving Zulu Lutheran Folkchurch in Rural Natal and Zululand 1902–c. 1914. 1999

LXXXIX *Johan Hasselgren*. Rural Batak Kings in Medan. The development of Toba Batak ethno-religious identity in Medan, Indonesia, 1912–1965. 2000

LXXX *Lian H. Sakhong*. Religion and Politics among the Chin in Burma 1896–1949. 2000

LXXXI *Carl Sundberg*. Conversion and Conceptions of Christ. A missiological study among urban converts in Brazzaville, Republic of Congo. 2000

LXXXII *Staffan Grenstedt*. Ambaricho and Shonkolla. From Local Church Independence to the Evangelical Mainstream in Ehiopia. 2000

LXXXIII *Jørn Henrik Olsen*. Kristus i tropisk Afrika – i spændingsfæltet mellem identitet og relevans. 2001.